Praise for *The Hellhound of Wall Street*

One of *Bloomberg*'s Best Business Books of the Year
One of *Library Journal*'s Best Business Books of the Year

"Page-turning history . . . Like a filmmaker, Perino cuts between squatter camps and the hearings." —*Bloomberg*

"Absolutely riveting! Michael Perino's account of the 1933 Pecora hearings—the sensational revelations of shady business practices at the highest levels on Wall Street—is a page-turner. No one can read about the many excesses of Wall Street in the 1920s without being struck with the similarities to today and wondering why we have allowed history to repeat itself."
—Liaquat Ahamed, author of *Lords of Finance*

"A brilliant and compelling account of how Ferdinand Pecora figured out—and exposed in nauseating detail—the malpractice of Wall Street. As we struggle to confront our modern financial demons, we should all pause to read and reflect on Michael Perino's account." —Simon Johnson, coauthor of *13 Bankers*

"Given the current economic downturn and the complicity of Wall Street banks in that downturn, Perino's book feels timely. As is often the case, history serves as a teacher, showing the past is prologue." —*USA Today*

"[In] reading Michael Perino's admirable study of the U.S. banking world after the Wall Street crash of 1929 . . . you may ask yourself more than once, 'Have we learned nothing?' for as Mr. Perino says, in today's financial difficulties there are echoes, so distinct as to be uncanny, of congressional hearings held seventy-seven years ago." —*Pittsburgh Post-Gazette*

"Fascinating . . . Perino plots Pecora's improbable rise to stardom like a Hollywood screenwriter." —*Barnes & Noble Review*

"Hats off to Michael Perino. *The Hellhound of Wall Street* is an excellent account of the Pecora hearings that should be read by everyone interested in financial reform. At the same time, it is a penetrating Wall Street morality tale that should evoke a strong sense of déjà vu in its readers."
—Charles Geisst, author of *Collateral Damaged* and *Wall Street: A History*

"Perino's recounting of Senate hearings where the banksters were put under oath and forced to come clean about their dirty dealing is gripping. Pecora emerges as the epic crimefighter—part Eliot Ness, part Sam Dash, part Perry

Mason—who fully understood the truth of Woody Guthrie's line: 'Some men rob you with a six-gun—And some with a fountain pen.' But what makes Perino's book a must-read is the outline it provides for what Obama and congressional Democrats should have done when they assumed power." —*The Progressive*

"[*The Hellhound of Wall Street*] will keep you entertained throughout, and you will come away knowing that we do not always learn from our mistakes." —*New York Law Journal*

"[A] lucid account of period banking and stock-market swindles and a crackerjack legal drama . . . Perino's book is a trenchant, entertaining study of the New Deal's heroic beginnings, one with obvious relevance to latter-day efforts to rein in Wall Street's excesses." —*Publishers Weekly*

"It has taken another economic meltdown to restore public recognition of Ferdinand Pecora as the most effective investigator of financial wrongdoing in American history. Michael Perino deftly recreates the dark days of 1933, when that shrewd New York prosecutor turned Senate committee counsel forced Wall Street's biggest bankers and brokers to admit how they contributed to the nation's slide into the Great Depression."
—Donald A. Ritchie, author of *The U.S. Congress: A Very Short Introduction*

"A thorough, well-written history that shows how the past can be prologue." —*Kirkus Reviews*

"Michael Perino's new work on Ferdinand Pecora powerfully amplifies our understanding of the pivotal role that Pecora played in leading the hearings that built the case for the New Deal's securities and banking laws. *The Hellhound of Wall Street* is a masterful evocation of the politics, finance, and personalities when Congress last addressed systematic reform of our financial system."
—Joel Seligman, author of *The Transformation of Wall Street*

"*The Hellhound of Wall Street* is an incisive and timely book about a man and period in our country's history when a presumptuous, reckless Wall Street elite, very much like the one that's caused such ruin today, met its match. We badly need a second Ferdinand Pecora now. Michael Perino provides brilliant analysis, telling anecdotal material, and wears his deep erudition easily. He has given us a vital cautionary tale from the past that is a pure pleasure to read."
—Steve Fraser, author of *Every Man a Speculator: A History of Wall Street in American Life*

PENGUIN BOOKS

THE HELLHOUND OF WALL STREET

Michael Perino is the Dean George W. Matheson Professor of Law at St. John's University School of Law. A former Wall Street litigator, Perino has testified in the United States Senate and the House of Representatives and has consulted with the Securities and Exchange Commission. He is frequently quoted in the media on securities and corporate matters. He has appeared on NPR's *All Things Considered, Morning Edition*, and *Marketplace,* on *Bill Moyers' Journal* on PBS, and on CNBC.

THE HELLHOUND
OF WALL STREET

How Ferdinand Pecora's Investigation of the Great Crash

Forever Changed American Finance

MICHAEL PERINO

PENGUIN BOOKS

PENGUIN BOOKS

Published by the Penguin Group

Penguin Group (USA) Inc., 375 Hudson Street, New York, New York 10014, U.S.A.
Penguin Group (Canada), 90 Eglinton Avenue East, Suite 700, Toronto, Ontario, Canada
M4P 2Y3 (a division of Pearson Penguin Canada Inc.) • Penguin Books Ltd, 80 Strand, London
WC2R 0RL, England • Penguin Ireland, 25 St Stephen's Green, Dublin 2, Ireland (a division
of Penguin Books Ltd) • Penguin Group (Australia), 250 Camberwell Road, Camberwell, Victoria
3124, Australia (a division of Pearson Australia Group Pty Ltd) • Penguin Books India Pvt Ltd, 11
Community Centre, Panchsheel Park, New Delhi – 110 017, India • Penguin Group (NZ), 67 Apollo
Drive, Rosedale, Auckland 0632, New Zealand (a division of Pearson New Zealand Ltd) • Penguin
Books (South Africa) (Pty) Ltd, 24 Sturdee Avenue, Rosebank, Johannesburg 2196, South Africa

Penguin Books Ltd, Registered Offices: 80 Strand, London WC2R 0RL, England

First published in the United States of America by The Penguin Press,
a member of Penguin Group (USA) Inc. 2010
Published in Penguin Books 2011

1   3   5   7   9   10   8   6   4   2

Excerpt from "Provide, Provide" from *The Poetry of Robert Frost*, edited by
Edward Connery Lathem. Copyright 1969 by Henry Holt and Company.
Copyright 1936 by Robert Frost, copyright 1964 by Lesley Frost Ballantine.
Reprinted by permission of Henry Holt and Company, LLC.

THE LIBRARY OF CONGRESS HAS CATALOGED THE HARDCOVER EDITION AS FOLLOWS:
Perino, Michael A.
The hellhound of Wall Street : how Ferdinand Pecora's inverstigation of the Great Crash
forever changed American finance / Michael Perino.
p.   cm.
Includes bibliographical references and index.
ISBN 978-1-59420-272-8 (hc.)
ISBN 978-0-14-312003-2 (pbk.)
1. Pecora, Ferdinand, 1882–   2. Stock Market Crash, 1929.
3. Stock exchanges—United States—History—20th century.
4. Financial crises—United States—History—20th century.   I. Title.
HB37171929.P47   2010
330.973'0916—dc22
2010019157

Printed in the United States of America
DESIGNED BY AMANDA DEWEY

For my mother and father

CONTENTS

INTRODUCTION

S aturday, March 4, 1933—Inauguration Day—was one of those raw March days when it seems that spring will never come. The thick layer of steel gray clouds sheathing the sky threatened rain, and a northwest wind whipped across Capitol Hill. Sunshine broke through on occasion, but it was dull and fleeting and did little to relieve the dreariness of that damp, chilly day.

Historians would later pinpoint that winter as the nadir of the Great Depression, but Americans hardly needed to be seers to realize that the economy could not get much worse. Thirty-eight states had closed all their banks, and everywhere else withdrawals were sharply curtailed. Outright bank failures numbered in the thousands annually. In those days before deposit insurance, one in four families lost their life savings. The economy was in full retreat, industrial production was half what it had been just four years earlier, and unemployment was an appalling 25 percent. Farm incomes were decimated after a decade of plummeting crop prices. Shantytowns of the dispossessed, sarcastically dubbed Hoovervilles, dotted the landscape, and breadlines stretched around many blocks. Homes were foreclosed, renters evicted, and signs of malnutrition among schoolchildren were increasingly evident. On Friday, March 3, the Dow Jones Industrial Average was 86 percent off its wildly inflated pre-crash peak in September 1929. At the end of trading that day, the New York Stock Exchange announced that it would be closed indefinitely.[1]

In the midst of the economic chaos, a shivering crowd of at least 100,000 gathered near the east portico of the Capitol to hear Franklin Roosevelt's plan of attack, some perched in the icy bare trees, others crammed in bleachers or crowded atop adjacent buildings. Pundits from all points of the political spectrum were openly calling for Roosevelt to assume dictatorial powers to address the crisis. In some parts of the country the possibility of revolution was openly discussed, and Lloyds of London was doing a booming business in riot and civil disturbance insurance.

The previous spring, tens of thousands of unemployed World War I veterans and their families had marched on Washington, demanding early payment of a promised bonus for wartime service, many protesting on the very spot where the inaugural crowd now gathered. The bonus never came, and in late July, the Army chief of staff, General Douglas MacArthur, let loose his cavalry, sabers and bayonets drawn, on the thousands still milling in the capital. Through clouds of tear gas, the tanks and soldiers drove the bonus army from the city and burned their encampment along the Anacostia River to the ground. Seven months later, Washington still had an ominous, wartime feel. Government buildings were heavily guarded, police patrols ringed the White House, and machine gun nests were strategically placed along the inaugural parade route.[2]

The new president made his way across the crowded platform, gripping his son Jimmy's arm with one hand and leaning on a cane with the other, giving the crowd the illusion that he was walking. After being sworn in by Chief Justice Charles Evans Hughes, Roosevelt turned to address the gathered crowd. Despite the chill March air, he shed his hat and overcoat. Grim-faced, his usual broad smile absent on this solemn occasion, he told the assembled crowd and radio listeners that the only thing they had to fear was fear itself—"nameless, unreasoning, unjustified terror which paralyzes needed efforts to convert retreat into advance." Roosevelt's address is rightly remembered for that hopeful phrase and for his call for the government to launch a war on the Great Depression. Positioning himself in stark contrast with Herbert Hoover, who sat stonily just a few feet away, Roosevelt pledged "action, and action now."[3]

The Inaugural Address, however, did more than just announce a vision for fixing the economy; Roosevelt used it to assign blame. Along with most everyone else at the time, Roosevelt pointed his finger at Wall Street, but his goal was not demagoguery. He wasn't trying to accrete power, but to stoke reform. The largely silent crowd stirred when Roosevelt told them that the "rulers of the exchange of mankind's goods have failed, through their own stubbornness and their own incompetence, have admitted their failure, and abdicated. Practices of the unscrupulous money changers stand indicted in the court of public opinion, rejected by the hearts and minds of men." Applause erupted for the first time when Roosevelt proclaimed that the "money changers have fled from their high seats in the temple of our civilization. We may now restore that temple to the ancient truths."[4]

Somewhere in Manhattan, perhaps sitting by the radio in his Upper West Side apartment, Ferdinand Pecora must have been smiling. It was Pecora, more than anyone else, who deserved credit for those lines. Though Roosevelt claimed that the lines had come to him a week earlier while he was sitting in a service at St. James Episcopal Church, it was Pecora—the man reporters called the Hellhound of Wall Street—and the Senate hearings he'd wrapped up just two days earlier that had made those lines true.

Few Americans today know who Ferdinand Pecora was, although he was once a media superstar, a nearly daily fixture in newspapers and radio broadcasts across the country. With the onset of our current economic woes his name has slowly begun to crop up again. In April 2009, House Speaker Nancy Pelosi called for a new "Pecora Commission" to investigate "what happened on Wall Street." The next week, the Senate invoked Pecora's name in voting to create an independent committee to investigate the financial crisis, and in January 2010 the Financial Crisis Inquiry Commission held its first hearings.

Pecora, a diminutive Sicilian immigrant and a former assistant district attorney from New York City, was chief counsel for the Senate Committee on Banking and Currency, charged with investigating the causes of the 1929 stock market crash. As he recounted in his own memoir of the hearings, *Wall Street under Oath*: "Before [the committee] came, in imposing succession, the demigods of Wall Street, men whose names were household words, but whose personalities and affairs were frequently shrouded in deep, aristocratic mystery. . . . Never before in the history of the United States had so much wealth and power been required to render a public accounting." In terms of rapt public attention, economic impact, and long-lasting legislative accomplishments, Pecora's investigation must rank as the most successful inquiry in the more than two-hundred-year history of congressional probes.[5]

Those hearings are largely forgotten now. Those few who have heard of them frequently get the basic facts wrong. And, of course, even at the time not everyone applauded Pecora's efforts. Raymond Moley, a key member of Roosevelt's Brain Trust, said that "Pecora was like a police chief who rounds up all the suspicious characters in town to solve a jewel robbery." Pecora was accused of grandstanding, with one writer calling him "three-quarters righteous tribune of the people [and] one-quarter demagogic inquisitor." Critics charged that his reckless unveiling of Wall Street's sins only exacerbated the banking crisis gripping the country.

Pecora was ambitious, and he certainly loved the limelight, but he was no more a demagogue than Roosevelt. He was avowedly liberal and reform minded; to those who knew him best he was an idealist with "an inveterate passion for justice." No Wall Street expert, his conclusions about the impropriety of certain stock market practices were sometimes off base. In the end, though, those missteps didn't matter. His success lay not in his talent for inciting passions and inflaming prejudices nor in the intellectual purity of his arguments, but in his ability to crystallize the zeitgeist of the early Depression years—the politicians' vague and vitriolic denunciations of Wall Street and the bitter grousing of a broken-down populace—into hard facts and concrete evidence.[6]

Ultimately, the acclaim Pecora garnered was justified because the hearings he led fundamentally changed the relationship between Washington and Wall Street. Before 1933 the federal government had taken a hands-off approach to the stock market. But the hearings, and the public clamor they created, changed all that. In his Inaugural Address, Roosevelt declared, "There must be an end to a conduct in banking and in business which too often has given to a sacred trust the likeness of callous and selfish wrongdoing," and he called for "strict supervision of all banking and credits and investments." Many would argue that the former is still all too true, but Roosevelt at least delivered on the latter. Over the course of Roosevelt's famous first hundred days in office and then in the year following, Congress passed and Roosevelt signed a flurry of banking and securities legislation, most of which still governs our financial markets today. The first federal securities laws, federal deposit insurance, and the creation of the Securities and Exchange Commission all trace their roots back to that fertile political soil.

Pecora made it all possible because his investigation created the sensational headlines necessary to galvanize public opinion for reform. As Benjamin Cohen, a lawyer and one of the primary drafters of those laws, put it, bankers were "so discredited in the public eye that Congress was ready to pass anything." Securities and Exchange Commission historian Joel Seligman argues that "effective securities legislation might not have been enacted had Pecora's revelations not galvanized broad public support for direct federal regulation of stock markets." Even Roosevelt drew a direct link between the wrongdoing Pecora uncovered and his ability to push through reform legislation. The legislative changes flowed right out of the hearings. "We built completely on his work," James M. Landis, former commission chairman and another drafter of the securities laws, observed. Most famous congressional hearings take the name of the committee chair, but Pecora's stellar performance was so dominating, his questioning so riveting, and his investigations so thorough that the Banking and Currency hearings eventually became known simply as the Pecora hearings.[7]

In short, the hearings played a critical role in our financial history. And they almost didn't happen.

Almost, that is, but for Pecora's prodigious legal skills mixed with a healthy dose of luck and what can only be described as impeccable timing. In fact, most of the Pecora hearings would never have occurred without a single, decisive turning point, a key moment that made the rest of the hearings and reform legislation possible. Before Pecora's appointment as chief counsel, the hearings had dragged on for nearly a year. Despite a great deal of early effort and promise, they had made little discernible headway and the resolution authorizing the investigation was about to expire. Nearly everyone believed the probe would limp quietly offstage, accomplishing nothing and leaving Wall Street untouched. The turning point—and the primary inspiration for Roosevelt's line about the money changers fleeing the temple—came in late February 1933, just a few short weeks after Pecora was first appointed counsel. It was just ten days, the ten days in which Pecora examined the officers from National City Bank (now, a few name changes later, Citigroup), particularly its chairman, Charles E. Mitchell. Pecora too recognized the key role this brief period played, writing that in those few days "a whole era of American financial life passed away."

Although he too has faded from memory, Mitchell was one of the best-known bankers of his day. Edmund Wilson, writing for the *New Republic* in 1933, said that "Sunshine" Charlie was "the banker of bankers, the salesman of salesmen, the genius of the New Economic Era." The son of a produce dealer and the onetime mayor of gritty Chelsea, Massachusetts, Mitchell started off as a $10-a-week clerk for Western Electric, moved to Wall Street, and made a fortune by fundamentally changing how it operated. He almost single-handedly pioneered the sale of stocks and bonds to middle-class investors. At the height of the bubble, he proclaimed that the market had nowhere to go but up, and he was constantly on top of his salesmen, hectoring, berating, bullying, and cajoling them to sell more and more of the securities City Bank "manufactured."

At first glance, the confrontation between Pecora and Mitchell hardly seemed like a fair fight, though the two men were not completely dissimilar. Both were smart, hardworking, and shared a burning ambition — Mitchell for wealth and Pecora for acclaim. But that's where the similarities ended. Mitchell had testified in congressional hearings before and had emerged unscathed. Pecora had been committee counsel for just a few weeks and had almost no time to investigate the bank's complex and far-flung operations. Mitchell was a world-renowned banker and an adviser to Presidents Harding, Coolidge, and Hoover on economic matters. Outside New York, almost no one had ever heard of Ferdinand Pecora. Mitchell was a member of New York's social elite, with all the trappings of Wall Street success — a Fifth Avenue mansion, houses in Tuxedo Park and the Hamptons, country club memberships, and a garage full of big, fast cars. Pecora was an Italian immigrant who was still struggling to overcome the bigotry and stereotypes of the day. After years of government service, he had managed to save just a few hundred dollars. Mitchell had the wealth and resources of City Bank at his disposal, and he strode into the hearing room surrounded by the most expensive legal talent in the country. Pecora had just cobbled together a tiny staff of first-generation immigrants, all earning the same meager salary he did. Nobody was expecting very much from Pecora.

Just ten days after the City Bank hearings began, Mitchell would walk out alone, discredited and disgraced. The bank quickly accepted his resignation. Pecora had shown that the bank and its securities-trading arm had engaged in all sorts of unsavory behavior. It sold worthless bonds to investors without fully disclosing their risks, manipulated its own stock price and the stock prices of other companies, and lavishly compensated its executives as the country plunged into depression. It's almost impossible not to hear in today's financial problems the echoes of those hearings held more than seventy-five years ago. Most Americans then blamed Wall Street and the banking sector for the ills facing the country. There was populist outrage over excessive executive compensation. The markets seemed to be awash in manipulative short selling, in favorable deals for the fortunate few, and in dodgy loans that were foisted on unwary investors. Against the backdrop of the then exploding banking crisis, the disclosures were riveting and, ultimately, revolutionary.

While the investigation continued to produce stunning revelations for months—including a dramatic confrontation between Pecora and J. P. Morgan Jr. later that spring—it was those ten days that set the tone for everything that followed. It was then, when banks across the country were shuttering, when City Bank's executives were in the dock, and when Pecora led America through the bank's financial machinations, that the federal government crossed its regulatory Rubicon. This was the turning point in which the relationship between Wall Street and Washington was forever altered.

Even more than that, it seemed to be a visible turning point in American society. In an ornate hearing room in Washington, one of the new Americans, so long dispossessed and marginalized, was firmly in control of the machinery of federal government. An Italian American, a member of a group almost universally regarded as crime-prone and lawless, was exposing the lawlessness of the Anglo-Saxons who ruled Wall Street. Those ten days were a vivid sign that something fundamental had changed in the power structure of the country.

This is the story of those ten days.

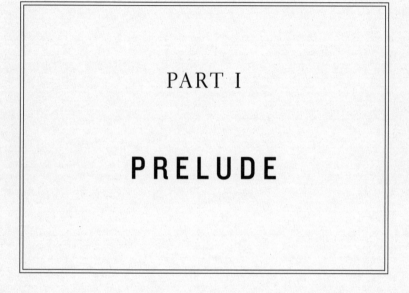

PART I

PRELUDE

Chapter 1

THE WELL-DRILLER
AND WALL STREET

On New Year's Eve 1932, Peter Norbeck sat behind his sturdy mahogany desk in the Senate Office Building, cigar in hand, dictating letters to one of his team of secretaries. Even on the last day of the year, the South Dakota Republican couldn't relax; it just wasn't in his nature, and, anyway, he was too far behind in answering the mail that constantly poured in from his constituents. Outside he could see the Capitol dome through the light rain that was falling on the city. The view was fitting for a senior senator of the majority party, as was his front-row seat in the Senate chamber, just to the vice president's left. Around him on the walls were the tokens of what he had accomplished in a quarter of a century in politics. The most prominent was the photograph of the work in progress on Mount Rushmore, George Washington's head emerging from the Black Hills' granite.

The senator had every reason to be content on that warm winter day. Six weeks before, he had somehow managed to emerge untouched from the "Democratic cyclone" that swept the country. He won reelection easily, which was more than most Republicans could claim that year. The 1932 presidential election had, naturally, been a stunning rebuke for Hoover. When Hoover was elected in 1928, the "Great Engineer" was hailed as one of the most competent and ablest men ever to win the office. Now his name was synonymous with poverty and depression. It wasn't just "Hoovervilles"—newspapers were "Hoover blankets," empty, turned-out pockets "Hoover flags." Depending on where you lived, the armadillos, groundhogs, or rabbits the desperately hungry caught and ate were "Hoover hogs." People who were left penniless in the Depression had been "Hooverized."[1]

Norbeck certainly didn't like to see Democrats elected president, and he was particularly unsure of this one. In his letters that year, Norbeck called Roosevelt "superficial" and "shifty," and he said that he had "absolutely no confidence in him or his Party." Indeed, just so everyone was clear on that score, Norbeck made sure to amend his biography in the Congressional Directory, which used to read "Roosevelt Republican"; it was now "Theodore Roosevelt Republican." Norbeck's wariness had more to do with a fear of the unknown than a real difference in political outlook. Norbeck viewed himself as a friend of the common man, particularly if the common man was one of the farmers who regularly voted for him. He was not averse to bucking party lines, and he regularly opposed the Republicans' conservative bloc. He was, in the words of a journalist of the day, "one of those prairie Republicans—half Democrat, half other ingredients, but less than one-half of one percent Republican."[2]

For all his suspicion of Roosevelt, Norbeck couldn't generate much sympathy for Hoover. The two had never seen eye to eye. Norbeck even refused to endorse Hoover in the 1932 election, a move that infuriated the president. Norbeck's decision to run his own campaign and remain uncommitted on the presidential election was driven by both his personal antipathy toward Hoover and his political pragmatism. The Depression had hit South Dakota farmers hard, and commodity prices had fallen to levels not seen in years. Wheat was twenty-five cents a bushel, oats less than a dime. By the time the farmer paid for shipping, he was lucky to make a few pennies. It was no wonder that some farmers simply left the crops in the field to rot. The letters Norbeck read from his constituents were brimming with ominous portents even more troubling than the current low prices—rainless skies, burnt and stunted crops, and swarming grasshoppers.

As Norbeck's reelection campaign crisscrossed the state that summer and fall, farmers gathered in mass rallies and blockaded roads with sharpened telegraph poles. Milo Reno, the leader of the militant Farmers' Holiday Association, was advocating that midwesterners withhold produce from the market or simply destroy it—all part of a strike to protest low agricultural prices and the wave of foreclosures sweeping the Great Plains. For months, raging mobs of desolate farmers interrupted foreclosure sales, and now self-help was turning violent—the dead body of a lawyer who had handled a foreclosure was dumped in a Kansas field; a sheriff and the representative of a New York mortgage company were beaten up in front of a courthouse; auctioneers were intimidated into selling farms back to their dispossessed owners for just a few dollars. For years Hoover regularly opposed the farm legislation that Norbeck tried to push through, and the senator did not have to look far to see just how unpopular Hoover was back home. If Norbeck held his nose and endorsed the incumbent president he might get dragged down along with him.[3]

The problem, of course, was that it was not just the presidential election that had gone so poorly—Democrats now controlled both the House and the Senate. Roosevelt's long coattails meant that Norbeck was going to lose the chairmanship of the Senate Banking and Currency Committee on March 4, 1933, the day the new Congress was to be sworn in and Roosevelt inaugurated. No, Norbeck was far from content on that last day of 1932, but it wasn't only because he was about to lose this plum and powerful committee chairmanship, the prestige that came along with it, and his view of the Capitol. Norbeck was unhappy because he had only two more months in the lame duck session of Congress to complete his Wall Street investigation, and it was going nowhere fast.

That Peter Norbeck was chairman of the Banking and Currency Committee was itself a bit hard to fathom. In fact, it would be hard to conjure up a more unlikely committee chairman. He was born in the Dakota Territories in 1870, the eldest son of Scandinavian immigrants. Raised on the family's farm with little formal education, he completed only three semesters at the University of Dakota, where he was doing mostly high-school-level work. He had a decent memory for facts, but he was neither an original nor a creative thinker.

He proved, however, to be a sharp and successful businessman. Norbeck made his fortune as a young man drilling artesian wells for farmers in the arid northern plains. He was the prototypical midwestern farm boy, a burly six-footer who tipped the scales at well over two hundred pounds. He had broad shoulders, a thick neck, and a pronounced Norwegian accent, which he made no attempt to conceal. In his Senate days a Washington journalist said that Norbeck "gave the impression of rugged strength and power. He wore his thick, bristling, iron-grey hair clipped short, and a heavy, full mustache completely covered his upper lip."[4]

When reporter Ray Tucker profiled Congress's progressive midwesterners (derisively labeled by many as Sons of the Wild Jackass) in 1932, he said that Norbeck's "greatest charm was his willingness to be himself. He puts on no airs and makes no pretense of being something that he is not." Despite that assessment, Norbeck was not above using his homespun manners to his political advantage. "Seemingly a naïve and childlike spirit," Tucker wrote, "'Pete' as he is known, is . . . one of the smartest politicians in the Senate; his naiveté is an affectation and armament."[5]

Norbeck entered politics in 1908 when he was elected to the South Dakota State Senate as a progressive Republican. In 1912 he supported Theodore Roosevelt's third-party bid for the presidency. Like Teddy Roosevelt, Norbeck was an ardent conservationist. In fact, it was Norbeck who insisted that Theodore Roosevelt, who remained Norbeck's political hero throughout his life, be enshrined on Mount Rushmore, the project Norbeck was single-handedly backing in Washington.[6]

In 1916, Norbeck was elected governor. Despite his avowed admiration for Roosevelt's moderate progressivism, Norbeck pursued an aggressive program of state ownership of private business. He, like other midwestern progressives, was hostile to the financial establishment. He thought bankers regularly gouged farmers on crop loans, so his largest venture was a system of rural credits that provided direct governmental loans to farmers at below-market rates. The program was a disaster because South Dakota proved to be an inept banker. In a time of falling farm prices, it made loans with little documentation. Bankers administered the law locally, and their primary mission was often shedding their own bad debts. By the mid-1920s, one-third of the state loans were in default, and taxpayers eventually bore the costs of bailing out the system.

The failure of the rural credits plan would, however, not come until later;

Norbeck was still by far the single most popular and powerful politician in South Dakota when he was elected to the United States Senate in 1920. In the Senate he focused primarily, although usually unsuccessfully, on agricultural issues, but was also assigned to the Banking and Currency Committee. It is not entirely clear how he got the post, and in his early years he showed virtually no interest in it. He was, though, at least frank about his ignorance, quipping that "as an authority on banking and currency he was the ablest well-driller in Congress." In the beginning, he did little more than show up at committee meetings. In 1925 he even offered to step down, but was reappointed.[7]

By 1927, however, he was the ranking Republican on the committee and therefore entitled to become its chairman. He continued to have little interest in the field, but was told that turning down the chairmanship might lose him considerable prestige. So he took the post, much to the surprise of his Senate colleagues. After his appointment, Norbeck still had only the most superficial understanding of how banks or Wall Street worked. His most common practice was to turn difficult problems over to Carter Glass, the Democrat from Virginia. The seventy-five-year-old Glass was a former Treasury secretary and generally acknowledged as the father of the Federal Reserve System. He had been Congress's resident expert on banking for three decades, and he became the real power on the committee.

As the stock market boomed to unprecedented heights in 1929, Norbeck did little to try to tamp down speculation. About the best he could muster was a rather lame warning that "what goes up must come down." It did, and as the country sank deeper and deeper into depression, more and more reform proposals came before the committee. At that point, Norbeck's lack of sophistication actually helped him, if not the rest of country. "I really begin to think I am fortunate," he wrote a friend, "in the fact that part of the stuff goes over my head—I do not understand it all. If I did, maybe I wouldn't sleep."[8]

In early 1932, while Norbeck sat bewildered in the Senate, Hoover was fuming in the White House. The embattled president needed to pin the blame for the failed economic recovery somewhere and he chose Wall Street short sellers as his scapegoats. They were, after all, tried-and-true villains; politicians have complained about short sellers in down markets since tulip bulbs were all the rage. The stock exchange in those early Depression years still seemed as lawless as the Wild West, and short sellers did everything they could to make sure that they came out on the right side of their bets that stock prices would fall. They circulated false rumors and formed shadowy conspiracies known as bear pools that would try to force prices down, just as during the boom years stock traders had used pools to drive prices up.

Hoover believed bear raiders were deliberately impeding economic recovery, both for their own financial benefit and to embarrass the administration. As one sympathetic Republican senator put it, "every time an Administration official gives out an optimistic statement about business conditions, the market immediately drops." Short sellers, the president insisted, were destroying "public confidence," and he appealed to their sense of duty. "If these gentlemen have some sense of patriotism which outruns immediate profit," Hoover lectured, "they will close up these transactions and desist from their manipulations." Many in Congress thought such attempts at moral suasion were bound to fail. They introduced a welter of proposals to curb short selling or ban it outright, even though those bills had little hope of actually being enacted.[9]

The notion that the market swoon and the Depression were solely the product of short selling was, in any event, delusional. Short sales certainly increased after Hoover speeches, but it was not a conspiracy. Bears had simply learned that investors now so thoroughly distrusted Hoover that whenever he predicted recovery the market would drop. Even the largest traders did not have enough capital to drive down and keep down the entire market if the economy were really recovering. Democrats began to openly mock Hoover's paranoia and his attempts to pin the continued Depression on a Wall Street conspiracy rather than his own failures. One senator elicited peals of laughter from his colleagues when he sarcastically suggested that "possibly after all the man who caused the panic will be located and shown to be some little broker over in Wall Street who has brought about the panic and now, through a spirit of willfulness, will not let us have prosperity back again."[10]

Hoover remained convinced that Wall Street was at fault, but there was little he was willing to do to rectify the matter. He wouldn't support the bills to limit short selling because he adamantly believed that the federal government had no business regulating the New York Stock Exchange. In fact, the president thought that such legislation was likely unconstitutional. So for two years Hoover did little but plead with the exchange's president, Richard Whitney, to take steps to rein in the short sellers. The patrician Whitney assured the president the exchange would act, but made only piddling changes to stock market rules.

Whitney even seemed to thumb his nose at the president. He continued to make speeches around the country proclaiming that "normal short selling is an essential part of the free market in securities" and ridiculing the notion of rampant bear raiders. In a national radio broadcast in October 1931, Whitney lashed out at the exchange's critics. "I would like to ask what proof there is—not blind prejudice, not vague assertions, but actual proof and evidence—that bear raiding has taken place in the stock market." Any attempt to ban short selling, he warned, would lead to Armageddon, the very "destruction of the market." Whitney was right that an outright ban on short selling was nonsensical, but his constant and very public intransigence infuriated the president.[11]

By the winter of 1931–32, Hoover had had enough. With the upcoming election, he was convinced that Democrats on Wall Street, prominent financiers and traders like Bernard Baruch and the Democratic National Committee chairman John J. Raskob, were planning huge bear raids that would crater the stock market and further dim his chances for reelection. In an angry meeting with exchange leaders, Hoover demanded immediate action. "Mr. Whitney made profuse promises, but did nothing," the president wrote. On February 16, 1932, Hoover issued a final ultimatum to Whitney—take substantial steps to stop bear raids or he would ask Congress to investigate "with a view to Federal control legislation." This was the first time Hoover had threatened an investigation, but given the president's views on the propriety of federal securities legislation, Whitney likely thought it was an idle threat. But Hoover did not back down. He told reporters that short sellers were bringing "discouragement to the country as a whole" and explained that he had asked the exchange to "take adequate measures to protect investors from artificial depression of the price of securities for speculative profit."[12]

A few days later, after yet another meaningless tweak to the exchange's short-selling rules, Hoover reached out to the Senate Banking and Currency Committee, although not to its chairman. Instead of contacting Norbeck, Hoover turned to Republican senator Frederic Walcott, the president's go-to man in the Senate. It was a natural choice. According to Washington columnists Drew Pearson and Robert Allen, Walcott was not only one of the president's fishing buddies, he was also his "most devoted henchman," a man who "gratefully does all the little chores which the President cannot get the Republican leaders to do, and [who] unquestioningly carries out under-cover legislative schemes for the President." It was Walcott that Hoover wanted to run an investigation of Wall Street, and the selection spoke volumes about the president's intentions.

Walcott was a conservative former investment banker from Connecticut who was in constant contact with Wall Street's leaders, frequently reporting their views back to the president. He was a staunch defender of wealth, privilege, and the economic status quo, hardly the man to conduct the kind of rigorous investigation of Wall Street misdeeds that would lay the groundwork for federal legislation. But federal legislation was not what Hoover was after, a point Walcott made explicitly just a few days later. The president really only wanted to scare and embarrass the short sellers so they would stop, in his view, driving down stock prices. When Walcott emerged from his meeting with Hoover, he made that intention clear to the assembled reporters, telling them that the committee would look at every angle of short selling and that "some of the outstanding bear raiders" would be called to testify. "We have the names," he gruffly told the press. The committee would disclose the identities of "these big professional raiders who have been deliberately taking the bloom off of every constructive enterprise for the last year."[13]

The Wall Street investigation, such as it was, was under way.

Ten months later, with authorization for the investigation and Norbeck's chairmanship both expiring on March 4, 1933, the South Dakota senator wanted to return to the probe, which had lain dormant since June 1932. The senator had expressed high hopes for the investigation when it got started in the spring. In early March, as the country obsessed over news of the Lindbergh kidnapping and of Al Capone being shipped off to jail for tax evasion, Norbeck and the other progressives on the committee seized control of the investigation. Unlike Walcott, they were not complaisant yes-men, and they saw little reason to limit a Wall Street investigation to short selling. The resolution they adopted permitted the committee to investigate virtually any aspect of stock exchange practices. By April, Norbeck had wrested control of the investigation away from Walcott. The South Dakota senator would run it himself.

In part it was a shrewd political move. There was no love lost for Wall Street in South Dakota, and Norbeck knew that investigating the stock market would sell well to his constituents back home. One political cartoon from his home state, captioned "Keep Norbeck on the Job," showed a South Dakota voter cheering as Norbeck, wearing overalls and brandishing a pitchfork, chased "Wall Street Gamblers." Norbeck, however, was thinking farther ahead than just the next election. After years of frustration over the failed farm legislation he had sponsored, Norbeck saw this investigation as his best chance to leave his mark in Washington. He was careful not to share those views publicly, telling reporters when asked what effect the inquiry would have on the stock market, "I don't know, and I don't care." Privately, however, he admitted the potential significance of what he was about to undertake. "This is the greatest opportunity I have had for broad work since I came to Washington," he wrote to his campaign manager.[14]

Seven months later, he knew that his aspirations had largely failed. Despite the expanded resolution, the committee had mostly confined itself to short selling, as Hoover wanted. Even with that limited focus, the hearings had not gone well. "This committee has spent a great deal of time trying to prove up on short selling as having a far-reaching effect on the market," Norbeck wrote. "Our best effort did not result in anything substantial, though everyone knows that." Then, at the end of June the committee announced without warning that it would suspend the investigation for the summer and fall. Norbeck had little choice; he needed to get back to South Dakota to wage his reelection campaign, and the other committee members insisted that they did not want hearings while Congress was adjourned. The press was both puzzled and surprised, especially since another $50,000 had just been appropriated to continue the probe. What exactly did this latest announcement mean? No one was sure. "What the future may hold for the investigation is unknown," the *New York Times* reported, but the paper was quick to point out that when Congress suspended investigations it rarely restarted them.[15]

In November 1932, Norbeck announced that he was ready to try again. A little more than a week after the election, he returned to Washington and told reporters that the committee would turn its attention to the Insull utility empire, which had collapsed spectacularly earlier in the year, taking 600,000 shareholders and 500,000 bondholders with it. The implosion of the Chicago-based company was billed as "the biggest business failure in the history of the world," the equivalent of an Enron or Lehman Brothers today. It wasn't hard to see the potential to score some political points. Even Roosevelt, in a campaign speech in California in September, had railed against "the reckless promoter, the Ishmael or Insull whose hand is against every man's." Several of Norbeck's political cronies, including his good friend and progressive colleague Senator Hiram Johnson of California, urged him to "cash in" on the scandal.[16]

Cashing in would not be easy. Samuel Insull, the mastermind behind the company, was in Greece, beyond the reach of the federal prosecutors in Chicago who had just indicted him for fraud. Many of the basic facts about the collapse were already well-known. The scandal had been thoroughly ventilated in the press and trustees were in charge of the company, sorting out the mess Insull left behind. Criminal enforcement authorities and "[e]verybody in Cook County running for office" had already been investigating for some time. It was more than a bit unclear what adding a set of congressional hearings on top of all those other investigations would accomplish.[17]

Norbeck said he would hold hearings anyway, even declaring that the committee might subpoena Samuel Insull if and when he was extradited from Greece. The New York bankers seemed unconcerned. "I am reliably informed," a member of Norbeck's staff wrote to him, "that Wall St. and the Exchange are well satisfied and believe nothing will be done." The press was similarly skeptical. This was a lame duck session of Congress, after all, and the committee was likely to find all its time devoted to new banking and reconstruction legislation. The press was right. In mid-December, the committee gave a banking bill sponsored by Senator Glass privileged status, a move intended to help speed it along. It meant that the banking bill would take precedence over almost everything else that came before the committee, with only Senator Glass having the ability to move it temporarily to the back burner.[18]

The ill-fated bill needed all the help it could get. It represented a major structural overhaul of banking regulation, and the ideas embodied in it had been kicking around in Congress since 1931, when Glass and a Columbia economics professor named H. Parker Willis began stultifyingly dry hearings on banking reform. The bill that emerged had something for everyone to hate, with two features at the very top of the list. Banking laws to this point reflected Americans' historical wariness of large concentrations of capital. They limited the ability of the largest banks to establish branches, and at the same time permitted small rural banks scattered throughout the South, the West, and parts of the Midwest to form and operate with tiny capital reserves. Naturally, those small banks took a beating when the economic downturn came, and most of the failures over the last few years had come from that group.

The Glass bill sought to solidify the creaking banking structure by reversing the previous policy, giving large urban banks greater leeway to open branches and increasing the capital requirements for small national banks. The presidents of the small local banks saw the branch banking provision as a death knell for their businesses, and they lobbied their senators hard to oppose it. As those bank presidents also happened to be major campaign contributors, the senators from those largely rural states were more than happy to oblige, including Norbeck, who was one of the most outspoken opponents of expanded branch banking.[19]

At the same time, Glass, a bitter and longtime critic of Wall Street "gambling," thought that large commercial banks had contributed more than their fair share to the speculative excesses of the 1920s because they had moved heavily into the stock-and-bond-selling business. Federal law technically prohibited nationally chartered banks from engaging in these investment banking activities directly, but big banks like City Bank and smaller ones, too, evaded those restrictions by forming securities affiliates, companies that were technically owned by the banks' shareholders but which the banks controlled. Glass's original bill simply proposed regulation, but the committee was flooded with so many letters complaining about securities affiliates that Glass ultimately decided that complete separation of commercial and investment banking was the only viable approach.

That proposal had a fair amount of support in Democratic circles—it had even been a plank in the 1932 Democratic platform. Republicans, at least publicly, favored only greater regulation and control, but even the most conservative of them had little good to say about the affiliates in private. The previous summer, Walcott told Hoover that the affiliates were "disgraceful affairs and ought to be done away with." Eugene Meyer, the Federal Reserve chairman, deplored affiliates. "These investment companies were doing more harm to the banks than they seemed to realize," he later said. "It was one of the vicious things that led to the disaster."[20]

Commercial bankers, naturally, saw matters differently. The American Bankers Association and the United States Chamber of Commerce opposed the bill; the ABA president went so far as to argue that Congress should repeal some of the banking laws already in existence, not pass more. In a magazine article entitled "Men, Not Laws, Make Sound Banks," he argued that Americans need only rely on the "honesty and efficiency" of the men who ran the country's largest banks. They were "the true strength of American banking" and they "continued to command public confidence . . . because they conformed conscientiously to principles of sound public service, which are better business guides than any statute ever written." With every quarter of the banking industry against some aspect of Glass's bill, it appeared to have little chance of success, although it would swallow inordinate amounts of time and energy in the Banking and Currency Committee.[21]

The same day that Glass's bill was fast-tracked, Norbeck again announced he was pushing forward with his investigation of Insull, even though members of his own committee were pushing right back. Some questioned the propriety of the committee poking around in the matter in the midst of an ongoing federal criminal investigation. Others argued that it was nonsense to do so while Insull remained in Greece. Many on the committee went even further, advocating that they should abandon the investigation altogether. With so little time left and so many other things to do, what was the point of continuing?

By the end of the year the investigation had foundered; the committee had not held a single hearing. Norbeck pressed on, announcing on December 28 that the Insull hearings would indeed be held, although he did not give a specific date. In private, he was much less sanguine. On that warm and rainy New Year's Eve, Norbeck wrote a friend: "I am having a dickens of a time here to get my Wall Street investigation started. There is so much 'inertia'; I find it in the

most unexpected places, even among those from whom I expected much help."
Norbeck knew that many of his fellow committee members did "not have any
relish for this work," but he was not yet ready to give up.[22]

The key problem now was finding a competent lawyer to lead the last two
months of the investigation. The search was proving much more difficult than
Norbeck had ever imagined.

Chapter 2

THE BEST
CROSS-EXAMINER
IN NEW YORK

erdinand Pecora, like Peter Norbeck, had every reason to be content as 1932 came to a close. For the past three years he had been a name partner in a small Manhattan law firm. After three decades in city politics, he was on a first-name basis with almost all of New York's leading politicians and lawyers. Married, with his only son at New York University, the good-natured lawyer with the easy smile was "Ferd" or "Ferdie" to his large group of close friends. In a week, the dignified and voluble attorney would turn fifty-one years old, and he was prospering. He had just moved to a nice apartment on the Upper West Side of Manhattan. Private practice allowed him to support his extended family, to put away some savings, and to contribute something to the charities that were then helping the army of unemployed encamped in the city. He wasn't anywhere near rich, but he was comfortable, and that, in itself, was an accomplishment given the Depression raging all around him. He had, by any measure, come a long way in the forty-seven years since he first sailed into New York Harbor.

. . .

Pecora was born in Nicosia, Sicily, a small Italian hill town due west of Mount Etna, on January 6, 1882, the third son of Luigi and Rosa Messina Pecora. Luigi was a shoemaker and at thirty-six had already been working at his craft for the better part of three decades. Rosa was only twenty when her third child, Ferdinand, was born, and just a year and a half later, Luigi left Sicily for New York. He was in the first wave of the great Italian exodus from the Mezzogiorno, the land south of Rome, which had always been economically the poorest part of the country. But it wasn't just economics that drove Pecora out of Italy. Protestant missionaries had just swept through that overwhelmingly Roman Catholic country and, in one of their few successes there, had managed to convert Luigi Pecora. In a country where the Catholic hierarchy denounced Protestantism as the equivalent of atheism or Satan worship, that conversion created enormous social strains for the family. They were outcasts, Ferdinand later said, shunned "by their friends and neighbors, and even by their own blood."[1]

His son described Luigi as a "strong-willed and stubborn individualist" who, rather than abandon his new religion, abandoned Sicily. He left alone for the United States in 1883 and in a little less than three years saved enough money to bring the rest of the family across. Rosa and the couple's now four children arrived aboard the *Alesia* on May 25, 1886, when Ferdinand was just four years old. It was seemingly an auspicious year to enter the country. The Statue of Liberty was dedicated that same year, and the great wave of immigration to the United States was cresting. But at the statue's elaborate dedication ceremony that October, not one speaker mentioned the Emma Lazarus poem written three years earlier. While that omission might seem puzzling today, the reality was that 1886 was an inopportune time to be one of the huddled masses yearning to breathe free.[2]

The United States was in turmoil. A decade earlier, the country had been largely rural, agrarian, and homogeneous. Now it was reeling, whipsawed by tectonic shifts in the cultural landscape. Urbanization, industrialization, immigration—they were all happening at once. The increasing tensions within America's rapidly evolving society were most sharply revealed in industrial-labor relations, which were growing alarmingly antagonistic. Violent confrontations among union activists, police, state militias, and federal troops were an all too common occurrence. As tensions mounted, a small but active band of anarchists, many of them European exiles, was beginning to garner public attention by pressing workers to escalate the conflict, to use any means necessary to improve their lot. Over the next generation, political violence—the Haymarket riot, the assassination of William McKinley, the attempted murders of various corporate chieftains, and the bombing of Wall Street—pervaded American society.[3]

Most Americans laid the blame for the violent radicalism and social unrest at the feet of the European immigrants pouring into the country, unleashing, in the words of historian John Higham, "a torrent of nationalist hysteria." The newspapers of the day whipped up this fervor with vicious editorials condemning the newcomers. These immigrants were "not Americans, but the very scum and offal of Europe." Americans weren't responsible for the increasing rate of labor violence; it was this "invasion of venomous reptiles" that was causing all the trouble. The country should shut its doors to any new "foreign savages who might come to America with their dynamite bombs and anarchic purposes." Those already here should be "crush[ed] . . . before they [had] time to bite."[4]

When Ferdinand and his family arrived in the United States, they had an additional strike against them. They were not just any immigrants; they were among this country's first wave of Southern Italian immigrants. Southern Italians, so different from the early waves of northern Europeans, were singled out for some of the harshest treatment during that time. "There has never been since New York was founded," the *New York Times* wrote around the time Luigi arrived in the United States, "so low and ignorant a class among the immigrants who poured in here as the Southern Italians who have been crowding our docks during the past year."[5]

That Italians were the object of intense bigotry, discrimination, and hatred is somewhat hard to appreciate today. After all, Americans with at least some Italian heritage number in the tens of millions. They have occupied virtually every position of power, influence, or prestige in the country. Hollywood, to be sure, still peddles stereotypes and will continue to do so as long as the public does not weary of Mafia movies. But no one today would blink an eye if they heard that an Italian American had been appointed as counsel for a high-profile Senate committee.

It was different in the late 1800s, when stereotypical views of Southern Italians were widely held. The *Times* viewed Sicilians, like the Pecoras, as "ragged, filthy and verminous." Many thought Italians were universally bloodthirsty criminals who lacked the intellectual capabilities of Anglo-Saxons or northern Europeans. "The disposition to assassinate in revenge for a fancied wrong," the *Baltimore Daily News* editorialized, "is a marked trait in the character of this impulsive and inexorable race." Italians were accused of creating the ghettos in which they lived because of their willingness to tolerate filthy and crime-ridden conditions. Even Jacob Riis, the muckraking journalist and ardent tenement reform advocate, wrote that the "hot-headed" and "swarthy" Italian "is content to live in a pig-sty" and frequently settled his quarrels at the point of a knife.[6]

Tales of Italian criminal activities were frequent fodder for urban newspapers, and many imagined that a secret Southern Italian crime organization, the Black Hand Society, extended its reach into every American city in which Italians were present. American immigration authorities classified Southern Italians as a distinct race on naturalization certificates, separate from the more favored Northern Italians. Unlike northern Europeans, olive-skinned Southern Italians like Ferdinand were not considered "white," and in the South they could not attend white schools.[7]

Occasionally racism erupted into violence. When the Pecoras were settling in New York during the early days of Italian immigration, many Italians, unable to find work elsewhere, served as strikebreakers, leading to violent clashes between them and the Irish and German workers they displaced. There were several Italian lynchings in the 1890s, the most infamous of which happened in New Orleans. The local paper justified the killing of eleven Italian immigrants: "Desperate diseases required desperate remedies." While it might be easy to chalk that response up to the Southern racism of the times, the lynchings were national news and those views were apparently widely shared. In an editorial sympathetic to the lynch men, the *New York Times* argued that the victims were "sneaking and cowardly Sicilians, the descendants of bandits and assassins, who have transported to this country the lawless passions, the cutthroat practices, and the oath-bound societies of their native country, [who] are to us a pest without mitigations. Our own rattlesnakes are as good citizens as they." Italian lynchings continued well into the 1900s.[8]

Those anti-immigrant and anti-Italian attitudes would wax and wane over the next half century, typically in harmony with the ups and downs of the economy, but they never disappeared entirely, and they would, as much as anything else, shape the future Hellhound of Wall Street.

Unlike most Italian immigrants, who took refuge in the emerging Little Italys on the Lower East Side and in East Harlem, the Pecoras moved to Chelsea, a largely Irish neighborhood. Most likely Luigi, having fled Sicily in the face of religious discrimination, was not keen on re-creating the same social ostracism that had plagued the family there.[9]

If Luigi's goal was instant acceptance into American society, he met with little success, especially as far as his third son was concerned. Ferdinand felt isolated in his new home. "Of course, we were in every sense strangers in a strange land," he recalled. The Irish residents of Chelsea, although themselves relative newcomers to the United States, did not think much of these Italian interlopers. Ferdinand was the only Italian in his school, and his classmates hurled the usual racial slurs at him—*wop, guinea, dago.*[10]

In truth, when he was young he was embarrassed at being Italian. Pecora simply wanted to fit in, to shed his foreignness, to become an American like everyone else. Even in the ethnic enclaves, the desire of a newly arrived immigrant child to assimilate was overwhelming. Pecora's isolation from the larger Italian émigré community made his craving to fit in virtually inevitable. For Pecora, a large part of discarding his minority status seemed to require proving the Italian stereotype wrong, at least as far as he was concerned. If most people thought Italians were unintelligent, he would excel in school. If most thought Italians lazy, he would be industrious. If most thought they were lawless, he would become a lawyer.

In his late fifties, Ferdinand discussed that desire to quickly assimilate to life in the United States in a short radio address for a series called *I Am an American.* All traces of an Italian or even a New York accent had long since vanished from his speech. His voice was rich and his articulation precise. He had perfected the mid-Atlantic accent of a well-educated, upper-class, urbane American; indeed, his tones and cadences were remarkably similar to Franklin Roosevelt's. Turning his father's decision to shun the Italian American community into an asset, he began with a boast of complete immersion in his new culture. He chided residents of ethnic enclaves, "who follow still the Old World ways and customs of life," and criticized those "who never learned *our language* well enough to really understand America." That last bit of phrasing is significant. He didn't complain that Italians weren't learning English; he complained that they weren't learning "our language." He really did think of himself as an American, not an Italian.[11]

Pecora's teachers almost certainly fostered that attitude. Public schools were at the forefront of Americanization efforts when Pecora began to attend them in 1888. As educators saw it, their job was to churn out loyal Americans by forcing children to forsake their cultures. In fact, in his first year at Public School 55 his teachers even made Ferdinand change the pronunciation of his name. In Italian, his surname is pronounced with the accent on the first syllable. But to Miss Anderson, Pecora's first grade teacher, that did not sound "euphonious." "Well," she told him, "it's easier to say Pe-cor-a than Pec-or-a." And that was the way that he, and everyone else, pronounced it for the rest of his life.[12]

Compounding Pecora's isolation was the family's desperate financial straits. Even when he was still quite young, Ferdinand could see that his family was far worse off than those around it. The Pecoras settled on Ninth Avenue, between 18th and 19th streets. For eight dollars each month, the family rented a basement cold-water flat that was originally intended as a storeroom for the shop above. The building sat in the shadow of the elevated train, the smoke and cinders drifting down on their apartment below. The basement was just one room, but thin partitions walled it off into three small areas. The front was reserved for Luigi's shoe repair shop, and the family squeezed itself into the little space that was left. The apartment was well below street level, and so dark that they could see only by waiting for their eyes to adjust to the feeble light from the kerosene lamps. The only heat was from the coal stove they used for cooking. The toilet was a pit in the backyard.[13]

Pecora's block was something of a borderland. To the south and west stretched a hodgepodge of tenements filled with the Irish working poor, industrial buildings, coal and lumber yards, meatpacking plants, and a bustling waterfront. Just north, however, Pecora could see a different New York—a middle-class, Anglo-Saxon New York of tidy, high-stooped brownstones. It wasn't long before Pecora came in contact with that other New York, when the family began to attend St. Peter's Episcopal Church, a short walk north from their apartment.

Eager to fit in, Pecora immersed himself in a host of church activities. He helped run the Young Men's Club. As an organizer of the Reading and Debating Club, he tackled the works of Shakespeare (he was fascinated by the speeches in *Julius Caesar*). He read all of Dickens's novels before he was fourteen, along with armfuls of histories and biographies. He excelled in the club's debates, where he argued about everything from American imperialism to whether Utah's representation in Congress should be tied to outlawing polygamy.[14]

Pecora loved being the center of attention in those debates and in the shows the boys put on for the parishioners. He had a strong need for approval, a craving for external affirmation. He began to develop a real love for dramatic performances. It was part of what later drew him to the courtroom. He thrived on the "drama of the law being performed in the trial courts" where he could see "the play of human nature."[15]

To get his drama fix when he was young, Pecora began going to the Grand Opera House on 23rd Street. He didn't have the money for admission, of course, but a classmate's father worked in the theater and was able to sneak him into the gallery for free. At one point, he even made it onto the stage, appearing as an extra in a production of *Julius Caesar*, which starred one of the leading actors of the day, Richard Mansfield. It was an "unforgettable experience" for Pecora, and a testament to his need for acceptance and acclaim. As he later recalled, there were "a number of occasions when the applause was terrific when I was on stage and I looked up hopefully, but then I saw Mansfield taking the bows."[16]

Most of his friends at St. Peter's were from, as Pecora called it, the "higher caste" that lived in those "very, very attractive" brownstones in the northern part of Chelsea and occasionally he would be invited to their homes. The visits "instilled" in him "a desire for a better kind of living." That desire to succeed also came from the church's rector, Reverend Olin Scott Roche. Before the ministry the plump Roche had a short career on Wall Street, and his sermons were still suffused with the American dream, although he did not define success only in material terms. Young people, he told the congregation, should have aspirations. "The trouble, especially with young men," he preached, "is that they set limits and bounds to their opportunities and capabilities. That is the reason they do not accomplish all that the Creator has fitted for them." Roche urged Pecora and the other young men to "help the world, attempt something, achieve something, and receive your reward—the thanks of men and the blessing of God."[17]

Pecora bought into Roche's philosophy wholeheartedly. "Individual initiative," he told radio listeners years later, "the hope of advancement through one's own efforts—these elements seem to me the fundamentals of progress in the American spirit." Pecora's determination to succeed, however, did little to improve his lot in the short term. In fact, the family's financial hardship quickly devolved into something much worse. Within two years of settling in New York, Ferdinand's oldest brother, Nicholas, died of pneumonia. Four years later, Ferdinand's older brother George drowned in the Hudson River, where the boys used to go to cool off in the hot summers, swimming off a busy pier at the foot of 22nd Street.

At ten, Ferdinand was now the oldest of the seven surviving children, and he was therefore expected to help support the family. He began to get up at six thirty in the morning to deliver quart milk cans throughout the neighborhood and after school he would hawk newspapers. When he was just eleven Ferdinand began to spend his summer breaks working in a shoe factory with his father, who had given up his struggling repair shop in the midst of a severe depression. Decades before New York began to enact effective laws regulating working conditions, the factory was brimming with dangerous machinery that frequently lacked even the most rudimentary of safety features. Ferdinand, who worked for as long as fourteen hours a day in those brutal conditions, saw "many sad cases of the workingmen being injured and carried out" of the factory.[18]

Encouraged by his parents, who had the "strongest desire . . . that all of their children should have as much of the advantages of education as they could possibly acquire," Ferdinand excelled in school and made long strides toward winning over his originally wary classmates. At the time the New York City public school system only went to the eighth grade, and when Pecora graduated, in 1895, he was both valedictorian and class president. Pecora was clearly smart and driven, and he wanted to continue his education and become a lawyer. Private prep school was out of the question; the free City College was the only realistic option. He sat for the entrance exam in June 1896, when he was old enough to enter, and ended up with the fifteenth highest score in the city.

Pecora enrolled briefly, but he didn't stay long. At St. Peter's, Pecora had caught the eye of Reverend Roche, who identified him as one of the church's "bright boys." Roche convinced Luigi that Ferdinand should study for the Episcopal ministry, and Ferdinand, the dutiful son, gave up his dream of becoming a lawyer. Through Roche's efforts, Pecora won a scholarship to attend St. Stephen's College in Annandale, New York, a classic liberal arts college for young men who planned to enter the Episcopal seminary, since renamed Bard College.[19]

Pecora enrolled in the tiny school—it had just eighty-five students—in September 1896. But his stay at St. Stephen's and his pursuit of the Episcopal ministry were nearly as short-lived as his City College career. Just before Christmas of that first semester, he learned that his father had been in a serious accident at the shoe factory, leaving him completely incapacitated. Workers' compensation was still decades away, and Pecora knew that "next to my mother, I was the only one who had any kind of physical capacity to be a breadwinner." Without consulting his parents, Pecora gave up his scholarship and hurried back to the city. He was the oldest son and his responsibility was to support his family. Just shy of his fifteenth birthday, Pecora's college career was over.[20]

For Ferdinand, leaving school was something of a mixed blessing. His mother was working in a Lower East Side sweatshop, and every night Ferdinand was appalled to see her trudge home bent under great bundles of unfinished work. After making dinner for the family, she would work well into the night stitching clothes. Rosa was exhausted and her face grew deeply lined from the stress and strain. Twenty years later, long after Rosa was able to quit the sweatshop, Ferdinand was amazed that his mother, then in her fifties, looked "far more youthful than she did in those photographs taken of her in the latter part of these so-called Gay Nineties."[21]

As a teenager providing the main economic support for his mother and six brothers and sisters, Pecora was under incredible strain. Unless you lived in the tenements, wrote Pecora's contemporary, the New York politician and labor reformer Robert Wagner, "you cannot know the haunting sense of insecurity which hangs over the home of the worker." But Ferdinand's heart had never really been in the Episcopal ministry. This was his chance to return to law. He replied to just two help-wanted ads, both for clerks in law offices, and he quickly landed one of the positions. Over the next twenty years, as he struggled to support his family and help put his younger brothers and sisters through school, Pecora would slowly ascend the legal ranks, first becoming a managing clerk, then going to law school, and finally becoming a member of the bar.[22]

With his interest in law and his prodigious speaking skills, he naturally turned to politics. In 1896, when he was just fourteen, Pecora had gone to Madison Square Garden to hear William Jennings Bryan, the Democrats' populist presidential nominee. He came away enthralled with Bryan's oratorical skill and captivated with his liberal politics. As he remembered in his oral history interview in the 1960s, "Mr. Bryan had the finest voice that I have ever heard on the lecture platform or any platform. He held that big throng just enchanted, partly by the wizardry of his voice I think as well as by the content of his speech."

Ferdinand gravitated to progressivism instead of the more radical strains of socialism, communism, or anarchism that had gained a toehold in the United States, particularly among disaffected immigrants. Pecora just couldn't "see any virtue in the fundamental principle of abolishing private property. I am a believer in the capitalistic system. I always felt that if the evils of capitalism could be excised from our economic system that the principle of capitalism is sounder than that of state ownership of the means of production and distribution." Progressivism did just that; it preserved the essential American structure but tried to smooth off its rough edges. Pecora's prescriptions reflected his own hard youth. What the country needed, Pecora thought, were "child labor laws; . . . workmen's compensation laws; [and] factory laws that would provide the workingman with a much safer place in which to do his work."[23]

That outlook led him to join the Progressive "Bull Moose" Party in 1912 and, like Norbeck, to support Theodore Roosevelt's unsuccessful third-party bid for the presidency. He became an active and accomplished stump speaker renowned for his extemporaneous speaking skills. When Pecora asked one political leader for suggestions for what he might say in a speech, the surprised reply was, "Since when did it become necessary for *you* to prepare a speech?" Indeed, sometimes Pecora could go on for more than anyone would have liked; "Pecora," Thomas Dewey complained, "was one of the most long-winded men God ever made." Unlike many great speakers, Pecora could also improvise, although that skill almost got him in trouble a few times. When a promoter mistakenly told a crowd that the well-known rabbi Stephen Samuel Wise was to speak at a rally, Pecora, at the promoter's urging, pretended to be the rabbi's assistant so as not to disappoint the gathered throng. Pecora quickly fled the scene after his impromptu speech as the crowd pushed in and began to speak to him in Yiddish. Wise thought the whole episode was hilarious and from then on he called Pecora his "Italian Assistant Rabbi."[24]

For all Pecora's hard work, New York's Progressive Party was a bust, managing to elect only a handful of state senators and assemblymen. When Teddy Roosevelt decided not to make another run under the Progressive banner in 1916, Pecora had a choice. New York had some progressive Republicans—men like Roosevelt and Fiorello La Guardia, who was elected to Congress for the first time that year. But Pecora decided instead to join the Democratic Party and support Woodrow Wilson for president. Here, too, Pecora faced a choice. Being a Democrat in New York City in 1916 meant either joining the city's notorious political machine, Tammany Hall, or becoming an independent Democrat. Most progressives abhorred the political machines, but the latter option probably meant continuing to lose. The ambitious Pecora joined Tammany.[25]

It was a calculated and pragmatic political decision, although Pecora could still claim that he was not completely abandoning his liberal principles. At the time, Charles Murphy ran Tammany. Murphy was no saint; he had grown wealthy in his stint as Tammany leader, mostly by making sure that his companies won city contracts. According to Murphy's rather nuanced moral system, those kinds of moneymaking opportunities were counted as acceptable "honest graft." Murphy clamped down on what he called "dishonest graft"—things like paying the police to look the other way while the bosses ran or profited from prostitution or gambling operations. Murphy's fine-grained distinctions certainly wouldn't pass muster today, but he was a vast improvement over prior bosses.

Murphy was also no ordinary political hack. He was very much an instrumentalist; all he wanted was to ensure the long-term success of Tammany, and to Murphy that meant making the machine respectable. He recognized, particularly after the tragic Triangle Shirtwaist Factory fire, in 1911, which killed 146 largely immigrant workers, that winning the fealty and votes of that burgeoning population was not simply a matter of providing patronage jobs, clambakes, and holiday food baskets. It involved giving them factory reforms and workers' compensation, providing women's suffrage and the direct election of senators. And that is just what Tammany did. Following the lead of his protégés, the future governor Al Smith and future senator Robert Wagner, Murphy helped push through the New York legislature some of the most progressive legislation in the country.[26]

Pecora threw himself into success in Tammany the same way he had thrown himself into winning over his classmates in Chelsea. "Pecora is the kind of man," one politician described, "who attends practically every dinner that is given." He began on the lowest rung of the political ladder, working in the local political clubhouse. In Pecora's case, recognition by the party's higher ups was not long in coming. With his verbal gifts, Pecora quickly joined Tammany's Speakers' Bureau, the crew of young political guns who gave stump speeches around the city on behalf of Tammany candidates. It was the same place where Smith and Wagner had started. Pecora's political career seemed to be taking off.[27]

A year later, Pecora successfully campaigned for Tammany's candidate for city comptroller, Charles Craig. On election night, Pecora sat with Craig and James Foley, a judge on New York's Surrogate's Court and the son-in-law of Charles Murphy. As it became clear that Craig was the winner, the talk turned to the role that Pecora should have in the new administration. Craig offered him a plum spot—chief deputy comptroller, the number-two man in the office, and Pecora turned him down flat. It was "a generous offer," the future interrogator of Wall Street told Craig, but he couldn't accept. "You've never had any banking experience," he explained, "and the chief deputy comptroller should be a man thoroughly trained in banking and finance. I probably know less about banking and finance than you do."[28]

Foley agreed that deputy comptroller didn't make sense. Besides, he had a better idea. The perfect perch for Pecora to launch a successful legal career was assistant district attorney in Manhattan. Pecora was equally adamant with Foley;

he couldn't think of a worse public office to hold. He found the atmosphere of the criminal courtroom "repulsive" and in private practice he had avoided criminal cases. "I don't believe that I could ever stand up before a jury of my fellow men and ask them to render a verdict that might mean the life or liberty of another person." Pecora turned down the job, but a month later it was offered to him again. This time his friends told him that prosecutors performed "very necessary work," work that "should be done always by persons of integrity . . . who would respect the rights of defendants." Pecora relented, and he was sworn in as a deputy assistant district attorney on January 1, 1918, just five days shy of his thirty-sixth birthday. The man who couldn't think of a worse job to have in government would spend the next twelve years in that office and would make a name for himself throughout the city as an honest, fair, and talented prosecutor.[29]

Indeed, when it came to respecting the rights of defendants, it took Pecora only a few months to prove his friends correct. He was asked to cover a simple one-day robbery trial for a sick colleague. Malcolm Wright was a young black man accused of robbing two women as they shopped on West 125th Street. The women convincingly identified Wright as the culprit. Wright's court-appointed attorney did little to shake their story on cross-examination, and he put just one witness on the stand, Malcolm Wright. Wright's alibi was that at the time of the robbery he was shooting craps with two people on the roof of a tenement building several blocks away. One of those two was a friend of Wright's, but he never testified. It wasn't much of a defense, and it shouldn't have been very surprising when the jury was back within the hour with a guilty verdict. It shouldn't have been, but as the foreman read the verdict Pecora got a "queer feeling" when he saw the look of "horror" on Wright's face.

On his desk the next morning Pecora found a scribbled note from Wright. "I swear to God I am innocent. Will you hear my whole story?" Pecora had Wright brought to his office and Wright revealed a tale of blatant police criminality. Wright had been picked up for the robbery a few days after it allegedly occurred and he protested his innocence to the detective who arrested him. "Well, maybe you're right," the detective told him, "but it will cost you $100 if you want me to believe it." When Wright failed to come up with the money, he was indicted.

Pecora believed Wright and brought the two women who had accused him in for questioning. At first they stuck to their story, but they were clearly uneasy. Then, after separating the women, Pecora told one of them that Wright was facing a twenty-year sentence. "[Y]ou look like the type of woman that wouldn't want to see anyone sentenced unjustly. Please think this over very carefully. I'm not going to ask you any questions for a few minutes. You just sit there and consult your own thoughts and then let me know if the story you've told, and the testimony you gave on the stand, was the truth."

The woman began to cry, and after Pecora promised that he would seek immunity for her for any perjury charge she told him what had really happened. Wright hadn't robbed her; she was conned out of the money by someone else. The police told her that the only way she would get it back was to finger Wright for the crime. Pecora went to the police station and there in the police blotter found the woman's original complaint, which corroborated her story. Pecora presented this evidence to the judge and asked him to set aside the conviction and to order a new trial, at which Wright was acquitted.[30]

Pecora had no tolerance for police misconduct. Prosecutors often say that their job is not to obtain convictions, but to see that justice is done. Pecora actually meant it. When he had evidence that the police had beaten a suspect to obtain a confession, Pecora didn't hesitate to testify on behalf of the suspect. It was his "solemn obligation," and although it probably won him no friends in the police department, he vowed that he would "do it again, and again, and again" if he had to.[31]

As a result of his work on the Wright case, Pecora was assigned to investigate another potential wrongful prosecution, this one involving a New York poultry dealer named Joseph Cohen, who'd been convicted of hiring assassins to kill his business rival, Barnett Baff. The murder and trial had been front-page news in all the city papers, and Cohen was on death row in Sing Sing when the district attorney learned that some of the testimony at the Cohen trial might have been perjured. He set Pecora to investigate the matter. In the face of obstruction after obstruction thrown up by the attorney general's office, which had originally tried Cohen and which seemed to be implicated in the perjured testimony, Pecora was relentless, spending almost all his time over the next two years tracking down evidence in the case. Thanks to Pecora's efforts, Cohen was eventually released from prison. (His execution had earlier been stayed just seven minutes before he was scheduled to go to the electric chair.)

Pecora obtained a perjury conviction against one of the witnesses in the Cohen murder trial. The day after the lengthy trial ended was a Saturday, and Pecora went to his then quiet office to clean up some paperwork. There was a timid knock on his door. A small gray-haired woman dressed all in black demurely asked whether he was Mr. Pecora. When he said that he was, she responded, "I am Mrs. Joseph Cohen." Mrs. Cohen clasped Pecora's hands and fell at his feet. As she sobbed uncontrollably, the only words she managed to get out were, "I came to thank you for what you have done for my husband." For the rest of his life, Pecora called it the biggest fee he ever received as a lawyer.[32]

In 1922, on his fourth anniversary as a prosecutor, Pecora was named chief assistant district attorney, the number-two man in the office. His boss and friend, the newly elected Joab H. Banton, had a serious heart condition and was often absent from the office. For long stretches over the next eight years, Pecora was in charge as the acting district attorney. Even when Banton was there, *Time* magazine wrote, Pecora's "brains really ran that office," and he was the go-to lawyer for handling tough trials. The one exception was murder cases, which Pecora refused to prosecute because he was fundamentally opposed to the death penalty. Tackling all those difficult cases, he certainly had his share of failures. But the difficulty of the cases made his success rate—he won convictions in about 80 percent of the roughly 1,000 cases he tried—all the more impressive.[33]

Pecora's first big success as chief assistant, and his first tangle with Wall Street, came when he led the prosecution of more than a hundred bucket shops—fly-by-night stockbrokers who sold fraudulent securities to unwary investors or simply took outright bets on market movements, a practice that was illegal under New York law. Despite the success of those prosecutions Pecora was convinced that New York's laws were ill-equipped to prevent this kind of fraud. "The only restrictive force" on those stock brokers, Pecora claimed, "was their own consciences." So he sat down to draft reform legislation with Samuel Untermyer, a prominent New York lawyer, informal Tammany adviser, and éminence grise among Wall Street reformers. The bill they proposed was mild, requiring only state licensing and inspection of stockbrokers, but the New York Stock Exchange, which jealously guarded its private regulatory prerogatives, "violently opposed" it, and it never made it out of committee.[34]

Pecora displayed the same idealism and reformist spirit that originally led him to the Progressive Party. Now it led him to police the corrupt and seamy underside of New York politics and big business. Early on, at least, his moralistic urges did not require him to make personally difficult political choices. Pecora indicted William Anderson, the head of New York's Anti-Saloon League, the country's first and, at the time, perhaps most powerful pressure group. Pecora learned that while Anderson was zealously pushing the cause of Prohibition and raising vast sums of money from the Rockefellers and other wealthy donors, he was engaged in a petty scheme to siphon off for himself fund-raising commissions earned by one of his underlings. After the prosecutor satisfied himself about the truth of the allegations, he didn't hesitate to charge Anderson, despite Anderson's political prominence and power. It certainly didn't hinder Pecora in making that decision that the Anti-Saloon League was a political thorn in the side of Tammany, which vehemently advocated for Prohibition's repeal.

The outspoken Anderson was indignant, accusing Pecora of pushing a purely partisan political agenda. He claimed the prosecutor was simply an errand boy for "an unholy triumvirate" of Tammany Hall, liquor distillers, and the Catholic Church, all of which were lining up Al Smith as an anti-Prohibition candidate for president in 1924. It wasn't true—Tammany boss Murphy did ask Pecora about the case, but only after Anderson had already been indicted. Murphy never sought to interfere, although it can't have escaped Pecora that a conviction would thrill the Tammany bosses. On the other hand, acquittal would be a major setback, so if Pecora was playing a political game, it was a very risky one.

None of those subtleties mattered much to Anderson, who was a "master propagandist," a "virtuoso," according to H. L. Mencken, in the arts of "sophistry and bellowing." Nearly every Sunday he preached his innocence at churches around the state and every Monday morning the New York papers were filled with his conspiracy claims. As he continued to proclaim his persecution, Anderson taunted Pecora, telling the press, "It will be a very, very cold day indeed when the District Attorney of New York County will dare put me on trial."

That was all the motivation Pecora needed. He quickly put Anderson on trial, even requesting that the governor appoint a Republican judge to hear the case in order to mute any claims of political bias. Anderson was an attorney and a gifted public speaker, and he apparently thought that Pecora was no match for him. He insisted, against his lawyers' advice, on taking the stand in his own defense. That decision probably cost him his freedom. In a withering day and a half of cross-examination, Pecora carefully dissected Anderson's direct testimony, showing at every step of the way how the League's documents and Anderson's own prior statements contradicted his sworn testimony.

Cross-examination was Pecora's métier. Bainbridge Colby, who was secretary of state under Woodrow Wilson and had been a member of the Progressive Party with Pecora, called the lawyer "the most brilliant cross-examiner in New York." Pecora had a prodigious memory; he seemed to remember every word of testimony and every piece of evidence. That gift allowed him to pounce on witnesses who tried, however subtly, to change their answers. With his love of acting clearly at work, he could assume various guises while questioning a witness. Mostly he was polite, even courtly; but when called for, he could quickly and effortlessly shift from friendly and innocuously curious to belligerent and sarcastic. He would doggedly ask the same question again and again until the witness finally conceded his point, and he would not hold back when confronting the rich and powerful.

J. P. Morgan Jr. would later complain that Pecora "has the manner and manners of a prosecuting attorney who is trying to convict a horse thief." One appreciative commentator noted that defendants "who came to face him with faint superciliousness, departed, however, chagrined, with respect for his capacity." Anderson was more resentful then respectful—he thought Pecora should have been removed from office and disbarred for his handling of the case. It is hard to imagine that he would feel otherwise. After Pecora systematically took him apart on cross-examination, the jury quickly found the Prohibition advocate guilty, a conviction that was later upheld on appeal.[35]

Other politically tinged cases hit closer to home for Tammany, but Pecora pursued them anyway. In early 1929, a small but politically well-connected bank in New York, the City Trust Company, collapsed within days of the death of its founder, Francesco Ferrari. It soon became apparent that many of City Trust's loans were fictitious, and Pecora helped lead the ensuing investigation. The inquiry quickly turned to the state superintendent of banks, Frank H. Warder. Pecora's investigation showed that Warder had been accepting bribes from Fe-rarri, including one a month before the bank's collapse, in which Warder got $20,000 for agreeing not to shut the bank down after a state inspection had un-covered its rickety finances. By the end of the year, Warder was indicted, con-victed, and shipped off to prison. One doesn't get to be superintendent of banks in New York without a good many friends in Tammany Hall, friends who were now quite upset with Ferdinand Pecora.[36]

In April, as the Warder investigation was ongoing, Banton announced at a mas-sive testimonial dinner that he would not run again, and, to the cheers of the 1,600 Democrats and Republicans in the room, he anointed Pecora as his hand-picked successor. "If in the good fortune of politics and public choice it falls upon our guest of honor to take that office," Banton told the crowd, "we will know that New York could not place it in better hands, cleaner hands." Banton's benedic-tion came as little surprise; Pecora was the consensus pick to be the Democratic candidate that year. Not only did he have all the experience, the judgment, and the honesty for the job, he even had all the right demographic qualifications. Part of the political leader's art was assembling a ticket that was sufficiently balanced to garner votes from all the disparate ethnic constituencies in New York. An Ital-ian Protestant was a godsend; he was a balanced ticket all by himself.

A Republican Party leader told Pecora, "Ferdie, if your party has enough sense to nominate you, we will not put up a candidate against you. We might even join in the nomination." Everything seemed to be falling into place, and Pecora, who felt the nomination was "virtually assured," liked the symmetry of entering the "office at the lowest rung of the professional ladder" and attaining the highest one. On August 8, 1929, when the Democratic leadership was to meet to deter-mine whom they would nominate, an Associated Press reporter walked into the district attorney's office just as Pecora was going out to lunch. The reporter had just been at Tammany Hall and had learned that Pecora would in fact be nomi-nated. With a now thoroughly "enhanced . . . appetite," Pecora headed off to lunch. He was back soon to await official word, and at three thirty the telephone rang. Tammany, it turned out, did not have the sense to nominate him.[37]

Pecora's brand of maverick idealism had been acceptable when Charles Murphy ran Tammany Hall. Unlike past Tammany leaders, Murphy treated the district attorney's office as something of a special case when it came to political interference. Murphy stayed out of prosecutorial decisions, leading Pecora consistently to turn down Tammany bosses and others who sought accommodations in his prosecutions. Unfortunately for Pecora, Murphy died in 1924, and Tammany had, by 1929, reverted to its old, crooked ways. After Murphy's death, Tammany had a weak and easygoing boss, George Olvany, who lost all control of the district leaders around Manhattan. The money to be made from protecting New York's speakeasies was just too tempting, and the tide of graft and corruption quickly ebbed back to its previous levels. Then, in early 1929, just as Banton proposed Pecora as his replacement, New York's mayor, Jimmy Walker, successfully pushed John Curry as Tammany's new leader.[38]

Curry was old-school; he was more interested in his own financial gain and the financial gain of his underlings than in the long-term success of the party. Reporters who covered New York politics in the 1920s and 1930s wrote that Curry was "full of personal loyalties and hatreds" and was afflicted with what could only be described as "stubbornly bad judgment." Curry prevailed in an election among district leaders by the narrowest of margins, just one and a half votes. When he took control, the cold-eyed boss with the square jaw and trim gray mustache could not have been clearer about shaking off whatever slim remnants there were of Murphy's more progressive Tammany Hall. "The New Tammany is a fiction," Curry told reporters covering his selection. "I will carry out the policies in which I grew up."[39]

If those one and a half votes had gone the other way, things might have turned out differently for Pecora. Olvany had already told Pecora the nomination was his. Now that Tammany was once again fueled by graft and corruption, however, the district attorney became one of the key offices—an ambitious lawyer who sought to go after public corruption regardless of the perpetrator's connections or party affiliation was a huge potential danger to the organization. Charles Whitman, a Republican Manhattan district attorney, put it best when he ran for the office in the early 1900s: "The only way you can throw the fear of God into Tammany Hall," he thundered in his campaign, "is by nominating and electing a man for district attorney who will do his full duty at all times." Curry had been among those Pecora had turned down for favors when he was chief assistant.[40]

The last thing Curry, who probably thought he was already sufficiently God-fearing, wanted was Ferdinand Pecora in the top job. He surprised everyone by announcing the nomination of Thomas C. T. Crain, a frail, elderly judge who had been a Tammany sachem for years. Frank Warder, the man Pecora had prosecuted in the City Trust collapse, apparently had a lot of friends in Tammany Hall. In one fell swoop, Curry and his cronies not only got revenge on Pecora, but they nominated a compliant and doddering figurehead who was not expected to cause any trouble. Pecora must have been bitterly disappointed, but he at least appeared equanimous, explaining that he had, in reality, "lost nothing." "No man ever lost what he never had," he said.[41]

Crain easily won the election, and Pecora stepped down from the district attorney's office on December 31, 1929. That same day, Banton gave his valedictory address in the hallway outside his office in the Criminal Courts Building. As the assembled reporters and assistants stood in front of Banton jotting down his comments, they could see behind the exiting district attorney a sign painter erasing the title "Chief Assistant District Attorney" from Pecora's office door. Crain was already fulfilling his campaign promise to abolish the position in which Pecora had so effectively served the city for so long. Pecora's public service career was seemingly at an end.[42]

When he left the district attorney's office, Pecora joined a law firm and his name was added to the letterhead. He handled a few criminal defense cases, including a couple involving allegedly fraudulent stock promotions, but the bulk of his practice was run-of-the-mill business litigation. Occasionally he would do some corporate work as well, mostly organizing new businesses or merging existing ones. About a year in, Pecora's old boss Banton joined the practice and Pecora reported that they "were all very happy together."[43]

Mostly, it seemed, he was just plain bored. Pecora had learned a great deal as a prosecutor, particularly about "the weaknesses and foibles of human nature." Being on the front lines of criminal activity for that long, he said, "enables one better to evaluate character [and] human nature." But reflecting back on his three years in private practice, he couldn't name a single incident or experience that helped him grow either personally or professionally. Pecora merely contrasted the excitement of the district attorney's office with the tedium of law firm work: "There isn't much occasion, [in private practice] for a lawyer to take part in any kind of litigation that is in any way out of the ordinary."[44]

Clearly, Pecora was itching for something more.

Chapter 3

SITTING ON THE LID

By the first week of January 1933, Senator Norbeck was growing increasingly frustrated in his quest to hire a new lawyer to run his Wall Street investigation, mostly because no one seemed to want the job. The senator had known, even before the first hearing was held eight months earlier, that getting the right lawyer—one who was smart, aggressive, courageous, and incorruptible—was perhaps his most important task. "You know these things generally turn on the lawyer who is employed," Norbeck wrote when the investigation began. The shaky start to the inquiry the previous spring was a strong reminder about how right his initial assessment was.[1]

Norbeck was hardly alone in the importance he placed on finding the right lawyer, but "right" had a different meaning depending on a senator's goals for the investigation. Back in March 1932, conservative members of the committee who had lost the fight over the breadth of the authorizing resolution knew there were other ways to squelch the investigation. They could starve the inquiry by making sure that the Senate appropriated only a small amount of money to conduct it or discourage the best lawyers from taking the job with stingy compensation. That was a particularly big hurdle in the early 1930s, because in those austere fiscal times salaries for the committee's employees were capped at $300 per month. As times got even tighter, that amount was reduced by another 15 percent, making for a princely salary of $255 per month.

Of course, some lawyers might do it for the prestige or to make a name for themselves. That was where a senator bent on restricting the investigation needed to be particularly cautious, because the committee's lawyer had almost boundless discretion to shape how it would be conducted. The resolution was now sufficiently broad that a lawyer could look into pretty much any aspect of Wall Street operations. Norbeck, or any senator who was interested in a mean-ingful investigation of Wall Street, would want a smart lawyer who was willing to go anywhere the evidence led. Finding a lawyer to do the laborious legwork was crucial because without documentary evidence to pin down a recalcitrant witness, it was easy for almost any witness to evade the questions put to him. And, of course, lawyers who already represented or hoped to represent Wall Street firms might shy away from tackling the biggest players for fear of harming their careers.[2]

Other senators simply objected to investigations as a matter of general principle. Carter Glass thought little of this kind of political theater, believing it was simply a Roman holiday that took time and attention away from passing his carefully crafted banking legislation. John W. Davis, the 1924 Democratic nominee for president and the founder of the prestigious Wall Street law firm that bore his name, shared Glass's skepticism. Davis, himself a former congress-man, generally thought investigations were a waste of time and good for little but generating publicity for the politicians who ran them. "[T]here will always be on committees," he wrote around the time of Teapot Dome, the bribery in-vestigation that rocked the Harding administration, "some persons whose daily prayer will be, 'Lord, let the limelight shine on me, just for the day.'" Davis was even more passionate by 1932 because he represented some of the most power-ful bankers in New York, including the most powerful private banking firm of all, J.P. Morgan.[3]

In March 1932, when the Senate first authorized the Wall Street investiga-tion, debate focused on precisely these issues and, as the progressives and con-servatives kicked around the possibilities, the investigation stalled. The key sticking point was how close a connection the lawyer could have to Wall Street.

Some conservative members of the committee were actually pushing for Davis. There was little doubt that he was one of the best lawyers in the country, but with his jaundiced view of congressional investigations, his muscular notions of economic liberty and rights of privacy, and his absolute faith in his clients' moral rectitude, he was clearly not the man to conduct a vigorous investigation. Other names were floated, but the senators were unable to reach a decision.

As the committee continued to dither for weeks, Norbeck was repeatedly forced to push back the start date for the hearings. "The bulls and bears," he announced, "may rest a few days more." At the end of March 1932, with the market continuing its downward dive, nothing had happened on the much ballyhooed investigation, and the press began to speculate that the senators had realized that they were in way over their heads. "Many Senators," the *New York Times* reported, "have expressed privately the opinion that those responsible for instigating the investigation, aimed primarily at short selling, figuratively 'have a bear by the tail,' and are unable either to dispatch it or let it go." Darker rumors swirled as well. The administration's ardor for the investigation, it was said, had cooled substantially when it learned that prominent Republicans and at least one cabinet member were among the short sellers.[4]

The latter rumors don't seem to have been true. If they were, President Hoover's reticence was short-lived. As the market continued to swoon, Hoover was growing antsy for the committee to publicly lambaste some short sellers. "I want the shorts investigated," he demanded on the last day of March, "and the quicker the better!" A week later, while Norbeck was in Chicago, Hoover called Senator Walcott, his confidant on the committee, and told him that George Barr Baker, a journalist and Hoover ally, had wired the president warning of a massive bear raid planned for the next day on the New York Stock Exchange. Hoover demanded the investigation commence immediately.

That same afternoon, Walcott called an impromptu committee meeting in the Senate Cloak Room. The Connecticut senator told the committee about the warning and his demand that the exchange's president, Richard Whitney, turn over a list of all short sellers. In the face of Whitney's refusal, Walcott convinced the committee to subpoena the exchange president, who was ordered to appear in Washington on Monday morning. The committee then named as its temporary counsel Claude R. Branch, a Republican lawyer who had worked in the Hoover Justice Department and was now a partner at a prominent Boston law firm.

Norbeck rushed back to Washington, convinced that the sudden urgency was a "well laid scheme" by Hoover and Walcott "to get a Wall Street attorney to do the investigating of Wall Street" while he was conveniently out of town. Walcott insisted to the press that the White House had nothing to do with the surprise start of the investigation, but Norbeck's hunch seems to have been right. On the same day that Hoover demanded action to investigate short sellers, he met in the Oval Office with one "C. R. Branch."[5]

Richard Whitney arrived at the appointed hour on Monday morning, the model of the Wall Street aristocrat, a man who seemed to stand far removed from the world of short sellers and market operators that the committee wanted to explore. For many, Whitney was the face of Wall Street. The Groton-and-Harvard-educated Boston Brahmin was the son of a bank president and traced his American lineage back to the Puritans who arrived on the *Arabella* in 1630. Whitney was tall, athletic, and perfectly attired (right down to the Porcellian Club gold pig dangling from his watch chain) and he played the roles of social elitist and country squire to a tee. On his five-hundred-acre estate in Far Hills, New Jersey, the Wall Street bond trader and broker to the House of Morgan raised prizewinning Ayrshire cattle and hunted foxes. Perhaps his most pronounced characteristic—and one that shone forth in all its glory that Monday morning—was his haughty noblesse oblige. According to his biographer, John Brooks, Whitney "had a toplofty way of being able to deal perfectly factually and equitably with people he considered his social inferiors—which meant most people—and at the same time leaving no doubt of just how he considered them."[6]

Branch and the senators were no match for the imperious Whitney, and the hearing quickly descended into farce. Progressives on the committee had been champing at the bit, insisting that they would conduct a vigorous investigation. "We are going into this stock market from top to bottom," said the Iowa Republican Smith Wildman Brookhart. "We are summoning Mr. Whitney because we think he knows the facts. We aren't going to stop with the bears. We are going to find out about the bulls, too." But the committee members had not conducted any investigation and were therefore forced to base their questions on hunch, rumor, and suspicion.

Whitney was able to deftly deflect their questions with little apparent effort, professing ignorance of wrongdoing at some points, at others gently lecturing the apparently baffled senators on the finer points of market operations. He had no knowledge of any planned bear raid, he told the five hundred reporters jammed into the hearing room, a room so crowded that spectators were sitting on file boxes and leaning against the back of Whitney's chair. Indeed, the stock exchange president claimed under oath that bear raids didn't exist, although he assured those assembled that "the New York Stock Exchange was doing its utmost as a body of men to prevent illegal practices." The soft-spoken Branch was little help. He asked only a few questions about the data that the exchange had assembled and mostly left the questioning to the senators, who, in their frustration with Whitney's unwillingness to concede anything, were left to posture and fulminate. By Tuesday, a committee member admitted that in two days the senators had learned "nothing at all."[7]

Norbeck quickly began to ease out the ineffectual Branch in favor of Branch's seemingly more aggressive assistant, William A. Gray, a Philadelphia lawyer who had a reputation for "bullyragging" witnesses. Gray took another crack at Whitney, with much the same results. Over the next several hearing days, Norbeck took out his frustrations on Whitney, complaining that the exchange leader was unwilling to "grant that anything in the market is illegal" and calling him "hopeless." But Whitney didn't have to admit to anything. Norbeck, the other senators, and their serial lawyers had absolutely no facts to back up their questions and therefore nothing with which to pin down the evasive Wall Streeter. At one point Norbeck lashed out at Whitney in frustration, "You make rules that are just paper rules." Whitney calmly asked for Norbeck's "proof" and the senator, who didn't have any, responded, "You attend these hearings for a while and we will give you some proof." The room erupted with laughter when Whitney replied resignedly, "I have." The South Dakota senator was so taken aback that all he could do was shout, "Yes, but up to now you have been running them!"[8]

A few minutes later, Norbeck dismissed the haughty exchange president, although he reminded him that he was still under subpoena. Whitney didn't want to leave; there were statements he wanted included in the record. "Oh, you will be back," Norbeck told him.[9]

The *Wall Street Journal* rebuked the senator for his tirades. "Chairman Norbeck's angry outbreaks while the president of the exchange was on the stand Thursday were nothing more or less than a confession of the committee's failure to date to prove against the exchange its presumption of guilt." The hearings, they concluded, were nothing more than a raw "abuse of inquisitorial power." Political cartoons pictured Whitney as a teacher lecturing a group of ill-informed schoolboys. Public interest quickly waned, in part, the *New York Times* surmised, "because of the somewhat foolish anticlimax that has been reached."

Norbeck tried to help his cause by taking to the national airwaves to excoriate the exchange, but it did little to sway public opinion. Those who already thought Wall Street was a den of thieves didn't need convincing. For everyone else, the speech underscored Norbeck's ignorance, and they dismissed him as a "vote-grabbing demagogue." Norbeck's poor radio delivery didn't help. The medium amplified his broad accent, which one listener described as sounding like that of a Scandinavian servant girl. Readers of the *New York Evening Post* were dismissive, accusing Norbeck of destroying public confidence in the market and ridiculing him for his pronunciation of "manipulators," which apparently came out "maniperlators." Conservative newspapers called on Norbeck to apologize to the stock exchange for his unfounded claims. Norbeck, however, was feeling neither contrite nor apologetic, and he vowed to "carry this investigation through to the end."[10]

By June, the hearings had produced no significant revelations, with only one exception. It came at the end of April 1932, shortly after the Whitney fiasco, and it was played up for all its dramatic possibilities. On Monday, Norbeck told reporters that a "surprise witness" would provide "sensational testimony" the next day. On Tuesday morning, the New York representative Fiorello La Guardia arrived at the jammed hearing room with two plainclothes policemen lugging a heavy brown trunk. The contents were apparently so explosive that La Guardia had kept the trunk in a police vault for the last three days. La Guardia directly contradicted Whitney's claims that it was impossible to manipulate stock, and he said he had the evidence to prove it. From the trunk, La Guardia pulled canceled checks and other supporting documents showing that a New York publicist named A. Newton Plummer had paid some of the leading financial journalists in New York nearly $300,000 over a ten-year period. Plummer was working with the pools trying to drive up the prices of sixty-one separate stocks. In exchange for cash and options, Plummer wrote favorable and not entirely accurate stories about the companies and then paid the journalists to publish them in New York's leading newspapers. It was all quite unseemly, but since everyone, even during the heyday of the stock market bubble, knew that pools did everything they could to rig the market, it is hard to say that anyone was all that surprised.[11]

After those scintillating disclosures, however, the hearings droned on with little discernible progress, with Gray and the senators continuing to focus solely on short selling and other market operations. Norbeck convinced the Senate to appropriate $50,000 to continue the inquiry, but John Marrinan, a former journalist and one of Norbeck's most trusted staffers, warned him that if he intended to continue he should do so without Gray. Gray, Marrinan told him, was too close to too many people on Wall Street. He accused Gray of trying "to divert the investigation away from the Stock Exchange and the insiders controlling its market operations" and of failing to follow up on Whitney's "misleading statements." He complained that Gray was a "personal friend" of Matt Brush, a famous short seller who had appeared before the committee, and that Gray "dined [with Brush] in the public dining room of the Willard Hotel and spent some time in his apartment on the day of the examination." This was the kind of close connection that Norbeck had tried to avoid.

Marrinan left the senator with a final warning—unless a change was made, there would be dire consequences for the investigation and for Norbeck. Norbeck and the committee would be condemned for "protecting the Stock Exchange" and for "wasting the funds of the Committee." Norbeck was convinced, and the committee abruptly dropped Gray without explanation at the end of June when it suspended the investigation for the summer and fall.[12]

Richard Whitney hated that the exchange was "being used as a political football," but he was delighted with the outcome. He told stock exchange members that he did "not wish to appear to be too critical," but it wasn't really true. Given the haste with which the investigation commenced, he said, "it was literally impossible for counsel and the accountants of the Committee to examine each case thoroughly in the time available, and, besides, they were handicapped by their lack of familiarity with the routine of the brokerage business. It is not surprising, therefore, that the record contains many inaccurate statements, but it is none the less regrettable." It was a polite way of saying that the committee and its counsel were ill-prepared, ignorant, and wrong. Reporters were equally unimpressed. Unless Norbeck could uncover "more sensational wrong-doings," the *Commercial & Financial Chronicle* predicted, there would be no federal regulation of Wall Street.[13]

After the November election, as Norbeck tried to get the investigation back on its feet, he faced the same problem that had vexed him in the spring. Whom could he trust to run a real inquiry?

The obvious choice was Samuel Untermyer, the lawyer who had worked with Pecora to draft the bill to toughen New York's securities laws. The seventy-four-year-old Untermyer was one of the highest-paid and best-known corporate lawyers in the country, but he was also a fierce critic of Wall Street. He had served as counsel to a Senate committee investigating the so-called "money trust" back in 1912. In those hearings, named after the Louisiana senator Arsène Pujo, Untermyer had famously cross-examined the elder J. P. Morgan, and the disclosures from those hearings laid the groundwork for the creation of the Federal Reserve.

As the grand old man of Wall Street critics, Untermyer considered himself, according to one biographer writing in the 1930s, "the stellar investigator of the age, if not of all history." He was a ruthless cross-examiner who often shouted at hostile witnesses. For the particularly recalcitrant, his favorite prop was his tortoiseshell glasses, which he would dramatically snatch off his face to stare down a witness, although in truth he was nearly blind without them. Outside the courtroom, he was arrogant, humorless, dictatorial, patronizing, and, not surprisingly, almost universally disliked. He was also quirky. Untermyer was an avid gardener with a collection of more than 60,000 orchids in the greenhouses of his Westchester estate, Greystone. The dapper lawyer wore one in his lapel every day, making sure that it matched his tie. On court days, his assistant carried spares in a damp paper bag so that Untermyer could have a fresh one for the afternoon session.

The grandstanding Untermyer frequently tried his cases in the newspapers and, although others might be able to match his investigative skills, his biographer wrote, "there is not the slightest doubt that he surpasses all his contemporaries in the art of making the first page." He knew how to work the press, usually by giving reporters the big, dramatic quotes they wanted. When Norbeck's investigation first got under way, Untermyer told reporters that the New York Stock Exchange was "the most despotic institution on earth," and that "its existence in its present form is . . . a menace and a disgrace. . . ." He blasted Congress too, arguing that it was Congress's failure to regulate the exchange as he had advocated that led to most of the market misdeeds: "The idea that such an institution should continue unregulated is repugnant to all conceptions of civilized government."[14]

Norbeck offered Untermyer the job in December 1932, but Untermyer immediately turned it down. Roosevelt had already asked him to draft the stock exchange legislation the president-elect planned to introduce once he took office. Untermyer offered Norbeck a host of reasons for turning down the job—the authorizing resolution was too narrowly drawn and the current committee lacked the determination to carry out a meaningful investigation. The truth, however, was that Untermyer was hoping to become counsel for the investigation when the chairmanship passed from Norbeck. Taking the post now with so little time left in the investigation and so great a possibility that nothing meaningful would happen would do nothing to enhance his chances of landing the job once Roosevelt took over.[15]

Untermyer did, however, make sure to keep his name in the press. Although he was supposed to be drafting stock exchange legislation, he spent most of his time publicly lobbying to run the investigation when Roosevelt took office. Just a few weeks after meeting Norbeck, Untermyer released a statement calling for federal regulation of the stock exchanges, predicting that a special session of Congress would pass such legislation, and criticizing what Norbeck had thus far accomplished. Untermyer clearly wanted to leave little doubt that he was the only man for the job.[16]

Norbeck next turned to Harold L. Ickes. The thin-skinned Ickes reveled in his ornery, argumentative personality, even calling his memoirs *The Autobiography of a Curmudgeon*. In December 1932 he was little known outside Chicago, where he had waged a long battle against Samuel Insull's control over Illinois and Chicago politics, urging Norbeck to open a full-scale Senate investigation of the wealthy utility magnate. Ickes thus made some sense as counsel for the committee, but only if it intended to wrap things up with Insull. Ickes knew Insull, but he was not an experienced courtroom lawyer. Ultimately, it did not matter, because Ickes, too, turned down the job.

True to form, Ickes responded angrily to Norbeck's plan to conduct only eight hours of testimony concerning Insull. He called it totally inadequate and refused to participate unless the hearings were dramatically expanded. Or so he said. Ickes, like Untermyer, already had his sights set on the Roosevelt administration. The Chicagoan had broken with Republican ranks to support Roosevelt during the 1932 election. He was already angling for the Secretary of the Interior post as his reward, making it highly unlikely he would be willing to become the committee's chief lawyer.[17]

In early January 1933, Norbeck reached the last name on his list, the white-haired, patrician judge Samuel Seabury. Seabury had just completed a series of high profile investigations of Tammany Hall that revealed massive corruption in New York City politics and led to the resignation of New York City's flamboyant mayor Jimmy Walker. Pecora's name never came up, and he was, not surprisingly, never linked to any Tammany corruption. He remained loyal to his Tammany friends, though, advising them on what to expect when they appeared before Seabury.[18]

While the New York probe had made the upright Seabury the country's best-known investigator, it wasn't entirely clear that he was the right man for the Banking and Currency Committee investigation. He was a stalwart reformer who had dedicated nearly forty years to the cause of good government, but, unlike Untermyer, he seemed to know little about the inner workings of Wall Street. In any event, Seabury didn't want any part of the assignment, either. He did suggest, however, that Norbeck hire one of his "boys" from the investigation, a young lawyer named Irving Ben Cooper. Although Cooper was then a few weeks shy of his thirty-first birthday, he was already a tenacious investigator, having worked two years for Seabury and, before that, on an investigation of ambulance-chasing lawyers. Cooper had a self-confident swagger, sported a pencil-thin mustache, carried a walking cane, and wore flashy suits that rivaled those of the New York mayor he helped to chase from office.

Cooper's élan didn't seem to bother the decidedly unflamboyant Norbeck, who thought he was "brilliant." To entice Cooper, Norbeck assured him that the $255-per-month salary limit would not apply to his work as counsel. Norbeck would try to get him $5,000 for the less than two months remaining in the investigation. Cooper accepted the job and his appointment was announced on January 10. He was noncommittal about his plans for proceeding with the investigation, but what he said suggested both nonchalance about the rapidly approaching deadline and an independence from the committee that might prove problematic. Cooper planned to read through testimony, and then he would "take up such phases of the inquiry as he deem[ed] necessary."[19]

Editorial writers saw Cooper's appointment as a hopeful sign that the Wall Street investigation would emerge from "lull and oblivion." Cooper had a chance to perform a "rare service" for the country. "A thorough investigation into the methods of high finance during the wild days," the New York World-Telegram declared, "will help defend future investors, and it ought to be highly useful to students of modern industrial economy and to the legislators alike in their efforts to help chart the country's progress out of its present travail."[20]

Norbeck must have welcomed that optimism. He was more and more distraught over the country's economic woes, which he pinned on the "destruction of public confidence" following the stock market crash. "People have no faith in the Government," Norbeck wrote, "and no faith in industrial leaders or bankers, in economists, statisticians, or even in themselves." Society was past fraying; now it was rending, and Norbeck was hardly alone in seeing it. A Youngstown, Ohio, lawyer noted in his diary that winter a rise in "begging and holdups and murder," not to mention lawyers who were disbarred for stealing client trust funds. "It seems," he wrote, "that all misdeeds and grievances are coming to the surface during this time of depression."

Property rights and the rule of law, once nearly universally respected, were flagrantly ignored. In coal country, out-of-work miners dug their own shafts on company property and sold whatever they could. When they were arrested for theft, juries refused to convict them, despite overwhelming evidence of guilt. The unemployed in Virginia and Detroit walked into company stores and simply took food off the shelves. One businessman expressed alarm "at the increasing undercurrent of hate directed against our bankers and big industrial leaders. The mention of revolution is becoming quite common."[21]

Norbeck saw federal banking and securities legislation as a small step that might help restore Americans' confidence. The *New York Times* and other newspapers, however, continued to criticize the idea that more laws might deter fraudulent behavior. Norbeck himself provided the impetus for one of the *Times'* editorials. As a way to jump-start the investigation, Norbeck had abruptly announced that the committee would hold hearings on the massive fraud perpetrated by the so-called Swedish Match King, Ivar Kreuger. Before his suicide in his Paris apartment, in March 1932, Kreuger was almost universally hailed as a financial genius; the securities of his companies were among the most widely held in the world. Within weeks of his death, Kreuger was reviled as the mastermind behind what was perhaps the world's greatest financial fraud. His companies— which had negotiated a series of match monopolies throughout Europe—proved to be nothing more than a massive accounting hoax. The shocking news further unnerved an already jittery public. Along with the British Insull, the Swedish Kreuger became the face of financial fraud, the poster boy for unscrupulous foreign businessmen who duped honest Americans out of hard-earned savings.

In his typical scattershot fashion, Norbeck left no time for investigation. As with Insull, he was just trying to cash in on a prominent scandal. Marrinan and Norbeck handled most of the questioning at the Kreuger hearing, which was just finishing as Norbeck was hiring Cooper. Naturally, without any investigation the two men relied solely on previously reported information. The picture they painted over two days of testimony was of foolish American investment bankers from the Boston firm of Lee Higginson who allowed themselves to be duped by this criminal mastermind. Norbeck and Marrinan saw the accountants as the heroes for uncovering the fraud, although in reality Kreuger lulled them into a lethargic stupor with fat auditing and consulting fees and lavish European trips. In any event, for the *Times* the real lesson of these hearings was that Kreuger was a "unique phenomenon," a criminal not unlike Al Capone. Kreuger was successful because he preyed on the trust inherent in modern business transactions. The *Times'* editorial writers warned the South Dakota senator: "You cannot legislate for business on the basis of a monstrous exception." Federal legislation might protect investors, but perhaps at the cost of killing the entire securities industry.[22]

If Norbeck was buoyed by the initial reaction to Cooper, his happiness was short-lived. Just a week after he was hired, Cooper quit in a huff, claiming that Norbeck had denied him a "free hand" in his investigation. Despite his laid-back initial response, Cooper had forged ahead aggressively. He hired seven lawyers to assist him, all former members of Judge Seabury's staff, apparently without consulting Norbeck. He then demanded five hundred blank subpoenas from the senator, which Cooper would then be free to serve on anyone he chose, without any input from the committee. Although the committee had issued only twenty-seven subpoenas over the previous nine months, Norbeck seemed initially inclined to issue them. But the senator quickly thought better of the idea. In fact, he suggested that Marrinan, the former journalist, should go to the New York office to supervise Cooper's activities until the lawyer had familiarized himself with how the committee had been conducting the inquiry.[23]

Cooper bristled; apparently, he was having trouble seeing that he was working for a Senate committee and that he was not some free-floating investigator. The enraged lawyer lashed out angrily at Norbeck, suggesting that Marrinan was really there to "sit on the lid" of the investigation. It wasn't true, of course. It had been Marrinan, after all, who had urged Norbeck to dump Gray lest the committee be accused of "protecting the Stock Exchange." Norbeck didn't know it at the time, but Cooper's reaction was perfectly in character. Cooper would go on to make a career of petulance and irascibility. Thirty years later, President Kennedy nominated Cooper for a federal judgeship, but most bar groups opposed his confirmation, not because of his legal qualifications but because of his volatile disposition and "persecution complex."[24]

Norbeck tried to make the best of a bad situation. He told reporters that it would have been "dangerous and unsound" to delegate that kind of unchecked subpoena power to one man. "By granting Mr. Cooper's demands for unlimited authority, the committee would have lost control of the investigation," Norbeck told them. "The resignation is not important," he assured the press. "The investigation will proceed."[25]

The damage, however, was done. Cooper came with Seabury's imprimatur, and so most seemed to believe Cooper and not Norbeck. That was particularly true of the *New York World-Telegram*. The paper's editorial page was a big Seabury booster and they seemed to view the Cooper debacle as a direct affront to the judge's integrity. Over the next three days, they blasted Norbeck for his efforts to "censor" Cooper. His "hamstringing," the editors wrote, "suggests that Senator Norbeck and his committee have no intention of going thoroughly into the devices by which huge pools and market manipulators have defrauded millions of people who assumed they were trading in an honest market." The paper concluded "that the investigation is dead as far as this session is concerned. Whether it will be pressed will depend on the Democrats and the Roosevelt administration."[26]

The public, or in any event those who wrote to Norbeck, were equally furious. One writer told Norbeck that it was "pathetic" that the country was so lacking in "honorable and patriotic leadership." Why, he asked, "should Mr. Cooper or any other investigator of honest character be hindered in bringing to light fraudulent and unethical practices whereby certain small groups are allowed to prey relentlessly upon the public in enriching themselves?" A concerned citizen named Sidney May wanted to know how Norbeck could expect any "self-respecting honorable man the type of Irving Ben Cooper to serve . . . under terms and restrictions laid down by you!" May "questioned the sincerity of the stock market investigation from its inception" and "this latest explosion is concrete evidence you have not venture[d] a genuine investigation, fearing to involve influential friends and possibly many affiliated with the present administration."[27]

Norbeck was in an enormous bind. Cooper's resignation had left him, with little more than six weeks left in the congressional term, with no lawyer, and with a public that seemed to believe that the whole effort was a sham. It was at this point that Norbeck nearly gave up. He reached out once more, this time to the former secretary of state Bainbridge Colby, who, like Norbeck, was a progressive and a former Theodore Roosevelt Bull Mooser. But now the task had changed. Norbeck didn't ask Colby to conduct new hearings but instead to prepare the committee's report, the summary of its investigative efforts over the previous year. The *World-Telegram* seemed to be right—the investigation was over.[28]

Colby was not interested in taking on such a limited assignment. He did, however, suggest one more lawyer to Norbeck, someone he knew from his days in the New York Progressive Party. His name was Ferdinand Pecora.[29]

Chapter 4

A SHORT-TERM JOB

Norbeck never recorded his reaction when he first heard the name Ferdinand Pecora, but there is a good chance it was less than enthusiastic. For all his progressivism, the senator was not above the bigotry of his times. He possessed a fierce pride in his Nordic ancestry and he generally held "Latins," as he called them, in disdain for what he viewed as their lack of industriousness. Although Norbeck constantly butted heads with the conservative wing of his party, he and other midwestern progressives voted hand in hand with them for the National Origins Act in 1924, legislation that effectively slammed the door on future mass migration from eastern and southern Europe. Five years after the act passed, when there was talk of amending those severe restrictions, Norbeck stood on the floor of the Senate and vehemently argued that it was bad national policy to restrict Scandinavian immigration while continuing to permit too many of the "agents of Mussolini" and the "friends of Capone" into the country.[1]

Norbeck's views would hardly have come as a surprise to Pecora, who had been living with them all his life. Perhaps Pecora's Bull Moose connections helped to overcome Norbeck's wariness, or perhaps with the clock ticking down on his investigation, Norbeck had nowhere else to go. Whatever the reason, on Sunday, January 22, 1933, Norbeck called Pecora at his New York apartment to offer him the position. In hindsight, it was one of the best decisions the senator ever made.

The call was out of the blue; Pecora had never met Norbeck and apparently had no inkling that his name had been mentioned as a possible counsel for the committee. Pecora knew little about the investigation; in fact, the hearings were so moribund that Pecora thought they were over. Norbeck conceded as much, offering Pecora the same six-week job he offered Bainbridge Colby—preparing the committee's report of what it had uncovered in the previous year. Norbeck told Pecora he could pay him only $255 per month, a pittance compared with what the senator had offered the younger and less experienced Cooper.

In the abstract, it didn't seem like much of an opportunity. Lawyers like Untermyer had certainly made names for themselves conducting governmental investigations. Instead of conducting his own investigation, however, Pecora's job would be simply to summarize what had already occurred. Still, Pecora jumped at the chance. It may have been a sign of his boredom in private practice, or perhaps he hoped that this small assignment might lead to real investigative work for the committee. He hastily called his partners, who said they would cover his cases during the next few weeks, and he was on a train that evening to meet Norbeck in Washington the next day.[2]

Pecora was in Norbeck's office on the third floor of the Senate Office Building at ten o'clock the next morning, and the burly senator led the lawyer to a steel filing cabinet "jammed full" of testimony and exhibits. To summarize it by March 4, Pecora told Norbeck, would require him to work "day and night." Pecora, however, was already angling to be more than simply a scribe. He asked Norbeck if he could see the Senate resolution authorizing the hearing. Although Norbeck confirmed that the committee had largely confined itself to short selling, a quick perusal of the resolution showed the lawyer that the committee could in fact investigate much more. Pecora latched onto language authorizing the committee to investigate the sale of securities. It was, he told Norbeck, "very broad authority" that would allow the committee to investigate not only short selling and trading on the exchanges, but also the initial issuance of securities by the investment banks to the public. Norbeck, Pecora said, was surprised. "We've got some might[y] fine lawyers on the committee," he told Pecora. "I'm surprised they didn't note that language."

"Under this language," Norbeck continued, "would it have been possible for my committee to inquire into the ways by which the people throughout my state were high-pressured into buying millions and millions and millions of dollars worth of securities that were sour?"

"Senator," Pecora replied, "it seems to me that under the broad language of this resolution, your committee has the power and was, in fact, authorized to do that very thing."[3]

There is no record of Norbeck's version of this first meeting, and it is, quite frankly, hard to know what to make of Pecora's account. Norbeck was unsophisticated about finance and not well-educated, but it's difficult to imagine that he had no idea how broad his investigatory powers were. Given the fight over the initial resolution, Norbeck must have known that the authorization that emerged from committee was broader than just short selling, although he never really exploited those powers. Other than its brief foray into the match company, Kreuger & Toll, the committee had focused its efforts almost entirely on ways to manipulate securities already trading on the organized exchanges. Pecora was suggesting a radically different focus—forget about the securities already out there and look at how they got there in the first place.

Pecora never revealed his suspicions, and he never explained what led him to suggest this change in focus. It's quite possible that he didn't have any tangible rationale; after all, but for his investigations of seamy boiler rooms, he knew little about the securities markets. He could have been doing nothing more than toeing the Democratic party line. In a speech in Columbus, Ohio, in August 1932, Roosevelt had called for greater disclosures in connection with public sales of securities, a reform that was repeated in the Democrats' 1932 party platform. Pecora may have seen the opportunity to create a factual record to demonstrate the need for precisely such reforms. There is simply no way to know for sure today. But whether it was through luck or the finely honed instincts of a seasoned prosecutor, Pecora had just made the proposal that would save the investigation.

For all his lack of sophistication, Norbeck was smart enough to follow Pecora's lead. Why he did so is just as unclear as why Pecora made the proposal in the first place. After years of deferring to Glass and with his keen awareness of his own limitations, perhaps it was his natural response to banking committee matters. Still, Norbeck was nothing if not a savvy politician, and he may well have realized that this change in focus would take the investigation directly into the heart of Wall Street's operations. Stock and bond underwriting wasn't the province of the shady market operators who had made up the bulk of the witnesses parading before the committee the previous spring. This was the exclusive club of patrician bankers who, from their offices around Wall and Broad and from the lofty confines of the Bankers' Club, ran America's markets. Later that spring, the most mysterious and, to the general public, most powerful of them all, J. P. Morgan Jr., pointedly told this same committee that he and his brethren were "a national asset and not a national danger." For Morgan, the power of the investment banker came not from his wealth, "but from the confidence of the people in his character." By attacking these bankers head on, perhaps Norbeck and Pecora saw the opportunity to discredit the entire enterprise, to break their stranglehold on financial policy, and to finally pave the way for federal regulation.[4]

Pecora's appointment was announced the next day. After the Irving Ben Cooper fiasco, Norbeck emphasized both Pecora's qualifications and the free hand he would have in running the investigation. Norbeck told the press that Pecora "has figured prominently in many important criminal and civil actions and he has been strongly recommended by outstanding members of the bar of New York." One of those was Pecora's old boss at the district attorney's office, Joab Banton, who called Pecora, in what must have seemed to reporters like more than a little bit of hyperbole, "the best qualified lawyer in the country" to lead a stock market investigation. To be sure, Pecora had handled securities cases before, but it was mostly low-level fraud. In none of his previous cases had he ever needed to dig deep into the everyday functioning of the stock market or of investment banking practices. He was facing a steep learning curve.

Norbeck assured reporters that Pecora "would have all the authority necessary to make a comprehensive investigation." In addition to the previously announced Insull hearings, Norbeck also signaled a shift in focus for the investigation. Following Pecora's lead, the committee would now turn its attention to "the issue and distribution of securities." Pecora announced no specific plans for the inquiry, although privately he wrote Norbeck that he was honored by the appointment and assured the senator that "in accepting this trust I shall give to its discharge my utmost ability and service." Pecora also struck a much more conciliatory tone than Cooper. "I shall be pleased," he wrote Norbeck, "to receive such instructions and suggestions as your Committee may desire to give me at any time, and shall endeavor to keep you currently posted as to our activities by written communication and otherwise."[5]

Pecora was back in New York later that same Monday, January 23. He set up shop in a small suite on the eleventh floor of 285 Madison Avenue, in the same building as his law office. It was "shabby-looking" with a decidedly slapdash and transient feel. The floors and walls were bare and the office furniture was a battered rental set from a secondhand dealer.

Pecora quickly assembled a handful of assistants. The first two were lawyers Pecora had known for years, Julius Silver from New York and David Saperstein from Union City, New Jersey. His "boys," as he called them, "were bright and industrious, and [he] felt quite certain they would welcome an opportunity to render this kind of service." He added an accountant, Ivan Lashins, and two other young lawyers Norbeck had already retained for the committee, James McDonough and J. F. O'Hanlon. Pecora knew a statistician then working for the New York attorney general's office named Frank Meehan. He had a "quick mind" and was experienced in bucket shop prosecutions, so Pecora added him to the staff as well. Rounding out the group in New York were John Marrinan, the ex-journalist who had so incensed Irving Ben Cooper, and Max Winkler, a former City College economics professor and expert on foreign bonds whom Norbeck had hired as a consultant to the committee a year earlier. It was, Pecora knew, a small staff to take on Wall Street, but he hoped it would "prove to be efficient."[6]

As Pecora began his investigation, Senator Glass's banking reform bill was undergoing a painful and very public death in the Senate. Its executioner was Louisiana's bellowing demagogue, Huey Long.

Debate on the fast-tracked Glass banking bill had opened on January 5, with Glass exhorting his colleagues to adopt his plan to take commercial banks out of the investment banking business but to permit them more leeway to add branches. There was a good deal of opposition to the former provision, with organized lobbying efforts arguing that investment banking was "a legitimate function of the banks and a necessary service to the industries and municipalities of the country." Liberal Democrats and progressive Republicans, however, were particularly opposed to the latter reform because they thought expanded branch banking would make it impossible for smaller banks to compete with larger ones, leading to greater concentrations of capital.

Norbeck still deferred to Glass, but he was growing tired of Glass's arrogance and condescension. Norbeck complained that Glass, who had been ill for about a year, was "not strong anymore and quite given to being irritable." The banking bill was more than just another piece of legislation to Glass—it was the capstone on his legacy as a banking reformer. Glass, Norbeck wrote, "seems determined to work out a 'perfect banking system' before he leaves the stage. He may know what that means, but I am sure that neither you nor I do."[7]

Glass's condescending attitude was on full display as the Virginia senator tried to impress on his colleagues the urgency of reform. As debate began, Glass, who had an odd habit of speaking only out of the left side of his mouth, argued that many small banks were on the verge of collapse, "choked with immobile, and in many cases, worthless securities." They were, he claimed, in even worse shape than they appeared, because many had failed to write off the losses they had suffered from the sharp declines in securities prices. Glass said he understood what motivated the plea for small rural banks, but he expressed little sympathy for their plight. "There have been 10,000 banks failed in the last few years," Glass argued, "of which 80 percent were banks whose capital did not exceed $25,000. They were merely pawn shops that were toppled over like tenpins at every disturbance of business." Without his branch banking reforms, Glass warned his colleagues, a colossal wave of bank failures would crash down on the already weakened financial system. The big New York banks signaled that if Glass dropped the provisions on securities affiliates they would not oppose branch banking. It was hardly a concession, since expanded branch banking was a reform they desperately wanted, and Glass refused to dicker.[8]

Huey Long, then just a thirty-nine-year-old freshman senator, rose to oppose the bill, principally, he said, because of his bitter opposition to expanded branch banking. In just a few short minutes, the brusque Long managed both to enrage Glass and to leave the remaining senators dumbfounded. Glass had studied banks for three decades, and it was an open secret that Roosevelt had offered him the job as Treasury secretary, a post he had occupied in the Wilson administration. There was no one in Congress more expert than Glass when it came to the financial system. Long, however, blithely announced that Glass was simply a stooge for J. P. Morgan; he claimed he knew "a good deal more about branch banking than does the Senator from Virginia."

The Kingfish (a name he took from a character in the wildly popular *Amos 'n' Andy* radio show) was no ordinary freshman senator. Although he often appeared buffoonish in his brightly colored shirts and garish ties, he was in reality a coldly calculating and ruthless politician who almost single-handedly ruled Louisiana. Ostensibly a voice for the downtrodden poor and lower working class, Long was preternaturally adept at using half-truths and bald-faced lies to whip up public anger as a means of cementing and enhancing his own power. To Roosevelt, the ambitious Long was "one of the two most dangerous men in the United States today." (The other was Douglas MacArthur, the general who had just rousted the bonus marchers out of Washington.) Roosevelt worried that Depression-weary Americans pushed to the limit and abandoned by government might, in desperation, succumb to Long's radical solutions.

Long was always ready for a fight. "Always take the offensive," was his constant refrain. "The defensive ain't worth a damn." Taking the offensive meant going after the "big man" first, and the big man on banking was Glass. In truth Huey, who could hold a personal grudge as well as anyone, needed little prodding to attack the aristocratic Virginian. The two men loathed each other. There were two opposing sets of Louisiana delegates at the 1932 Democratic convention, and Long had not forgiven Glass for his opposition to seating Long's slate. Glass never smoked or drank, two of Long's favorite pastimes, and he derided Long in his thick Virginia drawl as a "demagogic screech owl from the swamps of Louisiana." Long was a "creature who seems to have bought and stolen his way into the United States Senate." Glass would "vote to expel that scalawag without raising a finger to find out what the charges were against him."

Glass was hardly alone in his contempt for Long. Huey had arrived in the Senate only a year earlier, but in that short time he had managed to become a pariah. Long flouted the Senate's traditions with "wild antics" and "loud outbursts," all aimed at garnering publicity for himself rather than trying to push through the radical redistributive measures he claimed to champion. There were no holds barred when Long debated. With his unruly auburn hair falling across his forehead and sweat staining his suits, he pelted his opponents with savage personal attacks, often stooping to the role of high school bully by mimicking their mannerisms or mocking their appearance. Reporters loved him and crowds flocked to the gallery to see him perform, but the other senators disdained him. "I don't believe," one senator said, "he could get the Lord's Prayer endorsed in this body."[9]

Long wasn't pushing any legislation now; he just wanted to kill Glass's bill, and on January 10, when the bill came up for debate again, he began what would become a legendary filibuster in Senate lore. A tactic later made famous by Jimmy Stewart in *Mr. Smith Goes to Washington*, the filibuster allows a senator to use his or her privilege of unlimited debate to hold the floor indefinitely, bringing legislative business to a standstill. Long began with a four-hour sermon, quoting from two bibles he had on his desk in the back row of the Senate chamber ("two bibles is never too many," he said) and asserting that "the Lord himself" opposed branch banking. With help from only a few other senators and with lines of spectators queued outside the gallery doors to watch his performance, Long did everything he could to stall. He gave long-winded speeches about nothing, not even branch banking. He made numerous quorum calls. He asked the clerk to read lengthy documents into the record. Although Senate rules required Long to stay on the floor, rules meant little to the Kingfish, and as the documents were laboriously read, he would stroll out of the chamber to gossip with reporters.

Glass was the smallest member of the Senate, but he may have had its biggest temper. He was furious at Long, and a few weeks later only the intervention of another senator stopped the frail Glass from punching Long, thirty-five years his junior and half a foot taller. Glass dubbed the filibuster a "circus performance" filled with "oratorical rubbish." Slamming his fist against his desk he railed against Long's tactics: "Is the Senate reduced to that level of legislative depravity that it may be told by any member or group of members that it shall not legislate upon grave problems, that it should not pass a bill that the bankers know would prevent a repetition of this frightful crash and debacle?" Glass tried a slew of parliamentary tricks to thwart Long, but Long, who seemed immune to embarrassment, easily turned the tables on Glass. At one point, Glass demanded that Long, rather than the clerk, read documents into the record, arguing that the Senate would prefer to hear the senator from Louisiana's "mellifluous voice." Long was only too happy to oblige. He read the documents at a glacial pace, pausing every so often to ask Glass, "Am I going too fast?" As the filibuster dragged on, Glass sat slumped at his desk, despondent.

The only way to end debate was with a cloture vote, but at the time cloture required a two-thirds majority. The senators ended up just one vote shy, thwarted by a coalition of liberal Democrats, who wanted to kill branch banking, and conservative Republicans, who either opposed the requirement that national banks eliminate their securities affiliates or who were simply enjoying the public spectacle of internecine warfare among the Democrats. President Hoover, although he would in a few weeks urge passage of banking reform legislation, was thrilled with the outcome and, indeed, may have had a hand in it. "Now the Senate can keep wasting time, so far as I am concerned," he said after cloture was defeated. "I don't want them to do anything now. Whatever they might do would be bad legislation from our point of view." At times reduced to a hoarse whisper, Long warned his colleagues that he would wage this fight until the end of the congressional session: "You've got until March 4 to pass this bill . . . And you are not going to pass it by March 4. Put that in your pipe and smoke it."[10]

Long emerged victorious on January 25, when the Senate passed a watered-down bill that effectively emasculated Glass's branch banking reforms. Banking reform, at least for the lame duck session, would end there. With so little time left in the congressional session, the House announced that it would not act on the bill. Long was gleeful, confidently proclaiming that the Glass bill was "dead as a hammer."

In some ways, it was an unsurprising outcome. Delay and inaction are hardwired into the Senate's DNA, but in a time of unprecedented economic turmoil, editorial writers were appalled at the entire spectacle. They excoriated Long for his "unprincipled and tyrannical use" of the Senate rules and were equally harsh with the Senate as a whole. The "complete paralysis" of the Senate, the New York Times commented, was a "national disgrace." When an "impudent upstart . . . with a front of brass and lungs of leather" could hold the Senate hostage for days on end, it was no wonder that the Senate's prestige was shattered. "If the Senators feel themselves humiliated," the editors asked, "how do they suppose the country feels?" Even legislators were embarrassed by their own impotence in the face of this national calamity. "We're milling around here," Hiram Johnson wrote, "utterly unable to accomplish anything of real consequence."[11]

In truth, the overwhelming public anger over congressional ineptitude was firmly in place well before Long's virtuoso performance. The previous summer, Agnes Meyer, the wife of Federal Reserve chairman Eugene Meyer, had attended a hearing on a relief bill, which quickly bogged down into pointless debate. Agnes was a keen and intelligent observer of the Washington scene and a perceptive chronicler of the foibles of politicians and of her fellow members of the upper class. She was a social reformer who wrote for the *Washington Post*, a paper that her husband would later purchase and eventually pass on to their daughter, Katharine Graham. As the frustrated Meyer left the hearing room, she "passed a group of bonus marchers lying in front of the Congressional Library exhausted by their perpetual marching, ragged filthy, eating some horrible-smelling beans which were being cooked on the sidewalk in an army range. For sheer ignorance in the Senate . . . the picture was drab and discouraging beyond words. Of such materials is democracy compounded."[12]

On January 26, one day after the Senate passed the watered-down Glass bill, Norbeck announced that the committee's investigation would not be limited to Insull, but instead would explore other "important matters." Norbeck announced no specific names, but Pecora's attention had been turning to a single company and a single individual who were closely associated in the public's mind with the stock market bubble. The same was not true of Norbeck, who continued to suggest company after company the committee could investigate. Despite his failures in the investigation over the previous year, Norbeck still seemed not to appreciate how much time it took to investigate a company thoroughly, nor that such an investigation to pin down facts was essential to a successful hearing. Pecora was able to dissuade Norbeck from those other investigations, and on January 30, Pecora subpoenaed Charles E. Mitchell, chairman of the board of City Bank, and two other executives of the bank. The subpoenas required them to appear before the committee on February 21, 1933, just three weeks away. It was a remarkably short period of time given that Pecora somehow had to squeeze in the Insull hearings as well, but he had little choice. Authorization for the investigation ended in just thirty-five days.[13]

In the abstract, the subpoenas seemed like big news for the struggling investigation, but the immediate reaction was mild, in part because Pecora was undercutting expectations. He told reporters he was in Washington to do a constructive investigation that could lead to useful legislation. He was conducting "a fact-finding, not a head-hunting, exploration." Many reporters took that statement as confirmation of everything that Irving Ben Cooper had charged. There was just a month left in the inquiry, nobody had their heart in it any longer, and it was going to quietly whimper offstage as the new Roosevelt administration came into office. "We prophesy," the editors of the *Milwaukee Leader* wrote, "that the senate committee will put many, many thousands of words in print and eventually decide to straddle the subject and make a few minor recommendations that will only amount to a couple of tinker's damns."[14] As January 1933 came to a close, reining in Wall Street remained, for most observers, a pipe dream.

Chapter 5

SUNSHINE CHARLIE

Pecora's decision to subpoena Mitchell to appear before the committee was more serendipitous than calculated. True, Mitchell was a natural choice if Pecora's goal was to indict Wall Street's entire stock-selling operation; City Bank's investment arm sold more securities during the Roaring Twenties than any other investment banking operation. But the reason Pecora subsequently offered for his selection was far more mundane. The lawyer had just read that Mitchell was about to sail for Europe, "having been invited by Mussolini to come to Rome to give advice about the stabilization of the lire [sic]." Pecora "was anxious to have a subpoena served on Mr. Mitchell before he sailed."

Although seemingly haphazard, there can be little doubt that Pecora knew just how daring his choice was. There was certainly a big chance that Pecora would come away from the probe empty-handed. Mitchell was a veteran of congressional inquiries; he had even appeared before the committee in June 1932 to testify about City Bank's alleged participation in a pool to manipulate the stock of Anaconda Copper. City Bank's securities affiliate, the National City Company, offered Anaconda stock to the public at $125 a share in late 1929. In 1932, it was selling for $5. When William Gray pointed to that disparity Mitchell was indignant: "You don't hold us responsible for that?"

Mitchell treated Gray with contempt. He called the lawyer's financial calculations meaningless and he generally ignored Gray's questions and interruptions about manipulation, focusing instead on telling the committee about Anaconda's bright financial prospects and its long history with City Bank. Anaconda controlled 20 percent of the world's copper production and owned a third of the world's reserves. "In other words," he assured the senators, "we are not talking, as we sit here gentlemen, about a stock manipulation in some fly-by-night concern. We are talking about offering an investment of the primest [sic] quality in one of America's greatest industrial properties." Mitchell categorically denied any knowledge of an Anaconda stock pool; the securities affiliate's market activities were simply its attempt to meet the great customer demand for such a quality offering.[1]

Mitchell rode roughshod over Gray, and with so little time to investigate the bank, there was every chance that he would do the same to Pecora. Still, the payoff was potentially enormous. City Bank was a pillar of the banking community. The bank was an international powerhouse with almost a hundred branches in twenty-three countries. It had a hand in a fifth of all securities sold during the 1920s, and it was catering to more and more middle-class investors who entered the market in droves during that decade. Mitchell, one of the most powerful and well-known financiers of his day, was almost single-handedly responsible for creating that securities-selling giant.

Besides the new focus on securities sales, the City Bank subpoenas signaled another radical shift for the investigation. In its first year, Norbeck focused on short sellers and pool operators—men like Mike Meehan, Ben "Sell 'Em" Smith, and Jesse Livermore—financial pirates who most people assumed used any means, legal or illegal, to make money in the market. When he returned after the 1932 elections, Norbeck focused on Kreuger and Insull, scandals that had already been unveiled.

Pecora was attempting something quite different—something that was much more difficult but had the potential for a much greater impact. Mitchell had been criticized for his exuberant overoptimism during the bubble, but most of the public did not suspect him or his bank of any overtly unethical or wrongful behavior. Mitchell and City Bank occupied Wall Street's rarefied heights, the men and firms who, so far at least, had remained untouched by scandal. If Pecora could show improprieties at City Bank, if he could suggest that a swindler like Kreuger was not, as the *New York Times* thought, a "monstrous exception" but an all too common menace to small investors, then he would go a long way toward securing federal legislation of the stock market. With a little more than a month left in the investigation, what did he have to lose?

Founded two days before the outbreak of the War of 1812 essentially as a credit union for a group of New York merchants, City Bank had a rather shaky start and repeatedly came close to collapsing in its early years. The bank's heyday began about eighty years after its founding, when the famed banker James Stillman took over the reins. The enigmatic Stillman, known on Wall Street as the Sphinx, moved quickly to enlarge the bank and to attract big corporate clients, but the engine really fueling its growth was investment banking. After the Panic of 1893, railroad and other capital-intensive firms desperately needed to raise funds. Looking for a toehold in the field, Stillman formed an alliance with Kuhn Loeb, a leading private investment bank of the day, to help reorganize the faltering Union Pacific Railroad.

It was a good fit, with each bank complementing the other's strengths. As the more established investment bank, Kuhn Loeb had the relationships necessary to originate transactions, but it lacked City Bank's strong capital base. City Bank's rich clients were always looking to diversify their holdings and so provided a ready stable of customers for the firms' securities offerings. Eventually City Bank, like J.P. Morgan, became a consolidator of industries, orchestrating complex mergers in the copper and utilities industries.[2]

In 1909, the bank moved in to its palatial new home at 55 Wall Street. At the time, critics called it absurd that a bank should occupy an entire city block, but Stillman conceived the bank's headquarters as a monument to the firm's preeminence in banking and a testament to its durability and permanence. City Bank was indisputably the largest and strongest commercial bank in the country. Its clients were the dominant companies in a dozen different industries, from meatpacking and sugar refining to chemicals, oil, utilities, and railroads. At that point, Stillman retired from day-to-day operations of the bank. The new president was Frank Vanderlip, who wanted to extend Stillman's successes by transforming the bank into a worldwide, full-service financial supermarket, a one-stop shop for all its customers' financial needs.[3]

Vanderlip began opening City Bank branches throughout South America, Asia, and Europe, but investment banking once again drove the bank's success. With the advent of World War I, the United States became a creditor nation and as the European combatants increasingly sought to raise money here, New York surpassed London as the world's financial capital. City Bank and other New York banks flourished. Through its affiliated securities business, the National City Company, the bank pushed ahead in investment banking, forging relationships with the other leading investment banks, floating foreign government bonds, and underwriting risky offerings for emerging electric and gas utilities. The more established investment houses wouldn't touch these industries, but utilities provided City Bank with yet another way to expand its investment banking operations. The riskiness of such securities—technology was changing so rapidly that an established firm could become an anachronism nearly overnight—also made them harder to market to investors. That meant City Bank would have to look past the wealthy investors who were the traditional buyers of stocks and bonds. Vanderlip foresaw middle-class Americans as a natural outlet for all the firm's securities offerings and embarked on a plan to develop a broad, nationwide retail network to reach them. Vanderlip's chance for rapid expansion came in 1916 when National City acquired N. W. Halsey, a young and innovative firm that had pioneered the use of mass advertising to sell securities.

Although happy with his acquisition, Vanderlip was disappointed that he failed to convince the company's most promising executive, Harold Stuart, to stay on. Stuart decided to set up his own bond-selling firm in Chicago, which he named Halsey, Stuart & Co. Casting about for someone to run City Bank's newly acquired retail network, Vanderlip found an intelligent thirty-eight-year-old bond salesman "with a good eye and a keen mind," a man he felt sure would "prove of real strength to the whole situation." Charles E. Mitchell, Vanderlip thought, had "an astonishing capacity to create energy."[4]

·   ·   ·

Mitchell was born on October 6, 1877, in Chelsea, a "shabby and unfashionable" industrial suburb of Boston on the northern bank of the Mystic River. It was, fittingly, the hometown of Horatio Alger, and although Mitchell's was not quite a rags-to-riches success story, it was close. He had a comfortable, middle-class childhood. His father was a produce wholesaler who dabbled in local politics, eventually becoming mayor of Chelsea when Mitchell was ten. Although financially more comfortable, Mitchell's early life eerily echoed Pecora's. Both overcame hardships to become accomplished schoolboy speakers. Pecora had to learn English; Mitchell to conquer his early stuttering. Both became president of their class.

Mitchell went to Amherst, and although he was not a stellar student, he was diligent and determined. Like Pecora's, his family suffered a setback—his father's business failed in Mitchell's junior year. But unlike Pecora, Mitchell stayed in college, supporting himself by working part-time in a general store and teaching public speaking. The future Wall Street titan was tall and ruggedly good-looking. He had wavy hair, deep-set eyes, an "indomitable jaw," and an athlete's muscular body, with thick wrists and the hands of a "worker." He exuded strength, not only physically, but mentally. He never wasted words and he always locked eyes with whomever he was talking to. For all that steely strength, Mitchell remained an amiable man, one who was well-liked and whose many friends voted him "the greatest" when they graduated in 1899. Mitchell, never one to doubt his own abilities and accomplishments, responded, "I am."[5]

He left Massachusetts for Chicago to work for Western Electric, earning ten dollars a week as a clerk and spending a fifth of his salary on night classes in bookkeeping and commercial law. He quickly rose through the ranks and, six years after he arrived, the ambitious Mitchell came up with an idea to merge several manufacturing companies. He took that idea to the president of the Trust Company of New York, Oakleigh Thorne, who was so impressed with Mitchell that he hired him on the spot as his assistant.

Mitchell arrived on Wall Street just before the Panic of 1907 and he had a front-row seat for the good old-fashioned bank run then threatening his firm. Every day he saw the customers line up in the street to get their money out, and every night he worked with Thorne planning the next day's strategy. In those days, it was up to private bankers to avert financial catastrophe, and J. P. Morgan, City Bank's James Stillman, and other leading New York commercial and private bankers pumped millions into the firm, successfully preventing its collapse. "In five weeks," Mitchell later boasted, "I was given five years' training in banking."[6]

After a few years with Thorne, Mitchell set out on his own. C. E. Mitchell and Company sold bonds, and no one sold bonds more aggressively than the firm's namesake. He joined clubs, not to socialize, but for prospects, and he quickly developed a reputation as a young, high-energy go-getter. Mitchell was fantastically disciplined. With neither the time nor the inclination to join a gym, each morning he would walk the six or so miles to his Wall Street office at a blistering pace. It was a regimen he would keep up, rain or shine, for decades.

When he joined City Bank in 1916, Mitchell articulated a high standard for the affiliate's selling efforts, first in bonds and then in stocks as the market ballooned. It was a standard that was built on the trust and confidence that he knew its customers, most of whom were financial neophytes, placed in the bank. "The time will never come," the new president told a group of trainees, "when, pressed with the need for securities of our great selling organization, we will let down in our exacting requirements. . . . We are going to make more exacting our yard-stick," he told the trainees, because for the firm "the law of *caveat emptor* cannot apply."[7]

The old-line investment banking firms never advertised—J.P. Morgan was famous for not even having its name on the building. National City, however, was trying to reach a different audience—the "person of limited resources, all of whose capital and income are necessary to insure life's future comforts." So the firm placed advertisements in many of the magazines popular with the rapidly expanding middle class, right next to those for RCA radios and Lifebuoy soap. Mitchell even rolled out a nationwide billboard campaign. The advertising struck the same chord as Mitchell's speech to the trainees. In an age when advertising was viewed quite explicitly as a form of education and when consumers remained uncritically accepting of many advertising claims, the company offered an image of financial solidity, investment acumen, and "unquestioned reliability."

Tapping directly into investors' natural insecurity over making potentially devastating blunders in a field in which few felt comfortable, National City assured investors that they needn't "decide it alone." It could help investors choose safe investments in which "their principal is always safeguarded." National City's "world-wide investment organization" was there "for the asking" to help investors sort out the "perplexing range of possibilities" they faced. City was not just pushing generic investment advice, but individualized counseling. "National City judgment as to which bonds are best for you," one ad read, "is based on both strict investigation of the security and analysis of your own requirements." Indeed, the National City Company was pitched as a time-saving device, no different from the washing machines and vacuum cleaners then flooding the marketplace. Investors no longer needed "to make a prolonged personal study" of investments; they could rely instead on the company's "experienced advice" to help them choose from "broad lists of investigated securities." It all seems a bit quaint to modern ears, but in the 1920s the company's customers really did seem to believe that the investment banker was a man of probity who put his customers' needs and welfare before everything else.[8]

Those sentiments notwithstanding, Mitchell pushed his salesmen hard. If a salesman complained there were no buyers, Mitchell, universally renowned as "the greatest bond salesman who ever lived," would take him to the opulent Bankers' Club high atop the nearby Equitable Building and lead him to the window. "There are six million people with incomes that aggregate thousands of millions of dollars," he would tell the salesman, waving his hand at the city below. "They are just waiting for someone to come and tell them what to do with their savings. Take a good look, eat a good lunch, and then go down and tell them."

The biggest money in investment banking was in originating deals directly with the issuers. J.P. Morgan and Kuhn Loeb dominated the major issuers, so National City continued to underwrite the bonds of newer, riskier ones—utilities and airplane manufacturers, municipalities, and a host of foreign governments ranging from European countries devastated by World War I to shaky Latin American dictatorships. Some of these bonds looked like huge gambles, but they quickly became market darlings as the company continued to assure investors that its extensive research staff had examined them thoroughly and given them its seal of approval.[9]

Mitchell proved to be as good a motivator as he was a bond salesman, and his timing was excellent; he assumed the helm of the securities affiliate just before the sale of Liberty Bonds during World War I primed the burgeoning middle class to buy securities. Within a few years, the National City Company had 1,400 employees with branches across the country and around the globe. It was the largest securities distributor in the country, selling $1 billion worth of bonds annually in a decade when stock and bond sales more than tripled. Mitchell viewed his vast securities-selling organization no differently than he would any chain store. Like any large retailer, Mitchell's goal was to reduce his "unit cost" by generating a huge volume of business. "Our newer offices," he told the sales trainees, "are on the ground floor. . . . [We] are getting close to the public . . . and are preparing to serve the public on a straightforward basis, just as it is served by the United Cigar Stores or Child's Restaurants." City's chain stores, Mitchell insisted, should sell securities "like so many pounds of coffee." Indeed, not content to wait for customers to walk through the doors, Mitchell had his salesmen waiting for potential buyers in train stations, attending churches on Sundays, and "knocking at the doors of rural houses like men with vacuum cleaners or Fuller brushes." No one had ever sold securities this way before—Mitchell was transforming the investment banking industry.[10]

As Mitchell was overseeing National City's phenomenal expansion, Frank Vanderlip's term in charge of the bank came to an abrupt halt. City Bank's aggressive overseas expansion included heavy investments in Russia. After the 1917 revolution, the new government nationalized banks and City Bank took a major hit. James Stillman died just a few months later; his son James Jr. was named chairman, and he soon forced Vanderlip out of the presidency. Stillman the younger was nowhere near the banker his father was, but it hardly mattered. Times were flush and City Bank had just become the first billion-dollar bank.

The good times, however, evaporated with the recession of 1920–21. As the economy turned south, it soon became all too clear that no one during the boom years had paid close enough attention to the quality of the loan portfolio. The worst situation was Cuba. During World War I, Cuba had a monopoly on sugar in the United States market. After the war, prices continued to boom even as more land was converted to cane production and refineries sprouted everywhere. All that expansion needed capital and City Bank was there to meet the demand. In 1919 alone, the bank opened twenty-two branches in Cuba, telling its shareholders that sugar was produced there "under very favorable conditions economically" and that the industry was on a "sound basis." Soon City Bank held nearly 20 percent of the loans outstanding in the Cuban banking system. It had wagered an astounding 80 percent of its total capital on Cuban sugar, a huge, risky, and ultimately foolish bet. In November 1920, the United States lifted wartime controls, producers from outside Cuba came on line, and prices tumbled from twenty-two cents to a penny a pound. Sugar firms failed left and right, local Cuban banks closed, and the Cuban government eventually declared a debt moratorium that lasted into 1921.[11]

In the face of that disaster there was no way the younger Stillman, already in the midst of a very public and very messy divorce, could hold on to the presidency. He resigned in May 1921 and the board decided that Mitchell, then just forty-three, was the right man to clean up the mess. The new bank president wrote to Vanderlip that he was humbled by the selection. He had not sought the job "as it has been my feeling that the possibilities in the Company itself were sufficient to gratify my every ambition." City Bank's prominence and its importance in the economic structure of the country, he recognized, meant that he owed a duty not just to the bank's shareholders but to the public at large. "I am fully mindful," he wrote, "of the quasi-public position which The National City Bank must hold, and cognizant as I am of my own shortcomings, I can indeed approach the work with none other than a feeling of solemnity."[12]

Neither solemnity nor his lack of experience in commercial banking translated into long deliberation. The new bank president acted quickly and decisively, writing off bad loans, closing weak overseas branches, and instituting more stringent centralized controls. Mitchell's timing was again fortunate—the recession was short-lived, transforming once sketchy loans into solid ones. And although he claimed never to have aspired to his new position, he quickly consolidated his own power to ensure that he was the undisputed ruler of the bank. Immediately, he insisted that the board institute a bonus system for the bank's senior executives, telling shareholders that bonuses would "concentrate the attention of the officers upon service to the institution" and thereby reap "larger returns to the shareholders." In his pitch for bonuses, Mitchell never even mentioned how those bonuses might affect City Bank's "quasi-public position."

Knowing that failing to resolve the Cuba debacle "would have meant pretty nearly the destruction of our institution," Mitchell left for Cuba. He spent eighteen-hour days asking question after question at plantations and sugar mills around the country. Mitchell wouldn't write off the loans; doing so would have reduced the bank's capital too much, hurting its capacity to make new, sound loans and making it that much more difficult for the bank to right itself. Ever the gambler, Mitchell chose instead to invest even more money in Cuba. He consolidated the bank's holdings in a newly formed company, the General Sugar Corporation, which immediately became one of the largest sugar operations in the country. Going more heavily into the sugar business was a bold move for the bank, one that would only work if sugar prices rebounded. By 1922, Mitchell assured shareholders the strategy was working; the situation was "well in hand." To employees he was even more upbeat. "We are on our way to bigger things. The National City Bank's future is brighter, I believe, than it has ever been."[13]

Mitchell was true to his word, and over the next seven years he brought to the bank the same retail spirit he had used to transform the National City Company. "What General Motors was doing for the automobile and Proctor and Gamble for household products," Citibank's historians wrote, "National City now did for financial services." Mitchell envisioned City Bank as the "bank for all," and he scored huge public relations successes when the bank began accepting deposits of as little as one dollar and began making personal loans as small as fifty dollars. Those decisions were hailed as the "death-knell of the loan-shark business in New York" and a "new adventure in democratic finance." By 1929, the bank had more than 300,000 personal accounts, all waiting for City Bank and the National City Company to "tell them what to do with their savings." These "small but developing capitalists," as Mitchell called them, would be customers not only for banking and trust services, but also for the affiliate's securities offerings.[14]

Always pushing to reduce the bank's unit costs, Mitchell expanded aggressively. He sold large amounts of stock—increasing capital eightfold over the 1920s—and then used that money to acquire other banks and trust companies. He also took advantage of a change in federal law that finally permitted City

Bank to open branches. By 1929, the bank had dozens scattered throughout New York City. Mitchell stationed bond salesmen and trust officers in each one, making it that much easier to cross-sell to his customers. By the mid-1920s, City Bank wasn't just the largest bank in the country, it was one of the largest corporations, rivaling in size U.S. Steel and American Telephone & Telegraph. Affiliate offices continued to spread across the country—there were sixty-nine in fifty-one cities in 1929—all connected by 11,000 miles of private wire. There were company offices throughout Canada and in London, Amsterdam, Geneva, Tokyo, and Shanghai, all originating new bond offerings for the salesmen to peddle. The affiliate continued its run of record annual profits. In 1927 it had sales of $2 billion, was adding a thousand new customers a month, and had built its own new thirty-two-story office building.[15]

Through it all City Bank's stock price soared. In 1928, the stock was approaching $800 a share, too expensive for the middle-class investors Mitchell wanted most to attract. Mitchell split the stock five for one, but it rose again, this time to almost $600 a share. By the fall of 1929, in the midst of an enormous boom in bank mergers, Mitchell was negotiating a combination with the Corn Exchange Bank. The deal would give City Bank far more branches than any other bank in New York. More than that, it was a capstone for Mitchell's ambition. The deal garnered nationwide attention because it would, in Mitchell's words, make City Bank "not only . . . the largest and most powerful, but the most solid institution in the world." Shareholder approval was all that was needed to complete the deal, and it was widely assumed to be a foregone conclusion.[16]

With the booming stock market, Mitchell and other Wall Street leaders were celebrities, and the press chronicled their business pronouncements and their social lives with equal ardor. Mitchell employed a "highly organized publicity machine" to build him up as "a symbol of the great American banker of the twentieth century," a transformative figure who had revolutionized the way that commercial and investment banks did business. In a time when Wall Street was considered the stage on which strode "the aristocracy of American intelligence," Mitchell was front and center. He was "the ideal modern bank executive," someone who had risen faster than anyone else on Wall Street by the sheer force of his personality. Mitchell's successes and those outsize public perceptions of Wall Street genius spurred his own grandiose visions of his place in the financial and business pantheon. "He saw himself as a man of destiny," wrote a biographer at the time. "If John D. Rockefeller had become the master of oil he would become the master of money."[17]

With his celebrity and his wealth came all the trappings of Wall Street success—the limestone mansion on Fifth Avenue and the summer homes in Southampton and Tuxedo Park, all with their own live-in staffs. Mitchell lived flamboyantly and spent lavishly. He took annual European trips, shot grouse on the Scottish moors, and made six-week yacht cruises to the Caribbean. When Mitchell traveled for business, it was always by private railcar, complete with kitchen and chef. He was the epitome of the crass, nouveau riche gate-crasher. He drove big cars at reckless speeds. His wife was a music patron, but Mitchell called the opera a good place "to catch up a couple of hours' sleep."

In the 1920s, Tuxedo Park was still synonymous with high society and upper-class living. Mitchell outraged the town's old guard by building his massive home, aptly named Hillsdale, on the highest spot in town so that everyone had to look at it. They may have been annoyed, but they still came to his elaborate parties. The Vanderbilts, Hearsts, and Astors were frequent guests, as were President Coolidge and the Treasury secretary, Andrew Mellon. Even the queen of Romania, touring the country in 1926, requested to stay at Hillsdale, which she remarked made her own palaces look barren. Mitchell was in every way the great Wall Street success story. The handsome, powerfully built self-made millionaire was rugged individualism personified.[18]

On January 1, 1929, in a sign of his stature in the banking world, Mitchell was named a director of the New York Federal Reserve. Benjamin Strong, the bank's governor until his death in October 1928, had tapped Mitchell for the post. Mitchell, he thought, was "truly one of the ablest of our bankers" even though he had been, to that point, a "bitter critic" of the Federal Reserve. The relentless market booster was now a caretaker of the solidity and safety of the financial system, and he wasted no time in shaking up the place.

The Federal Reserve was becoming concerned that stock market speculation, much of it driven by margin stock purchases, had gotten out of hand. At the time, investors could buy stocks for as little as 10 percent of their value, borrowing the rest from the broker and putting up the purchased stock as collateral. The broker would in turn borrow the money in what was known as the call loan market. Call loan rates had skyrocketed to 12 percent by the end of 1928, and companies like Standard Oil, General Motors, and RCA decided that this was the best way to invest their idle cash. New York banks were equally ebullient; they could borrow from the Federal Reserve for 5 percent and immediately lend the money at 12. It was a great system for everyone concerned so long as stock prices continued to rise. The lenders were making easy money with little risk because the collateral underlying the loans could be sold immediately. Margin magnified the stock buyer's gains. A 10 percent rise in price would give the investor a 100 percent return. Of course, a 10 percent decline would wipe the investor out, but no one, apart from the Federal Reserve, seemed very worried about that possibility in early 1929. This was the New Era. Many uttered what nearly always proves to be the most expensive phrase in investing: "This time is different."

The Federal Reserve was in an unenviable position. If it raised rates it could harm the broader economy, not just put a crimp on stock speculators. And, of course, if the market came crashing down it would be the Federal Reserve that would take the brunt of the criticism, a prospect that no regulator relishes. So it took more timorous steps. In February, it twice warned member banks not to borrow money "for the purpose of making speculative loans." On March 4, 1929, when Hoover was inaugurated, he urged the Federal Reserve to do more, prompting daily meetings of the board. The Federal Reserve made no announcements, but after an unprecedented Saturday meeting on March 23, the market was spooked. That Tuesday, prices plummeted on huge volume, and as banks reduced their call market loans, rates zoomed to 20 percent. It looked like the party was over.[19]

Strong's recommendation of Mitchell had been contingent on having a "nice talk" with Mitchell that emphasized that "so long as he is a member of the board of directors he should be willing to accept the decision of the directors in all matters and not indulge in outside criticism." Apparently the talk didn't take, because Mitchell came to the rescue of the staggering stock market, announcing that City Bank would borrow $25 million from the New York Federal Reserve to prevent liquidation of margin loans, "whatever might be the attitude of the Federal Reserve Board." Mitchell's edict, in the words of the economist John

Kenneth Galbraith, was "the Wall Street counterpart of Mayor Hague's famous manifesto, 'I am the law in Jersey City.'" The Federal Reserve and Hoover remained silent, unwilling to openly challenge Mitchell. Or at least that was the way it seemed to outsiders. In truth, Mitchell had acted with the approval of the New York Federal Reserve's new governor, George L. Harrison.[20]

After City Bank's intervention, call loan rates declined and the market continued its upward trajectory. Senator Carter Glass, never a fan of the stock market and always protective of his Federal Reserve, was livid at Mitchell's apparently defiant attitude. Mitchell, the senator said, slapped the Federal Reserve "squarely in the face," treating its policies "with contempt and contumely." He was unfit to serve on the board and should resign immediately. But to everyone else, Mitchell was a hero. A *New York Times* editorial proclaimed that Mitchell had "saved the day for the financial community. No one can say how great a calamity would have happened had he not stepped into the breach at the right moment." Mitchell, it seemed, had refused to be browbeaten by know-nothing Washington bureaucrats. He had single-handedly prevented a panic and saved the great bull market. Maybe he was indeed the heir to J. P. Morgan.[21]

The market euphoria of spring barely survived the summer. Stock prices were choppy in September but unmistakably trending downward after the market's peak just after Labor Day. In October 1929, the Yale economist Irving Fisher uttered what would prove to be one of the more durable quotes linked to the Great Crash. "Stocks," Fisher confidently predicted after an alarming dip in early October, "have reached what looks like a permanently high plateau." Mitchell and Fisher saw eye to eye. The two were "Wall Street's official prophets," but they were far from alone in their optimistic assessments. Most everyone was exuberant; Mitchell and Fisher were simply more visible and more insistent.

In September, as he boarded a liner for a European vacation, Mitchell assured investors "things have never been better"; there was simply "nothing to worry about in the financial situation of the United States." As late as October 21, after a particularly bad day on the market, Mitchell, now arriving back in New York, tried to calm welling public panic. The market readjustment, he told reporters, "had actually been an encouraging sign" and, in fact, had already "gone too far."

The crash began two days later, not as a nauseating one-day plummet, but as an agonizing weeklong plunge into the abyss. The sell-off that began in earnest on the afternoon of Wednesday, October 23, fed on itself as speculators abandoned their positions and margin accounts were sold out. On Black Thursday, almost 13 million shares changed hands, three times the previous record. As the averages continued to fall, the Morgan partner Thomas Lamont, Mitchell, and other leading bankers tried to support the market—just as J. P. Morgan had done to stave off the Panic of 1907. They pooled resources and sent Richard Whitney out to the floor of the New York Stock Exchange to ostentatiously purchase U.S. Steel and other leading industrial stocks at above-market prices.

Could Mitchell save the market again? He tried to say all the right reassuring things, insisting that he was unconcerned about what he viewed as a "purely technical" market adjustment. Sunshine Charlie had been right many times before—this time he was dead wrong. With the bankers' organized support the market stabilized, but only temporarily. On Monday, as thousands of frightened investors congregated outside the police barricades surrounding the New York Stock Exchange, the market dove a record 13 percent. Another 12 percent drop on Black Tuesday, on volume that easily beat the record of the previous Thursday, meant that the market had lost $30 billion in value in a week, ten times the annual federal budget.[22]

There was no way that Mitchell, after his unbounded optimism and failed attempt to stem the crisis, could avoid some well-earned rebukes in the aftermath. Senator Glass did not mince words, charging that Mitchell was "more responsible than all others together for excesses that have resulted in this disaster." The New Yorker did its best to supply a little humbling derision. Parodying the New York Times's Neediest Cases column, it told the story of "Charlie," who "likes nothing better than to tell everyone that the prices of securities in Wall Street are grotesquely conservative." Charlie was now forced "to subsist on a diet of crow and raspberries. What he needs for Christmas is some good, serviceable prestige." Publicly, Mitchell maintained the requisite stiff upper lip, but in private he "accused the country of crucifying him."[23]

The reprimands and ridicule, however, were aimed at Mitchell's lack of foresight, not his villainy. Almost no one seemed to believe that Mitchell had deliberately deceived investors—he was simply overly optimistic. "When Mr. Mitchell was broadcasting his roseate dreams to buy stocks," one author wrote at the time, "he thought he was walking in a new world." Mitchell's public optimism mirrored his private comments. The banker had wired the Wall Street financier Bernard Baruch in August 1929 that stocks looked "exceptionally sound" and likened the market to "a weather-vane pointing into a gale of prosperity." Baruch proved to be the savvier investor—with Mitchell's predictions still reverberating in his head, he chose to sell all his remaining stocks and managed to get out of the market before the crash.[24]

Even with this colossal blunder, Mitchell's position at City Bank was never in jeopardy. Percy Rockefeller (John D. Rockefeller's nephew) was a City Bank director and one of its largest stockholders, and he called rumors that Mitchell would resign in the wake of the crash "too absurd to be considered by any sensible person." Even a magazine as liberal as the Nation could still call the "imaginative and unconventional" Mitchell "courageous" for his "progressive" attempts to democratize banking. Sure, he was only doing it to make money, but Mitchell had, nevertheless, convinced his bank "to lend to common people in small amounts, at reasonable interest" and to "sell securities to even the least investor." He had "done as much as any one . . . to socialize banking." Mitchell was still a banking visionary.[25]

Within a few months, Mitchell's reputation would rebound, and by 1932 he was far from a pariah. His place in society and in the power structure of the country appeared both secure and undiminished. In 1930, he was on a list put together by a wealthy corporate lawyer and former ambassador to Germany, James W. Gerard, of the fifty-nine men—mostly bankers and industrialists—who, "by virtue of their ability" actually "ruled" the United States. Publication of the list caused something of a sensation. Some scoffed at Gerard's assertion that these men were "too busy to hold political office but they determine who shall hold such offices." Still, New York's Governor Roosevelt felt compelled to announce that he was tired of a handful of men controlling the destinies of 120 million. Whatever the truth, Mitchell's inclusion on the list reflected his secure position among the business and financial elite. He served out his term as a director of the New York Federal Reserve, despite Glass's finger-pointing. In many quarters he was still praised for his courageous stand against the Federal Reserve.[26]

A year later, Mitchell prominently came to the rescue of New York City. As the Depression worsened, cash-strapped owners stopped paying their property taxes, while relief efforts sent the city's expenses skyrocketing. In no time, New York City was on the brink of financial collapse. Mitchell led a team of bankers in negotiating potential loans to the city. When Mayor Walker was summoned to a meeting at Mitchell's Fifth Avenue home, the banker read him the riot act—he needed to cut salaries and purge the city's bloated payroll of patronage appointments. "Cut your budget," he bluntly told Walker, "or go elsewhere for your money." Despite Walker's popularity with the voters, it was clear where the power lay. Walker was so nervous that he pulled all the tacks out of the antique French chair on which he was sitting. He hastily retreated, the city slashed salaries, and the loan was made.[27]

That same year Hoover consulted Mitchell and other leading bankers on ways to address the credit crisis then gripping the country. Mostly, Mitchell thought the government did more harm than good. Taxes were damming "the natural flow of wealth," and he advised the government to simply stay out of the way. "[E]very experiment in Government management," he lectured, "demonstrates its disqualification in that field." By 1933, Mitchell's knee-jerk optimism remained, for the most part, undimmed. He was "moderately hopeful" that the storm would soon be over. The banking panic, he said, had been overcome and the United States' economic system was "essentially sound, the most efficient in the world, and capable of providing a higher standard of living for the people than yet has been known in any country." A few days before the Long filibuster killed Senator Glass's banking bill, Mitchell warned City Bank's shareholders about the dangers of severing securities affiliates from commercial banks. Affiliates were an "essential element in the financial machinery of the United States" and eliminating them would, he confidently asserted, make it that much more difficult for the country to emerge from depression.[28]

Bankers' reputations among average Americans were certainly battered and bruised at the end of January 1933. Father Charles Coughlin, the popular radio priest, grew even more popular when he began to blame Wall Street and international bankers for the Great Depression. As the Depression wore on, Coughlin's commentary turned violently anti-Semitic, leading some commentators to dub him the father of hate radio. But in the early 1930s, at the height of his popularity and influence, Coughlin's targets were "greedy bankers and financiers." When Coughlin called Hoover "the Holy Ghost of the rich, the protective angel of Wall Street," tens of thousands of letters, many stuffed with donations, inundated his church in Royal Oak, Michigan. In January 1932, another priest, Father James Cox, led a ragtag group of unemployed men to Washington. After an audience with Hoover, Father Cox confidently declared that the United States had "a government of the bankers, for the bankers and by the bankers." Being a banker, the *American Mercury* noted, was "formerly regarded as a mark of esteem in the United States," but was now synonymous with "rascal" or "scalawag."[29]

There was, at the time, a tendency, wrote journalist Anne O'Hare McCormick, "to blame the bankers for almost everything." Mitchell was still thought of as a "rampant bull" and he and other bankers, once heroes, were now the scapegoats of the crash. In bad economic times, Americans have traditionally suspected Wall Street's motives and its morals, but now the country doubted its intelligence, too. "An eminent financial expert," one wag noted, "declares that conditions are improving. Nevertheless we think conditions are improving."

When Pecora subpoenaed Mitchell to appear before the committee, it remained clear that the public's simmering and unfocused anger at Wall Street and the lingering animosities about Mitchell's role in the boom days had done little to dent either the power he wielded or his stature in the banking community. Americans were angry and suspicious. Demagogues like Father Coughlin were eagerly denouncing bankers as "gangsters" who were "perfectly organized for their own selfish ends." But no one had yet provided proof that Mitchell or any other leading Wall Street banker had in fact acted illegally or unethically.[30]

The day after he was subpoenaed, Mitchell called Pecora directly. Seated in his wood-paneled office with its black marble fireplace, the banker was in full salesman mode, apparently feeling no need to interpose a layer of lawyers between himself and this neophyte senatorial investigator. Mitchell wasn't taking Pecora too seriously—when he wrote Pecora a few days later, he didn't even get his address right. On the phone he "told [Pecora] a persuasive story about the urgent necessity" of his trip to Italy and of his plan to sail in just a few days. The banker assured Pecora that he was unnecessary; the other executives of the bank had all the information the committee needed. If the committee released him from the subpoena "he would return on March 1st and submit himself for examination before the close of this session of Congress." In exchange, the banker held out a big carrot. Mitchell promised Pecora that the bank would fully cooperate with the committee's investigation. "Mr. Mitchell agreed," Pecora informed Norbeck, "that the investigators and accountants of the Committee's staff should have complete access to all the records that we regarded as relevant to the Committee inquiry."[31]

Mitchell was trying to stall, to run out the clock. He knew that authorization for the investigation expired on March 4, and if he returned from Europe on March 1, at best the committee would have just two days to question him. And that was a big if. Less than a decade earlier, Harry Blackmer had fled the country rather than testify in Congress about Teapot Dome. On that last day of January 1933, he was still safely beyond the reach of the United States legal system, splitting his time between Monaco and Cannes. Samuel Insull, currently under indictment in Chicago, was still successfully fighting extradition from Greece. Mitchell would have a much easier time avoiding the committee.[32]

Pecora surely realized all this, but he also must have wanted to keep his options open. He certainly did not want to reject Mitchell's request while the banker was holding out the promise of unfettered access to the bank's records. There is, of course, nothing glamorous about document review—most of the time it's mind-numbing drudgery. Lawyers typically dread the countless hours it consumes, the incessant, patient sifting of stacks and stacks of documents necessary to reconstruct the facts of a case and to unearth the few gems that may make or break it. Pecora thrived on courtroom forensics, so he was probably no different. He knew, however, that the flashy and effective cross-examination couldn't happen without the long slog through reams of paper. There are few surprises for great cross-examiners, who almost invariably know the answers to their questions before they ask them. It is really the only way to pin down evasive witnesses, who are unlikely to concede anything important unless confronted with the documentary evidence that leaves them with no other choice. It was the failure to do that kind of legwork that had made Richard Whitney's appearance such an abject failure for the committee. With the investigation hanging in the balance, Pecora was not about to make the same mistake with City Bank.

Naturally, none of this was news to City Bank's lawyers, and it was certainly possible that Mitchell was lying; perhaps he had no intention of allowing Pecora's staff to run untrammeled through City Bank's books and records. The senator and later Supreme Court justice Hugo Black wrote that business executives at the time had "built up the fiction that they have a right to enjoy some special privilege of secrecy" from governmental investigations. Pecora decided he could wait and see, at least for a little while. On the off chance that Mitchell really was going to provide Pecora with exactly what he wanted, he would remain noncommittal. He told Mitchell that he "would consult with the Committee and take the matter under advisement myself." He agreed to let Mitchell know by Thursday—two days later and two days before Mitchell was due to sail—about whether his appearance could be postponed.[33]

Those two days let Pecora test Mitchell's cooperation, and it quickly became clear that it was not forthcoming. When Pecora's staff went to City Bank headquarters the next morning, they met with delay and dawdling. City Bank was not so shortsighted as to refuse outright. "While there was no abrupt or disagreeable obstruction," Pecora informed Norbeck, "ways were invented to kill time by reason of objections to various lines of our inquiry." It was much the same treatment that committee investigators received in the spring of 1932 when they investigated the bank's participation in the Anaconda Copper stock pool. At that time they were told that they could look at selected documents, but only under the watchful gaze of a City Bank officer, and under no circumstances were they permitted to take notes. Why William Gray, the committee counsel at the time, would agree to such restrictions is a mystery, but it is some measure of the deference accorded to the theoretically omnipotent leaders of Wall Street. City Bank was trying the same tactics again. Now Garrard Winston, a partner from City

Bank's outside law firm, Shearman & Sterling, and a director of the securities affiliate, would have to review and approve all requests before the investigators could look at a single document. If there were any doubts about City Bank's strategy, those doubts were now gone.[34]

Norbeck wasn't pleased with the delaying tactics and he decided to turn up the heat on the company. Right after getting off the phone with Pecora, Norbeck told reporters that the committee intended to focus its inquiry on how City Bank sold its own stock. That wasn't quite right—Pecora wanted to examine all the stocks and bonds City Bank sold, not just its own. Norbeck then placed responsibility for the stock market bust—and by implication for the ensuing Depression—right at the feet of City Bank and Mitchell. The investigation showed that the participation of large banks in stock promotions was "highly responsible for the wild stock market boom." The Federal Reserve tried to slow down the stock market, Norbeck argued, but Mitchell "defied the board and speeded up the boom. He took a 'go-to-hell' attitude toward the Board and got away with it."[35]

Norbeck's press gambit backfired. Bank employees told Pecora's staff that "the picture has now changed." From there on in, they intended to focus on the precise language of the Senate resolution in analyzing document requests. The message was clear: City Bank would look for any basis on which to shield material from the committee.

After a day of fruitless attempts to gain access to the City Bank records, Pecora summoned Shearman's managing partner, Guy Fairfax Cary, to his office. Sitting in Pecora's tattered armchair, the patrician Cary, who had been a City Bank director since 1919, could not have been more out of place. Cary looked the part of the serious, formal, somewhat tightly wound Wall Street lawyer, with his down-turned mouth, bald head, and frameless pince-nez. Indeed, other than the fact that they were both New York lawyers of about the same age, it is hard to imagine two men with more different backgrounds. Cary was part of New York's business and social elite. His maternal grandfather was a partner at one of the leading investment banking houses, Brown Bros. & Co. Cary attended prep school at Groton before going on to Harvard and Harvard Law. Now approaching his third decade of practice, he catered to the legal needs of large corporations and wealthy New Yorkers. Cary lived on Park Avenue, summered in Newport, was a fixture on the New York social scene, and belonged to some of the city's most exclusive clubs, the kind of clubs that did not allow lawyers with vowels on the ends of their names to join.[36]

For Cary to feel uncomfortable was just what Pecora wanted. He knew it was a "crude" psychological trick, but it was usually effective. Pecora would later use the same tactic in his initial meeting with J. P. Morgan Jr. Morgan famously went nowhere for meetings—if someone wanted to meet, he or she would invariably come to Morgan at 23 Wall Street. Pecora, however, insisted that he was too busy to make the trek down to Lower Manhattan; Morgan would have to come uptown. It had the desired effect. "I felt," Pecora said, "it might be a good thing to do something which might convey to Mr. Morgan the impression that he was not going to meet Ferdinand Pecora, the individual, but that he was to meet a representative of the United States Government."[37]

Cary may have felt uncomfortable, but he remained recalcitrant. He told Pecora that according to his own reading of the resolution, the committee's authority was severely limited; it could only investigate "listed securities." That meant City Bank would not turn over any documents involving transactions in securities not listed on the New York Stock Exchange. Norbeck's misstatement concerning the thrust of the committee's interest—the issuance of the bank's own stock—also gave Cary a big opening. If that was the case, Cary told Pecora, then the committee had no authority to investigate any matter involving the bank after January 11, 1928, the day City Bank had delisted from the New York Stock Exchange, ostensibly to prevent manipulation of its own stock.

Cary's argument was aggressive; he was trying to excise from the investigation all of City Bank's activities around the crash, effectively gutting the investigation. Unlike the supine Gray, however, Pecora wasn't going to back down, and he wasn't going to get hemmed in by every mistaken utterance that came out of Norbeck's mouth. Pecora told Cary that his position was unsound. Yes, the resolution referred to listed securities, but it also authorized the committee to investigate the effect stock exchange trading had on "the operation of the national banking system and the Federal Reserve System," of which City Bank was most certainly a part. The resolution also didn't limit the committee to investigating listed securities; it authorized the committee to investigate buying and selling of listed securities. Whether City Bank was listed was irrelevant, because City Bank was clearly in the business of buying and selling listed securities. Pecora was right, but Cary wasn't looking to be right. He only needed a plausible argument that would allow him to slow down Pecora's investigators.

Not surprisingly, the two men decided nothing that evening, and the meeting ended with Pecora no closer to inspecting the bank's records than he was before. The lines were drawn, and Pecora had no reason to believe that Mitchell or City Bank had any intention of cooperating. Now it was Pecora's turn to turn up the heat. He immediately notified Mitchell that his appearance before the committee on February 21 was "imperative." Il Duce was simply going to have to wait for Mitchell's advice on the lira. The next day he told the press: "[T]he committee staff has encountered certain recalcitrants who are attempting to obstruct the inquiry. . . . I shall not hesitate to employ every legal means to ascertain all facts essential to the investigation." There was little doubt who Pecora was referring to.[38]

Pecora was still pursuing evidence from other sources, things like Mitchell's tax returns and other documents in the hands of federal agencies, but he wasn't going to get very far without the bank's documents. And it wasn't just documents relating to City Bank transactions. John Marrinan suggested getting "a line on salaries and bonuses paid to officers of the National City Company." Cary and Garrard Winston clearly weren't going to let them see those documents without a fight—even shareholders didn't know what the officers made. On Saturday, Cary and Mitchell continued to duck Pecora's calls, perhaps thinking that he, like Gray, would give up in the face of their stonewalling. They didn't know Pecora very well.[39]

Pecora asked Norbeck to issue a new set of subpoenas requiring the bank's employees to produce everything in Washington the following week. If they failed to show or failed to bring all the documents, they would be held in contempt and thrown in jail until they complied. Norbeck readily agreed to issue the subpoenas. In truth, he was likely in a sour mood, particularly unwilling at that moment to be conciliatory toward a bunch of New York bankers. Not when the news from home was so disturbing. Protesting farmers in Sioux City had just shot and killed a sixty-eight-year-old man who had tried to run their blockade.[40]

The subpoenas went out on Tuesday, February 8, and City Bank caved the next day, agreeing to give Pecora and his staff complete access to its books and records. Cary's argument for limiting the scope of the committee's inquiry didn't prevail, but he bought his client a week. Now Pecora had only twelve days to get through City Bank's documents while simultaneously trying to conduct an inquiry into the Insull utility collapse. To forestall any other attempted delays, Pecora would go to City Bank's headquarters himself.[41]

Chapter 6

A MINE OF
INFORMATION

February 9 was brutally cold in New York City. The temperature hovered in the mid-teens, but the windchill made it feel below zero as Pecora made his way down to Wall Street. He traveled through a city devastated from three years of depression. "No one can live and work in New York this winter," Rexford Tugwell, a member of the Roosevelt Brain Trust, wrote, "without a profound sense of uneasiness. Never, in modern times, I should think, has there been so widespread unemployment and such moving distress from sheer hunger and cold." Pecora didn't have to look far to see it. Beginning just below his Riverside Drive apartment was a massive encampment of squatters that stretched nearly forty blocks north. Pecora could watch the crowds gathered at the dumps that lined the Hudson, waiting to scavenge bits of food from the next load off the garbage trucks. President Hoover said that no one was starving, but he was wrong; New York hospitals reported more than thirty starvation deaths in 1933.

That kind of hunger certainly wasn't limited to New York. In Chicago, crowds fought over the garbage bins behind restaurants. In the coal fields of Appalachia, miners were earning less than $2.50 a day and were lucky if they could work three days a week. Hunger was a constant presence, with most diets consisting of little more than beans and bread. When one schoolteacher in an impoverished mining camp told a faint young girl to go home to eat, she replied, "It won't do any good . . . because this is my sister's day to eat."

As Pecora made his way farther downtown, he would have passed the empty hulks of half-finished office buildings. Foreclosure sales were now a daily occurrence; three weeks earlier the Pierre Hotel had been sold off to the highest bidder. Bryant Park, the once trim little square of green just around the corner from his office, was choked with weeds. To the west were Army and newspaper trucks pressed into duty as soup kitchens in Columbus Circle and Times Square. There, men in what were once fashionable suits and hats, long since tattered and frayed, stood with their collars turned up against the cold, burlap wrapping their shoes, their eyes fixed on the sidewalk. They waited patiently in lines that wrapped around the block—the columnist and Algonquin Round Table member Heywood Broun called the lines "the worm that walks like a man." When they accepted the bread or thin soup or just coffee and doughnuts, they would shuffle silently away, their faces "flat, opaque, expressionless."

For all the unfocused anger at the financial community, this was still the heyday of rugged American individualism; success and failure were supposed to be about personal character, not broad economic forces. Business leaders were frequently heard blaming the poor for their plight, accusing them of failing to practice "habits of thrift and conservation" and of foolishly gambling "their savings in the stock market." Many of the jobless blamed themselves as well. They were failures and they were ashamed.

The homeless weren't just along Riverside Drive; they were everywhere, in missions and municipal shelters, in subways and bridge abutments, on park benches and in doorways, and even in the cheap speakeasies, where for the price of a single drink you were welcome to sleep on the sawdust-covered floor. On the Lower East Side there were so many evictions that you couldn't walk down the street without seeing furniture on the sidewalk. In Queens, foreclosed homeowners barricaded their front doors with barbed wire and sandbags, daring the sheriff to try to evict them. In Central Park, hard behind the Metropolitan Museum of Art, were two hundred scrap-wood-and-tin shacks, their occupants often seen roasting the birds they managed to catch in the park. "Jungletown," the *New Yorker* reported, was on the corner of West and Spring streets, "a whole village of shacks and huts . . . made of packing boxes, barrel staves, pieces of corrugated iron, and whatever else the junkman doesn't want." Everywhere people were afraid, afraid of the unknown, afraid that this skimping and saving, this perpetual gnawing uncertainty and hunger might be the norm for the rest of their lives.[1]

Mitchell, luckily, was able to avoid the brutal cold of that February day. He and his wife had decided to take a short trip to Bermuda now that the Italy trip was off. The fall and winter had been quite busy socially for the Mitchell family. Mitchell's daughter, Rita, came out that year, one of the honored debutantes at Tuxedo Park's lavish Autumn Ball. The debutante season ended just after Christmas with a supper dance at the Mitchell home on Fifth Avenue. The Mitchells struck a holiday theme for Rita's party, bedecking the house in evergreens, poinsettias, and holly. Rita greeted her nearly four hundred guests (it was a small party because only her friends were invited) in a traditional white lamé gown augmented with a corsage of white orchids. The Mitchells, of course, did their part for charity as well. That winter, for example, they attended a performance by the Italian marionette troupe Teatro dei Piccoli, the proceeds of which benefited the Italy America Society and the Italian Welfare League.[2]

Pecora may not have known much about corporate finance and stock and bond offerings, but he was on familiar ground when he reached Wall Street that morning. When he quit St. Stephen's and his pursuit of the Episcopal ministry in 1896, Pecora had quickly landed his first legal job just down the block from where he now stood. At fifteen, he signed on as a law clerk for a "kindly . . . single practitioner" named J. Baldwin Hands.

Hands's office was at 18 Wall Street, catty-corner from J. P. Morgan's famous one at 23 Wall, and Pecora quickly developed a fascination for Wall Street celebrities. Pecora had, of course, heard of the famous financier—everyone had—and his boyhood curiosity led him to keep his eyes peeled for a glimpse of Morgan as he went to and from his job. One morning soon after Pecora started working for Hands, Morgan pulled up in an open carriage attended by his uniformed driver and footman. Like everyone else, Pecora was taken aback by the glowering financial tycoon's appearance. "He was, to a certain extent, an impressive-looking man, but to me his general appearance was of a forbidding nature," Pecora remembered. "He looked grim. He looked something more than merely human."[3]

Pecora's curiosity and reaction were natural. The portly Morgan had fierce eyes, a wicked temper, and a grotesque, bulbous nose hideously transformed by rhinophyma. By 1896, Morgan had also reached a pinnacle of power and wealth unsurpassed in the country. To a boy who quit school to support his family, whose mother worked in a sweatshop, whose father was crippled in an industrial accident, and who had just moved out of a dank basement, Morgan must have seemed like a being from another planet. Pecora's brief glimpse of Morgan on Wall Street was not the only time their paths crossed. Pecora's love of great oratory led him to attend Sunday services at churches that "had eloquent preachers," including on several occasions St. George's Episcopal Church, where Morgan was a warden. Pecora was always sure to get a seat on the center aisle. He knew that Morgan carried the collection plate there and it amused the impoverished teenager to hand out money to the plutocrat.[4]

Landing the job with Hands offered Pecora much more than proximity to a financial legend. Hands had a general practice and Pecora was his only employee. Pecora helped with everything, including accompanying his boss on trials, and he quickly began to learn about practicing law. Hands immediately liked his earnest young clerk and took "almost a paternal interest in" him. In fact, after a year, Hands convinced Pecora that it was time for him to move on. Hands's practice was simply too small and too limited to give Pecora the breadth of experience he needed if he really wanted to become a successful lawyer. Soon, with Hands's help, Pecora was the managing clerk in a larger practice just down the block. By 1902, he was earning $25 a week, enough for his mother to quit the sweatshop.[5]

He also started studying at New York Law School, just around the corner on Nassau Street. The school was one of an emerging crop of night law schools and, for Pecora, it was the only practical choice. He had the brains for Columbia or Harvard, but those schools were full-time only and he couldn't very well quit his job and send his mother back to the sweatshop. Both schools also required a college degree. Ostensibly the degree requirement was designed to raise the standards of the bar, but in reality it was intended to weed out the immigrants who were then flocking to law school.[6]

Like Pecora, other immigrants, especially eastern European Jews, saw a legal career as a path to financial security and social mobility. Many members of the established bar, however, were not nearly as open-minded as J. Baldwin Hands. For the most part, they reacted to the influx of immigrants in much the same way as the broader society. Elite lawyers complained about the "pestiferous horde" of immigrants seeking to become lawyers, "boys . . . [who] can hardly speak English intelligibly and show little understanding of or feeling for American institutions and government." The best law schools adopted strict quotas on "foreign lawyers," on the theory that foreigners were intellectually and morally inferior. The result, according to Jerold Auerbach, who chronicled turn-of-the-century discrimination in the bar, was that a "poor deserving" Jewish boy had a small chance of getting into Harvard. "If he was Italian, Polish, or Greek—or a black American," Auerbach concluded, "his chances were virtually non-existent."[7]

So it was New York Law School for Pecora, and for the first time in his life, he was not the model student. He was bored and disappointed with the lectures, which were geared toward giving students just enough information to allow them to pass the bar. "They sought," he later complained, "to teach the principles of the law without giving any thorough consideration to the philosophy that underlay . . . those principles." By his second year he never bothered attending class, and he appears not to have been officially enrolled. Pecora never graduated from the school's two-year law program. A law degree was not required for bar admission, but he still had a long way to go before he could practice.

The delay was again the product of the bar's antagonism toward this influx of budding immigrant lawyers. New York lawyers complained the state had become "the dumping ground of the world," and that it needed to adopt more stringent standards for bar admission than those of "more favored states" with fewer immigrants. Although New York City had created its first public high school only a few years earlier, the state now required a high school diploma or a so-called law student's certificate, a sort of high school equivalency diploma. Portrayed as a way of ensuring that only men (it was almost uniformly men at the time) of the highest quality were permitted to practice law, the new standards, bar leaders concluded, meant that only "morally weak" candidates or "the idle, the lazy, and the unprepared" would be excluded. In truth, the burden of these admissions standards fell predominantly on the urban immigrant poor like Pecora. The credits Pecora had accumulated in grade school and in his brief stay at St. Stephen's, he soon discovered, didn't cover all the courses he needed to get his certificate.[8]

As managing clerk, Pecora's workload was becoming heavier, making it that much harder for him to satisfy those course requirements. He soon, however, had another motivation for getting it all done. In the summer of 1906, Pecora needed a break from working and studying and, along with hordes of other New Yorkers, he fled the steamy city for Long Island. Pecora headed for Sea Cliff, one of the island's most popular summer destinations. Situated on the North Shore and reasonably close to the city, the town's travel posters boasted: "Beautiful Sea Cliff 250 Ft. Altitude No Mosquitoes." What more could a New Yorker in those pre-air-conditioned days ask for? Pecora and his friends were short on cash, so they got permission to pitch a tent in a vacant lot, and they spent the summer weekends there, hopping on the Long Island Railroad after they finished work. It was there that Pecora met Florence Louise Waterman, also twenty-four years old. Florence lived on the Waterman family farm in Evans, New York, on the shores of Lake Erie south of Buffalo. The family was apparently reasonably well-off, because they summered in Sea Cliff in a cottage that just happened to be across the street from the vacant lot where Pecora was camping.

Florence was beautiful; he later described her as a "Gibson girl, [who] has had offers to pose for artists." The two courted and seemed to quickly fall in love, but Pecora told her he was not wealthy—a fact that must have been painfully obvious when she saw his tent across the street—and that he was continuing to support his parents and younger siblings. They could not marry, Pecora insisted, until he was making enough money for them to set up their own household. The only way to do that was to finally start practicing law. With that additional spur, Pecora buckled down and, after four years, completed the requirements for bar admission. Ferdinand and Florence were married on November 30, 1910. A few months later, at age twenty-nine, Pecora finally became a lawyer.[9]

Pecora, it quickly turned out, wasn't much of a family man. He poured himself into his work, hustling for fees representing property owners in Brooklyn and Queens who were suing the city in eminent domain cases. A judge involved in those proceedings reported that the neophyte lawyer handled them "magnifi-cently." When he wasn't working, he was building his political career, taking care of matters for the local bosses, giving speeches, and attending numerous dinners and events. It left him little time for Florence or his son, Louis, born in 1915. In fact, Pecora never matched the rectitude he showed in his legal career in his private life. He was reportedly a notorious womanizer who had a string of extra-marital affairs. According to one story, Pecora had taken "one of his darlings" to a camp in Pennsylvania when "his family happened to walk into the camp." Pecora caught sight of them before he was spotted and sneaked away. During the Wall Street investigation, Pecora was allegedly involved with Frieda Hennock, a former law partner of his assistant, Julius Silver. In those days philandering was subject to a double standard. Rumors of the affair never affected Pecora, but they likely cost Hennock, the first woman named a commissioner of a federal admin-istrative agency, a later nomination for a federal judgeship.[10]

Despite the widely held notion of immigrant lawyers flocking to the bar en masse, Pecora remained a rare bird. In 1900, around the time he started law school, New York had about 15,000 lawyers; only 39 of them were Italian Amer-icans. There were surely more than the records show; many Italians anglicized their surnames to escape the bigotry of the day. Lawrence Richey, then a Secret Service agent and later Hoover's appointments secretary, started life as Law-rence Ricci. Nobody would have been fooled, however, if Pecora became Peck. As the *Christian Science Monitor* would later put it, his "personal appearance is somewhat singular, and bespeaks his ancestry." He was stocky and under five and a half feet tall, with dark eyes and jet-black hair just beginning to gray, which he wore swept back in a slick pompadour; *Time* magazine described him as a "kinky-haired, olive-skinned, jut-jawed lawyer from Manhattan." If it weren't for his dapper suits and his impeccable English, nearly everyone would have pegged him as one of the millions of Italian laborers who had flooded New York and other Northeast cities.[11]

The Dillingham Commission—a congressional committee formed to study immigration—had just concluded that those millions posed a severe threat to American society. Southern Italians, the government reported in 1914, three years after Pecora became a lawyer, were "revengeful . . . excitable, impulsive, highly imaginative, impracticable; as an individualist having little adaptability to highly organized society." Perhaps, the sociologist Edward A. Ross wrote that same year, these character traits were due to the "distressing frequency of low foreheads, open mouths, weak chins, poor features, skew faces, small or knobby crania, and backless heads. Such people lack the power to take rational care of themselves; hence their death-rate in New York is twice the general death-rate." Italian immigrants, "chiefly the undersized, illiterate overflow from half medieval Naples and Sicily," were a "direct menace to our Government because they are not fit to take part in it."[12]

The number of lawyers with Italian surnames didn't get much larger over the next decade. Even as late as the 1930s, Italian American lawyers still numbered in the hundreds in New York, the U.S. city with the largest Italian population. So it was faint praise indeed when, in early 1933, a few weeks after his trip to Wall Street, *Time* would call Pecora the "most brilliant lawyer of Italian extraction in the U.S." Pecora's emergence, first on the metropolitan stage as a prosecutor and now on the national stage in the Wall Street investigation, made him a pioneer. He wasn't the first Italian American lawyer, but he was the most visible, and he practiced his craft on a pinnacle that no Italian American lawyer had yet attained. Thanks to a phone call from a South Dakota senator who really had no business chairing the Banking and Currency Committee, Pecora was back on Wall Street, just down the block from where his legal career began.[13]

The Greek Revival building at 55 Wall Street radiated money and power with its imposing two-tiered façade of columns, each carved out of a single block of Quincy granite. Successively the home of the New York Merchants' Exchange, the New York Stock Exchange, and the Custom House, the building now housed City Bank's main branch office. Pecora crossed the immense banking room, his heels reverberating off the gray marble floor. The lawyer didn't walk so much as march—his head and shoulders back and his arms swinging confidently at his sides. He strode under the soaring coffered ceiling and the central, Pantheon-inspired dome, past the tellers in their bronze cages, the clattering typewriters, the secretaries taking dictation, the clerks checking the ticker tape, and made his way to the offices of the bank's primary outside law firm, Shearman & Sterling.[14]

Founded in 1873, the law firm was one of the most prestigious and largest in the city—the polar opposite of Hands's tiny practice and precisely the kind of firm that would never dream of hiring an immigrant lawyer from a night law school. Like the handful of other large firms that had flourished over the previous sixty years, Shearman specialized in corporate work. It had prospered representing Jay Gould, Henry Ford, and the Rockefeller family. James Stillman, the former chairman and president of City Bank, retained his personal lawyer, John Sterling, for the bank in the 1890s. Sterling quickly became Stillman's most important adviser and, although the lawyer had died fifteen years earlier, at the time of Pecora's investigation the bank remained Shearman's single largest and most important client.[15]

As soon as Pecora sat down in Cary's office, the investigator explained that he wanted to review the minute books for all board meetings for both the bank and its securities affiliate starting in October 1929 and going back five years. "There are quite a number of minute books you'd have to examine," Cary replied dryly. Pecora was unconcerned: "If you'll kindly make them available to me, I'll proceed to do it." Pecora stared in shocked silence when a few minutes later Cary's assistants hauled in stacks of large books that stood "about a yard from the floor." Pecora was "appalled by the magnitude" of information he had to review in just a few short days.[16]

Cary led Pecora to Shearman's spacious library, where he could review the books, and then Cary made what Pecora considered a puzzling request—that only Pecora review them. Perhaps Cary's goal was to make it more difficult to get through the material before the upcoming hearing. Cary, after all, knew better than almost anyone what Pecora would find there. Of course, he said none of that, but instead aimed right at the investigator's vanity: "Well, Mr. Pecora, we know about you. You're a figure in the public life of this community, from the district attorney's office, and so forth, and you can well appreciate the confidential nature of these books. We wouldn't want to have any eyes read them but those of persons whom we know something about."

The rationale was more than a little odd. After all, Pecora's assistant counsel, David Saperstein, and a "corps of accountants" had just that morning hauled a huge Photostat machine to the bank's office on Exchange Place and were busy copying and reviewing other City Bank documents. Pecora and his staff were there to gather evidence for a public hearing to be held in less than two weeks in the Senate. A good part of the country was about to hear precisely what was in those books, and the committee had subpoenaed them, which meant that the bank would have to bring them to the hearing. No, it didn't make much sense, but Pecora, perhaps realizing that with his staff immersed in the banks' other documents there was no one else to read them anyway, acceded to Cary's request.[17]

Pecora read all day, poring through the minute books for the bank and its securities affiliate, the summary of their activities during those boom years. They "were a mine of information," he later recalled. At six o'clock, when the office was scheduled to close, Pecora asked politely if he could remain. He was sorry to put any of Cary's employees to any inconvenience but he had very little time to do his work, he explained. Cary agreed, and Pecora remained at that table reviewing City Bank's minute books until about one in the morning.[18]

He was back at Shearman the next morning and sat at the library table until well past midnight again. Still worried about the press of time, Pecora did not try to take notes on everything he learned. Instead, he tried to make a "quick selection of items" about which he wanted to question City Bank officers. As Pecora sat taking notes, Cary would occasionally wander back into the room and hover in the area. Pecora continued to scribble on his pad and Cary would peer over, clearly trying to see what had caught the investigator's attention. Every once in a while, Cary would edge closer, until Pecora worried that he might see his notes. "So on those occasions I professed to be a little bit weary, and I closed the book and relaxed for a few minutes. And he would walk away."

Pecora spent a third day with the minute books before leaving Saperstein and the accountants to comb through the bank's other records. He had to get back to Washington to conduct the Insull hearings. Pecora knew that whatever he and the other investigators found in City Bank's documents would constitute the bulk of what Pecora would be able to present in Washington. "I had no volunteers to give me information," he later complained, although he did look for some.

Two years earlier, a former City Bank securities salesman named Julian Sherrod had written *Scapegoats*, a tell-all book about the company. It was a 1930s version of Michael Lewis's *Liar's Poker*, but it was far too general to be of any real help to Pecora in putting together a cross-examination. Pecora wired Sherrod and asked him to come to Washington, but Sherrod refused—the National City Company had laid him off a few years earlier and, in the midst of 25 percent unemployment, he had finally landed a job in Houston. He wasn't about to leave it to help with the investigation. Pecora also tried to enlist a New York University finance professor to help in the effort. NYU, however, refused to make up the difference between the professor's normal salary and what the committee could offer him. It wasn't the money they objected to; NYU wanted nothing to do with the dangerous game that Norbeck and Pecora were playing. The deans there were unwilling "to be a party to any investigation that might result in the receivership of any company as important as the one in mind, under present economic conditions." The economy was sliding toward the cliff. Many people believed that revelations of pervasive wrongdoing at City Bank might just push it over the edge.[19]

The long hours in Shearman's library had another benefit for Pecora—they allowed him to maintain some distance from the rapidly deteriorating situation in Washington. When Pecora first went to Shearman's offices, Norbeck confidently announced to the press that the committee "has now been given full access" to City Bank's records "so our investigators are getting at the important facts." He projected the image of an investigation moving forward surely and swiftly, but it didn't last the day.

That afternoon, David Olson, a committee accountant, abruptly and noisily resigned, charging the senators with trying to cover up Wall Street misdeeds. The previous July, Norbeck had hired Olson, a former Price Waterhouse auditor, to investigate certain income tax matters, and he had proved to be troublesome from the start. Olson focused mostly on making himself indispensable and trying to profit off whatever he uncovered. "Olson's attitude," Norbeck's staffer James Stewart wrote the senator, "is still the same as before, namely he wants to handle the case himself and is trying to keep himself in a position so that no one else can present it to the committee." Stewart was even forced to subpoena Olson when he refused the committee's request to turn over documents from his investigation.[20]

While Olson was a major headache, what he claimed to have uncovered was potentially a huge political scandal for the Republican Party. According to Olson, the ambassador to Great Britain and former Treasury secretary Andrew Mellon, the current Treasury secretary Ogden Mills, and other government officials had hatched a scheme that permitted Gulf Oil (which was run by Mellon's nephew) and various other companies to underpay their taxes by $220 million. Norbeck now had an enormous dilemma. Olson's allegations went well beyond the scope of the committee's authority to investigate Wall Street, but Mellon was one of the wealthiest men in the country and a major contributor to the Republican Party. If Norbeck didn't pursue Olson's claims, it would look like a cover-up. To make matters worse, it was not clear that Norbeck could trust Olson, who so far had proved to be a sloppy and unreliable investigator. After reviewing Olson's work, Stewart concluded that it was impossible to substantiate Olson's sensational claims. The documentation was "incomplete" and the investigation unfinished. "Whether the case represents an evasion, an avoidance, or whether there is no basis for the charge," Stewart wrote the senator, "I am not prepared to say." Eventually, when word of Olson's accusations began to leak out, Norbeck convened the committee to hear the accountant's evidence, and they ultimately determined not to pursue the matter.[21]

Olson promptly quit, accusing the committee of evasion and ineptitude. The committee's inquiry, he claimed, was a "whitewash" designed to uphold Wall Street practices that he considered blameworthy. "I have been forced to conform," he angrily told reporters, "to a standard of incompetence and procrastination which is entirely new in my experience and from which no definite result of any merit can possibly be expected."[22]

Norbeck accepted Olson's resignation and fired right back. He had "hoped that [Olson's] services would be very useful to the committee," but "these hopes have not been realized. Mr. Olson's tendency to exaggerate and his inaccuracy as to facts have largely offset the value of his other services." Norbeck assured reporters that the "committee has taken the tax matter seriously" and his assessment of Olson eventually proved correct. Olson filed his own whistle-blower suits against Mellon—it turned out that he made a tidy living filing such claims—and he stood to recover as much as 10 percent of any taxes paid in those actions. The lawsuits were promptly dismissed as baseless.[23]

The same day as Olson's angry outburst, a group calling itself the New York

Stock Exchange Reform Committee demanded that the entire Senate investigate Norbeck's conduct of the stock exchange probe. Reportedly an arm of the Manhattan Board of Commerce, the group charged in a letter sent to every member of the Senate that Norbeck's committee "has completely collapsed and is and has been doing nothing more than practicing a deception upon the people of the United States." In what was clearly a jab at Pecora, the report lambasted the committee for refusing to employ attorneys who were skilled in financial matters. The committee was "sitting on the lid," the report charged, and wanted only "to satisfy the public with a few headlines and with as much lethargy as the public will tolerate." The Banking and Currency Committee, the report concluded, should "be relieved" of its investigatory efforts until after the Roosevelt administration took office.[24]

It was a scathing denunciation. There was only one problem—no one had ever heard of the New York Stock Exchange Reform Committee. It seemed clear enough that the group was not a front for the NYSE, but no one seemed to know precisely who they were. "I don't know whether those who claim to be reformers are actually reformers," Norbeck told the reporters when asked about these charges, "but I am suspicious because so many things have been thrown in our way lately." He was right to be suspicious. The man behind the organization was a Bronx real estate developer named Logan Billingsley, brother of the Stork Club owner Sherman Billingsley. Logan Billingsley was a former bootlegger with a host of arrests and convictions who had now remade himself as a respectable Bronx businessman. Billingsley organized the Manhattan Board of Commerce in 1930, listing as members a score of prominent New Yorkers. The Better Business Bureau later became suspicious of those claims, and with just a few phone calls found out that most of the influential people the board had named had never even heard of it. When the Better Business Bureau discovered Billingsley's criminal record, it labeled the Manhattan Board of Commerce a fraud.[25]

No one in Washington seemed to know any of this, but rumors were flying that the report was really the handiwork of Samuel Untermyer, the wizened securities reformer who had turned down Norbeck's offer of the counsel job but who was still gunning to run the investigation once Roosevelt came into office. Although Untermyer told Norbeck that he had nothing to do with the Reform

Committee, the coincidence was remarkable. The report advocated a plan that suited Untermyer's ambitions perfectly—an immediate cessation of the hearings until Roosevelt came into office.

Untermyer was also sure to give Pecora rather halting praise, a tactic he frequently employed when another attorney dared step on his investigatory preserve. He told Norbeck, "I am an old friend of Mr. Pecora, about whose integrity of purpose in anything he undertakes there can be no question." In other words, Pecora was well-meaning, but couldn't get the job done. In a letter to a member of Roosevelt's Brain Trust, Untermyer was a good deal more explicit in his criticism of his "old friend." Writing near the end of the City Bank hearings, Untermyer dismissed the significance of what Pecora accomplished. "The mere exposure of Wall Street's sins would produce sensational headlines but would serve no useful purpose in laying the basis for constructive reform," he said. "Pecora unfortunately understands absolutely nothing about intricate exchange machinery and could not lay [a] foundation."[26]

In hindsight, it is easy to see that the charges lodged against the Wall Street investigation were frivolous, but that was not how it seemed at the time. With the Olson and Reform Committee accusations coming on the heels of Irving Ben Cooper's hasty resignation as counsel, it was beginning to look as if the committee really didn't have any intention of conducting a meaningful investigation. One political cartoonist accused Norbeck of arming his investigators with only a tack hammer to attack Wall Street's impregnable fortress.[27]

That was the way the public saw things as well. Letters rushed into Norbeck's offices, accusing him of everything from mishandling the investigation to outright corruption. One writer informed Norbeck that his committee was "smitten, stricken and afflicted with incompetence and the dry rot of political imbecility." He charged the committee with "official malfeasance, with a conspiracy to cover up public criminality on the part of men within the jurisdiction of Congress." James Nue of Akron, Ohio, was sure he saw a conspiracy. "From the time you started your investigation of The New York Stock market [I] have been very much interested in how far you would go before some of the big 'fellows' would stop you, it would be interesting to know just what was done to silence you."[28]

Editorial writers and columnists around the country were a bit less strident, but no less critical. As they saw it, despite all the time and expense, the investigation had, in the end, not amounted to very much. Mostly, they blamed Norbeck, who had turned out to be a "far more cautious crusader than might be inferred from his belligerent promises some months ago." The papers saw no reason why they should expect anything of importance in the last few weeks. "The impression grows here," wrote the syndicated columnist James McMullin, "that the stock market investigation will finish spending its $50,000 as rapidly as possible and shut up shop." Real investigative action, wrote the editors at the *New York World-Telegram*, would have to wait for the next Congress, "when the Committee on Banking and Currency may be made up of more courageous men."[29]

Part of the reason most outside observers had written off the investigation was because the infighting on the committee was now an open secret. "Behind the scenes it is known that the Senate committee has been driven by dissension," the *Christian Science Monitor* wrote. "The group is sharply divided over the wisdom of the hearings, and some members are apathetic." The most outspoken critic was Senator Frederic Walcott, the man Hoover had originally tapped to run the investigation. The former investment banker accused Norbeck of using the committee staff to write his campaign speeches and even went so far as to suggest that it was Norbeck who had interfered with his attempts to get the investigation up and running in the spring of 1932. Now Walcott sought to distance himself from the apparently collapsing effort, pointing out that he was no longer a member of the subcommittee.[30]

Walcott's charges made no sense. When the hearings started, he wanted to focus solely on bear raids, while Norbeck and other committee members fought to broaden the investigation. Norbeck was a prairie well-driller with an almost preternatural antipathy to the eastern financial elite, while Walcott was a former investment banker with strong ties to Wall Street. It simply didn't ring true that the conservative Walcott had tried to push the investigation hard while the progressive Norbeck held it back. But none of that seemed to matter to reporters, who were thrilled with the spectacle of such a pitched battle. Word had even leaked out that warring staff members had to be dispatched to separate cities, leading one writer to marvel, "If that committee gets to the March 4 deadline without any broken skulls it will be a miracle."[31]

In all this Norbeck saw a well-orchestrated attempt to discredit his investigation. He even heard from his brother back in South Dakota that "Wall Street men" were there looking for dirt on him. Norbeck was livid and he lashed out at his critics. He complained bitterly that there was "too much money on the other side" being used to thwart his efforts, and he predicted that "there will be more resignations as the enemies of the investigation are able to reach them." But he refused to give in.[32]

Then, just when it looked like things couldn't get any worse, one of the men Pecora had subpoenaed for the City Bank investigation, John D. Ryan, died from a massive heart attack. The sixty-nine-year-old Ryan was a director of City Bank and the chairman of the board of Anaconda Copper, one of the stocks City Bank had allegedly manipulated. It certainly looked like his unexpected death might seriously undermine the investigation, but Pecora tried to assure reporters that it was not a problem. Ryan had fully cooperated with the committee, promptly turning over all documents the committee requested. "At no time did he join with other officials of the bank in resisting our efforts to get at the facts in the National City situation." But those denials hardly helped. After all, if he had been cooperating when others weren't, wouldn't that necessarily impede the investigation?[33]

Besides, after everything else that had happened, it was not entirely clear that anyone believed Pecora anymore. That was particularly true in the heartland, where the natural reaction of many people was to distrust anything or anyone from New York. The *Aurora Monitor*, a Missouri newspaper, thought that Pecora's selection damned the whole investigation. For his prosecution of the Anti-Saloon League's William Anderson, the paper said Pecora "ought to be serving a life sentence in state's prison." The paper, no fan of Wall Street, wondered "just how much conscientious ruthlessness can be expected of this cheap little heeler, since discarded even by Tammany?" The "idea of getting a cast-off Tammany legal hack to investigate the Stock Exchange . . . is so ridiculous and in addition so tainted with suspicion of its good faith that even the United States Senate brand of intelligence ought to have comprehended it." They even saw fit to attack his religious convictions—the convictions that had made Pecora an outsider in the Italian community in New York. "Pecora claims to be a Protestant," the *Monitor* declared, and "if he is it is probably because he can be more useful to Tammany as a professing Protestant than as a frank Romanist."[34]

Pecora, like Norbeck, had to do his best to disregard the criticism and the setbacks. He had to this point poured almost all his energies into City Bank, knowing that those hearings would make or break the investigation. It was the right strategy, but it meant that Pecora had largely ignored the next big task that was looming before him—conducting the Insull hearings. Although Pecora knew they were just the opening act, they would still be wickedly complicated. With his first public appearance as the committee's counsel now just days away, he could ignore them no longer.

Chapter 7

JUNIOR

orbeck had made elaborate promises for the Insull hearings, telling reporters that they would be "the most sensational yet." Rumors swirled that the testimony might implicate "scores of prominent persons." Insull was the biggest corporate collapse of the day, and the Senate hearing room was packed tight with dozens of reporters and photographers. The latter, with their flashes constantly blazing, jostled for the best views, a contemporary reporter wrote, of the "many, many celebrities . . . celebrities among the witnesses, celebrities among the sitting senators, celebrities among the correspondents, celebrities among the thrilled onlookers." They were all there waiting for a bombshell.

With Samuel Insull still safely in Greece and with the nearly daily disclosures from the criminal case and the bankruptcy proceedings, the reality was that there probably wasn't much new to discover. These hearings were simply a three-day dress rehearsal for City Bank. Some of Pecora's performance, however, suggested that he might not yet be ready for opening night.[1]

Not that Pecora wasn't trying, but he was working at a distinct disadvantage. This was his first time on the national stage, and unfortunately he was operating in an area about which he knew comparatively little. It wasn't even his investigation. Although Norbeck's staff had been working on it for months, they really hadn't turned up anything new. With all his work on City Bank, Pecora could devote little time to understanding Insull's devilishly complex organization. The Insull utility empire was a towering pyramid, with layer upon layer of holding companies, sometimes with ownership interests in each other, piled atop a welter of operating systems that stretched from Maine to the Midwest. The utility companies Insull controlled produced about one-eighth of the country's electricity. Even the most adept and sophisticated corporate practitioner would need months even to begin to understand it all. Pecora had just a few days.

As the hearing date grew closer, Pecora quickly read through as much of the company's records as he could, but it was futile. No matter how much ground he covered, no matter if he read documents until dawn, there was no way he could do justice to the topic in the short amount of time he had. Of course, the truth was that the whole enterprise was misguided from the start, just as the Kreuger investigation had made little sense. The only thing to be gained from Senate hearings on those already disclosed scandals was the chance for senators to express some righteous indignation and to satisfy Norbeck's repeated promises that he would investigate the collapsed utility companies. The most Pecora could hope to accomplish was to reveal a few more details about a story everyone already seemed to know.[2]

Nor could the retreaded Insull hearings compete with the other news that would soon dominate the papers, almost totally eclipsing the celebrity witnesses in Washington. That week, the Senate voted to repeal Prohibition, good news for a population that was greatly in need of a legal drink. The excitement over that development was short-lived, however. On Valentine's Day, the eve of the first hearing day, Michigan's newly elected governor William Comstock announced that he was shutting down the state's banks for eight days, euphemistically dubbing it a "holiday." A month earlier, Ernest Kanzler, the chairman of one of Detroit's largest banking chains, had told the chief national bank examiner from Chicago: "We have got to get considerably more money or the whole group is going to collapse." The money did not come; indeed, over the next month millions continued to flow out of the banks and a holiday was the only way to prevent their complete collapse. The announcement was front-page news across the country, although this was hardly the first warning sign that the bank-ing sector was in serious trouble.[3]

There had been a host of bank failures before Michigan—more than 5,300 since the start of 1930. The biggest was the grandly named Bank of United States in New York, a bank with more than 400,000 depositors, largely Jewish and Italian immigrants, who when they opened their accounts had mistakenly thought it was affiliated with the federal government. On December 10, 1930, there were runs as word began to leak out that the bank was in trouble. Depositors, many of whom were unemployed in the Depression, raced to the bank and stood in long lines in a cold, wet rain to get their money. The state banking superintendent Joseph Broderick tried to get Wall Street firms, including City Bank and J.P. Morgan, to come to the bank's rescue, but the elite Wall Street institutions appeared to have little interest in aiding a retail bank, "especially," a Wall Street historian noted, "one run by outsiders that catered to immigrants." New York banking authorities shut it down without warning the next morning.[4]

The depositors, it soon became clear, were right to be worried about their money. The bank was the victim of massive criminal mismanagement by its major-ity stockholders, two former garment merchants named Bernard Marcus and Saul Singer. They were using the bank's capital to speculate in the bank's own stock, which they then tried to sell to depositors and friends through high-pressure sales techniques. When that failed, they would sell it to the bank's own affiliated com-panies. There were, in addition, millions in bad real estate loans, suspect and shady loans to board members, and a host of other risky banking practices. Marcus and Singer eventually went to prison, not for their criminal mismanagement of the bank, but for their fraudulent attempts to cover it up.[5]

Over the next year after the high-profile collapse, the frequency of bank failures accelerated as people began to wonder about the safety of the banking system as a whole. In just one week in June 1932, twenty-six Chicago banks went under, pushed along by the Insull collapse. The bank failures spurred runs on both insolvent and solvent banks, including the city's largest, and presumably most stable ones. By October 1932 the situation looked better, and Hoover's Treasury secretary, Ogden Mills, confidently proclaimed that the administration had saved the banks. It proved to be a temporary reprieve. Bank failures and runs were again mounting after the election, and citizens in small towns and large cities across the country saw "armored cars rushing to threatened banks" and "moneybags unloaded by guards with guns."

By December 1932, the Reconstruction Finance Corporation, a government agency established earlier in the year to make loans to cash-strapped banks, had to rescue banks in Wisconsin, Pennsylvania, Minnesota, and Tennessee. In part, the upwelling in bank runs was due to Congress's disclosure of RFC loan recipients, a move prompted by popular anger over the decision to bail out politically well-connected banks but to leave the unemployed largely on their own. The RFC was derided as "Wall Street's three-billion-dollar soup kitchen." Unfortunately, disclosure of the RFC recipients only increased pressure on the named financial institutions and created even greater public uncertainty over the solidity of the nation's banks. Bank runs were infectious and the contagion spread from largely rural banks, to small cities, and then to larger ones. Soon Hoover administration officials were staving off bank runs in Iowa (where twenty-six banks failed in a single day), Illinois, and Minnesota. Then came Chattanooga, Little Rock, Mobile, St. Louis, and Memphis. A month later more runs were cropping up, this time in San Francisco, Baltimore, Kansas City, Nashville, and Boston.[6]

There were local and state holidays before Michigan. On Halloween 1932, Nevada ordered a voluntary bank holiday that ultimately lasted until well into December. The Nevada banks were small with interconnected ownership and big undiversified portfolios of livestock loans. In a time of rapidly falling commodity prices, those banks were doomed—with sheep selling for just twenty-five cents a head, the ranchers were simply not going to pay back the eight dollars a head the banks had lent them. In fact, many ranchers who could no longer even afford to feed their herds resorted to wholesale slaughters, dumping the carcasses in nearby canyons. At the time, however, the Nevada holiday was considered a "minor," largely local problem without national implications.[7]

Other states tried their best to disguise their interventions. Two weeks before the Michigan holiday, the Hibernia Bank and Trust Company in New Orleans was teetering on the edge. Fresh off his success in killing the Glass banking bill, Huey Long came to the bank's rescue, helping to arrange a $20 million loan from the RFC and the Federal Reserve. Federal funds were due to arrive on Monday, February 6, but the bank was too short on cash to make it through its Saturday hours. Not wanting to disclose the bank's precarious position, Long needed a pretext to keep the banks closed. After his aides talked him out of declaring a holiday in honor of the Louisiana pirate Jean Lafitte, Long roused the city librarian from bed, instructing him to find some significant historical event on February 4 that would justify the governor declaring a state holiday. The groggy librarian found nothing, although he did determine that the United States had severed diplomatic relations with Germany on February 3, 1917. That was enough for Long, who decided that such an important decision must have taken two days rather than just one. Governor Oscar Kelly Allen, Long's flunky, declared February 4 a state holiday in honor of the sixteenth anniversary of that event, much to the surprise of the local German consulate. Few were fooled by this transparent ruse.[8]

Michigan was different and far more serious than these previous tremors. There were, to be sure, logical reasons to view Detroit as an anomaly, to treat it not as a harbinger of the demise of the entire banking system but as an isolated crisis like Nevada or Louisiana. Detroit was a one-industry town hard hit by the Depression. It had the highest unemployment rate of any major city in the country and its banking system was none too stable. Most of the nominally independent banks there were chained together into two competing holding companies, one controlled by Henry Ford and the other owned by a group of Detroit business leaders. When one bank in a chain was imperiled, as was the case in February 1933, the whole structure was likely to topple.

Yes, it was possible to argue that Detroit was unique, but that was not how Americans saw it. Detroit was for them the industrial heartland of the American economy—booming automobile production was a huge part of the boisterous economy of the 1920s. If a statewide closure could happen in Michigan, many reasoned, it could happen anywhere. A bank closure wasn't just a bank closure. All sorts of other businesses closed as well; with their money frozen in the bank they simply couldn't operate. Steel, copper mining, railroads—virtually every industry in the United States was all but shut down. The economy had ground to a screeching halt. And, if businesses couldn't operate, that meant they laid off even more employees.

Bank closures meant that those merchants who stayed open would no longer accept checks, and in those days nearly everyone paid for nearly everything with checks. If families were low on cash, how would they pay the rent or buy food or gas? After these "holidays," banks invariably paid depositors pennies on the dollar. With no federal deposit insurance, that kind of failure might wipe out a lifetime of savings overnight. The unemployed who were just scraping by with meager savings might quickly find themselves evicted from their homes or in the breadlines snaking through the cities. It was no wonder that, first in nearby Ohio, Indiana, and Illinois and then across the country, people rushed to their banks, regardless of whether they seemed solvent or shaky. They wanted their money and they wanted it now. Whatever remnants of trust Americans had in the financial system were stripped away. Michigan was the tipping point that transformed public unease into full-blown panic.[9]

President Hoover, in a futile attempt to get Roosevelt to come out in support of his economic agenda during the interregnum, captured the worsening mood of the country, a mood that Roosevelt would later echo in his own Inaugural Address. "The major difficulty," President Hoover wrote to Roosevelt, "is the state of the public mind, for there is a steadily degenerating confidence in the future which has reached the height of general alarm." If Roosevelt spoke now to support Hoover, the president-elect could remove that fear, preventing "the fire" from spreading. Hoover was essentially asking the incoming president to support his economic program, to repudiate the New Deal before he even assumed office. Roosevelt had no intention of endorsing policies he had run against and he certainly wasn't going to take responsibility without the power of office. His response to Hoover was delayed, but his assessment of the financial system was even graver. It was, Roosevelt asserted, common knowledge that a great many banks were unable to pay their deposits in full; that problem, however, was so "deep-seated that the fire is bound to spread in spite of anything that is done by the way of mere statements." Roosevelt was right—after Michigan the fire had become an inferno.[10]

Even repeal prospects and the Michigan bank closures, however, were soon crowded from the front page when, on the first day of the Insull hearings, a delusional thirty-three-year-old unemployed bricklayer from New Jersey named Giuseppe Zangara made an unsuccessful assassination attempt on Franklin Roosevelt. All six shots missed Roosevelt, who had just finished a brief speech in Miami's Bayfront Park, but the Italian immigrant fatally wounded Chicago's mayor, Anton Cermak, who was standing on the running board of the convertible carrying Roosevelt. The papers were filled with tales of Roosevelt's fearless heroism—how the president-elect insisted that the Secret Service drive back to retrieve the fallen mayor, how Cermak was rushed to the hospital cradled in Roosevelt's arms, and how, later that evening, Roosevelt was completely at ease, sleeping soundly throughout the night. The near miss and Roosevelt's poise under fire did more than just bolster his popularity; they gave Roosevelt an ineffable but powerful mystique. Letters to Roosevelt suggested that God himself had spared Roosevelt so that he could be "the Saviour of Our Country." Here, it seemed, was the man destined to lead embattled Americans out of their troubles.[11]

A few weeks later, *Time* magazine published their assessment of Zangara, the would-be assassin: "Most illiterate dagoes have the killer instinct, especially when their animal comfort is disturbed."[12]

Pecora's first witness was Samuel Insull Jr. When Junior was a boy he had dreamed of becoming a poet or a playwright. On February 15, he was probably wishing he had gone one of those routes. Instead, by the early 1920s he had become his father's heir apparent and, up until the utility organization went into receivership, the president of one of the holding companies. The son of the disgraced utilities czar did his best to maintain a polite and smiling façade; he was humble, although hardly humiliated, and earnest in the face of this searing public inquiry. Junior was short, balding, and impossibly young—he was just shy of his thirty-third birthday when he appeared before Pecora. To Pecora, Junior seemed "more bewildered than anything else"; he lacked "the knowledge that might have been expected of one in his position." Junior may have been hazy on some of the details, but he managed to come across as reasonably forthright and honorable. He looked, in other words, nothing like the villain Norbeck wanted him to be.[13]

Perhaps, at least in this case anyway, there was no single villain. Samuel Insull Sr. would soon be captured off the Turkish coast and returned to the United States to stand trial for fraud. In 1934, he was acquitted of all charges. Even before that jury verdict, Owen D. Young, the chairman of General Electric, founder of RCA, and a leader of the Insull creditors, told Pecora that Insull was no rogue. Although Americans' faith in the business community was shattered, scandal had not touched Young, whose name was floated as a potential presidential candidate or perhaps secretary of state, and he retained an air of authority and propriety even in the winter of 1933. But Young was widely criticized when he told reporters after testifying before the bankruptcy trustee, "After all, the most you can say of that old man [Insull] is that he had too much confidence in this country and his own companies."

That was not what the public wanted to hear; they presumed Insull guilty, a presumption that was only strengthened by his hasty flight for Europe. Young, however, did not change his view. He told Pecora that Insull was simply a "victim" of the byzantine corporate structure he created, "which got even beyond his power, competent as he was, to understand it." Young admitted that even he could not understand how all the utility's intricate parts fit together, and if Young couldn't understand it, that effectively meant no one could. There was no way, Young concluded, to "get an accounting system which would not mislead even the officers themselves of that complicated structure."

For Young, the utility company's collapse was the product not of fraudulent financial shenanigans but of that complex structure and Insull's ill-advised decision to borrow heavily as the economy continued to head south. But the very impenetrability of the utility empire raised a concern more fundamental than finding the one single miscreant responsible for the debacle, a concern that was at the heart of what Norbeck and Pecora were trying to accomplish in the hearings. "If I am right in thinking," Young testified, "that Mr. Insull himself was not able ultimately to understand that structure, how can the ordinary investor, buying shares or buying obligations . . . be expected to know, or even to inform themselves, conscientious and able as they might be, really as to the value of those securities?" Couldn't federal regulation of these securities sales help to rectify this problem? Pecora asked. Young agreed; it would be useful to have a federal law providing "for very complete publicity, so that investors themselves may know exactly the situation."[14]

With no overt criminality to uncover, Pecora's examination of Junior was limited mostly to pointing out the huge paper profits Junior and other members of his family earned on an option to buy the stock of one of the Insull holding companies. Pecora, in his first public test, was clearly trying, perhaps a bit too hard, to deliver on Norbeck's promises of sensational disclosures, but he was faced with an intractable factual problem—Junior never sold his stock.

Junior naturally and, indeed, quite persuasively argued that his paper profits were irrelevant: "I don't think you can just saw off the transaction at any one time and say a fellow got a benefit which he did not exercise, when he has stuck with the ship and gone down with it." He explained that he never felt "free to sell the stock. Although I might have legally done so, morally I felt bound, and I lived up to that moral obligation." Because Junior stood by the shareholders, he patiently explained, he should not be treated with obloquy. "I consider that a man who is an officer of the company, who may have been said to have gotten privileges from that fact, but who held his stock right down through the crash, is in a different position than if he . . . sold that stock."

At this point, Norbeck jumped in to help Pecora, but if anything he made matters worse. "Not knowing the crash was coming," the senator sneered, "that is what he gets credit for. If he had known it was coming, then there is no certainty that he would have held it." Junior would not budge—he "sank with the ship," he again explained. Norbeck continued to bluster, just as he had with Whitney the previous spring. He now heaped the pent-up anger of weeks of criticism about his investigation on the young businessman: "It does not take courage to stick with it, if he does not know the ship is going to sink."

In the end, Junior may not have been as honorable as he was trying to make himself out to be, but he certainly wasn't the kind of greedy and unscrupulous executive that Norbeck hoped to parade before the American public. Pecora, for his part, seemed to be trying too hard. He appeared to want to prove himself on this first day, and he ended up pushing a weak hand too aggressively. Hectoring Junior was not a great start; it made both Pecora and Norbeck come across not as tenacious investigators, but as bullying and abusive.[15]

By the second day, however, Pecora seemed more at ease. At one point in the afternoon, Owen Young was reflecting on his own purchase of $48,000 in Insull holding company stock in the late 1920s. "You will remember," Young told the committee, "that at that time there was a great boom on. Some of us can only barely recall it." Pecora quickly cut him off, "And others painfully recall it."[16]

In fact, Pecora generally had much more success with the bankers who took the stand on day two than he had with Junior. First up was Charles G. Dawes, perhaps the biggest celebrity among the celebrity witnesses. Dawes had been Coolidge's vice president, a former ambassador to Great Britain, former head of the RFC, and, to top it all off, a Nobel Peace Prize winner for his work restructuring German war reparations. None of that, however, was why he was there. Dawes was the recently resigned chairman of the Central Republic Bank and Trust Company of Chicago, which had loaned buckets of money to Insull.[17]

There was a good deal of anger at Dawes and his bank going into the hearing, anger that had nothing to do with its Insull loans. In the Chicago banking panic the previous year, the RFC lent $90 million to Central Republic only weeks after Dawes had resigned as RFC chairman and took over control of the faltering bank. It was far and away the RFC's biggest loan. Chicago had a 40 percent unemployment rate at the time and this one loan was actually three times larger than all the loans the federal government made to the states for direct relief to the unemployed, homeless, and hungry in 1932. When the public learned that Hoover had personally authorized it, they concluded that politics, not need, was driving the federal response to the Depression. That the bank subsequently failed despite the massive infusion of cash did nothing to improve the public's mood.[18]

Now as Dawes faced Pecora, he admitted that his bank had violated "the spirit" of an Illinois law that prohibited banks from lending more than 15 percent of their capital and surplus to any one company. Technically, the bank did not violate the statute, because the loans were made to separate legal entities, but Pecora was able to draw a stark picture of reckless lending by a bank that ultimately had to be bailed out by the federal government. All told, the bank lent close to 50 percent of its capital and surplus to various Insull companies in forty-one distinct loans.

Dawes's bank was hardly alone in its earnest desire to lend money to Insull, even if doing so ran afoul of those lending restrictions. The president of Illinois's Continental Bank once cornered Junior at a party and told him, "Say, I just want you to know that if you fellows ever want to borrow more than the legal limit, all you have to do is organize a new corporation, and we'll be happy to lend you another $21,000,000." Insull's bookkeeper, Phil McEnroe, said the bankers were no different from the grocers who used to accost his mother as she shopped. "We have some nice lettuce today, Mrs. McEnroe; we have some nice fresh green money today, Mr. Insull. Isn't there something you could use maybe $10,000,000 for?" To the extent that the investigation succeeded at all the previous spring, it had shown short sellers and other market operators engaged in unethical or outright illegal practices. This was hardly news to the public, for whom those actors were already highly suspect. Now, for the first time, Pecora showed commercial bankers engaged in a reckless grab for profits that pushed hard on the boundaries of legal behavior. With those revelations coming right on the heels of the Michigan closures, there seemed, at last, to be some hope that the investigation might actually succeed.[19]

The hopeful signs in Pecora's performance on that second day of testimony weren't just from the disclosures about imprudent lending. Most of those were already well known anyway. On that second day, he began to show why Bainbridge Colby had called him the best cross-examiner in New York. Pecora had been relentless with Junior; in fact, he was too relentless, continuing to push the Insull heir even after it was pointless to do so. That initial experience might have chastened another lawyer, but not Pecora, who refused to let Dawes downplay the significance of his bank's actions. Unlike the first day, however, Pecora now had more to work with.

Puffing on his underslung pipe as he sat through the questioning, Dawes insisted that, despite the violation of the 15 percent limit, his bank had acted prudently and responsibly. Dawes was as theatrical as Pecora and he insisted as he pounded on the table, "At the time these loans were made, all of them were supposed to be well secured on the basis of existing values." After his failure with Junior, it would have been understandable if Pecora let Dawes get away with that justification. After all, this was the former vice president of the United States and a Nobel laureate. Pecora, however, seemed unfazed by Dawes's star power, and he politely cut the heart right out of Dawes's justification.

"It is agreed," Pecora asked, "is it not, that the policy underlying these banking laws . . . bears no relationship, as such, to the question of security underlying loans so made?"

Dawes puffed on his pipe and responded in the only way he could, "That is true." And it was true—there was nothing in the statute that permitted greater loans when they were properly secured.

"It simply establishes the principle that a bank should not put more than 10 or 15 percent of its eggs in one basket," Pecora continued. "So that principle was violated, regardless of the security underlying the loans?"

The Nobel laureate stared at Pecora and answered matter-of-factly, "Certainly." In just a few questions, Pecora had neatly eliminated Dawes's entire defense. All Dawes could try to do was to absolve himself of responsibility. The loans, he said, were made at a time when he was unconnected with the bank.[20]

On Friday morning, Pecora faced his last substantial witness in the Insull hearings. Across the table was Harold Stuart, Insull's white-haired and distinguished investment banker from the Chicago-based Halsey, Stuart & Co. Stuart, too, was under indictment in Chicago for mail fraud, although he too would be acquitted in 1934. Stuart, the man who refused to join National City when the bank acquired his bond-selling firm in 1916, had built Halsey, Stuart into a scaled-down, midwestern version of the National City Company. Stuart, like Mitchell, helped forge a vast retail bond-selling network. He prospered by specializing in utility securities, one of the emerging industries that the more established investment banks avoided. Like Mitchell, Stuart was not shy about employing less than genteel methods to sell securities, and he too had been wildly successful as a result. Over the years, Stuart and his team of bond salesmen hawked hundreds of millions of Insull securities to middle-class investors and small country banks. Halsey, Stuart, therefore, provided a great test run for the next week's City Bank hearings. Here too Pecora showed flashes of great legal ability and hints of what approaches and inquiries might work in the City Bank hearings. But, even more than with Junior, there were also signs that Pecora was way out of his depth.[21]

No stunning revelations came out of Stuart, but Pecora was at least able to get some sense of what testimony worked with the press and what didn't. His first efforts were largely a failure. Pecora started with a whirl of testimony about the creation of one of the Insull holding companies. To anyone not well-versed in the intricacies of corporate finance, the testimony was only so much gibberish about debentures, detachable warrants, and prior preferred stock. It took hours and either it went over the heads of the assembled reporters or they were thoroughly bored by it. Their stories the next day gave it, at best, only a cursory nod.

Reporters instead focused on two more basic themes: how much money Halsey, Stuart made and what the bond dealer did and failed to do when it sold all those Insull bonds to small investors. Instead of dissecting and explaining complex transactions, they latched onto simple anecdotes. Most of the next day's news stories repeated the tale of Evaline MacNeil, the Halsey, Stuart customer who lost money when the firm induced her to replace government bonds with Insull securities, never bothering to tell her that Halsey, Stuart owned a big stake in the utility giant. Reporters also didn't want to dwell on nuances, but rather to regale their readers with simple and straightforward deceptions, such as the way Halsey-Stuart tried to disguise its ownership interest in Insull by placing its holdings in the name of a midlevel corporate executive. The press loved to ridicule the inanities of the 1920s. One of their favorites was Halsey, Stuart's attempt to drum up business by putting a University of Chicago professor on the radio to dispense investment advice. Dubbed the Old Counselor, the professor, who taught English, not economics, was chosen for his mellow voice, not his investment acumen. His knowledge was irrelevant anyway because Halsey, Stuart wrote all his lines.

These were the lessons from the Stuart testimony. Keep it simple. Don't dwell on the details. Humanize the story. If Pecora was going to succeed, those were the lessons that he would have to put to good use when Charles Mitchell took the stand.[22]

The Insull hearings proved to be a good dress rehearsal not just as a way to test themes for his audience, but also when it came to the mechanics of the hearings. This was Pecora's first experience sharing the courtroom floor with, in effect, a coterie of co-counsel, the senators on the committee, and he was beginning to see that his goals for the hearings might not always match theirs.

His first lesson came early in the Stuart testimony when the North Carolina Democrat Robert Reynolds strolled into the hearing room and plopped himself down at the table. Reynolds was a gregarious playboy who was then married to his fourth wife, a former Ziegfeld Follies dancer. Although banking was not high on Reynolds's agenda, he rarely missed an opportunity for self-aggrandizement. After just a few minutes of listening to the testimony, a reporter quietly handed

Reynolds a note suggesting a question the senator could pose. Reynolds immediately jumped to his feet, silenced Pecora and bellowed at Stuart, "Is it not true
that you took money from one pocket and put it in the other pocket?" Stuart
could only stare at the debonair senator and never, in fact, even answered the
question. Reynolds nonetheless immediately resumed his seat, looking quite
satisfied as the photographers rushed to snap his picture. Pecora returned to his
questions, and about five minutes later, Reynolds turned to the reporters behind
him and whispered, "Hey, give me some more dope."[23]

Pecora had successes in those three days of Insull hearings, and he certainly did not seem cowed when facing off against celebrity witnesses. But his
performance was troubling on a much deeper and much more fundamental
level. It was more than his shaky start with Junior. It was his inexperience with
the inner workings of Wall Street. The testimony involving the Chicago commercial bankers was easy. Illinois had a clear statute and it wasn't hard to tote up
the loans and show how the bank had evaded the limits placed on them. Stuart,
too, was easy, in at least some respects. It was not hard to see the silliness of the
"Old Counselor" or to point out what investors were never told when Halsey,
Stuart offered them securities. But to really examine Stuart, to really provide a
foundation for constructive federal legislation, Pecora needed to be comfortable
with bond-and-stock-selling operations. If he wasn't, it would be all too easy for
witnesses to keep him off balance and prevent him from showing where they
had strayed. It was the kind of knowledge, to borrow Pecora's line about Junior,
that might have been expected of one in his position.

It was the kind of knowledge that Pecora didn't seem to have or at least
wasn't showing. Indeed, at times Pecora seemed glaringly ignorant of even the
most basic facets of stock and bond underwriting. He seemed surprised, for example, that investment banks formed syndicates of underwriters, each of whom
took a small piece of the offering, as a way to reduce their risk. This simple
strategy had a long history, but it seemed entirely new to Pecora, who attempted
to portray it as a nefarious scheme to deceive investors.

At one point, Pecora even seemed baffled about whether a particular syndicate agreement was an attempt to manipulate the price of a security already
trading on the New York Stock Exchange (what he claimed) or an offering of
entirely new stock (what it actually was). Senator James Couzens, perhaps the

most knowledgeable person on the subcommittee when it came to corporate finance, was incredulous at the entire line of questioning. "What is counsel trying to do?" he asked Pecora. "To prove by this witness that the market is rigged or maintained without customer demand?" Yes, Pecora responded, that was exactly what he was trying to do.[24]

Missteps like that may have given knowledgeable observers reason to worry about whether Norbeck had chosen the right lawyer. Sure, Pecora had little time to prepare for the Insull hearings and there certainly wasn't any doubt about Pecora's ability to handle himself in the hearing room. But maybe Untermyer was right; maybe Pecora, as well-meaning as he was, simply wasn't up to the task. Maybe he didn't know the securities markets well enough to be effective. After all, if he was struggling with Stuart, how was he ever going to be able to handle Mitchell?

Pecora finished the Insull hearings at five o'clock on Friday, February 17. The clock was still ticking. Mitchell was due on the stand at ten o'clock on Tuesday morning. Pecora's staff had been hard at work for the last week sifting through City Bank's records and preparing briefing memos for the "chief," but Pecora had been completely absorbed with Insull and still had a lot of "spade work," as he called it, to finish if he was going to conduct a meaningful examination of Mitchell or, for that matter, any of the other City Bank officers. So he boarded a train that evening and headed back to New York, to meet with his staff and get ready for the hearings that would make or break the investigation.

Pecora took a few hours off from his preparations to give a dinner speech at the Elks Club, where he was a member. His talk reflected at least some of what he had gleaned from City Bank's documents and foreshadowed, for anyone paying attention, what would take place in a few days in Room 301 of the Senate Office Building in Washington. He told the crowd of eight hundred at the Hotel Commodore that his recent investigation revealed "how men of might— not because of principle but because of economic power and wealth—have by the waving of a hand and the adoption of a resolution taken millions and millions of the hard-earned pennies of the people and turned them into gold for themselves." And he signaled his desire for what he hoped the hearings would accomplish. "When the nation again comes to days of plenty and prosperity," he concluded, "let us seek to make it impossible for water and hot air to be sold to men and women of America for gold taken from their life savings."[25]

That goal was still a long way off, and most outside prognosticators were still predicting that Pecora wasn't going to get there. "You can expect," one nationally syndicated columnist wrote, "National City's forthcoming inquisition by Mr. Pecora to be mild—if it takes place at all."[26]

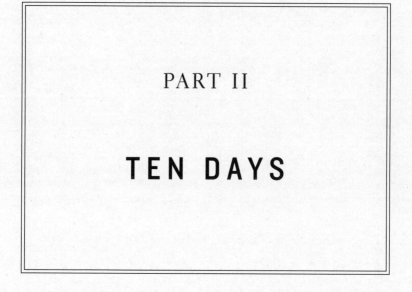

PART II

TEN DAYS

Chapter 8

DAY ONE:
UNIMPEACHABLE
INTEGRITY

Room 301 was neither the largest nor the most familiar hearing room in the Senate Office Building. That distinction belonged to the Caucus Room right down the hall, which had served as the backdrop for the headline-grabbing Senate investigation of the Teapot Dome scandal a decade earlier. In later years it would be the setting for everything from the Army–McCarthy hearings to the Watergate investigation and the Clarence Thomas confirmation. The Caucus Room, however, was reserved for the most significant events with the biggest expected turnouts, and Mitchell's appearance before the Banking and Currency Committee apparently didn't make the cut.

What Room 301 lacked in size and history it made up for in classic elegance. It was, and remains, one of the most beautiful rooms on Capitol Hill. The sky-blue, barrel-vaulted ceiling rose more than thirty feet from the floor and veined Italian marble pilasters ringed the walls. High atop the east and west ends of the room were nautical murals, each fronted by a detailed model ship. Columbus and the *Santa Maria* discovering the New World were on one end; the War of 1812 and the U.S.S. *Constitution* occupied the other. In between, three ornate crystal chandeliers punctuated the ceiling. The room faced south toward the Capitol dome and on that clear Tuesday morning, late winter sunlight flooded in from a set of large French doors.[1]

Pecora was already there when Mitchell, nicely tanned from his Bermuda trip, strode briskly into the room surrounded by his retinue of lawyers and bank assistants, the latter hauling the stacks of documents the committee had subpoenaed. It was a tremendous display of legal firepower. Flanking Mitchell were the two partners from Shearman & Sterling, Guy Cary and Garrard Winston. With them was James Harry Covington, a former congressman and founder of the powerhouse Washington law firm that bore his name, Covington & Burling.

This was the first time that Pecora and Mitchell had met face-to-face and, like many before him, the New York lawyer was struck by Mitchell's powerful appearance and brash self-assurance. Mitchell towered over the pocket-size Pecora. With his thick neck, firm jaw, and iron-gray hair he had the air, in the words of one of his salesmen, of a "commanding officer," a man "of indomitable will . . . who would not surrender." Pecora professed not to be intimidated by the legendary banker. He claimed that he never was "consciously overawed by being suddenly brought among persons whose names meant something," despite his teenage attempts to glimpse J. P. Morgan. "[T]here were many persons who may have been considered great by large segments of the public, and who have turned out to be stuffed shirts. I found a number of those in the course of my investigation." That assessment had the benefit of thirty years of hindsight. It is hard to imagine that Pecora was totally free of trepidation as he stood there that morning, and word was that many of his meals of late had gone untouched.[2]

When we see congressional hearings today the legislators are invariably arrayed behind a large, curved dais. The witnesses sit at a small table set in the well and the spectators are in the chairs at the back, very much like a courtroom. Room 301, however, was configured much differently in 1933. In those days there was no dais; instead, a large, baize-covered mahogany trestle table occupied the center of the room. The senators—sometimes as many as a dozen but at other times only one or two—sat around the long table. Pecora was to Norbeck's right, a cigar, ashtray, and matches in front of him and a glass of water within easy reach. There was nothing separating the senators from the witness; Mitchell was right there at the table, senators on either side of him and Pecora across the way. Mitchell's lawyers were sitting just behind him. With all the reporters, assistants, and spectators crowded around the perimeter of the room, it felt less like a trial and more like theater in the round.[3]

The room looked much as it did for the Insull hearings, with one glaring exception—the photographers were gone. Pecora, whom many accused of sensationalizing the hearings, had banned them, concluding that they had been disruptive and "disconcerting" to the witnesses. "There is no reason," he later said, "why a person who takes the stand in response to a subpoena should be subjected to any of the unpleasantness beyond that which might be embodied in the examination itself." While that ban may have protected the witness, it had another benefit as well—it was now much harder for senators to mug for the camera.[4]

Although Pecora may not have been intimidated by Mitchell, it was clear that he faced a formidable task on that small stage. Bankers had certainly taken their lumps since the crash. Membership in the Investment Bankers Association was plummeting about as fast as the stock market indices as firm after firm collapsed. Those that remained found their already tattered reputations disintegrating even further for their failure to uncover the Kreuger & Toll fraud, for selling Insull securities, and in the face of the worsening banking crisis. Indeed, just that morning, Federal Reserve officials in Chicago reported that the city's banks would have to close before the week ran out if public calm could not be restored. By the afternoon, Cleveland bankers were reporting that withdrawals were increasing at an alarming rate and they asked the state's governor to declare a statewide holiday. New Jersey passed an emergency law authorizing state banks to require a ninety-day notice for withdrawals, and the Guarantee Trust Company of Atlantic City immediately put limitations in place. The reverberations from Michigan were spreading.[5]

Still, as far as the public was concerned, the worst problems remained at regional banks. City Bank was still considered a fortress, its balance sheet "the envy of every bank in the United States." Men like Mitchell, the leaders of the largest New York banks, and the banks themselves still retained at least some vestiges of the aura of invincibility that surrounded them at the height of the market bubble. "The prestige and reputation of these institutions," Pecora wrote, "was enormous. They stood, in the mind of the financially unsophisticated public, for safety, strength, prudence, and high-mindedness, and they were supposed to be captained by men of unimpeachable integrity, possessing almost mythical business genius and foresight."

Indeed, it was that image more than anything else that City Bank had been selling for the past fifteen years. National City's advertisements told investors that they could have confidence in the reliability and integrity of City Bank and its securities affiliate. From their first days in the company's bond-selling class, neophyte salesmen "were sold good and hard, all day long on the soundness—if not infallibility—of the wonderful old institution we were going out to represent. . . . We were told to sell the Institution to people *first* and then it would be easy to sell them securities." Over the next few days, Pecora had to prove to the American public that the bank's sterling image was and always had been a mirage.[6]

It was not going to be easy. Pecora still knew very little about the inner workings of Wall Street. Nonetheless, he had several distinct advantages over previous counsel. Most important, he had done his homework on City Bank; he was far more thoroughly prepared than he had been for Insull. He was also much more comfortable after his earlier trial run. Sure, he would have liked to interview Mitchell and the other witnesses at least once before the hearing. Without those interviews he would have to improvise, but that didn't bother Pecora. He was incredibly fast on his feet from years in the courtroom and years of extemporaneous stump speeches for Tammany Hall. In fact, the prospect of jousting with Mitchell on the fly "exhilarated" him.

The only continuing unknown was the senators. In a criminal trial, Pecora commanded the floor and he had nearly total control over the flow of testimony during his examinations. Here, the senators could jump in at any time. At their best, the senators functioned almost like a Greek chorus, commenting on the significance of the facts Pecora had just pulled out of a witness. At their worst, they just got in the way. Pecora saw it during the Insull hearings—senators like Robert Reynolds awkwardly and ineptly trying to score debating points or grandstanding for the assembled reporters. Maybe there would be less of that now that the cameras were gone, but Pecora couldn't be sure.[7]

The lawyer also had no shortage of inspiration on that late February morning. Success would mean enormous acclaim, the continuation of the hearings into the next Congress, and a good chance that the federal government would finally regulate the financial markets. There was another motivation as well. Since the committee's announcement in late January that it would investigate City Bank, Pecora and Norbeck had received hundreds of letters from former customers and investors, all with tales of ruin from following the bank's advice. To be sure, many of those letters hardly qualified as inspiring. Some were from obvious cranks and spun wildly implausible conspiracy theories. A fair number were angry and spiteful, urging Pecora to "go after these unscrupulous crooks with gloves off." Many suggested that Mitchell needed to go to prison (preferably one with hard labor) and one thought that having a "few Bankers shot at Sunrise" might be in order.[8]

Other letters, however, contained incredibly moving tales of personal and financial loss as well as severe economic deprivation. Years later Pecora recalled how important those letters had been to him during the course of the investigation. They came from people who had been utterly devastated by investing with City Bank and who were barely hanging on as the economy tumbled into the abyss. Many mentioned Mitchell by name, painting him as an incredibly callous man, indifferent to the losses they had suffered.

Helen Kirst, a widow from San Francisco, told a tale that was repeated again and again in that thick file of letters. The bank's sales force convinced her to sell her portfolio of safe government bonds in order to buy the bank's stock, which they assured her was not only safe, but would yield her a much better return. "Naturally believing them to be honorable and a bank of highest standing and integrity I was [gullible]." The longer she held the stock the more nervous she became. She repeatedly asked the local manager to sell the City Bank stock and he repeatedly refused to do so. When the stock collapsed she was left penniless and she wrote Mitchell to complain. Mitchell wrote back a short reply. He was, he claimed, "sorry" that she had lost money, but it was really her own fault. After all, she "shouldn't have gambled."[9]

A. H. Nicander from Douglaston, New York, also trusted the bank and its affiliate. "The fact that the National City Co. is a subsidiary of the National City Bank, one of the largest banking institutions in the country, led me to believe that any issues sponsored by them was [sic] of unimpeachable security," he wrote. "I am one of the army of unemployed, having had that status for almost three years, have three dependents, have come to the end of my resources and am attempting to obtain relief work. I had faith in the industries of the country and invested the larger part of my savings in them, and due to this faith I have now been reduced to indigency."[10]

And then there was Christopher Lane, an elderly Brooklyn man. "I am writing this from McGrath's Funeral Parlor [in] Brooklyn," he told the investigator. "My wife is lying in her casket in the next division. She died of pneumonia. Had I hoarded my $10,000, I could have taken her to the South for the winter. . . . When you see Mr. Mitchell, you might ask him if it comes within your jurisdiction, why his Company or Bank, so trusted, could palm off such poor stuff on an old retiring teacher."[11]

Pecora needed to begin to tell those stories to two related audiences that day. The first was the flagging members of the committee. Other than Norbeck, most of the senators still seemed to have little enthusiasm for continuing the investigation, especially with the congressional session ending in less than two weeks. If the investigation were to continue into the next Congress, Pecora would have to convince those indifferent senators of one of two things: either that investigating Wall Street was necessary in order to implement crucial reform legislation, or, if nothing else, that it was great publicity for them amid the ever worsening economic crisis.

The other audience was, of course, the cadre of reporters in Room 301 and, just as important, their readers across the country. As hard-bitten as many of the reporters seemed, they were, after all, not immune to the devastation around them. "I come home from the hill every night filled with gloom," one Washington reporter wrote in his diary. "I see on streets filthy, ragged, desperate-looking men, such as I have never seen before." After the Insull hearings, Pecora knew the way to make his case was not to dwell, at least on that first day, on the minutiae of complex securities transactions. There would be time for that kind of testimony in the coming days.

Instead, his initial focus had to be money, favoritism, inequity, and privilege. If he was going to succeed in puncturing that aura of invincibility surrounding the bank, he would have to show that Mitchell and his fellow officers were greedy men who cared little about the consequences of their actions and thought that they were above the law. If he could tell that kind of simple morality tale, he could create the kind of outrage he needed, the kind of outrage that would enable him to plumb more arcane securities matters, to continue the investigation into the next Congress, and, perhaps, to provide a bit of vindication for Mr. Lane and the others. As Frances Murphy, another elderly widow, put it in a letter to Pecora, "I can only hope that it will be within your power to make the offenders realize the extent of their guilt and that justice, in some form, will be accorded to the innocent, and ignorant, depositors."[12]

For now, though, the investigation was hanging by a thread.

Pecora knew he needed to make a splash that day, but he still started slowly, easing into the examination by quizzing Mitchell about the organization of the bank's securities affiliate, the entity that allowed it to engage in the kind of investment banking functions otherwise forbidden at nationally chartered banks. The friendly, cooperative pose that Mitchell struck with Pecora in their first phone call had vanished, replaced by a tone that was both arrogant and condescending. He had the manner of a powerful man irked at wasting his time on a mundane and insignificant task. When in the first few minutes Pecora asked him when the agreement organizing the affiliate was prepared and when it became effective, Mitchell responded dismissively: "I assume that it did at the time of the organization, Mr. Pecora. I can not conceive it as being otherwise, but I would have to look it up."[13]

Pecora was unfazed; he had handled countless hostile witnesses before. In fact, Mitchell's arrogance and disdain were precisely what Pecora wanted to show. So he continued to ask more detailed questions about the affiliate's organizational structure and the relationship between it and the bank. Mostly, Mitchell claimed not to know the answers; he had not "refreshed" his memory about those matters. Pecora saw it differently; he thought Mitchell was "not giving evidence of complete candor." Perhaps that was so, but it seems more likely that Mitchell considered this just one more tedious visit to Congress, one that would require little preparation since the others had gone so well. When Pecora pressed him for answers, Mitchell would simply turn to Garrard Winston. Winston would check the assembled documents or consult with the bank employees in attendance and whisper the answer to the banker, and Mitchell would repeat it for the record.[14]

As this laborious process was repeated, it became clear that the bank's lawyers were still attempting to run out the clock. They told Pecora that due to an inadvertent "oversight," the minute books for the securities affiliate had not been brought to Washington. That oversight claim is hard to accept. Pecora had spent hours with those books at Shearman & Sterling and they were at the core of the investigation. A few days earlier, one of Pecora's assistants had specifically instructed the bank's lawyers to bring them to the hearing. These were supposed to be the best lawyers in the country. They simply forgot to bring the documents to Washington?[15]

In the first hour that morning Pecora's deliberate pace, Mitchell's vague grasp of details, his constant hushed conferences with his lawyers, and the missing documents all slowed the hearing to a crawl. A journalist who sat through the hearings described "the monotonous flow of questions and answers" during these slack interludes as "like the mumbling of bees pecking at the flowers in a summer garden on a sultry afternoon." The reporters were bored and the senators were getting antsy; they wanted drama and, so far, they weren't getting any. Of course, Pecora had a purpose—before he got too confrontational with Mitchell he wanted to lay a foundation for questions he would ask later on in the hearings. It was what a careful lawyer did. The senators, on the other hand, wanted to cut to the chase, and so Senator James Couzens, the white-haired and jowly Michigan progressive, decided to jump in.[16]

In some ways, there was no one in the room more qualified than Couzens to question Mitchell. Many politicians are business neophytes, but not James Couzens. He was one of Henry Ford's original partners and the former general manager of Ford Motor Company. He had helped build the company from the ground up, and there were more than a few knowledgeable observers who gave Couzens as much credit as Henry Ford for the company's success. Like Mitchell, Couzens had even built up a nationwide network of salesmen, although they sold Model Ts instead of stocks and bonds. After a decade of building Ford into one of the largest corporations in the country, however, Couzens had grown restless. "There comes a time," he told an interviewer, "when the fun of making money is all gone. . . . The battle is won; the goal is achieved; it is time for something else." It was a sentiment that Mitchell never came close to uttering. Ford and Couzens had famously split a few years later, with Ford buying out Couzens's stake. That made Couzens a multimillionaire, by far the richest man in the Senate when he arrived there in 1922.[17]

In his public life, Couzens espoused a simple philosophy, one that seemed diametrically opposed to Mitchell's. "I want," Couzens explained, "to do what I can to see that life is not made a burden for the many and a holiday for the few. I want to do that which will contribute the greatest good to the greatest number." That statement was more than just empty political rhetoric. Couzens's most famous act at Ford was his crusade for a more equitable sharing of profits between the shareholders and employees. He instituted a plan that reduced the hours of Ford employees while at the same time raising the company's minimum wage to the then unheard-of amount of five dollars a day.

Couzens was well aware of how bad things were in the country. As a result of his great wealth and prominent position, he was inundated with letters from people asking for small gifts, most of which contained harrowing stories of distress. Each received a courteous and sympathetic reply explaining that the senator confined his giving to charitable organizations, and he was as good as his word. He gave away nearly $30 million of his own fortune to provide indigent children with health care. Accounting for inflation, Couzens's philanthropy put him on a level of generosity equal to the gifts of Bill Gates and Warren Buffett.[18]

In the Senate, Couzens quickly became a thorn in the side of the rich and powerful. He famously battled Andrew Mellon in the mid-1920s over the Treasury secretary's plan to reduce income taxes on the wealthiest Americans, an early iteration of "trickle-down" economics. Couzens actually thought the government should raise their taxes, and his opposition to Mellon's proposal led him to investigate the Internal Revenue Bureau, an inquiry that publicized a host of tax loopholes. Couzens's high-profile investigation of a Treasury Department bureau incensed Mellon. In retaliation, he authorized a tax suit against Couzens, claiming the senator had underpaid his taxes when he sold his Ford stock. Much to Mellon's chagrin, the suit showed that Couzens had actually overpaid. There was a hint of the lingering animosity over that episode in the hearing room that morning. Garrard Winston previously worked at Treasury for Mellon. In the Washington–Wall Street revolving door at the time, Winston was named a director of the affiliate the day after he left Treasury, in 1927. While still in government, Winston had publicly defended the retaliatory tax suit against Couzens. At one point in the hearings that morning, Winston was giving so much assistance to Mitchell that Couzens asked if he was a City Bank employee, and proposed that the committee could make everybody's life easier if they just put Winston directly on the stand. The Shearman partner simply winked at Couzens and went back to advising Mitchell.[19]

Like other midwestern progressives, Couzens had long been a critic of Wall Street. As early as 1928, Couzens warned President Coolidge that Wall Street was headed for disaster. Couzens possessed a rigid moral code and firmly believed in conservative commercial banking. Banks, he thought, took in deposits and made short-term loans. They shouldn't be stock and bond promoters. Couzens couldn't help but believe that had business leaders acted less recklessly and more ethically, the crash might have been avoided. Because of these and other progressive views, Couzens was accused of being a radical. Some called him a "scab millionaire" and, like Roosevelt, a traitor to his class. His response was straightforward: "Yes, I'm radical as hell when I see an evil that ought to be ended."

As he sat in Room 301 that morning, Couzens was exhausted. He was in the thick of the frantic efforts to prop up the collapsed banks in his home state. Indeed, it was Couzens's rivalry with Ford that helped spark the Michigan bank closure in the first place. Couzens, who had been investigating improper RFC bank loans, insisted that Ford subordinate his substantial deposits in a Michigan banking group as a condition for the RFC loan that would have kept the banking group open. Ford refused and threatened to withdraw all his money from Detroit banks, a move that would have precipitated a full-blown panic. It was then that Michigan's governor stepped in and declared a holiday. The senator was under most circumstances belligerent, blunt spoken, and downright crotchety. "I've never known a man," one contemporary remarked, "whom you could count on to be unpleasant to the extent that you could him." Couzens relished a good fight, and now, a week after his confrontation with his former business partner, the already caustic business critic seemed even more ornery. With the banks back home shuttered—in his opinion because of the dishonesty and greed of the men who ran them—and with Couzens already getting heat in the press for the role he played in the Michigan crisis, the senator appeared to be in no mood for coddling bankers, especially prominent ones from New York.[20]

While Couzens undoubtedly had the business stature to challenge Mitchell, he was not a lawyer, and his initial attempt to quiz the Wall Street banker was inept. Couzens wanted to talk about how the affiliate made all its money. When a corporation sells securities to the public, in most cases it doesn't do so directly. The corporation retains an investment bank and sells the securities to it. The investment bank is essentially a wholesaler; it turns around and sells those securities to investors at a somewhat higher price, profiting on the markup. Peering at the banker seated across the table from him through his large round glasses, Senator Couzens asked how City Bank went about determining the difference between those two prices, known as the "spread."

Mitchell responded vaguely: "The necessities of a situation, of course, were constantly under discussion in each particular issue. The officer in charge of the negotiations was the man who ultimately negotiated the spread."

Couzens pressed on: "And, then, I suppose, you had different acquisitions of securities, where the spread was small in one case, and larger in another case, and intermediate in another case?"

"Oh, quite so," Mitchell readily agreed.

That was when Couzens tried to go in for the kill. The spread depended "upon the gullibility of the public, or the ease with which the sale of securities might be made, or the soundness of the securities, I suppose?"

Most likely Couzens just wanted to make Mitchell squirm, but Mitchell was not a man who squirmed easily. If, instead, it was an attempt to get an admission out of Mitchell, it was a terribly clumsy one. Whatever else Mitchell might have been he was far from dumb. One of his associates wrote that when he met with Mitchell, what struck him most was that his "remarkable mind functioned as a huge machine. I could almost see it spinning as a great wheel in a Power House." Senator Couzens's question didn't trip up the banker for even a moment: "I would not grant your expression, gullibility of the public." Mitchell then carefully and patiently explained the many factors that went into determining a spread: "I think you will grant very readily, Senator Couzens, that there is a great deal of difference between selling, for instance, a bond of the State of New York and selling a bond of the primest [sic] of our railroads. Sales requirements, methods of distribution, are very different, and different in their cost, and that is all represented in the spread."[21]

If Pecora was chafing at the senators' amateurishness, he didn't show it. He stuck with his plan. A good showman knows that you have to leave the audience wanting more. And, as the lunch break approached, Pecora appeared to want to leave the assembled reporters with something juicy to write about. It was time to establish Mitchell's motive for pushing the affiliate to churn out $20 billion in securities in the ten years before the crash (nearly $3 trillion in today's dollars).[22]

Pecora asked Mitchell about the management fund—the bonus pool at the bank—and what it was designed to do. Mitchell was more than happy to explain; indeed, he seemed eager to demonstrate how clever he had been to devise it. The securities affiliate wasn't really a commercial bank, he informed Pecora, it was an investment bank and it "selected as its executives men who would normally be of the type to hold partnerships in private banking and investment companies." Those private partnerships were "extremely lucrative," and for City Bank to compete with them it had to offer the executives of its affiliate "some share in the profits that they should make."

Mitchell's explanation was more than just incomplete; it simply didn't make sense. The management fund, as Pecora quickly showed, applied not just to the employees at the affiliate, but also to the commercial banking executives. That, and the generalities of Mitchell's answer, raised a host of questions. What incentives did the management fund create for those executives and were those incentives the right ones for a bank that was a "quasi-public" institution? If City Bank was attracting executives who would normally "hold partnerships in private banking and investment companies," how would their different investment approaches and greater appetites for risk change the bank? What did the shareholders know about the operation of this bonus pool? How big was "some share" of the profits?

From his investigation, Pecora had a pretty good idea what the answers to those questions were. Now, he continued to grill Mitchell on the details of how the bonus pool operated. What was immediately apparent as Mitchell spoke was that his conceptions about appropriate compensation were radically different from those of the average American. He explained that to properly incentivize his men their salaries "were held at what was regarded as a low figure," just $25,000. That low figure was more than twice what Pecora made in his best year and thirty-three times the average annual income in 1929.

The primary compensation for Mitchell and the other officers was the management fund. After deducting an initial 8 percent return for the shareholders, the officers collectively shared 20 percent of all the remaining profits. In broad strokes, City Bank's management fund looked similar to compensation in hedge funds today, and for Pecora, it provided the same incentive for excessive risk taking. In fact, it might have created even greater incentives for risk. A hedge fund typically collects 20 percent of all profits, but the executives at City Bank had "nothing to gain and everything to lose, individually, by a conservative policy" because their profit sharing did not kick in until the bank had crossed that initial 8 percent threshold.

There was another factor, as well, that pushed the executives to ever riskier securities offerings. Every year it took more and more sales to get the management fund into the black. Mitchell was continuously expanding his far-flung securities-selling network. By 1929 it had offices across the country linked by the latest information technology of the day. The overhead on the system was enormous, and City Bank had to sell larger and larger amounts of securities just to break even. "I say without fear of contradiction," the former City Bank salesman Julian Sherrod wrote, "that hundreds of millions of dollars have been lost through investments that were originated primarily to pay operating expenses of a large, expensive and unnecessary system of distribution."[23]

Payments out of the management fund were made twice a year, so the executives eligible to participate in it had incentives to focus on short-term profits, not long-term performance. As Pecora had Mitchell spin out the details, Senator Couzens was nonplussed and jumped back into the questioning, this time much more effectively. Couzens had authorized his fair share of bonuses back at Ford. Bonuses in and of themselves didn't bother him. What bothered him, especially given his deeply ingrained suspicion of financiers, were the incentives these particular bonuses created. "And, as you look at it in retrospect," the senator asked Mitchell, "do you think that was a good system to set up for a financial institution?"

Mitchell adamantly believed that it was; it created, he thought, a wonderful "esprit de corps" among the bank's officers.

Couzens was not convinced, and he offered his own perceptions about the incentives he thought those bonuses created: "Does it not also inspire a lack of care in the handling and sale of securities to the public, because each individual officer has a split?"

Mitchell said he understood why Couzens might take that view, and he conceded "that it must have some influence, Senator Couzens. At the same time, I do not recall seeing it operate in that way."

"You would not see it," Couzens replied. "Only the customers would see it after they had gotten the securities."

That scornful gibe worked, because it made a simple and powerful point about Mitchell's testimony. Mitchell had originally pitched his bonus plan as a way to "concentrate the attention of the officers upon service to the institution." Later, his justifications for the bonus system spoke volumes about his own personal motivations. "Unless the man of energy and perhaps ability," he said, "can see within the organization for which he is working a point that he can possibly reach that has great material benefit attached to it, I say unless he can see that his work is going to be somewhat . . . dulled."

Couzens and Pecora saw it very differently. The officers at City Bank were paid potentially enormous amounts, but only if they were able to sell vast amounts of securities. And, since they did not bear the cost of securities that went down in value, they had incentives to sell as many securities as possible, even if they were of dubious quality. The affiliate, Pecora wrote, was "a gigantic, foolproof device for gambling freely with the stockholders' money, taking huge profits when the gambles won, and risking not a penny of their own money if they lost."[24]

To be sure, the institution as a whole might be concerned about preserving the reputation that it was trying so hard to sell to investors. After all, every failed deal that City Bank pawned off on its customers tarnished that reputation a little bit more, presumably making it that much harder to make the next sale. But with bonus checks calculated every six months and the market booming, such long-term considerations were probably only distant, fleeting thoughts to the average City Bank executive, if they occurred at all.

All of these disclosures were clearly rubbing Couzens the wrong way, so the truculent senator pushed his point even further. "I understand," he said, "you have quite a national reputation as a salesman and a financier, both. . . . Which are you, a better salesman or a better financier?" It was classic Couzens, confrontational and in-your-face. Mitchell tried to shake it off. He smiled and asked whether Couzens thought that was a fair question. Couzens, never one to back down, said he thought it was and that he would be willing to answer it himself.

Mitchell responded diplomatically: "I have rarely seen an executive who had to do with the public and the management of a great corporation who was not inherently, by personality or otherwise, in the class that might be called a good salesman."

"I should judge you to be," Couzens responded, "a better salesman than a financier—and that is no disparagement on your financial ability at all."

"I thank you for the compliment," Mitchell muttered gamely.[25]

Now it was Pecora's turn to jump back into the questioning. He cleverly played off Mitchell's reluctance to describe himself as a salesman to lay a trap for the banker. Mr. Mitchell, he asked innocently, since the affiliate was primarily in the business of selling securities, didn't he earn his salary more as a salesman than as a financier? Mitchell, as expected, again denied he was just a salesman. In his "loftiest moral tone" Mitchell explained to Pecora that City Bank did not just sell securities, it "manufactured" them.

Couzens, the former auto executive, didn't think much of that analogy; manufacturing, he said, was an "unfortunate" word for a securities business.

But Mitchell stuck with it; he had been describing City Bank's business in these terms for years, a fact that Pecora surely knew as he questioned the banker that morning. "It may be in your mind Senator Couzens," Mitchell reiterated. "At the same time, that has an analogy that I do not consider amiss. A large part of the business of the National City Co., and a large part of the executive brains, is devoted to the development of long-term credits suitable for public investment."[26]

According to Mitchell, City Bank's job was no different than Ford's. It didn't manufacture cars; it manufactured another kind of consumer product—investment securities. And not just any securities; City Bank "manufactured" securities that were "safe and proper" for investors. It was the same rhetoric City Bank used in its sales training classes and in its advertisements. Trainers told the new recruits that the company had its own "yardstick" by which it measured the quality of its offerings. That yardstick, the trainer assured his class, "would never be shortened." The company's advertisements touted its "sound securities," which were offered to the public only after they had been thoroughly investigated by its expert staff. It was a claim that Pecora intended to test over the course of the hearings, and Mitchell's boasts about creating only securities that were "suitable" for its customers gave Pecora a great launching point for that inquiry. Indeed, this little bit of testimony would come back to haunt Mitchell and the other City Bank executives in week two of the hearings as Pecora marched them through the long list of securities that City Bank thought fit that criterion.[27]

Just before the noon lunch break, it was time for Pecora to show just what City Bank's compensation scheme meant to Mitchell's bottom line. He first wanted to know how Mitchell and the others divvied up the management fund. There were some minor differences between the bank and the affiliate, but basically it was done in two ways, Mitchell said. The board's executive committee allocated half the fund, deciding the share each executive would get based on his value to the company. Since Mitchell was a member of that committee, he had a strong hand in determining his own bonus for the year. It was an enormous conflict of interest. For the second half of the fund, however, Mitchell tried to cast himself as an enlightened business leader. Mitchell gave his subordinates the opportunity to anonymously vote on his share. "I do the rather bold thing of placing myself on a pedestal," he proclaimed, "where the officers can throw all the stones that they will at me without my knowing from whom the stone comes, and I take their final net as the maximum which I will receive."

While Mitchell may have considered himself enlightened, it is not entirely clear that Mitchell's subordinates relished the opportunity to throw those stones, a point that Pecora was quick to make. Mitchell had "a voice in fixing the apportionments" of the management fund that the bank awarded to his stone-throwing subordinates, didn't he? Mitchell conceded he did, but maintained that he did not know how they voted for him. That promise of anonymity, however, may have been small solace to Mitchell's underlings. Mitchell was famously autocratic, ruling the bank by fear and the constant threat of dismissal if someone's performance dipped.[28]

When his subordinates anonymously voted on Mitchell's share, they signed a ballot indicating what share they thought their fellow executives should get of the remaining fund. It probably would not have been very difficult to match up the anonymous ballots with the signed ones. In constant anxiety about the security of their own jobs, were Mitchell's subordinates confident enough in the anonymity of the process to vote Mitchell the share they thought he really deserved? It is hard to know today, but each year Mitchell took home about 40 percent of the bank's management fund and about 30 percent from the securities affiliate. "Mitchell," Pecora wrote, "asked for stones, but was given bread."[29]

How much bread did he end up with? Through the management funds and his "low" salary, City Bank paid Mitchell over $3.5 million from 1927 to 1929. It is hard to even contemplate what those numbers must have sounded like to the people gathered in Room 301. Pecora was making $255 a month as counsel for the committee. The senators were earning $9,000 a year, congressional pages about a tenth of that amount. Newspapers had cut reporters' salaries in half as they began to feel the economic squeeze. Factory workers, if they were lucky enough to have a job in February 1933—unemployment in the manufacturing sector was 45 percent—were making about $17 a week. If you were able to get relief in New York, you could expect to get $10 a week. Even in the bubble years, Mitchell's income put him in rarefied company. Of the four million or so tax returns filed each year from 1927 to 1929, only a few hundred had income above $1 million. Measured in current dollars, Mitchell earned nearly a half billion dollars in those three years.[30]

Senator Brookhart, the progressive Republican from Iowa, who had been largely silent during the morning, was shocked. "Congress is making a big noise about reducing the salaries of these $1,600-a-year Government clerks. Would not it be a good idea for them to consider regulating the salaries of these national-bank presidents, first?" Mitchell wisely avoided answering. "That is something," he said, "you will have to answer yourself."[31]

But regulating salaries was not what Pecora was after. Just before the chairman called the noon recess, Pecora spelled out precisely the point he was trying to make in case anyone in the room had missed it that morning. It wasn't just shock value, although that was certainly part of his calculus. Pecora was trying to show, as Senator Couzens had suggested earlier, that the bonus plan created inordinate incentives for "unwise security selling methods, and unwise and unsound banking methods."[32]

After lunch, Pecora returned to the kind of factual details he started off with in the morning session. As the hearing went on, it became clear to Mitchell that this appearance before the committee was radically different from his earlier one, and that Pecora was a lawyer far different from Gray. As Pecora asked one precise and detailed question after another, he gradually saw a change in Mitchell, who, as he later recalled, "seemed to be wondering where I got the information from upon which I based these questions. I don't know whether he had been told . . . that I had spent three days from morning till midnight examining these minute books." Mitchell thought someone had given Pecora "a lot of inside information," and so as the hearing wore on, Mitchell became more frank and candid in his answers. He had no choice; Pecora already knew what he would say. Indeed, by the afternoon Pecora must have known that he couldn't have asked for a better witness than the "self-confident" Mitchell, who "was convinced of his own integrity" and seemingly clueless about the impressions his answers made.[33]

Two significant disclosures dominated the early part of the afternoon. Pecora stuck with his questions about the management fund, this time focusing on 1929, the year of the crash. The securities affiliate made its initial profit distribution to executives in July, as the stock market continued to boom. The October crash wiped out those profits and the executives should have been entitled to nothing for the year. But Mitchell, who had again taken the lion's share of the fund, recommended to the directors that he and the other officers be allowed to keep the money they had received in July. They would just call it an advance on future bonuses.

Would it "not have been fairer to the company," Pecora asked, "for [the officers] to have made a refund?" Mitchell refused to concede the point. He tried to argue that the executives were entitled to keep the money despite the affiliate's losses for the year. What about those "advances"? Pecora queried. Did Mitchell or any of the other executives have their subsequent bonuses reduced because of the advances? Mitchell had no choice but to admit that there had been no profits in the past three years and, he was "sorry to say," no prospects for any in the current depression. Calling the distributions advances thus "proved a very inexpensive gesture." Mitchell and the other executives never returned any of that money, showing about as much regard for their duty to the shareholders of the bank, whom they theoretically worked for, as for its customers. Indeed, as would become apparent in the next few days, Mitchell never even saw fit to disclose to the bank's shareholders just how much he and the other officers were taking through the management fund. Why should he? "Mr. Mitchell's whole attitude," Pecora wrote, "was not that of the servant, but of the master, of his institution."[34]

In the afternoon, Pecora also began to lay out some of the unwise securities-selling methods this compensation scheme created, focusing first on the slim information City Bank typically provided to investors. The former Bull Moose progressive was adhering closely to the progressive playbook. *Other People's Money*, Louis Brandeis's then two-decade-old chronicle of the Pujo investigation, advocated increased disclosure as the best way to clean up Wall Street abuses. "Sunlight," the future Supreme Court justice wrote, "is said to be the best of disinfectants; electric light the most efficient policeman."

If investment bankers had to disclose not only their fees but also all the material information about the securities they offered, investors would be adequately equipped to make up their own minds about what to buy and what to shun. Like much of progressivism, it was a modest and moderate reform. The government would not be in the business of deciding what securities were safe enough to sell. Disclosure was simply an attempt to make the market for securities function more efficiently. It was also the reform Roosevelt pushed during his presidential campaign. Perhaps burned by some of his own investment failures, Roosevelt once described stocks as "a package too often sold only because of the bright colors on the wrapper." Candidate Roosevelt proclaimed that federal law should "let in the light."[35]

To make this point, Pecora returned to the spreads that Senator Couzens had brought up in the morning session. Spreads were a focal point in Brandeis's critique and now Pecora walked Mitchell through a standard bond sale. In a hypothetical deal, City Bank would buy a bond with a face value of $100 from the issuing company for $90, and then sell that bond to investors for $97.50. So, in a $10 million bond issue, City Bank would immediately pocket $750,000. Did the affiliate, Pecora wanted to know, tell investors about the spread?

The answer, of course, was no; City Bank never told customers what it was making on the deal. Nor, for that matter, did any other United States investment bank. Mitchell, who viewed securities selling as no different from any other form of retailing, was "perplexed" at the point Pecora was making: "If I go in and buy a pound of coffee there is no indication as to what the grocer paid for it and what profit he got for it."

Pecora quickly rejected that analogy: "But when a person goes to a store to buy a pound of coffee he knows the merchandise that he is buying, doesn't he?"

Mitchell tried humor to throw the lawyer off his point. "Well, from some of the coffee that I have drunk I wouldn't think he did."

But Pecora kept at him, refusing to be put off. "And that usually is the fact with regard to the average investor, isn't it?" he asked Mitchell. "He doesn't know the offers except as to such information as is vouchsafed to him by the offering house?"

Mitchell had to agree; he had been saying the same thing for years. The company's customers knew very little about the securities it offered and the firm encouraged investors to rely on its "experienced advice." So, Pecora asked Mitchell again, did he think buyers should have information on spreads? Mitchell was at least candid: "I have been unable myself to really see the desirability of it." He did claim that he thought investment bankers "ought to work toward giving additional information to the public. But whether [information about spreads] is pertinent, whether it is something that would really aid a buyer to determine the true intrinsic merit of that which he buys, I must say I am very much in doubt."

Was there harm in providing the information? Pecora asked. "No," Mitchell replied, "but it would not be harmful or beneficial as to whether the circular was printed on red paper or gray paper or yellow paper."

Pecora didn't care for that answer at all, and he rebuked Mitchell with a flash of anger that had not been seen in the morning. "I am not discussing the best color. The color of the paper gives no information, does it, of the security to the public?"

Mitchell remained unconvinced. "I do not consider that spread is pertinent information. Maybe it is." It was, in other words, a mystery to this Wall Street tycoon why a customer, trying to evaluate the advice it was getting from City Bank, would care about the company's profit margins on the various securities it offered. Wouldn't the company have an incentive to push the securities on which it stood to make the most money? Mitchell apparently could not, or would not, see the issue. Despite his pronouncements to the bond training class at the company that caveat emptor was not good enough for the sacred relations between the securities affiliate and its customers, that seemed to be precisely what the firm was practicing.

Mitchell was hardly alone among business and financial leaders on this score. Many of them, despite the progressive call for greater disclosure, still seemed to adhere to the contemptuous sentiments of Henry O. Havemeyer, the president of the American Sugar Refining Company. He thought that the public had no right to know anything about the internal operations of the company before buying its securities. "Let the buyer beware," he proclaimed at the turn of the century. "That covers the whole business. You cannot wet-nurse people from the time they are born until the day they die. They have got to wade in and get stuck and that is the way men are educated and cultivated."[36]

Because of Mitchell's blindness on the importance of spread information, Pecora pushed back on the banker's claim that he was "heartily in favor of fuller information." Wasn't City Bank the largest investment bank in the world? "It would not have been unbecoming," Pecora suggested, "for the National City Co. to have taken the lead in bringing about a change in custom with regard to putting out fuller information to the public?"

Mitchell insisted that the bank was "trying to blaze a trail with respect to that." Now it was Pecora's turn to be sarcastic: "When did you commence to blaze that trail?"

About eighteen months earlier, Mitchell said, and explained that City Bank had "learned much" from its mistakes during the boom years. Of course, City Bank was hardly alone in making errors: "We have all made mistakes, and

a man that can not profit by it certainly is not very worthy." Now, Mitchell repeated, the bank was trying to lead the way to a better investment banking industry: "We are trying to blaze the way for investment finance into a higher
ground than it has been."

Pecora was dubious and he gently reminded Mitchell of his response from
only moments ago. "But you have not yet blazed the trail to the point where you
are giving the investing public information concerning the price at which the
company acquires these securities that it offers to the public?"

No, an annoyed Mitchell answered, the bank had not yet blazed the trail
quite that far.[37]

L ate in the afternoon, as the light began to fade outside, Senator Smith Wildman Brookhart, a lame duck insurgent who would be out of the Senate on
March 4, decided to change topics. Brookhart was one of the most colorful
characters on the Banking and Currency Committee. It was said that his ten
years in the Senate had changed neither his pants nor his philosophy. Nominally
a Republican, he viewed the members of the party's right wing "old guard" as
his mortal enemies, and he had long advocated "control of Wall Street." He
introduced one of the bills to criminalize short selling. A crack rifle shot, a great
political barnstormer, and an "incorrigible Progressive," Brookhart was, according to a Washington journalist of the day, "one of the best inflamers that Iowa
ever produced." Unfortunately, he was far from an intellectual powerhouse, and
he knew little about the financial and banking communities that he continually
railed against. Norbeck said that not only was Brookhart "the most easily fooled
man in Washington," he never even realized afterward that it had happened.[38]

The Iowa senator had been shocked at Mitchell's salary, and he had heard
at lunch from at least a dozen of the spectators filling Room 301 that they had
lost their life savings when City Bank's stock collapsed. How much of the bank's
stock did Mitchell own, Brookhart asked, and did he sell any of it before the
crash? Anyone who had done his homework would not have asked the question,
at least not that way. In his defense, Brookhart had just returned from Iowa,
where he had been confined to bed with a case of double pneumonia. Still, the

senator had, however unwittingly, given Mitchell the perfect opening to explain how honorably he had acted toward the shareholders. In fact, Mitchell proclaimed, he was the largest buyer of City Bank stock in 1929; he had boldly stepped in to buy the bank's stock in the middle of the crash to sustain the share price and "protect our shareholders."

Ever the firebrand, Brookhart scoffed at that response. He accused Mitchell of being unsympathetic to the shareholders who were wiped out when the bank's stock cratered. Forgetting or ignoring for the moment the bonuses he had raked in during the boom years, Mitchell shot right back. His response wasn't sympathetic, it was indignant. "If anybody here in the room, or anybody that you know, has suffered a loss in gross that I have in City Bank stock, then you know somebody that I do not," Mitchell insisted. "I, individually, have suffered a greater loss from the market failure in National City Bank stock than any other individual in the United States."[39]

If Mitchell was looking for sympathy or commendation, he wasn't going to get it from Pecora. In the coming days, Pecora would reveal that Mitchell's actions were not quite as honorable as the banker claimed. For now, however, Mitchell's boasts about his stock purchases gave Pecora the opening he needed to throw his last bomb of the day. Pecora's next question highlighted the real difference between the average grandstanding senator and Pecora, the skilled courtroom advocate. Brookhart had no idea what Mitchell would say when he asked his question; he only hoped the banker would be embarrassed by the answer. Pecora knew precisely what had happened when he asked Mitchell, "Well, Mr. Mitchell, did you also sell during the year 1929 any substantial portion of your holdings of National City Bank stock?"

At first Mitchell ignored the question and went right back to trumpeting his purchases. He owned more stock now than ever, he finally concluded after a long, rambling response. That kind of answer might have worked with the committee's former counsel, but it wasn't going to throw off Pecora. Pecora patiently let Mitchell finish his answer and then politely repeated his question. "No . . . my question was: Have you also sold very extensively of your holdings in that period or before the end of that year?"

Mitchell hedged, but finally conceded that there had been some "personal transactions" in the later part of 1929. Pecora pressed on and a few questions later, the truth tumbled out. At the end of 1929, Mitchell sold 18,300 shares of City Bank stock to establish an investment loss and then turned right around and bought the stock back for exactly the same price in early 1930. There was absolutely no economic reason for the transaction; it was a sham, done with only a single goal in mind.

"I sold this stock," Mitchell conceded, "frankly, for tax purposes."

Brookhart thought Mitchell was putting a bit too fine a point on his motive. The "sale was really just a sale of convenience" to reduce his income tax, wasn't it?

Mitchell hedged again: "You can call it that if you will."

"Well, is that right?"

"Yes, it was a sale, frankly, for that purpose," Mitchell finally admitted.

No one in the room could have expected this. A cold hearing transcript rarely provides clues as to the reactions of the spectators, but there were really only two possibilities—either stunned silence or shocked murmuring. This was supposed to be a hearing about stock-selling practices, but Pecora had just succeeded in making one of the leading bankers in the country—a man of theoretically "unimpeachable integrity"—admit to what might have been criminal tax evasion. The confident man who walked into the committee room irked at the banality of yet another congressional hearing was now facing the real prospect of incarceration for a personal transaction that had nothing to do with stock exchange practices, but had a great deal to do with public perceptions of his character and his motives.

Pecora didn't want to leave any doubts about the transaction Mitchell had just admitted, so he had Mitchell spell out all the details. How big a loss did Mitchell report on just this one transaction? There was a bit of jockeying, but the number that finally came out was large even by today's standards; in early 1933 it was colossal—$2.8 million. Yes, Mitchell admitted, due to that single transaction he did not have to pay a penny of taxes for 1929, the same year he took home $1.1 million in salary and bonuses. Pecora had just one final question: "By the way, that sale of this bank stock that you referred to in the latter part of 1929 was made to a member of your family, wasn't it?"

"It was; yes, sir," Mitchell replied.[40]

Pecora was gentleman enough not to disclose that the member of Mitchell's family on the other side of this trade was his wife, Elizabeth. The portrait of a greedy banker willing to use any artifice to hang on to every cent of his enormous salary was now complete, and Pecora had Norbeck adjourn the hearings for the day.

It was all over before five o'clock. In a little more than four hours of testimony, Pecora, in concert with the senators on the committee, had managed to punch some gaping holes in the veneer of invincibility and respectability surrounding City Bank and in the unimpeachable integrity of Charles Mitchell. Mitchell and his associates were not dispassionately looking out for the interests of depositors, securities customers, or even the bank's shareholders. Pecora was understated when he described their motives in his memoirs; they had, he said, "a lively interest in their own financial profits as well." In truth the picture Pecora painted on that first day of testimony was of a corporation run with only a single purpose in mind—to maximize the financial returns of its officers, especially its chairman. Nothing else seemed to matter. Not the shareholders, who were kept in the dark about how much the officers were raking in; not the customers, who trusted the institution to provide them with sound financial advice; and certainly not the federal government, whose tax bills could be easily evaded with a couple of ledger entries.[41]

If Pecora's goal was to create outrage, he succeeded magnificently. The only thing dividing most newspapers was which part of the testimony was more outrageous. The *Washington Post* went with the bonuses (the paper ran the line "Huge Pay Told" over Mitchell's picture). For the *New York Times*, it was the taxes— "Mitchell Avoided Income Tax in 1929 by '$2,800,000 Loss,'" its headline read. Given Mitchell's prominence, the most common reaction was surprise and shock. "Charles E. Mitchell, president of the National City Bank, and a man who has always been held in high regard," one paper wrote a few days later, "admits a cheap dodge to avoid paying income taxes in 1929." The *Wall Street Journal*'s coverage was, perhaps not surprisingly, notably different. It thought the most significant aspect of Mitchell's testimony was his huge purchases of City Bank stock during the crash. The *Journal* gave only cursory treatment to the bonuses and, as for taxes, merely buried near the end of the article that there had been "temporary transactions in connection with taxation."[42]

The New York papers reported the news stories, but their editorial pages were strangely silent. This was not true in the Midwest, where editors typically needed little prompting to criticize Wall Street. The *Capital Times* of Madison, Wisconsin, for example, praised the "strong calcium light" Pecora was shining on City Bank. The editors saw the bonuses as a "vicious accelerator" of the Great Depression. "Perhaps few things could be worse or more corrupting and insidiously devastating," the editors wrote, "than paying officers of a bank, which underwrites extensive bond issues, a bonus. That is one institution where a bonus shouldn't even be permitted in the front door."

The mood in Congress was ugly. Brookhart was furious, although that was hardly a surprise since he believed that Wall Street "was the particular invention of the devil." As he devoted more time to the Detroit banks, Senator Couzens faded from the hearings, but he was especially indignant about Mitchell's tax dodge given his own running battles with Treasury. The idea that a business leader like Mitchell would try to avoid paying his proper taxes through this kind of ruse infuriated him.

On the floor of the Senate the next day, Burton K. Wheeler, the progressive Montana Democrat, roared, "It seems to me that the best way to restore confidence in banks would be to have them take these crooked presidents out of the banks and treat them the same as they treated 'Al' Capone when he avoided payment of the income tax." Soon bankers everywhere were derided with a new nickname—"banksters." Carter Glass, a vehement states' rights advocate, offered his own peculiarly Southern quip: "There is a big scandal down in Georgia. The fact has just been discovered that a white woman is married to a banker."[43]

The previous summer, Agnes Meyer, that perceptive Washington chronicler, had expressed her anger at "New York bankers" who had "proved that they are no heroes. The wealthy classes as I have learned to know them through the depression are not much to be admired. They are overcome by fear and selfishness." The worst were the bankers. "If the general public realized the ignorance, smallness, futility and greed of the average N.Y. banker," she wrote in her diary, "I think they would certainly hang a few of them, beginning I hope with Charlie Mitchell."[44]

That was precisely what Pecora had shown on that first day of testimony. There was still much more to come.

Chapter 9

DAY TWO: MORALE

By Wednesday, the sham stock sale had clearly emerged as the biggest story. Reporters were desperate for more information on the transaction, especially the identity of the mysterious family member on the other side of the trade. As the day wore on it became clear they weren't going to learn that information from either the committee members or from Mitchell. The 1930s were far more gallant than the present times, and the senators on the committee refused to divulge Elizabeth Mitchell's name because they were reluctant "to bring that person unnecessarily into a public investigation." Mitchell clammed up entirely, most probably on the advice of his lawyers, who must have known he was now facing a potential tax evasion charge. When reporters asked him about the sale, Mitchell would only say, "I shall make no statement as to that while these hearings are still in progress."[1]

Not everyone was happy with Pecora's first day of work on the City Bank hearings. One critic dashed off a handwritten note to the committee to complain vehemently about the unfair treatment that Mitchell suffered at the hands of Pecora and the senators. "If ever a man was crucified that man was C.E. Mitchell." The leaders of the investigation were a "bunch of ward politicians" who only knew how to spend "money like a lot of drunken Indians. . . . One of the finest men in the country has been sacrificed on the altar of political ambition." That kind of opinion, however, was decidedly in the minority—most everyone who wrote to the committee for the remainder of the City Bank hearings was angry, but their anger was directed at Wall Street, not Washington.[2]

Over the course of the day, Hoover administration officials saw the banking crisis worsen appreciably. People across the country were rushing to banks, withdrawing in aggregate tens of millions of dollars each day, and hoarding it to prevent it from possibly being lost forever if their bank failed. The United States was still on the gold standard in those days, permitting depositors to exchange their paper money for bullion. In those sketchy times, precious metals seemed like a more certain bet than paper money, so many customers insisted on the former or on the gold coins that were then still in circulation. European central banks were also pulling gold from the United States at alarming rates. The huge outflow of gold—into European government coffers, sock drawers and strongboxes, and in jars buried in the backyard—put yet another strain on the already strained banks. Federal Reserve banks were required to maintain a certain amount of gold, and some were coming close to dropping below that mandated level. Banks in Cleveland, Toledo, and Baltimore were particularly hard hit by wave after wave of panicked withdrawals. All sent urgent appeals to the RFC for emergency loans.[3]

M r. Mitchell, are you an officer of the General Sugar Corporation?" With his first question on Wednesday, Pecora revisited the crisis that led to Mitchell's selection as the bank's president, in 1921. The bank had foolishly wagered 80 percent of its total capital on the Cuban sugar industry and in the face of plummeting sugar prices the bank had nearly collapsed. In characteristic Mitchell fashion, he decided to invest even more in Cuba. The bank consolidated its holdings in the General Sugar Corporation—in effect City Bank was going into the sugar business—and waited for sugar prices to turn around, at which point it might be able to sell its holdings at a smaller loss.

Mitchell told City Bank's shareholders over the next several years that the Cuban situation was "well in hand" and had "continued to improve," but it wasn't and it hadn't, at least not in any meaningful way. Prices never really came back; they bounced between two and six cents per pound throughout the 1920s. Many of City Bank's loans were made when sugar was selling for twenty-two cents a pound. It is hard to imagine that an intelligent businessman of Mitchell's caliber could have ever thought they would reach that level anytime soon. Those were monopoly prices under wartime conditions. Most likely Mitchell simply wanted to postpone the day of reckoning until the bank was in a more stable financial position. If he could grow the bank sufficiently in other areas, writing off the sugar loans would end up being a much smaller percentage of the firm's capital base.[4]

By 1926, General Sugar was consistently losing money, and, with the bank now otherwise thriving, Mitchell decided to finally close the books on the Cuban sugar fiasco, halting any further loans to the country's mills. Federal bank examiners had been after him for years to write off the loans but Mitchell dismissed their suggestions, apparently believing that the examiners' views were barely worthy of consideration. "[W]hat a bank examiner could know about the detail of operation of these great properties in Cuba," he said disdainfully, "was always a question in our mind." Even after deciding to shed the loans, Mitchell still didn't want to write them off entirely, because doing so would reduce the bank's capital too drastically. Nor did he have any great interest in publicly disclosing the enormity of the bank's Cuban losses. So he fixed on another plan, a plan that Pecora briefly explored in the hearings the previous afternoon.[5]

On February 15, 1927, City Bank sold 250,000 new shares for $200 each. Half the $50 million it raised was allocated to the securities affiliate, the National City Company. The very next day, National City purchased all of General Sugar's 1.5 million shares for precisely $25 million. General Sugar in turn then paid off the vast bulk of what it owed to City Bank. Through this simple transaction, City Bank had neatly excised the Cuban debt from its books and placed it in its affiliate, with the bank's shareholders picking up the tab. This shift, Mitchell conceded, was the primary motivation for increasing the company's capital—to get the bank out of its exposure to Cuba.[6]

On Tuesday, Pecora asked Mitchell if the bank classified the Cuban sugar loans as bad loans. Mitchell would only say that they were "slow and doubtful," although he did admit that in 1931 the company had written down the value of the 1.5 million General Sugar shares it owned to $1, essentially conceding that the shares were worthless. Of course, that $25 million came directly from the shareholders—that was the whole point of the stock offering. Hadn't City Bank, Pecora demanded, simply bailed itself out of a bad loan?

Mitchell was unwilling to concede that the bank's shareholders had squandered $25 million. "It was," he said, "a transfer at the time of a short-term questionable investment that the bank had . . . into a long-term investment in the City Co." The transaction, he continued, was "a contribution by shareholders in cash to make up for losses which would otherwise have affected the capital and surplus and undivided profits, the capital structure of the bank." The shareholders were, in Mitchell's view, simply repairing "the condition of the institution." Because shareholders had an equal interest in the bank and the affiliate, transferring the loan between the two was simply a matter of accounting; "the stockholders when they got through it," Mitchell argued, "had exactly what they had before." Indeed, this shift in accounting arguably made a positive difference; the shareholders were actually better off with these loans in the affiliate to the extent that the bank's capital was now freed up to make additional profitable loans or investments.[7]

Mitchell was right, but only to a point. The National City Company never published an annual earnings statement, and Mitchell was clearly using the affiliate to obscure City Bank's mistakes, both to outsiders and to the bank's own shareholders. As Mitchell confided to one of his bond salesmen, "We wash our dirty linen on the back porch rather than on the front porch." Having the affiliate there to quietly take care of those mistakes created an insidious problem. If the executives at City Bank never really had to worry about being held accountable for their mistakes they would inevitably, as one newspaper noted, take "risks they would never have dared or cared to take as bankers."[8]

Pecora now raised a similar point, returning again to the importance of disclosure in securities transactions. When City Bank sold the shares in 1927, Pecora asked, were the shareholders "told that they were going to make this sort of a reparation that you have just referred to?" Mitchell ignored the question: "I called your attention to the fact that it was the transfer of a questionable short-term investment that the bank had into what we hoped was a good long-term investment, which we intended to permanently keep in the City Co."

Among Pecora's greatest attributes in the courtroom were his patience and his persistence. The hellhound was more of a pit bull, tenaciously pursuing a line of inquiry until he got his answer. When the shareholders were asked to buy this stock, Pecora repeated, were they told that the proceeds "were going to be used to enable the National City Co. to take over these slow and doubtful loans of the bank?" No, Mitchell reluctantly acknowledged, they were not.

Perhaps the shareholders would have agreed with Mitchell that shoring up the bank's capital was a good investment for them, but they never got the chance to decide. The bank never told them what it would use the capital for and no law required such a disclosure. As Pecora later wrote, "In Mr. Mitchell's view, apparently, the stockholder's function was to put up the money, and it was none of the stockholder's business what was to be done with it thereafter." And besides, Pecora added, wasn't it true that the Cuban sugar industry "has been in a state of collapse" since 1920? Other than a "slight breath of hope" in the mid-1920s, Mitchell agreed, Pecora was "deplorably correct." Yet, Mitchell could now claim that when the bank transferred its interest he thought it was an "excellent" long-term investment for the affiliate? Given the company's write-down of the entire value of the investment just a short time later, it certainly seemed that Mitchell's claim was an outright lie or at least a wild exaggeration.[9]

Now on Wednesday morning, Pecora circled back to Cuba, but before he could Mitchell wanted to contest nearly everything that happened the day before. The mood quickly turned confrontational. What was clear right from the start of the hearings that morning was that Mitchell was enraged at the treatment he had received on Tuesday and he was aiming to get control of Pecora, just as he controlled Pecora's predecessor. Pecora's questions, the banker angrily charged, had created "incorrect impressions" and Mitchell wanted a chance to clear them up. Mitchell didn't care for Pecora's claim that the National City Company was "bailing out" the bank, and he was particularly incensed that he had been "forced" to answer questions about matters that he only vaguely remembered. It was, he said, "unfair" when Pecora knew that there were City Bank officers in the hearing room who were better able to answer.

Pecora was furious over that charge. "Wasn't it you that made the answers to the questions that I put to you, that created whatever impression is in your mind concerning them?"

With that, the two men immediately set to sniping at each other, until

Mitchell finally appealed to Norbeck to intercede: "I presume, Senator Norbeck, your committee is after the facts, and not after the creation of a wrong impression in regard to these matters." The banker demanded that he be permitted to make a statement clarifying his testimony from Tuesday. He wanted to mitigate whatever damage he had caused himself.

Pecora wanted none of it. "Whatever wrong impression was created yesterday," Pecora again countered, "was created by your testimony, because you were the only witness who testified yesterday, isn't that a fact?"

Mitchell again tried to blame Pecora and his leading questions, but Pecora cut him off after just a few words: "I was not testifying. I was asking you questions, and certainly if anything that I assumed in my questions was incorrect you had every opportunity in answering those questions to point that out. Now, you want to point it out, after twenty-four hours."[10]

Norbeck gave Mitchell a chance to make a short statement, but Pecora continually interrupted to contradict the defenses Mitchell now offered. As he had done with Gray, Mitchell tried to ignore Pecora. At one point, Mitchell referred to General Sugar's estimated earnings, and Pecora asked whether those estimates had ever been realized. Mitchell didn't answer, and Pecora kept at him, asking the banker some variation of that same question six times in a row until Mitchell finally conceded that he did not know the answer. "Well," Pecora responded, "if you are going to give us a complete explanation of these things, wouldn't it be better to first fortify yourself as to the facts of actual earnings instead of taking merely estimated earnings?" Mitchell again charged that Pecora was being "very unfair."

It was the same claim that Insull and Stuart had made a week before. And although Pecora had seemed bullying at times during those hearings, he didn't now. Having so thoroughly discredited Mitchell on that first day, Pecora now came across as a dogged and fearless investigator, unwilling to cower before this famous New York banker. Mitchell, on the other hand, seemed like a powerful man who had been caught in a moment of unguarded candor and who was now furiously trying to backpedal his way out of trouble.[11]

Pecora was particularly keen to make sure that Mitchell did not downplay the lack of disclosure to the shareholders. When Mitchell noted that the shareholders "furnished" the $25 million for the transaction, Pecora again cut him off: "One moment there. You say the $25,000,000 was furnished by the share-holders. You do not mean by that that when the shareholders put up that $25,000,000 they knew it was going to be used to finance this sugar transaction, do you?"

Mitchell still seemed perplexed as to how the purpose for the offering was any of the shareholders' business. "I hardly think there was any necessity for [them to know]."

Pecora bore in: "Just answer my question: Did they or did they not know what was going to be done with it?"

"As far as I know," Mitchell responded, "they did not."

Whenever Mitchell tried to squirm out of his answers, Pecora pinned him back down, frequently relying on his incredible memory for the details of the material he raced through in Shearman & Sterling's library. When for example, Pecora said that the "sugar industry was in a state of collapse," Mitchell denied it: "Oh, I hardly think you can say that." Pecora did not miss a beat. "Let me read your own language out of your minute book right on that." There, repeated sev-eral times, was the word "collapse." Here was the crucial difference between Pecora and Gray: Pecora had all the facts at his fingertips and if someone tried to dodge and weave he was ready.

When Mitchell completed his statement, he remained unapologetic. Yet again, he said, it was "unfair to look upon this as something that has been foisted on an unsuspecting public or that there is anything criticizable in this. . . . [T]here is nothing which from the standpoint of the banker, in that which he has done, that is criticizable. If there is, I cannot find it." Mitchell appeared both puzzled and offended. Why should he have to explain the reasons for his busi-ness decisions in this hearing room in Washington? How could this former prosecutor question his motives? Perhaps Mitchell truly believed he and the bank had done nothing wrong, but that was the point. Mitchell could only see the deal "from the standpoint of the banker"; the standpoint of the investor was something that did not seem to enter his consciousness or affect his conscience. Mitchell's explanation had done nothing to undercut the impression Pecora made on the first day of the hearings—City Bank and Mitchell had a cavalier disregard for the bank's shareholders.[12]

Pecora was now completely in charge of the hearing room and at times he genuinely seemed to be having fun. Pecora wanted to return to the Anaconda Copper pools that Gray had questioned Mitchell on the previous spring. Mitchell was astounded. "I cannot conceive of the committee having further interest in it."

Pecora's response was playful: "Have you any further interest in it?"

Mitchell was emphatic: "Most decidedly no."

It is easy to imagine the smile on Pecora's face when he replied, "No. Well, I have just a little additional interest in following up certain lines that apparently were not pursued when you were before the committee last year."

The previous spring, Mitchell had dismissed Gray's attempt to question the propriety of the transactions used to manipulate Anaconda stock with only thinly veiled contempt. Within a few minutes of answering Pecora's questions and apparently still reeling from the first day's testimony, Mitchell was willing to concede that "on the back-look" it was "unfortunate" for the bank to be involved in these kinds of stock market operations. "I would not do it again," Mitchell concluded. "I would rather look to the time when we would be completely out of that sort of thing. I do not believe that it is a thing that we should be doing, Mr. Pecora."

"When did you first reach that conclusion?" Pecora wanted to know.

"Oh," Mitchell replied, it was just recently, at about "the same time that many of us began to feel the headache from that which had gone before."

Pecora reminded Mitchell that "the headaches of some people have been so extensive they have forgotten when they commenced." Mitchell murmured his assent, but he apparently believed that contrition or real regret were unnecessary. The public should be satisfied with his admission of error, no matter how belatedly it had come.[13]

As Pecora took charge, the senators were much less intrusive, seemingly content with their Greek chorus role. Pecora showed, for example, that at the time the securities affiliate was participating in an Anaconda Copper stock offering, worldwide copper prices were dropping by a third. It was still a good investment, Mitchell said, prompting Senator Brookhart to chime in: "Were you selling your own stock then?"

When Mitchell said that City was indeed selling, Brookhart retorted with derision: "Had you reached the conclusion that it was about time to get rid of it; is that the idea?"

Mitchell's anger rose for the second time that day. "That is not the way," he responded hotly, but Brookhart cut him off: "That is the way you did it."

It happened rarely to the smooth-talking bond salesman, but for a moment he seemed to splutter: "That is not the fair way to do it."

Brookhart and Mitchell had finally found something on which they could agree: "I admit it is not," the senator replied.[14]

That afternoon, for the first time since the City Bank hearings had begun, someone other than Mitchell occupied the witness chair. Right after the lunch recess, Norbeck swore in Gordon Rentschler, the forty-seven-year-old president of City Bank. The son of an Ohio manufacturer, Rentschler grew up in a small Midwest town and then attended Princeton, where he graduated, as class president, in 1907. Like Mitchell, he was a tall, physically imposing man, although Rentschler's thick, round glasses, jovial smile, and "boyish enthusiasm" tended to soften his appearance.

A few years after returning to Ohio to take over the family business, he met Mitchell, and the two men quickly became friends. Indeed, it was Rentschler—his company manufactured, among other things, sugar-processing equipment—whom Mitchell sent to assess local conditions in Cuba. It was Rentschler's idea to form General Sugar, and he was one of the men put in charge of it. In 1923, Rentschler became the youngest City Bank director and shortly thereafter began working for the bank full-time. He was soon tapped as Mitchell's heir apparent. The two men were extremely close; they were frequently spotted walking together on Mitchell's daily constitutional from his Upper East Side home to his Wall Street office, immersed in conversation about City Bank business. In 1929, Rentschler became president of the bank when Mitchell was named its chairman.[15]

Given Rentschler's history with the bank, it would have been quite natural for Pecora to start by asking him about General Sugar, but he didn't. Pecora asked Rentschler if he remembered a City Bank board meeting held in November 1929, about two weeks after the crash. The bank's executives were overextended in the market. They had been buying the bank's stock on margin and it, along with everything else, was tumbling. The executives were getting hit with margin calls and, if they didn't come up with the money, the stock would be sold. So the bank's board decided to help them out. It authorized lending the top one hundred executives up to $2.4 million (hundreds of millions in today's dollars), most without security, all interest-free. A City Bank official later conceded that to get that kind of loan without security—let alone interest free—a borrower "would have to have some really good story." The story here, at least according to the board resolution, was about the need to keep up the executives' spirits in those trying times. The loans were necessary, the board stated, for "protecting such officers in the present emergency, and thereby sustaining the morale of the organization."

Many of the loan recipients were the same men who had received bonuses from the management fund, men, Rentschler argued, with earning power and assets. It looked like "their obligations were good obligations to take." Unfortunately, the executives proved to be poor credit risks. By the time of the hearing, only about 5 percent of the loans had been paid back, and City Bank never tried to collect the remainder. "[N]ow taking a hind look at it," Rentschler conceded, "it is a different picture." So different in fact that the bank wrote off a substantial portion of the loans and, in a process that at this point must have sounded familiar to the assembled audience, transferred the balance to the National City Company. "[W]ould you say," Pecora asked, clearly unperturbed by his row with Mitchell that morning, "that the bank was bailed out of those loans under that process?"

Rentschler didn't care for the question any more than Mitchell: "Whatever word you wish to use. The bank was relieved of these loans; yes, sir."

Pecora seemed to enjoy taunting the City Bank executives with that phrase, so he kept at it: "You have heard that term used before, 'bailed out,' haven't you? . . . It is used in the common parlance of Wall Street, isn't it?"

"Well, I suppose so. But I do not use it."

"You think it has a harsh sound to the ear, is that it?"

Rentschler did not answer; he just smiled at Pecora. What could he say?

The lawyer had just shown how the bank's executives had, in effect, helped themselves to the shareholders' money.[16]

What amazed the committee even more than those generous interest-free loans was Rentschler's candid admission just a few moments later that at the same time the bank was granting them to its executives, it was selling out the accounts of its customers, the customers whom it had convinced to buy City Bank stock. Rentschler seemed puzzled by the question. Of course they were selling out the customers; "it is the absolute rule of the bank," he said, "to preserve its assets that are secured in any manner." As a business matter, the bank had little choice but to do so. What it didn't have to do was to extend loans to its executives simultaneously. The combination, more than anything else, solidified the impression that the market was not a level playing field and that these bankers were coldhearted and greedy. Only small, unconnected investors would bear the costs of their imprudent investments; the insiders would simply bail themselves out.[17]

City Bank proved less solicitous of its lower-level employees' morale. On the same day in February 1927 when it sold stock to fix its Cuban problem, City Bank instituted a stock purchase plan that permitted certain higher-level bank employees to buy City Bank stock. Suddenly, in December 1929, the bank decided to extend the plan to lower-level employees, permitting them to buy stock on installment over four years while paying interest on the unpaid balance. Under the plan, those employees purchased 60,000 shares for $200 a share. The monthly payments were then deducted directly from the employees' checks.

City Bank was still requiring the employees to meet their obligations under the plan. The market for City Bank stock, Pecora quickly established, was $40 per share and it had recently traded as low as $25 per share. "And the National City Bank has not done anything to sustain the morale of its employees with regard to those stock commitments of theirs under this plan, has it?" Pecora asked.

Rentschler insisted that the employees were "entirely well satisfied" with their participation in the plan and that City Bank's morale was as "strong and fine" as any in the country.

It was a ludicrous claim that would have been hard for anyone in the room to believe, so Pecora decided to take advantage of it. "As a matter of fact," Pecora followed up, "after paying their installments as they have fallen due since December of 1929 to date, most of the employees who subscribed for stock under this installment plan still owe more than the stock is worth in the market; isn't that so?" Rentschler admitted that was true.

"And the only way they could be relieved of payments is by resigning their positions; isn't that so?"

"Yes," Rentschler replied.

In a time of 25 percent unemployment, snaking breadlines, and massive homelessness, it is hard to imagine that many employees would have taken that step. It would have been "practically the equivalent," Pecora later wrote, "to voluntarily enlisting in the ranks of the unemployed." The City Bank clerks were certainly stuck; "content" seemed a bit of a stretch. In fact, the true situation may have been much worse than Pecora presented at the hearings. One Chicago man wrote to Norbeck charging that when employees satisfied their obligations, they were fired. "I knew one man, married, and with a family, with a salary of $175 per month forced to turn over $60 of that amount for his stock. At the completion of it he was discharged. Many of the employees are destitute— practically all of them in want."[18]

As Rentschler sat in the Washington hearing room more than three years later, he still failed to see the inequity of the situation. Executives, he claimed, had purchased under the installment plan as well and just like the lower-level employees, they too were required to pay the full purchase price. All the employees, he insisted, were "treated exactly alike." After the testimony about the morale loans, Pecora failed to share Rentschler's assessment of the equity of the situation. "It is not recorded," he noted sarcastically in his memoirs, "what the faithful employees, in the privacy of their own hearts, thought of these noble and equalitarian sentiments."[19]

Why did the bank do it? Pecora's theory was simple—Mitchell and the other officers were indifferent to anyone but themselves. That certainly seemed to be the case, but there was a more immediate motive, a motive that Pecora did not address in the hearing room that day. When the stock market crash came, Mitchell was still trying to complete his blockbuster merger with the Corn Exchange Bank, the deal that would transform City Bank into the largest financial institution in the world. Under the terms of that deal, Corn Exchange shareholders could elect either to get 0.8 shares of City Bank stock for each of their shares or to get $360. So long as City Bank's stock price remained above $450, the Corn Exchange shareholders would take the stock. But the price was dropping fast; as the stock market crashed it was already well below $450 and heading further south. A cash deal would have cost City Bank $200 million, money that it had no desire to spend. So Mitchell and the other executives launched a concerted effort to push the stock price upward.

"Flashes" hummed over National City's private wires during the last week of October 1929, urging its salesmen to push the bank's stock. The heavy selling of the previous few days, the president of the securities affiliate, Hugh Baker, argued, "has produced a situation which we regard as distinctly opportune for our customers and our prospects. . . . Remember our stock sold recently around $580 a share." The "exceptional conditions which made this price possible," Baker concluded, "are fast disappearing and in fact are about gone." At the same time, the affiliate and the bank's officers jumped into the market and began heavily buying the bank's stock.

Mitchell, too, was part of the effort. On Tuesday, October 29—the last day of the crash—Mitchell went to see George Whitney, a Morgan partner and the brother of the New York Stock Exchange president Richard Whitney. He established a $12 million line of credit with the firm, drew down $10 million, and began to buy City Bank stock furiously. Months after the City Bank hearings, J. P. Morgan Jr. would explain to Pecora that his firm made the loan to Mitchell and loans to other leading bankers because, "They are friends of ours, and we know that they are good, sound, straight fellows." Mitchell and Morgan were apparently quite good friends, because the loan was incredibly risky. It was, to be sure, well secured by Mitchell's City Bank stock. The Morgan firm was not nearly as optimistic about that stock as Mitchell; it valued the stock at $200 a share, well below what it was then trading for in the market. Nonetheless, the loan still amounted to more than 5 percent of Morgan's net worth.[20]

The buying spree proved to be a futile effort and, in hindsight, it never had a chance of succeeding. The tsunami of selling was simply too strong; the millions that Mitchell and the other executives poured into City Bank stock made absolutely no difference. City Bank stock was at $320 by the end of that Tuesday and settled at around $300 in early November. Mitchell abandoned the effort, paid $4 million of the $10 million back to Morgan, and prevailed on the bank's

stockholders to vote down the Corn Exchange deal. A month later, with the affiliate holding a large number of the City Bank shares it had purchased in the
open market, the installment-buying plan was opened to lower-level employees.
Putting the stock in the hands of the employees rather than selling it back into
the market would, the bankers thought, take additional downward pressure off
the stock. Of course, they were wrong about that, too.[21]

Mitchell had been correct at the hearing on Tuesday; he was the largest
buyer of City Bank stock in 1929. But it wasn't a bold move to "protect" City
Bank's shareholders; it was a desperate bid to save a tottering merger, a reckless
attempt to preserve Mitchell's ambition to rule the world's largest financial institution. It was the same kind of bold strategy he had tried with the Cuban sugar
loans and it, too, had failed. But failure here was not simply a matter of raising
new capital from the shareholders. Failure ultimately left Mitchell on the verge
of financial ruin. The morale loans apparently covered at least some of the executives' losses, but not those of the lower-level employees. They were saddled
with staggering obligations they could barely shoulder as the country sank into
depression.

By four o'clock, day two of the hearings was over, and Pecora was off to his
next task.

The Hoover administration had, to this point, not been very helpful to the
City Bank investigation. Most of the relevant information in its possession—
national bank examiner reports and inspection records—were in the hands of
the Treasury Department, then under the control of Ogden Mills. Mills was a
wealthy New Yorker, a Republican who ran in the same social circles as Mitchell
and the other New York bankers. Because of his personal wealth, Mills received
the same letters asking for assistance as Couzens. Nothing could more underscore
the difference between the two men than their respective responses. Despite his
surface gruffness, Couzens gave away millions to charity and had his staff courte-
ously reply to each letter; Mills dismissed the requests as "begging." Many went
unanswered or received the curtest of replies.

Since replacing Andrew Mellon as Treasury secretary, Mills had become
one of Hoover's most trusted allies, and, in an administration overflowing with

Wall Street supporters, he was one of the most zealous. Treasury was, to be sure, stretched to the limit as it tried to contain the mounting banking crisis, but it certainly looked like it was trying to obstruct the investigation. Mills, who was extremely close to Mitchell's lawyer, Garrard Winston, originally opposed Pecora's request for Mitchell's income tax returns, and he released them only after much pestering from the committee. It had been twenty days since Norbeck and Pecora had first asked for copies of the comptroller of the currency's reports on City Bank. After the end of testimony on Tuesday, the committee passed a resolution again calling for Mills to turn over those documents. Despite the damning testimony coming out of the hearings, Pecora had still gotten nothing.[22]

So Pecora went to see Mills in person. The two knew each other from New York. In fact, Mills had vehemently criticized Pecora's handling of a graft case involving milk sales in New York City when Mills unsuccessfully challenged Al Smith in the 1926 gubernatorial election. Now Pecora wanted to force a showdown with Treasury, but he did it smoothly, without histrionics. He told Mills that he wanted access to the bank examiners' reports. Mills remained reluctant. He brought into the office his undersecretary, Arthur Ballantine, a stuffy and shrewd Wall Street lawyer just back from trying to rescue the Detroit banks, and the two had a whispered conference. Contemporaries said that Mills often acted like an arrogant "spoiled child" and that he was a "natural bully." With this investigator, he now decided that he wouldn't budge.

"Well, Mr. Pecora," he said, "the law, as it has been interpreted, and as I have been advised by Mr. Ballantine, would not compel us to produce those reports." Mills's resistance was surprising; in the last throes of the Hoover administration, as the president was trying to save whatever remained of his legacy, it should have already been clear that it was politically foolhardy to stonewall Pecora. Still, it wasn't totally out of character—Mills fancied himself a shrewd political operator, but, in truth, his machinations were consistently unsuccessful, and he displayed, according to one observer, not "a glimmer" of "political sense."

Pecora knew the law, but he also knew that legal duty was not the only lever he could use on Mills.

"If you would prefer to have me do it, I will have a subpoena signed by the chairman of the committee served upon you for the production of these reports at a hearing before the committee tomorrow, if you feel you can't let me have

a look at them now," he told Mills. "Perhaps this would give us a nice opportunity to raise the question again in a form and manner that might bring about a
clarification of the law on that subject by the Supreme Court."

Pecora, of course, didn't actually want a showdown between Congress and
the Treasury. That would take years to wend through the courts, and he had only
a few days. It was Pecora's threat to go to the committee for the subpoena that
caught Mills's attention. Mills smiled.

"Well, I suppose, Mr. Pecora, we'll be damned if we do and we'll be
damned if we don't," he said appreciatively. "If you report to the committee that
we have denied you access to these reports, it'll be in the headlines of papers all
over the country."

Now it was Pecora's turn to smile.

"Well," he admitted, "that conceivably might follow, Mr. Mills. We don't
control the newspapers."

"No, of course not," Mills replied. "But the newspapers are following everything that's going on before your committee." Mills smiled again and turned
to Ballantine: "Arthur, I think we might just as well let him look at them right
here and now."[23]

Pecora's friends had warned him, "Ferd, you're making enemies of powerful
people by this investigation. Don't you think that might hurt you in the
future?" If Pecora was afraid he wasn't showing it. It was the same thing he had
done when he was an assistant district attorney. As Mitchell's treatment of Jimmy
Walker in New York's fiscal crisis showed, the Wall Street banks were hardly bit
players in New York politics, and neither was Mills, despite his political clumsi-
ness. Within a year of leaving office his caustic criticisms of the New Deal were
widely reported in the press. Pecora's fearless and conscientious prosecution of
this investigation ran the risk of killing off any realistic hopes he had of ever
successfully running for elected office.

Pecora's willingness to attack Wall Street and Treasury without quarter
made him appear incorruptible, precisely the kind of counsel that Norbeck had
hoped to get to run his stock exchange investigation. And the general view in
New York political circles was that Pecora was as honest a man as Tammany Hall

had ever spawned. Not everyone, however, saw it that way. Years later some of his political rivals claimed that Pecora was far from the model of rectitude that he appeared to be. Pecora, one claimed, "has been at the public trough for a great many years." Others said Pecora was "a real spender," with one rumor claiming "he was making $15,000 a year as an assistant district attorney and spending $50,000." Was it true? Was the moralistic Pecora who was so busy demonstrating the greed and cupidity of the City Bank executives no different? Was he just another Tammany grafter?[24]

It is difficult to say with any degree of certainty, but the available evidence suggests that, at least in 1933 and before, Pecora was financially honest. The allegations of corruption were made by rivals in the midst of New York's bitter mayoral campaign in 1950 (Pecora was a candidate in that election) and so may well be no more than the usual political mudslinging. There is certainly no documentary evidence of graft, although this is hardly the sort of thing that anyone would write down. Judge Seabury's investigation of Tammany corruption was completed just before Pecora was appointed counsel to the committee and it never implicated Pecora in any wrongdoing. Indeed, almost two decades later, in that same bitter mayoral campaign, Seabury endorsed Pecora. Police graft was a big issue that year, and Seabury said that Pecora was the kind of man of "integrity and character" who could tackle it. It is hard to imagine that the stalwart good government advocate would make that statement if he knew Pecora had taken graft in his district attorney days. And, of course, Tammany's decision not to nominate Pecora for district attorney in 1929 is perhaps the best evidence that Pecora was fairly resistant to this kind of corruption. Even Pecora's political rivals acknowledged that Pecora "knows party 'loyalty' and its rewards. He learned the hard way. He knows that the way of the party 'ingrate' is political death or very hard."[25]

Pecora was not a paragon of virtue; his string of extramarital affairs is evidence of that. He was a man who was confident in his abilities, politically ambitious, but ultimately insecure about his place in society and about his background and heritage. That last trait made him occasionally fawning, even unctuous, with those in positions of power, a trait that was amplified in some ears by his overly formal speaking style and dignified mien. When Roosevelt sent him a signed photograph, Pecora wrote to the president that it would "occupy the place of honor in my house, just as you do in my esteem and affection." On another occasion, Pecora offered Roosevelt his opinion on the local political scene in New York with the qualification that "my views may lack an intrinsic value worthy of your attention. It may be that I am guilty of a presumption in even thinking you might care to know what they are, in which event I would tender my apologies."[26]

But none of his obsequiousness made Pecora economically corrupt; he craved public acclaim, not material wealth. He took the counsel job even though it paid him only $255 per month, far less than he was earning in private practice. And, at least by his own account, he turned down a number of bribes in the course of the investigation. Sometime in 1933 a "prominent figure in the financial world" offered Pecora $250,000 in cash if Pecora refrained from putting him on the stand. Pecora never revealed the man's name, but he turned down the bribe and the banker appeared at the hearings. Which one of the many bankers who traipsed before the committee was it? There were easily a dozen men who had the financial wherewithal to afford such a generous bribe, but without any other evidence it would be pure speculation to identify the culprit. In any event, whoever offered that bribe was not alone in trying to buy his way out of having to face the tenacious investigator in the glare of that Washington hearing room.

Pecora recorded another attempted bribe a few months later. An unnamed "important financial figure" approached a friend of Pecora's and asked, "What is Pecora's price?" At first Pecora's friend didn't understand, but the banker explained, "All through my lifetime I have learned that every man has his price. The difficult thing, sometimes, is to find out what it is, and that is why I am asking you. What is Pecora's price for not putting me on the stand?"

The friend obviously knew Pecora well, because he replied, "You don't own all the gold in the world, but if you did, that wouldn't be enough."

"Let's talk realities," the financier persisted. "Would a million dollars do the trick?" Pecora's friend didn't report any of this to Ferdinand until after the man had already been put on the stand, explaining, "I didn't want to tell you beforehand. I knew you were going to put him on the stand and I didn't want you to kill him."[27]

As the hearings wound down in 1934, the senators on the committee began to regret the tiny salary they were paying Pecora, and they were embarrassed when they thought of what the lawyers he was regularly facing were paid. Senator Glass, who would butt heads with Pecora throughout the investigation, proposed that the Senate appropriate a "special allowance" in recognition of the great work the lawyer performed. The other senators enthusiastically agreed, but Pecora urged them not to do it. The thing that had given him "great compensation, although not in the coin of the realm" was the letters of appreciation he received from the public, many of which applauded him for taking on the job while being paid so little.

"If this resolution were to be adopted," he told the senators, "I feel that a lot of those persons who honored me with their letters of commendation might feel that I let them down. . . . The comfort that I've derived from those letters . . . [has] been of more value to me than could any special compensation the Senate might see fit to award me."

Senator Couzens and others urged him to reconsider, but the Hellhound of Wall Street would not be dissuaded.[28]

Chapter 10

DAY THREE:
MANIPULATION

Next on the stand for Pecora was Hugh Baker, the president of the securities affiliate. Bald and severe in appearance, Baker was fifty-one, the same age as Pecora. He had worked for City Bank for nearly two decades, starting with the bank in 1914 and then becoming a salesman for the affiliate in 1916. Baker became National City Company's president in 1929 when Mitchell was named chairman. Baker was one of the recipients of the City Bank morale loans, although his financial crisis couldn't have seemed very acute, at least not to investors who had just been wiped out in the crash. Just a month before Black Tuesday, he purchased the top two floors of a new apartment building going up on Fifth Avenue. At the time, it was the largest cooperative apartment ever sold in New York City.[1]

Baker had been sitting in Room 301 for two days watching Pecora dismantle Mitchell and Rentschler. Both were still there. Mitchell had temporarily retired to the spectator's row directly behind Baker. The "personification of American rugged individualism," one reporter noted, now stayed close to his attorneys, all of them sitting politely and quietly with their hands folded in their laps. It would, the reporter noted, "unquestionably take a steamshovel to get

[Mitchell] away from the enclosure of those high-priced, wise looking lawyers." With the committee room still jammed with spectators, many loitering around the door because they had nowhere to sit, the soft-spoken Baker seemed afraid to answer even the simplest question for fear that Pecora would do to him what he had just done to Mitchell and Rentschler. Within the first few minutes of his testimony, Baker consulted a memorandum handed to him by his lawyers, and Pecora asked an innocuous question about whether the banker had a good or poor memory.

"Well, I would not boast about it," Baker replied.

Pecora tried again and this time Baker said his memory was "probably about the average." From there, the interchange between the two men quickly descended to the absurd.

"I do not know what the average is," the lawyer explained, trying to get Baker to just answer his simple question.

"Neither do I," Baker responded.

"I merely want to know the state of your recollection," Pecora persisted. "Is it generally good or is it generally bad?"

"I do not know how to answer that question, Mr. Pecora."

"You can not tell us whether you think you have a poor memory or a good one, is that it?"

"No; I can not answer that question."[2]

It was a fitting start to a laborious day. Baker constantly battled Pecora on every point. Getting nowhere with him, the lawyer brought the company's corporate secretary, Harry Law, to the stand. He was no more helpful. Law couldn't answer a question without long pauses and whispered conversations with lawyers and the other executives from the bank. He incessantly twirled company documents in his hands as the whole room waited for his answer. Pecora was sure that Baker in particular was not being candid with him, and the lawyer wanted the record to reflect how long both men were taking to answer his questions. At one point he admonished Baker for the constant coaching he was getting: "Mr. Baker, do you consider yourself qualified, as the president of the company, to answer these questions, or do you think that someone else can answer them more accurately?"

As he was about everything else that day, Baker was unsure. "Well, probably there are others who can answer better—"

Pecora interrupted impatiently: "Is there anyone who knows more about the company's transactions than you?"

"I don't think so."

"Then suppose you answer these questions and not have Mr. Law whisper the answer in your ear. Will you?"[3]

What Pecora was trying to pull out of Baker and Law was the story of how the National City Company ceaselessly flogged City Bank's stock. The sales push during the crash, it turned out, was not an anomaly. Starting in 1928, the company intensely marketed City Bank stock to the public, not only to raise the price of the stock, but because broad stock ownership benefited the bank. Stockholders became just another group to whom the bank could cross-sell its other financial products. Rentschler put it somewhat more diplomatically, testifying that there were "a great many collateral conditions flowing to the bank because of it" so that "it was a very desirable thing for [the bank] to broaden our contacts [and] to make it possible for more people to become stockholders in our bank." Broad ownership was an integral part of the bank's financial supermarket strategy, and the number of City Bank shareholders mushroomed from 15,000 in 1927 to 86,000 at the time of the hearing.[4]

The National Banking Act, the federal law governing nationally chartered banks, prohibited City Bank from directly trading in its own securities, but Mitchell and the other executives saw no reason why the company could not trade the bank's shares. It was not, after all, a national bank. As Pecora had begun to show late the previous afternoon with Rentschler, however, the bank was walking a fine line. In bank branches without employees of the affiliate, bank employees would take orders for stock. The affiliate benefited enormously from the bank's large capital base. It could borrow up to 10 percent of the bank's capital to finance its activities in the securities markets. In 1928, as City Bank's stock price skyrocketed, Mitchell split the stock five for one, decreasing its price by 80 percent, so that more middle-class buyers could afford it. National City salesmen were constantly pushed to sell the bank's stock, and even received premium commissions when they did so, giving them even greater incentives to urge the stock on their customers. Because the trustees who ran the company were City Bank officers and directors, the line prohibiting national banks from securities trading was, at the very least, decidedly smudged, if not entirely obliterated.[5]

Rentschler, of course, didn't see it quite that way, although he conceded that the company had cut back on trading City Bank stock after the crash and said that it was not nearly as aggressive as it had been at the time of the boom. Pecora reminded Rentschler that "a national bank may not buy or sell its own shares" and then asked, "Do you consider that those provisions of the national banking act were violated in spirit if not in letter through this medium of its investment affiliate . . . engaging in those transactions?"

This wasn't the bank buying its own shares, Rentschler insisted, because it had been done through the artifice of the affiliate. But he did acknowledge that "in the light of experience I am perfectly willing to say to you I prefer that the National City Co. not sell shares." Even Rentschler thought it was unwise for the bank to be pushing its stock so aggressively. That concession, however, was not enough for Pecora, who still wanted to explore the details of just what the affiliate had previously done to market the bank's shares. And it was on that point that he was getting nowhere with Baker or Law.[6]

It didn't help matters that neither Pecora nor the senators had a firm grasp on the mechanics of stock transactions. At various points, the senators, for example, seemed to be assuming that City Bank was issuing new stock to investors, thereby reaping huge windfalls as the bank's stock price continued to climb, when in reality it was simply acting as a broker for sales of already issued stock. Pecora did manage to show that the company had borrowed 30,000 shares of stock from Mitchell in the spring of 1929, paying him interest in the process. By the time the company returned the stock in July, it owed Mitchell $128,850, another little payday for the bank's chairman. It would have made a nice point about the many ways that Mitchell was able to profit from his position as chairman of the bank (for lending his stock for three months, the company paid him five times his annual salary), but Pecora had a different point in mind. Wasn't this, he asked Baker, an example of the company shorting the bank's stock? Given all the hostility toward short sellers at the time, it was an explosive charge. Baker denied it and the two battled for the better part of the day over what constituted a short position.

After two hours of persistent questioning, Baker finally conceded that National City was technically short at one point in 1929, but he remained adamant that it was only a temporary imbalance between the purchase and sale transactions it was executing for customers. Pecora's questioning was tenacious and he ultimately got the admission he wanted, but in truth his theory made no sense. Pecora was trying to show that the aggressive promotion was designed to push City Bank's stock price higher. If that was what the company was doing, why would it sell City Bank stock short, a bet that the stock price would go down? It wouldn't. Nonetheless, the newspapers dutifully reported the next day that City Bank had shorted its own stock. Apparently, the reporters didn't understand the stock market any better than Pecora did.[7]

Despite the false steps, Pecora was able to draw a compelling picture on Thursday that City Bank had consistently tried to control trading in its stock—control it apparently used to run up the price. The most significant step in cementing that control was in 1928 when the bank removed its stock from the New York Stock Exchange, the largest, most prestigious stock market in the country and the natural place to list shares if the bank intended to broaden ownership as much as possible. Baker claimed the bank was concerned that leaving the stock on the exchange might allow it to be manipulated, but that claim seemed implausible on its face. He pointed to only a handful of small trades and price movements that alarmed him. It sounded like a pretense, an impression that Pecora immediately tried to underscore.

"The fluctuations that you had observed," Pecora asked, "were five-point fluctuations in small lots?"

"Yes," Baker replied. "There were sales, I think five sales, one right after another."

"And what was the aggregate of those five sales?"

"Fifty shares."

Pecora liked to repeat answers to emphasize their significance: "Fifty shares?"

"Yes; ten shares each."

"And you thought that indicated manipulation of the stock on the floor of the exchange?"

Baker thought that the trades "seemed to offer those possibilities," but Pecora highlighted how ridiculous that contention was. "And what were the number of shares the bank had outstanding at that time?"

The answer, which Pecora well knew, was 750,000. "And from a total volume of sales aggregating fifty shares on that date," Pecora asked, "you thought there was a manipulation in the stock of the bank?"

"Thought it was possible that there was," Baker said meekly.

Pecora remained incredulous. "Thought it was possible? . . . Did you complain to the exchange authorities about that manipulation?"

It would have been the natural thing for City Bank to do if it really suspected manipulation, but Baker conceded that there had been no complaint.[8]

On the basis of that slender reed—on trades constituting a minuscule fraction of the outstanding City Bank stock—Baker contacted Mitchell, who also claimed that he had "been much disturbed regarding recent speculative movement" of the bank's stock. Mitchell agreed that delisting the stock was necessary. Activities on the New York Stock Exchange, he wrote, "only intensify speculative interest which can not be of any possible advantage to us." The New York Stock Exchange at first refused—it said investors relied on the existence of the market, which made it easier to buy and sell City Bank shares. Without approval from City Bank's shareholders, the exchange would not delist the stock. It was only a temporary roadblock. The bank obtained approval and the stock was delisted in January 1928.

If the bank's goal was to prevent a wild run-up in the stock price and to lessen speculative interest, it was singularly unsuccessful. Delisting turned the company into the primary market maker for City Bank stock. City Bank stock, once only thinly traded on the New York Stock Exchange, was now in some weeks being sold by the company at a rate of more than 90,000 shares. The numbers seem small by today's standards, but they were huge in 1928 and 1929. The National City Company was the largest investment bank of the day, and it did more business in City Bank stock than in any other individual stock. And although the whole purpose of delisting was theoretically to limit speculative interest, Baker admitted that City Bank did nothing to dampen this activity; in fact, the company encouraged it. Throughout 1928 and 1929 National City was engaged in an "extensive campaign" to sell the bank's shares. The sales pitch

In early 1933, Ferdinand Pecora was one of only a handful of Italian immigrant lawyers in New York. He arrived in the United States in 1886, a time of fierce anti-immigrant and anti-Italian sentiment—sentiments that lingered into the 1930s.
The New York Times

"If immigration was properly Restricted," the original caption of this 1890s cartoon read, "you would never be troubled with Anarchy, Socialism, the Mafia and such kindred evils!" *Corbis*

Convinced that short sellers were interfering with his efforts to revive the economy, President Herbert Hoover (left) in early 1932 asked Frederic Walcott (below), a conservative Connecticut Republican and member of the Senate Banking and Currency Committee, to investigate them.

Library of Congress

Walcott, a former investment banker, insisted that the committee had no intention of proposing legislation to regulate the stock market.

Library of Congress

Senator Peter Norbeck, a progressive former artesian-well driller from South Dakota, was the chair of the Banking and Currency Committee, although he had very little knowledge of how banks or the stock exchange worked. He seized control of the investigation from Walcott, seeing it as a chance to make his mark in Washington.

Library of Congress

New York Stock Exchange President Richard Whitney was the first witness in the investigation. The imperious Whitney ran roughshod over the committee, leading editorial writers to mock the hearings as foolishly inept and a raw "abuse of inquisitorial power."

AP/Worldwide Photos

After the 1932 election, Norbeck was desperately trying to restart his now dormant Wall Street probe, but most commentators accused him of trying to protect Wall Street. Outside observers had almost universally written off the investigation as dead, as this January 1933 cartoon suggests. *Rollin Kirby Post/New York Public Library*

With a little more than a month left in the congressional session, Norbeck hired Pecora (right) to complete the investigation. A host of other lawyers had already turned down the job, including Samuel Untermyer (below), the éminence grise of Wall Street reformers. Pecora, shown here when he was chief assistant district attorney in Manhattan, was a highly experienced prosecutor, but unlike Untermyer, he knew little about Wall Street's inner workings.

RIGHT: *New York Historical Society;*

BELOW: *Library of Congress*

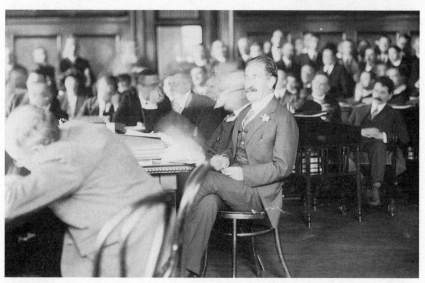

The winter of 1932–33 was the nadir of the Great Depression. Shantytowns of the dispossessed, sarcastically derided as "Hoovervilles," and breadlines were everywhere, including these in New York City. ABOVE AND BELOW: *Library of Congress*

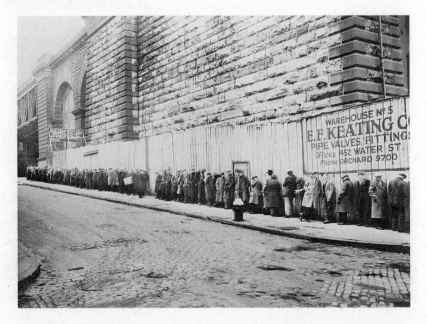

The banking system was in dire need of reform. Bank failures and runs, such as this one on the Bank of United States in 1930 (above), skyrocketed during the Depression. On February 14, 1933, Michigan declared a statewide bank holiday, sparking a wave of similar measures that would all but shut down the country's banking system over the following two weeks. Days before Franklin Roosevelt assumed office, the police in New York were holding panicked crowds at bay at the country's largest savings bank, the Bowery (below).

ABOVE AND BELOW: *Library of Congress*

The pugnacious senator Carter Glass (above) was desperately trying to pass his banking reform legislation in the waning days of the Seventy-second Congress. The bill would have revamped the entire scheme of banking regulation, but it died in Congress after Louisiana senator Huey Long (below) waged a lengthy and colorful filibuster in January 1933 to defeat it. The death of the bill was welcome news to the banking industry.

ABOVE: *Senate Historical Office*; BELOW: *State Library of Louisiana*

Charles E. Mitchell, chairman of the National City Bank, started his career as an investment banker and was reputed to be "the greatest bond salesman who ever lived."

Library of Congress

Mitchell was nicknamed "Sunshine" Charlie for his ebullient market views. A month before the Great Crash in October 1929, Mitchell and his wife, Elizabeth, sailed for Europe. Before leaving, Mitchell assured American investors that there was simply "nothing to worry about in the financial situation of the United States."

Library of Congress

Mitchell transformed City Bank's securities affiliate, the National City Company, into the country's largest investment bank by trading on the bank's sterling image and appealing to a broad swath of middle-class investors, many of them investment neophytes.

Pecora had prodigious courtroom skills and was called the best cross-examiner in New York. His forensics were built on a foundation of thorough investigations. Working from a "shabby" office in New York, Pecora had only a few weeks to study City Bank's far-flung operations before the hearings began. ABOVE AND BELOW: *Corbis*

A trio of New York's and Washington's best-known and highest-paid lawyers represented City Bank at the hearings. James Harry Covington (top left) was a former congressman and a founding partner of one of Washington's premier law firms, Covington & Burling. Guy Cary (top right) was a partner at New York's Shearman & Sterling and a City Bank director. Garrard Winston (right) was a Shearman partner and a former assistant Treasury secretary.

ABOVE RIGHT: *Shearman & Sterling*;
ABOVE LEFT: *Library of Congress*;
RIGHT: *Library of Congress*

Mitchell (below) had nothing but disdain for the Senate Banking and Currency Committee's investigation, but he faced sharp questions, not only from Pecora but also from progressive Republican senators James Couzens (left) of Michigan and Smith Wildman Brookhart (right) of Iowa. ABOVE AND BELOW: *Library of Congress*

President-elect Roosevelt followed the City Bank hearings closely. Five days before the inauguration, he posed for this photograph examining the family Bible he would use to take the oath of office. Later that evening he would sit at this same table to work on the address that would set the tone for his presidency. *FDR Presidential Library*

On March 4, 1933, two days after the City Bank hearings came to an end, the new president assured Americans that the "money changers have fled from their high seats in the temple of our civilization. We may now restore that temple to the ancient truths." *Library of Congress*

After the City Bank hearings, public demand for federal regulation of Wall Street reached a fever pitch, as this cartoon in the *New York World-Telegram* depicts.

Rollin Kirby Post/New York Public Library

The first meeting of the newly created Securities and Exchange Commission, the new federal watchdog of the securities industry. Joseph P. Kennedy (seated center) was named the commission's first chairman, and Pecora served as a commissioner until he was appointed to the bench in New York. *Corbis*

was the usual palaver—a hint of insider knowledge and a smattering of exclusivity combined with an overwhelming sense of urgency. "Charles Mitchell had confided to certain trusted National City salesmen," one customer was told, "information to the effect that the National City Bank stock was a good buy. This was to be passed along to special clients only."[9]

With the company aggressively pushing the stock and with the stock split, the volume of City Bank trading nearly doubled and the price skyrocketed, reaching a peak in 1929 of $580. Accounting for the split, City Bank's stock was now selling for the equivalent of nearly $3,000 a share. Baker denied that the company tried to control trading in City Bank stock, "except when the market seemed to be moving too fast in one way or the other, and then we would undertake to do it." As of January 1928 the stock had nearly quadrupled in price in a little over a year and a half. That growth rate apparently suited the bank and the company just fine.

For Senator Brookhart the conclusion was obvious—City Bank was far more efficient at "booming" its stock than the New York Stock Exchange had been. Norbeck agreed; hadn't the company encouraged investors to buy City Bank stock and helped along the price run-up? Baker remained unsure how to answer, but his response hardly helped his case: "I didn't—I certainly was not trying to stop business."

"You were interested in selling and not in protecting the public," Brookhart interjected.

Baker claimed he "was interested in both," but Brookhart didn't believe him. "What did you do to protect the public?" the Iowa senator demanded. "I have not seen anything yet that was done to stop all this vast loss they have sustained as a result of all these transactions."

"Well," Baker stammered, "I haven't any answer to that. There was not anything we could do that we did not do, as far as I know, to protect the public as regards its investments."[10]

As usual, Brookhart had overstated the case—the general market bubble, not just City Bank's activities, played a huge role in the bank's soaring stock price. Still, most listeners probably agreed with the senators—the bank did everything it could to push things along.

The affiliate's central market role and its great desire to see a soaring City

Bank stock, Pecora also showed, created a huge conflict of interest for the company, both with respect to pushing City Bank stock and in pushing the securities the affiliate had underwritten. City Bank's depositors frequently sought the bank's advice on investments. "And in order for a bank to give that kind of advice disinterestedly," Pecora wanted to know, "it should not be interested in pushing any particular security, should it?"

Baker tried to duck the question, but Pecora kept at him: "Mr. Baker, you would not hesitate to say, would you, that the advice which a bank gives to a depositor, in response to the depositor's request for such advice concerning investments, should be wholly unselfish and disinterested on the part of the bank and should be designed to serve the depositor's interests?"

"It should certainly serve the depositor's interests all the time," the investment banker offered.

"And do you think that a bank which has an affiliation with an investment company, sponsoring its own issues or the issues of others, is in a position to give that kind of unselfish and disinterested advice to a depositor seeking such advice?"

The conflict was patently obvious—of course the bank would prefer the securities its affiliate offered. Baker would not, however, admit the obvious; he thought the bank could give "unselfish and disinterested advice." Pecora didn't; he was sure that the "temptation" to act in the best interests of the bank was too strong. Even though a few moments earlier Baker had testified that the company's employees "were interested in promoting the interests of the bank in any way we could," he never quite admitted that those interests colored the investment advice it offered its customers. He didn't really have to; Pecora had made his point.[11]

Pecora ended the day by showing that just a few months after the stock market crash, the company participated in a stock pool—euphemistically known as a trading account—to boost the price of City Bank's stock. It was just the kind of manipulative activity that Baker had so forcefully claimed earlier in the day that the bank had sought to avoid and the reason it had delisted its stock from the New York Stock Exchange. Now, in the company's bid to drive up the stock price after its disastrous post-crash plummet, the company granted an option to a brokerage firm called Dominick & Dominick (a firm that just happened to be owned by one of the bank's directors) to buy blocks of City Bank stock at progressively higher prices. As in any pool, the members would then trade the stock back and forth with each other in an attempt to stimulate buying interest and increase the stock's price. Baker denied any knowledge that the option was part of a pool operation, a claim Pecora easily deflected.

"When you got the letter did not the letter contain sufficient information to indicate to you that [the shares subject to the option] were to be used in a trading account and not in an investment account?" Pecora asked.

Baker started to deny it, but the investigator cut him off: "Now look at the caption of the letter itself and read what it says."

Baker hemmed: "That is what the caption is, but I discussed—"

Pecora cut him off again: "Read it."

"I had discussed this—"

"Read the caption out loud," the exasperated lawyer finally demanded, "so the record will show it."

The sheepish banker dutifully read the words "National City Bank of New York Capital Stock Trading Account" into the record.

After a long, tedious day, Room 301 burst into laughter.[12]

Pecora never explored the reason for the pool, but it seems clear that the primary intended beneficiary of this manipulative scheme was none other than Charles Mitchell. Just two months before the letter was sent, Mitchell had borrowed millions from the J.P. Morgan company in his failed bid to save the Corn Exchange merger, pledging his City Bank stock as collateral. Mitchell still owed Morgan $6 million. If the bank's stock price fell any more, the stock Morgan held (it was now, temporarily at least, the second largest City Bank shareholder) would be worth less than the outstanding balance on the loan. Mitchell might be a "good friend" of Morgan, but money was money. Morgan might well demand additional collateral or even foreclose on the loan to limit its losses.

A rising stock price would alleviate that risk; it was an effect that the option was clearly designed to achieve. By setting the exercise prices of the options at successively higher tiers, City Bank was encouraging Dominick & Dominick to drive the price upward; it was the only way for the trading firm to continue to profit on the option. "Our only desire," Baker admitted, "was to see the stock move up." This, of course, was the same Baker who, after seeing fifty shares trade on the NYSE, was so concerned about manipulation that he recommended delisting the stock. Now he was granting an option on 32,000 shares to facilitate a pool to help boost the stock price. And this was the same Mitchell who wrote that manipulative trades "can not be of any possible advantage to us." Fear of manipulation apparently no longer applied when Mr. Mitchell's money was on the line.

The pool worked, but only briefly. Dominick & Dominick made a tidy little profit of about $350,000 as City Bank's stock price began to rise. The increase, however, was short-lived. As 1930 wore on, the stock price dropped further in value and Mitchell eventually gave Morgan a mortgage on his Fifth Avenue home and his houses in Tuxedo Park and the Hamptons to secure the outstanding loan. By 1933, virtually none of that balance on the Morgan loan had been paid, but Morgan had not yet foreclosed on its good friend.[13]

The third hearing day was a slog and lacked the riveting disclosures of the first two days. There was, however, little doubt that Pecora had already accomplished much of what he set out to do. In the space of three days, Pecora showed that City Bank—that paragon of banking virtue, one of the largest and most respected banks in the world—was engaged in the same kind of petty stock promotions as the Bank of United States, the failure of which helped spark the banking crisis then gripping the country. Just like that much smaller and less prestigious retail bank for immigrants—the bank that City Bank would not deign to rescue when it got in trouble late in 1930—City Bank was speculating in its own stock and selling it to the bank's own depositors. Were the Bank of United States' bad real estate loans any different from City Bank's bad Cuban loans? Hadn't the two banks done precisely the same thing with their mistakes—dumped them into their affiliates? The Bank of United States authorized highly suspect loans to its board members. Were they really any different from the City Bank "morale" loans? And hadn't the former garment manufacturers who ran the Bank of United States, Marcus and Singer, been shipped off to jail?

The *Nation* made that connection. It called the City Bank revelations "the largest bank scandal . . . since the failure of the Bank of United States. It all recalls the ancient music-hall quip: 'If you steal $25, you're a thief. If you steal $250,000, you're an embezzler. If you steal $2,500,000, you're a financier.'"[14]

Less than two months before the City Bank hearings, the president of the American Bankers Association argued that there was no need for Congress to pass new banking laws, especially laws that would strip commercial banks of their affiliates. Americans need only rely on the "honesty and efficiency" of the men who ran the country's largest banks, who "continued to command public confidence . . . because they conformed conscientiously to principles of sound public service." Was there anyone who still believed that was true? Certainly not Joseph Kennedy, who lamented, "The belief that those in control of the corporate life of America were motivated by honesty and ideals of honorable conduct was completely shattered."[15]

And certainly not the editors who had been shocked in Wednesday's testimony to hear how shabbily City Bank had treated its own employees, forcing them to continue to pay for now nearly worthless stock at greatly inflated prices. The "morale" loans to the higher executives stood "in ugly contrast with the manner in which the same officials are still compelling their lower-caste employees to repay loans for similar purposes, but at the original high mark of the market prices. There can be no sympathy with men who do such things." The "indecent callousness" with which these high-level bankers treated lower-level employees "marks them as men set apart from their fellows as betrayers of their trust not merely as bankers, but as human beings."[16]

The editorial sections of the New York papers remained quiet, but the president-elect, making his last cabinet selections and preparing to enter the White House, had taken notice. He was amazed at what he heard and astounded by the lack of editorial comment in New York—a silence he would later attribute to the press's lack of "moral indignation." Outside New York, the papers were beginning to express that precise sentiment. The *Philadelphia Record* called the "disgusting revelations . . . cheap skullduggery." The *Hartford Courant*, which had to this point been a reliable defender of Wall Street, now saw why the public had become so disenchanted with the financial community. The "average citizen . . . sees himself as the innocent victim of the catastrophic consequences of the wild speculation that characterized an era of false prosperity," the editors observed. Even the *Wall Street Journal* thought that the failure to inform the bank's own stockholders of the size of the bonuses the executives were collecting from the management fund was troublesome. "Certainly, Mr. Mitchell's testimony affords further basis for demands for greater corporate publicity," they dryly noted.[17]

Even more than the papers, the American people were angry at what they had heard over the past few days. Letters flooded the Senate Office Building, some addressed to the senators, some to Pecora, almost all praising Pecora's performance, expressing outrage at the testimony, and calling for federal legislation to address the abuses. John S. Campen, a former National City Company salesman, rued that he had been recommending City Bank stock to "everyone in North Carolina. . . . I want to say that I think that [Mitchell's] action constitutes one of the dirtiest and lowest passages in our Financial History—and that I hope you prosecute him and his associates who helped along that line to the very limit." Dr. J. W. Gould lost his life savings and now found himself "in my old age an utterly ruined man. Is there no justice in the land? Is there any redress for me? Can you, will you advise me what to do?" Gould was not alone in asking Pecora for help, but to all of them Pecora was forced to express his regret and his helplessness. It was, he wrote, "beyond the province of the Committee or Counsel to function for a private litigant."[18]

Many of those writing to the committee were convinced that federal legislation was the only way that these kinds of abuses could be remedied. Indeed, many thought Mitchell was emblematic of bankers as a class, not an isolated aberration. It was, Silas Green wrote the committee, "a disgrace to the people and the authorities of this country that many men of Mitchell's stripe can do our people the way they do and keep out of jail." Green pointed to the law strictly regulating securities sales in Britain and urged Norbeck to prevail on Congress to follow Britain's lead. "If you could get Congress to pass a similar law in this country," Green concluded, "it would do more to protect the American public from dishonest bankers and Wall St. crooks than all the investigations ever held."[19]

While most people seemed angry at the disclosures coming out of Washington, others were terrified. Constant Eakin, a Frigidaire executive, had a nervous breakdown when he heard Mitchell's confessions of wrongdoing. Most of his money was at City Bank, and he thought it all might vanish.[20]

On the Senate floor on Thursday the mood was angry. Senator George Norris of Nebraska, a gray-haired Republican senator who had been reliably progressive for over two decades, hauled out an eight-foot-square chart depicting the "Spider Web of Wall Street." The legs of the large black spider that dominated his chart were the eight Wall Street banks—including J.P. Morgan and City Bank—that Norris claimed controlled most corporations and industries through a web of interlocking directorships.

Although most of Norris's comments focused on that old-money trust claim, there was plenty of anger about the disclosures coming out of the Pecora hearings as well. Norris compared investment bankers to muggers preying on elderly widows and expressed sympathy for a public desire for physical revenge against them.

> Suppose the Senator from Oklahoma were walking down the streets of Washington and a widow should come along whom he knew had in her pocketbook the proceeds of a life-insurance policy on her dead husband, which she was probably taking to the bank to deposit. Suppose the Senator would knock her down and steal the money from her and undertake to escape. The people roundabout, if they saw what happened, would seize the Senator from Oklahoma, and if they did not tear him limb from limb—if the mob did not kill him on the spot—he would be sent to prison.

Senator David Walsh, a Massachusetts Democrat, complained that corporations "have paid their entrenched officials unconscionable salaries, that they have speculated and gambled with private financial resources they have been intrusted [sic] with, and have carried on their functions in disregard of the public interest and without an effort to do justice to their employees or even to their stockholders." Congressional anger led to some radical, infeasible, and almost certainly unconstitutional proposals. Kentucky's freshman Democrat, Marvel Logan, proposed that the government confiscate the profits of industry above a mandated fair return to capital and labor.[21]

It was not surprising that Roosevelt and progressive legislators were outraged by what they heard coming out of Room 301. What was surprising was the fact that Pecora had even managed to sway the incumbent president. Back in

December in his State of the Union message to Congress, Hoover spoke of systemic, not individual failures. Indeed, Hoover thought that thousands of individual banks and bankers "have shown distinguished courage and ability" though they were working in a fundamentally flawed and unstable banking system that was in large part responsible for the bleak state of the economy. Now in January, writing to United States Attorney General William D. Mitchell (no relation to Charles Mitchell), Hoover was so disturbed by what Pecora uncovered that he completely changed his view.

> If only part of the things brought out prove true, these men have done the American people more damage than all the incidental operations of Al Capone. Capone had the merit of confining his robbery and the infliction of physical violence to the wicked. . . . [I]f these stories are true these men are not bankers, they are banksters who rob the poor, drive the innocent to poverty and suicide and do infinite injury to those who honestly work and strive. Worse than that, they are traitors to our institutions and national ideas.

Despite his personal views, Hoover maintained his public silence. He thought it inappropriate for the president to "publicly judge individuals" and he remained somewhat skeptical about the truth of Pecora's charges. Still, he asked the attorney general to start a formal investigation of City Bank. It was too little too late. There were only a few days left in his administration, not enough time to do anything meaningful. But Hoover, who had started the hearings a year earlier simply to chase the short sellers into hiding and who was now no doubt thinking about his legacy, decided not to leave these allegations for the Roosevelt administration to handle. He told the attorney general that his letter would "indicate to you the seriousness of my feeling about it and how anxious I am that even in the few days left to us we shall not fail in our duties for upon proof that either the implications of these exposures are untrue, or that being true, these men land in jail, depends the faith of the American people in our institutions."[22]

By the inauguration, Hoover seemed even more convinced of bankers' culpability. Perhaps his comments weren't genuine; maybe he was still trying to shift blame for his own failures and inadequacies, but, whatever the motive, the now former president privately complained that he and the Federal Reserve chairman Eugene Meyer "have tried everything on behalf of the bankers but they have fought us, haven't tried to [cooperate], haven't even told us the truth. They are without ability and without character."[23]

Chapter 11

DAY FOUR: LEGAL LEGERDEMAIN

On Friday, Attorney General William D. Mitchell launched a formal investigation of City Bank, Charles Mitchell, and, for good measure, Insull. The Justice Department's first step was to piggyback off Pecora's work. It announced that it would obtain copies of the testimony and analyze whether there were violations of the National Bank Act, the tax laws, or other federal statutes. At the same time the United States attorney in Manhattan, George Z. Medalie, announced that he, too, would investigate, and would focus on whether Mitchell's 1929 wash sale amounted to a criminal tax evasion.[1]

By the weekend, the Internal Revenue Bureau, which had originally signed off on Mitchell's return, launched its own investigation. Indeed, ever since Tuesday's disclosure, the bureau had engaged in some serious backpedaling. Ambrose W. Hussey, the Internal Revenue agent who had "personally okayed" Mitchell's tax return, was now furiously trying to explain his actions. Mitchell's statements at the hearing, he explained, completely contradicted his original statements to the Internal Revenue Bureau. The bureau reviewed the transactions "thoroughly on account of it being a sale between a husband and a wife," Hussey explained. Mitchell assured the examiners, however, that his wife was financially capable of purchasing the City Bank shares and the bureau thus allowed the loss as a bona fide transaction. The 1930 return did not disclose the repurchase of the 18,300 shares, and the bureau apparently decided that they could simply take Mitchell at his word, because they did nothing further to investigate the transaction.[2]

The banking situation in Michigan had not improved appreciably by Thursday. Despite constant conferences between banking officials from Washington and Michigan and rumors that the RFC would loan up to $150 million to the wobbliest of the Detroit banks, nothing had happened yet. The bank holiday was still in place, although Governor Comstock revised his order to permit some very small withdrawals. A few of the more secure banks allowed their depositors to take out no more than 5 percent of their money. It helped a little, but 5 percent was tantamount to a closed bank, and no one seemed to take the change as a positive sign.

With negotiations over the Michigan banking closures still stalled, governors in other states were beginning to address rumors that they were next. The passage of emergency legislation in New Jersey and the restrictions in place at banks in Atlantic City and Maple Shade was not, according to Governor A. Henry Moore, a cause for concern. "There is no thought," he assured a reporter, "of a banking moratorium in this state." Officials in other states made similar pronouncements, but they did little to calm fears, either among the depositors or the bankers. "Few bankers slept soundly," one Arkansas banker noted about those tense days in early 1933. "Confident as they might be of their own bank's safety, they were never free from the fear that rumor would start one run which would trigger a reaction to engulf all." And in Washington, those fears were looking more justified with each passing hour. Ogden Mills reported a rash of bad news to the Federal Reserve Board—the situation in Cleveland was critical, with the possibility of a large bank closure by the next day; there was trouble in Kansas City and the possibility of closures in Baltimore; two banks were on the verge of collapse in the District of Columbia and they were likely to bring down four or five smaller banks with them.[3]

A t ten that morning, Norbeck gaveled the hearing to order, his opening line nicely summing up Pecora's dominating performance that week.

"Mr. Pecora," he asked, "who will you have this morning?"

Pecora wanted Baker again. He quickly led the soft-spoken and thoroughly flummoxed head of the National City Company through his bonus and salary for 1927 to 1929. He was a piker compared with Mitchell—he earned a little over $750,000 compared with Mitchell's $3.5 million—but few others in the day could match even that sum. Pecora didn't dwell on the numbers; he didn't need to at this point. Instead, he returned to the topic that had consumed most of the previous day—the manipulation of City Bank's stock price and whether the bank was indirectly trading in its own stock in violation of the National Bank Act.[4]

Baker was still terrified of answering any of Pecora's questions, even the most basic ones. It seemed clear that City Bank's lawyers had drilled him long and hard about not admitting anything unless absolutely forced to do so. Returning briefly to the decision in 1927 to delist City Bank's stock from the New York Stock Exchange, Pecora asked, "Isn't it easier to control the over-the-counter market for a security than the Stock Exchange market?" The answer was obviously yes; over-the-counter stocks, generally speaking, have fewer shares outstanding and are more thinly traded—far fewer shares change hands in any given day, making it much easier to move the price precipitously. Baker, however, professed not to know, leaving an exasperated Pecora to ask, "You are market wise, aren't you?"

The president of the world's largest investment bank was unwilling to admit he knew anything at all about the basic operation of the stock market: "I don't know that I am."

"Do you think that you would be the president of the National City Co. if you were not a keen student and observer of the markets for securities, all markets?"

Baker refused to answer. "Well, I certainly don't know the answer to that question. That is somebody else's decision to make."

Even on this minor point, Pecora refused to give in, so he tried a different tack: "It is not an unfair assumption that you were chosen for the chief executive position of this great investment company because you were market wise, is it?"

"Well, I doubt if that was the consideration of it. I don't think that was the idea, as to whether I was market wise or not."

Like Pecora, Senator Brookhart was having trouble believing Baker could be so recalcitrant, and he too tried to pry an answer out of Baker: "That was one of the things, wasn't it?"

It was no use. "I do not know Senator," Baker said. "I was not there when the matter was being discussed."[5]

The testimony all that morning was desultory, with the senators constantly wandering off topic to ask Mitchell, who took the witness chair after Baker, about balancing the federal budget. In between the digressions, Pecora spent most of the morning trying to analyze a series of transactions in which City Bank granted what were termed "over certifications" to a brokerage firm named J.R. Schmeltzer & Co. The transactions themselves were routine. New York commercial banks ordinarily made day loans to brokerage firms to finance stock purchases, loans that the brokerage firms would repay by the end of the day when they delivered the securities to their customers and collected payment. When a broker needed more money than the normal line of credit it had with the bank, it asked for an over certification, which was regularly granted if both the broker and its customer were good credit risks. Day loans were an easy way for the banks to make some extra money. The loans didn't pay much interest—just 1 percent per year—but they were, for all intents and purposes, riskless. "Since I have had any connection with the National City Bank," Mitchell told the committee, "we have never lost a penny in all of our day loan accommodations." Not even during the crash? Pecora asked. "Not a penny," Mitchell replied.

Although Senator Brookhart and others tried to suggest that such loans fostered speculation, they were missing the point. It was not so much that City Bank made these day loans, it was the timing and the security involved. Schmeltzer, it quickly became apparent, was purchasing large amounts of City Bank stock on behalf of the National City Company in October 1929, just as the stock market was beginning to crash. This was, of course, the time when National City was furiously buying the bank's stock in order to stabilize its price and save the Corn Exchange merger. By helping to finance these trades, it certainly seemed as if City Bank was further blurring the line between impermissible trading on its part and permissible trading on the part of National City. City Bank was, after all, lending money to a brokerage firm hired by its own affiliate to purchase City

Bank stock. Didn't this, at a minimum, constitute financing the purchase and sale of its own stock? Mitchell, unlike Baker, at least was candid with Pecora. City Bank, a bank organized under the National Banking Act, was not trading in its own stock; the National City Company, which was not a national bank, was trading in City Bank stock.

It was, of course, a slim distinction, but it was a distinction that Mitchell probably felt confident in making because it had two decades of history behind it. Shortly after the turn of the century, the bank's president, Frank Vanderlip, wanted to transform City Bank from simply a commercial bank into a financial supermarket—a one-stop shopping place for all its customers' financial needs. It was the only way, Vanderlip thought, to meet the increasing competition from two sources—state-chartered banks, and trust companies organized under liberal state corporate laws. The latter were the real financial services innovators at the time. Unburdened by the laws that prohibited nationally chartered banks from engaging in anything other than commercial banking, they quickly expanded from their traditional role of administering estates and wills to offering their customers a host of financial services—they took deposits, provided financial planning, offered safe deposit services, and started distributing securities. Customers loved them because they could do all their financial business under one roof. State-chartered banks quickly pressed their legislatures to loosen the legal restrictions imposed on them, and they too began to offer these allied services. Both had lower capital requirements and so could offer higher interest than national banks, and both had branches, making them much more convenient than national banks, which were limited to a single office.[6]

Nationally chartered banks were at a huge competitive disadvantage. Not only were national banks prohibited from engaging in lucrative trust and asset management services, by the turn of the century the United States comptroller of the currency was beginning to crack down on their nascent securities-selling efforts. As an early proponent of banking reform measures that would loosen the strictures on nationally chartered banks, Vanderlip got nowhere in Congress and he turned to plan B. If City Bank was prohibited from engaging in certain activities, why couldn't the bank form an affiliate corporation that was not a nationally chartered bank, a corporation that was not bound by the same restrictions? Writing to the bank's shareholders in 1911, he told them that it would be a "material advantage" to establish a separate corporation to "make investments and transact other business, which though often very profitable, may not be within the express corporate powers of a National Bank."

Pecora's take was somewhat more colorful. He viewed the affiliates as an attempt to take profitable business away from private investment banks like J.P. Morgan rather than as a way of competing with trust companies and state banks. Commercial banks, he wrote, "looked with hungry eyes upon the savory meats that had hitherto been the virtual monopoly of the private investment banker, and they decided to share more liberally in the feast."

This idea was not original to Vanderlip; he modeled City Bank's affiliate on the First Security Company that George Baker of First National Bank had formed in 1903. By the time City Bank got around to forming its own affiliate, there were more than two hundred bank affiliates in existence. The key to business success was to ensure that the executives of the bank completely controlled the affiliate without actually owning it, which would violate federal law. National banks turned to their Wall Street lawyers, who came up with an ingenious solution. The shareholders of the bank formed a separate corporation; in City Bank's case it was called the National City Company. Rather than retaining control of those shares, however, the bank's shareholders agreed to place their shares with three trustees, all officers or directors of City Bank, who had the ability to vote on any matters that would normally be submitted to the company's shareholders, including electing the board that would run the company. The trustees also agreed to distribute through the bank any dividends the company declared. Legally, the affiliate was a separate corporation in which the bank had no ownership interest. In reality, however, because the bank and the affiliate had precisely the same management, this structure was the functional equivalent of the bank forming a wholly owned subsidiary to pursue these business ventures. Indeed, City Bank was literally inseparable from the company—National City's stock was printed on the reverse side of the stock certificate for the bank.[7]

Pecora read that history and concluded that the structure effectively nullified the restrictions built into the National Banking Act. "Surely," he wrote, "the suave legerdemain of the corporation lawyer in the service of high finance has scarcely, if ever, achieved a more hairsplitting triumph!" Now with Mitchell back in the hot seat, he wanted to drive that conclusion home with the loans the bank made to finance purchases of City Bank stock. "Wasn't that a species of trading by the bank in its own stock?" the lawyer asked.

Mitchell remained adamant; the bank and the affiliate were separate legal entities. That was true, Pecora pressed, but shouldn't we look past those formalities? The company, he insisted, "is inseparably interwoven with the bank, is it not? . . . It is like one body with two heads, isn't it? It has the same body; it has the same blood, meaning the capital derived from the sale of the capital stock of the bank. . . . But instead of having one head it has two heads, and the two heads seem to be the one head in your personality. You were the chairman of both institutions. But in form it had two heads, didn't it?"

It was not Pecora's most elegant question, but it made the essential point: any real separation between City Bank and the National City Company was illusory—a mere legal fiction—because Mitchell was the driving force behind both companies. Even Mitchell had to concede that the two were hardly distinct; they were one "institutional entity."[8]

When Hugh Baker resumed the stand in the afternoon, Pecora switched gears from the independence of the National City Company to its operation during the 1920s. Just what were the consequences of allowing national banks to use these legal expedients to engage in what would otherwise be prohibited activities? It quickly became apparent that Mitchell (and his fellow executives) really did believe that securities could be sold like coffee or vacuum cleaners. Like any other sales organization, National City used financial incentives to drive its salesmen. If some stock or bond "was considered more difficult to sell" or if the company "desired to accelerate sales of any particular issue," the company would suddenly offer premium commissions, sometimes a third higher than its standard commissions. The premiums were always, of course, for the securities the company sponsored or for the stock of City Bank.

For a firm that had pitched its "unquestioned reliability" to magazine readers across the country for years, it was a jarring disconnect. At the turn of the century, when trust companies began hawking securities for the first time, many industry observers began to worry about the inherent conflict of interest they faced between giving disinterested investment advice and promoting their own interests. Those concerns were frequently dismissed; the honesty and integrity of bankers, it was widely thought, would be enough to prevent abuses. Perhaps that faith and confidence had been misplaced.[9]

Those promotions went out to the affiliate's scattered offices in flashes sent over its 11,000 miles of private wires, but this was only the mildest means used to spur on the sales staff. The company liked "to keep the salesmen on their toes" with sales contests, an innovation for which Mr. Baker claimed credit. "I suppose our sales organization," he testified, "is like all other sales organizations. There are times when they seem to slow down and are tired. In order to inject new life into the organization we would develop what we called sales contests, to add some competition." There were any number of contests that Pecora could have questioned Baker on, but he chose one that was announced on September 27, 1929, just one month before the crash. Pecora's choice was not subtle, but it was an effective way to link that calamity to those hard-sell efforts.[10]

One of Baker's 350 salesmen was Julian Sherrod, the man who had written the tell-all book about the company two years earlier and whom Pecora unsuccessfully tried to enlist as an assistant in the investigation. Sherrod's name never came up in the hearings, but Baker's testimony on Friday afternoon seemed to confirm everything he had revealed. Sherrod's experience seemed typical. Like a Fuller Brush man, Sherrod started by selling securities door to door. He called on customers early in the morning and late at night when they were not at work and he even made sure to visit certain churches on Sunday to maximize the number of potential clients he could pitch. Despite attending the affiliate's bond class, he was ill-prepared, and he found a population that seemed equally ignorant about investments. "He did not know what he was buying and I did not know what I was selling," Sherrod wrote afterward, "I was just merchandising." It didn't matter; Sherrod was successful anyway. He sold nearly $700,000 in bonds in his first six months. The key was not to focus on what he was selling but to focus on the reliability and integrity of City Bank. "I had mastered the gospel and talked so much about the greatness of our

Bank," Sherrod wrote, "that a man would finally give up and say 'all right, send me some.'"[11]

But inside the securities affiliate, the harried employees weren't simply dispassionately and clinically analyzing the quality of bonds and securities. The scene Sherrod described in his book and Baker described at the hearing was a 1920s version of *Glengarry Glen Ross*; precisely, Pecora noted, "like that of any nonbanking large-scale sales organization." The first order of business was generating the pool of potential customers. The company had an entire department dedicated to drumming up new leads—culled primarily from voter lists and automobile registrations—leads that were constantly fed to the salesmen. Of course, the company also had a ready-made list of new securities customers—the depositors of City Bank. The bank, after all, had started its personal loan department and had begun accepting tiny deposits from customers not just for the positive public relations it generated, but because these "small but developing capitalists" were potential stock and bond customers.

Just a day earlier, Rentschler testified that the bank wanted to create a broader base of potential clients for the affiliate. On Friday, however, Baker seemed squeamish about admitting that reality. He denied ever seeing a list of depositors, but even his testimony showed National City and the Bank working closely together. It was the inseparably interwoven single enterprise that Mitchell had testified to earlier in the day, and it left, to Pecora's way of thinking, these "prospects" with their guard down. The company's salesmen, he reasoned, "came to them clothed with all the authority and prestige of the magic name 'National City.'"[12]

"Would it surprise you to know," Pecora asked Baker, "that many of the bank's depositors who never before had had any business with the company were approached directly by the salesmen or representatives of the company and greeted with the remark that the salesmen knew that they were depositors of the bank?"

Baker did "not dispute that at all," but he insisted that the bank did not simply hand a list of its depositors over to the company. It would, however, transmit the names of customers interested in investments to the company and the company would immediately contact that depositor.

Pecora realized at once that the close connection Baker had just revealed gave him an opening to reexplore the conflict of interest that existed between the bank and the investment company, and he quickly took advantage of it. "And if that depositor or customer then followed up that suggestion by calling upon the National City Co. for advice as to his investments, it was not an unusual thing for the National City Co. to suggest investment in securities that the company was sponsoring, was it?" Pecora asked.

Unlike the day before, Baker was caught off guard on this issue: "That is right."

"In fact, it was the usual thing, wasn't it?"

Baker realized what he had admitted and tried to back away. "That is right. But he did not recommend—"

Pecora never gave him the chance to finish that justification. "And do you consider, as a director of the bank, that that was a disinterested and unselfish way for the bank to advise a depositor concerning the making of investments generally?"

Even with his testimony about promotions and sales contests, Baker was unwilling to admit that either the bank or the company had done anything improper. He, like Mitchell in his first day of testimony before the committee, relied on the company's internal "yardstick" for measuring investment quality; the one that Mitchell claimed would never be shortened while he was in charge in order to meet the business needs of the bank. The National City Company, Baker insisted, had "facilities . . . for study of investments, and based upon that we made our recommendations." Pecora wasn't quite ready to challenge that claim about the quality of the affiliate's offerings. There was still next week.[13]

Instead, Pecora continued to paint a picture of a company that never overlooked an opportunity to make a sale, no matter how small. A memorandum sent to salesmen entitled "Loaves from Crumbs" discussed the problem of small cash differences in favor of customers that sometimes occurred when trading stock. Those cash balances, the executive who wrote the memorandum worried, often went "into the customer's bank account to be lost sight of or spent." With the lower cost of City Bank stock as a result of its split, the memorandum advised salesmen that they "should make it a point to see that the crumbs resulting from an exchange of securities go at once into one or more shares of the stock. If the amount is insufficient to buy one share you can have the customer put up the remaining cash." Buying City Bank stock "ties the customer in closer than ever." The memorandum recognized what Baker seemed loath to admit—broadening the stockholder base would create new customers for the affiliate. "By using the crumbs of cash resulting from exchanges to buy new stock of the National City Bank . . . you will work these crumbs into a loaf of substantial size with consequent advantages to the client, the National City Co., and yourself."[14]

There were some lighter moments during the day, such as when Pecora's notes incorrectly transcribed a flash sent to the sales staff. "We necessarily will deal recklessly," Pecora quoted from his notes, "in executing orders—"

Uncharacteristically, Baker interrupted him: "I did not say 'recklessly.'"

"What did you say?"

"Ruthlessly," Baker replied.

"Ruthlessly?"

"Yes."

Pecora was more than willing to admit his mistake. "We have it 'recklessly,'" he said, "but we will adopt your term 'ruthless.'" Laughter rippled through Room 301. "Thanks for the correction."

"I like that much better," Baker offered.

"So do I," Pecora agreed.[15]

With all the pressure to sell, the pace in the affiliate's offices was grueling and relentless. The former National City salesman Julian Sherrod gave a taste of it in his memoirs:

All day long our private wire was busy. All day long the message was the same—hurry up, hurry up, hurry up—send some orders—send in some orders—send in some orders. . . . When things slowed up a little, some genius would hatch up a contest of some kind and then we would be under extra pressure from every direction sometimes for weeks.

Top salesmen were rewarded, everyone else was shamed. With the threat of dismissal constantly hanging over their heads for lackluster performance, the salesmen lived in fear of the dictatorial Mitchell. A typical internal memorandum noted dryly, "I should hate to think there is any man in our *sales crowd* who would confess to his inability to sell at least some of any issue of either bonds or preferred stocks that we think good enough to offer. In fact, this would be an impossible situation and, in the interest of all concerned, one which we would not permit to continue." One legend claimed that Mitchell fired a young employee who had the temerity to tell the world-renowned banker that his pants were unbuttoned. "In those days," wrote the critic Edmund Wilson, "the trousers of Charles E. Mitchell could no more be unbuttoned than Louis the Fourteenth's grammar could be at fault." All in all, it was hardly the kind of probity, rigor, and "unquestioned reliability" that the company had tried so hard to project for so many years.[16]

How could the bank engage in and even control these activities indirectly when it was prohibited from doing so directly? Hadn't federal banking examiners been able to see through this patently transparent artifice? Apparently, they had, or at least someone in the federal government had. Pecora asked Mitchell if he was familiar with an opinion written in 1911 by the solicitor general of the United States, Frederick Lehmann, to the then attorney general, George W. Wickersham. Mitchell had read it "many, many years" earlier and he did not remember the details. Pecora was more than happy to remind him.

The opinion was lengthy, but Pecora hit the highlights, reading a series of excerpts into the record. In 1911 President Taft requested an opinion on "the legality of the agreements and arrangements existing between" City Bank and the National City Company. The Lehmann opinion was a full explanation for the decision that Wickersham and Lehmann had already reached and conveyed to Taft—the bank and the affiliate were in violation of the law. Lehmann (whom Wickersham considered "one of the most intelligent men I know") discussed the affiliate's participation in general investment banking business, pointing out that the affiliate "has no independence of action" and was controlled entirely by the bank's executives. "The temptation to the speculative use of the funds of the banks," Lehmann wrote, "will prove to be irresistible."[17]

The main point of contention, however, was not these generalized invest-ment banking activities. Other national banks had already formed investment banking affiliates. City Bank's was the largest, but it stood out for a different rea-son. Several of the bank's shareholders transferred shares they owned in other banks and trust companies to the National City Company, instantaneously trans-forming the affiliate into the nation's first bank holding company. The National City Company was a nascent interstate banking chain, and its existence imme-diately riled those who were constitutionally opposed to large concentrations of economic power. Wickersham thought that holding companies should be pro-hibited, so it was not terribly surprising when Lehmann concluded that "the National City Co. in its holding of national-bank stocks is in usurpation of Fed-eral authority and in violation of Federal law."

With all the testimony over the last several days describing the affiliate's sales practices and the bank's financing of its operations, Norbeck was convinced that Lehmann was a "prophet." Pecora tried to put a more nefarious cast on the opinion. The lawyer could only submit a carbon copy as an exhibit, he said, because the original was "not to be found among the files of the Department of Justice." In his memoirs six years later, Pecora wrote that the opinion had been "buried," the result, no doubt, of a political conspiracy or, at the very least, "the complaisance of governmental authorities toward powerful financial and busi-ness groups during the lamented pre–New Deal era." Lehmann's opinion "had disappeared—*spurlos versenkt* [sunk without a trace], to borrow a wartime phrase—leaving only a carbon copy as a ghost to haunt the conscience of the Bank."[18]

Mitchell was silent in the face of these suggestions, but his lawyer James Covington was not. The sixty-two-year-old former congressman from Maryland and former judge was one of the best known lawyers in Washington and a founder of one of the city's largest law firms. Covington demanded to be heard, and he and Pecora immediately got into a rancorous debate about just what the Lehmann opinion signified. This was, Covington argued, just an opinion. If "so high-minded a man" as George Wickersham never pressed charges against City Bank, then "he must have differed with it." Pecora thought it was a "gratu-itous assumption," to which Covington immediately responded, "Not so much a gratuitous assumption as some that you have made from time to time." Covington got an immediate rebuke from Norbeck, who told him, "We want no more of that."

Pecora, however, would not back down, and his response dripped with sarcasm. The opinion, Pecora repeated, said that Lehmann and Wickersham were in agreement. "[F]or the benefit of the learned gentleman who has just placed his observation on the record," Pecora sneered, "I will repeat—"

Covington dismissively cut him off: "I heard that, Mr. Pecora."

Now Pecora was furious, and he read directly from a portion of the opinion where Lehmann explained that he and Wickersham had "concurred that the agreements and arrangements in question were made to enable the bank to carry on business and exercise powers prohibited to it by the national banking act." Pecora looked up from his copy of the opinion and glared at Lehmann: "Did you hear that Judge Covington?"

"I heard that, Mr. Pecora."

"And you still say that the Attorney General did not concur, do you?"

"I did not say that he did not concur."

"Then I misunderstood you," Pecora replied derisively. "Excuse me." Covington had indeed said that, and now he said it again. Wickersham must have ultimately come to a different conclusion than Lehmann because he never filed an action against City Bank and "the fair presumption is that Mr. Wickersham always obeyed the law."[19]

Pecora had refused to be intimidated by Mitchell, and he certainly wasn't going to let Covington walk all over him. In truth, however, neither man was precisely right, although of the two, Pecora seemed to have the better of it, at least when it came to what Wickersham thought of securities affiliates. Formation of the National City Company prompted the congressman Charles A. Lindbergh Sr., father of the famed aviator, to call for a congressional investigation of the "money trust." That investigation would eventually be dubbed the Pujo Committee, the investigation that gave Samuel Untermyer his first taste of national fame. At around the same time, Wickersham also launched an investigation of City Bank and its investment affiliate, without ever bothering to consult with the Treasury secretary, Franklin MacVeagh, who oversaw nationally chartered banks. The investigation revealed a strong difference of opinion in the Taft administration. Wickersham was an ardent trustbuster who called the Supreme

Court's decision to affirm the dissolution of Standard Oil "one of the most important ever rendered in this country." He generally favored greater government regulation of economic matters. MacVeagh, by contrast, was sympathetic to the complaints he was hearing from the national banks—federal regulation was hamstringing them as they tried to compete with state banks and trust companies. MacVeagh was ready to hold that City Bank's affiliate was legal.[20]

In the summer of 1911, Taft's advisers battled to convince the president that they were right. MacVeagh told Taft that the secretary of state, Philander Knox, shared his assessment of the legality of the affiliate. The attorney general urged Taft to authorize an action against City Bank. This "flagrant evasion of the statute," he wrote the president, needed to be "brought to book" at once.[21]

The dispute between Justice and Treasury left President Taft in an awkward political position. If he sided with MacVeagh he would be portrayed as capitulating to the "money trust"; if he sided with Wickersham he risked destabilizing the banking sector, which was only a few years past the devastating Panic of 1907. So like any good politician, Taft said he would resolve the dispute, and then never did. At some level he didn't have to. The primary concern the City Bank affiliate raised was the propriety of its functioning as a bank holding company. All the governmental attention now focused on the bank was too much for Vanderlip. By the fall of 1911, he had divested the company of all its domestic banking stocks. Over a year later, Taft finally informed Wickersham that he had decided to take no action against City Bank. The affiliate survived; it was free to engage in a host of investment banking activities, all with the apparent acquiescence of the federal government, although it was no longer a bank holding company.[22]

The Pujo Committee ultimately found that national banks like City Bank were subject to severe conflicts of interest when they underwrote and sold corporate securities through affiliates, the same concern that was earlier expressed about trust companies. The committee, however, was not so sure that the integrity and honesty of bankers would be sufficient to minimize abuses. Its report recommended that national banks be prohibited from dealing in securities. It would have been the death knell for securities affiliates, but again the federal government failed to act. Congress never passed legislation incorporating that recommendation.

In fact, over the next decade, the federal government's tacit acceptance of securities affiliates shifted to outright approval. During World War I state banks and trust companies were, for the first time, permitted to join the Federal Reserve System. Those that joined were not required to give up any of their allied financial services, and national banks took this as an obvious signal that it was all right for them to continue to engage in investment banking. In 1920, the comptroller of the currency again warned that securities affiliates of national banks were a "menace" and he again called for their abolition, but this warning was ignored. Indeed, the comptroller office's view soon reversed; worried that national banks would leave the system unless they could compete with state banks on more even footing, the comptroller called for a substantial loosening of the restrictions imposed on national banks.

In 1927, Congress did exactly that when it passed the McFadden Act. Its primary innovation was to permit greater branching opportunities, but it also formally recognized securities affiliates. The provision engendered little debate because it appeared to ratify already existing and well-entrenched practices. But the effect in a time of burgeoning stock market values was enormous. Securities affiliates nearly doubled their participation in offerings and quickly became the dominant players in investment banking. Covington was wrong about Wickersham, but he was right about the federal government—it ultimately came to the conclusion that the affiliates were acceptable. Washington, it seemed, was just as much at fault for the abuses of the 1920s as Wall Street.[23]

Pecora implicitly blamed all the unsavory sales practices he cataloged that afternoon on Washington acquiescence, although strictly speaking that was not the case. Some practices—pushing depositors into the securities markets and aggressively hawking City Bank stock—would not have occurred but for the fact that the company was the bank's alter ego. Many of the sales practices that the senators and the public found so objectionable, however, had nothing to do with affiliate status. Mass advertising, door-to-door sales, and sales contests were the by-products of trying to peddle securities to the middle class. Other investment bankers, like Halsey, Stuart, used similar techniques but were not affiliated with nationally chartered banks. These practices may well have existed even if the Taft administration had cracked down on affiliates. Still, Pecora wasn't totally wrong when he equated the two. After all, it was City Bank's reputation for integrity that had made its aggressive sales efforts so successful, a reputation it would not have but for its status as a safe and sound national bank.

At least that was how the *New York Times* and other leading papers saw matters. After the Kreuger testimony six weeks earlier, the *Times* warned that legislation was pointless because it would do nothing to deter the handful of individuals who were responsible for these frauds. Congress "cannot legislate for business on the basis of a monstrous exception," the paper warned. Now, after a week of Pecora's relentless questions, the *Times* was willing to recognize more systemic problems, problems that it said arose from the proliferation of securities affiliates:

> The sensational disclosures at Washington, not yet complete, show what happens when vast banking resources are made available for excesses of speculation. Through their subordinate companies, the so-called "affiliates," too many banks were infected by the mania of the time and became more like agencies for the flotation of securities than organizations for the regular supply of loans and discounts in ordinary business. But there is now reason to believe that the lesson of that folly has been learned and that at least for a long time to come the principles of conservative banking will be recognized and lived up to. The abuses of recent years, some of which the Glass banking bill would remove or correct, will certainly have fewer defenders after the wholesome publicity which has now set them in so vivid and startling a light.

While the *Times* suggested that further legislation was unnecessary to address those problems—presumably they still thought the integrity and honesty of bankers would be sufficient—by Friday afternoon, Wall Street knew what was coming. "The general impression in the financial district today," the *New York World-Telegram* reported, "was that the security affiliate of a banking institution will soon become a thing of the past." Affiliates, to columnists Drew Pearson and Robert Allen, "had become a festering sore in the financial structure of the country."[24]

It was just what Senator Carter Glass had tried to accomplish in his banking bill and, in all fairness, he deserved a good deal of the credit for uncovering Lehmann's obscure, twenty-year-old legal opinion. Carter Glass—the senator who, more than any other, consistently and vigorously denounced this kind of political theater—had disclosed the opinion nine months earlier. Indeed, in May 1932 Glass had been even more incendiary than Pecora, charging in a speech on the Senate floor that Wickersham and another unnamed Democratic attorney general suppressed the opinion, a stark demonstration, he said, of the "power and blandishment of inordinate wealth." Affiliates, Glass charged, were one of the greatest contributors to the Depression, and he urged his fellow senators to separate them from national banks. But as willing as Glass was to attack politicians on the Senate floor, he was unwilling to attack bankers in the hearing room. In his own banking reform hearings in 1931, Glass played down evidence of personal wrongdoing. He wanted a dispassionate analysis of the banking system, not a public pillorying of prominent financiers or financial institutions.[25]

Glass must have been a little chagrined about the success Pecora was having. He knew more about the banking system than Pecora ever would, and most of the same critique of securities affiliates had been made in Glass's earlier hearings. Pecora had the advantage of marvelous timing—the banking crisis created something of a teachable moment, a time when the entire country seemed to be talking about the banks. But his success was built on more than just good luck. Pecora was a far more effective teacher than the more knowledgeable Glass because he moved the analysis from the abstract to the particular. Pecora wasn't talking about what affiliates might do; he was talking about what this particular affiliate did. On one level it worked because Pecora was vilifying the National City Company—angry and frustrated Americans could now focus on a single individual and a single institution. But more than that, he was using Mitchell and National City as a device, a concrete example, one that was easier to grasp and much more immediate and powerful for everyone trying to come to grips with what was wrong with the banking system.

Glass may have been vexed at this neophyte's overwhelming success, but the astute politician knew how to seize a propitious moment. He lashed out at the Senate opponents who had first emasculated and then killed his banking bill. The disclosures, the senator said, provided concrete evidence of the need to reform the nation's banking laws. "These disclosures . . . prove conclusively the truth of what I said on the Senate floor four years ago—at the height of the boom—namely, that the Federal Reserve System was being used to aid the speculators rather than those for whom it was created." As his bill languished in the House, Glass again pressed for its passage. To him, it was "utterly incomprehensible" why the House, in light of all these new revelations, was continuing to do nothing.

His avowed hatred for sensational congressional hearings notwithstanding, Glass was apparently not above using the disclosures Pecora generated to achieve his own political aims. Indeed, he was not even averse to privately shaping those hearings to the extent he could so long as his own personal reputation for being above such crudities was not sullied. During the hearings the following Monday, one of Norbeck's staffers handed Pecora a note: "Reminding you of two questions to be asked of Mr. Mitchell at the suggestion of Senator Glass, whose connection is not to be disclosed."[26]

W eek one was over. It had been by turns riveting and dull, funny and dramatic, eye-opening and mundane. Pecora's performance was triumphant, although hardly flawless. He sometimes painted with too broad a brush. His ignorance about the finer details of Wall Street practice could be frustrating, and it occasionally led him astray. A few times he was flat-out wrong. Generations of critics trying to undermine the entire enterprise would latch onto those mistakes, but none of them mattered very much in the end because, while some of the details were not quite right, the overall picture was accurate.

The first four hearing days in Room 301 had become, according to the legendary journalist I. F. Stone, an "instrument of democratic education"; it had "turned the nation into a vast class in economics." Not rarefied economics with complex formulas and elegant graphs, but practical, real-world economics. After three years of depression, Americans had certainly developed doubts about the prudence, foresight, and high-mindedness of the rulers of the nation's financial markets. Pecora gave them proof—proof that the honesty and integrity of the financial establishment was inadequate—proof that laissez-faire didn't work. If

Wall Street could not or would not regulate itself, Washington would have to regulate for them. For his part, Pecora said that his work gave him "a feeling of pride, I hope pardonable pride, that I had been the means for bringing about this education of the public."[27]

Class would be back in session on Monday.

Chapter 12

DAYS FIVE AND SIX:
INTERMISSION

The economics lessons coming out of that Washington hearing room were resonating throughout the country, amplified and intensified by the ever worsening banking crisis. All week, states expanded the authority of their banking regulators to restrict withdrawals. The new statutes stoked the spreading banking panic as depositors rushed in to remove their money before the restrictions went into effect. Now even larger metropolitan banks were starting to feel the strain of heavy withdrawals. On Saturday, the Union Trust and Guardian Trust in Cleveland were inundated with panicked depositors, who by closing that day had managed to remove half their money from the beleaguered banks. The president of Cleveland Trust, Harris Creech, temporarily stemmed the panic at his bank with nothing more than impassioned rhetoric. Standing on the teller counter above the swirling mob, Creech implored the crowd to remain calm, telling them that the bank intended to honor all withdrawal requests.

Creech was apparently a persuasive speaker, because many customers, satisfied that the bank would not fail, walked away without withdrawing any money. Creech's promise, however, was short-lived. At an emergency meeting at midnight on Sunday, Cleveland's banking leaders agreed that when the banks reopened on Monday morning, they would limit withdrawals to 5 or 10 percent of deposits. Nearly every bank in the city, including Cleveland Trust, adhered to that restriction.

Reports from Detroit, where the bank holiday had now been in effect for eleven days, were grim; officials there had made absolutely no progress in their struggle to reopen the banks. Labor unrest had rocked Detroit a year earlier, and now Senator Couzens and the secretary of commerce, Roy Chapin, predicted that serious rioting might break out at any moment. While state officials had allowed very limited withdrawals to individual customers, there was little currency to be found anywhere. The city was bankrupt, nearly incapable of providing relief, and unemployment had been so bad for so long that starvation deaths in the city were an almost daily occurrence. "Cash for milk is scarce or not obtainable," Secretary Chapin, he too a former Detroit auto executive, wrote, "and I foresee by the first of the week the possibility of very serious disorders." Perishable food was rotting in railroad cars because there was no way to pay for it, and automobiles that had run out of gas were left abandoned in the streets.[1]

The Saturday morning newspapers made no one feel any more secure. Although editors everywhere had done everything they could to downplay the news of bank failures, hoping not to inflame fears even further, there was no way to suppress this story. Maryland's banks would be closed for the next three business days. Governor Albert Ritchie had been pleading for calm in radio address after radio address, but to no avail. It wasn't just the small depositors in the lines snaking through the streets of downtown Baltimore; many of the banks' largest customers, including the Baltimore and Ohio Railroad and the city and state governments, yanked all their money, further destabilizing the already wobbly financial institutions. A dozen Baltimore banks had no money at all. The moratorium, state officials said, was the only way to prevent the complete collapse of every bank in the city. Maryland was now the second state to declare an official bank holiday, and the closure of its banks virtually ensured that more states would follow.[2]

In Washington, Hoover and Mills were still trying to manage the crisis, but other governmental officials had all but given up. The Federal Reserve chairman, Eugene Meyer, hated going to the office and thought the efforts to prop up the banking sector futile. He was, his wife Agnes wrote, "too wise to try to conduct an earthquake." His colleagues at the Federal Reserve were far harsher; they said Meyer seemed "dazed," that he "had nothing to offer" in terms of solutions, and that he "acted like a whipped dog!" Meyer may not have known how to stop the crisis, but he was sure about what he thought of the testimony coming out of Room 301 that week. Mitchell, he concluded, had grievously injured the Federal Reserve System. That Saturday Meyer confided to a colleague that the previous June he had, without the board's knowledge, tried to have Mitchell removed as chairman of City Bank, an effort that obviously went nowhere.[3]

Agnes Meyer could see that Hoover was growing despondent, and she thought the dénouement appropriate for Hoover's failed presidency. "Hard on H to go out of office to the sound of crashing banks," she wrote in her diary that Saturday. "Like the tragic end of a tragic story. . . . Looking back it seems like nothing but blunder after blunder. He has been perversely and stubbornly wrong and short-sighted from start to finish."[4]

In the midst of the banking crisis—what Roosevelt had already called an "inferno"—some argued that the committee's decision to continue hearings was more than just pointless. Showing this kind of deep-seated wrongdoing at one of the nation's largest banks at a time when the banking system was in free fall amounted to pouring gasoline on the flames. The conservative *New York Evening Post* said that Congress had "done nothing to restore public confidence" and had "chosen the worst of all possible times to throw further doubt upon banks." Pecora and the committee had broken "the faith of the people in their financial leaders"; but even the *Post* concluded that the revelations "could not be ignored."[5]

The *Evening Post* wasn't alone in urging the committee to proceed with more caution than it had demonstrated in the first week; business leaders were also worried. The president of the Chicago and North Western Railway warned Norbeck that the investigation was leading to panic: "The disclosures to date are causing the rank and file out through this country to distrust all banks, the good along with the bad; hoarding is starting in again; withdrawals are becoming very heavy; the whole financial structure seems to be sitting on dynamite." Perhaps, he wrote Norbeck, it might be better to adjourn the hearings for a short time "to give people an opportunity to quiet down, and possibly relieve the situation."

It was not terribly surprising that business leaders were upset by what Pecora was doing in Washington, but less august citizens also urged restraint. A New Yorker named William Purnell told Norbeck that the disclosures were frightening the people, and would soon create outright panic. Purnell thought that the country had its hand "in the lion's mouth, we should be very cautious and not stick him or make him bite us before we get our hand out of his mouth." There would be, he thought, plenty of time later to "convict the criminals."[6]

Many agreed that the disclosures heightened public fear about the solidity of the banking sector, but thought it was better to reveal those problems than to cover them up. "Only with knowledge of what is being done," the *Washington Herald* editorialized, "can it be hoped that legislation will be devised which will lift the tone of prevailing business methods and make impossible the continuance or recurrence of such practices as are now being unfolded to us. Indeed, it is a period of tragic disillusionment through which we are now passing!" The disclosures, an editorial in another paper claimed, were "highly salutary. . . . The small depositor will get over his apprehension and cheer up—[a] better order and greater safety for depositors can come only through a wholesome purging." Norbeck heard that same view directly from his constituents as well. "Feel that your exposure of malpractice by banks is doing great good," one person wired him. "Must come sooner or later. Keep it up. To discontinue now would be unfair to public."[7]

To the extent that there were Mitchell defenders—and they were getting harder and harder to find—they took pains to point out that however unseemly the disclosures might appear to be, they were common, if not accepted, practices in the 1920s. James Paul Warburg, a member of the Warburg banking dynasty who worked closely with Roosevelt early in his administration, said that Mitchell and other bankers "made money hand over fist for themselves and did things which are now considered immoral, but which, in the days when they did them, were not uncommon. We were still living in pretty much the jungle rule in Wall Street."[8]

It was more than just a change in standards, however; the truth was that none of the acts that were causing so much anger were illegal. That was certainly true as far as City Bank's banking and securities-selling practices were concerned.

Affiliates were permissible under federal law, no federal laws required disclosures in securities offerings or prohibited participation in pools, and the bank had broken no laws in paying bonuses. Financing the affiliate's trading in the bank's stock skirted the line, but it too was probably technically permissible. Even Mitchell's tax sale may have been lawful. This kind of wash sale was apparently quite common at the time and, if it was shown that Mitchell acted in good faith, relying on the advice of his lawyer in structuring the transaction, he would not be criminally liable for tax evasion. Trying "to inflate such a charge to the heights of dastardliness," one financial newspaper noted, "is overdoing things in a fanatical sense."[9]

That defense, however, was really no defense at all. "The reason there are no laws against such things," *Business Week* explained, "is that no lawmaker ever imagined such laws might be necessary." Indeed, the magazine wondered "if the imagination of Congress ever can anticipate all of the queer things certain types of bankers can think of during the infection of a boom." From day one, Pecora said he was trying to provide a sound framework for necessary federal legislation. Doing that required the investigator to show just where current law was inadequate. "If some of the practices disclosed are not in violation of the law," the editors at the *Baltimore Sun* wrote, "then so much the worse for the respect in which law should be held. The country would like the practices and the law to be examined jointly. . . . The Senate's committee should plug away until the whole story is unfolded."[10]

The continuing furor over the City Bank testimony was fueled in part by Senator Burton Wheeler, who took his scathing attack on bankers from the Senate floor to the national radio waves. Mitchell and his colleagues, he said, "shocked the moral conscience of the entire nation." The investigation wasn't destroying public confidence, he argued, not for the long haul anyway. "[N]othing will restore confidence in our banking structure," Wheeler told his audience, "more promptly than demonstrated proof that we have a government that has the courage and integrity to prosecute with equal vigor these malefactors of great wealth as well as the humbler offenders." After the crash, Mitchell had been derided for his foolish optimism, but the week's revelations were more than simply an attack on his judgment. "An adventurous American people,"

Wheeler explained, "will not criticize too harshly mistakes of judgment, or even unwise speculation, but they will not condone the violation of a fiduciary trust. These men, trusted by their depositors, stockholders and investment clients, traded on that sacred confidence to their own profit and to the ruin of those who trusted them."[11]

The attention the City Bank hearings garnered was hardly surprising, what with Wheeler's continuing attacks and the week's dramatic revelations unfolding as they did against the backdrop of that ever worsening banking crisis. Room 301 had become the crucible in which the American economic system was being tested. "Capitalism," the editors at the St. Louis Star-Times wrote on Friday, "is on trial for its life." As compelling as that story line was, there was more to the media's fascination with the hearings. It was the man who was prosecuting capitalism. Reporters already were captivated by Pecora, who they viewed as simply "splendid." The first week of hearings, Newsweek wrote, was "four packed days of crackling testimony on the boom-time practices . . . pieced together by the Committee's sharp-witted counsel, Ferdinand Pecora." With a nod to the ongoing Japanese invasion of China, the Washington Herald remarked that "Mr. Ferdinand Pecora goes through the National City Bank like a Japanese tank through the Great Wall of China. How vulnerable the famous 'Wonders of the World' are, after all!"[12]

Americans have always loved a good underdog story, and reporters knew that this had the potential to be a great one. It was a story about class and ethnicity in the United States, a story about who wielded power in American society in the 1920s and about how that power was shifting right before everyone's eyes.

Part of the fascination was simple novelty. An Anglo-Saxon Protestant lawyer conducting the same examination as Pecora would not have been nearly so compelling. Nor would there be anything particularly unusual about a stellar performance by a Jewish lawyer. Although anti-Semitic views were likely far more durable at the time than anti-Italian ones, Jewish stereotypes tended to coincide with legal aptitude. There were plenty of precedents for outstanding Jewish lawyers. Samuel Untermyer, after all, had cross-examined Morgan twenty years earlier and remarkably, given Pecora's commanding performance, Untermyer continued to lobby to take over as committee counsel. On Saturday, he wired Norbeck claiming (inaccurately) that in those earlier hearings he had "uncovered" City Bank's affiliate and that he "repeatedly denounced [affiliates] as unlawful and dangerous and vainly sought to suppress them in their infancy." In a national radio speech, Untermyer delivered a "scathing indictment" of the Stock Exchange and the House of Morgan. It seems amazing to think that after that first week, Untermyer could have seriously believed he still had a shot at becoming counsel once the new Congress was in session, but Pecora was in fact far from assured of keeping his job. One Democratic member of the committee reportedly reached out to the incoming administration to tell them that if Roosevelt requested it, the committee would retain Untermyer.[13]

Other Jewish lawyers, like Max Steuer, had established nationwide reputations as courtroom magicians. Steuer was considered the greatest trial lawyer of the day, the man to call when you were really in trouble. He had just obtained convictions as a special prosecutor in the Bank of United States scandal, and that victory led Norbeck's staff to float his name as a potential replacement for Gray. Some columnists, in fact, were still spreading rumors that Steuer, who was looking to take on more public-oriented work now that he was near the end of his career, was interested in the job and would take it once the new Congress convened. A blockbuster performance by Steuer would have surprised almost no one, although there is little doubt that his appointment would have engendered a fair number of anti-Semitic letters to the committee. But who had ever heard of an Italian lawyer?[14]

Pecora's performance was surprising not only because there were so few Italian lawyers but because it played so strongly against the prevailing stereotype of Italian Americans as lazy, unintelligent, and ungovernable criminals. There was no shortage of irony in the public spectacle of a theoretically lawless Sicilian demonstrating the pervasive lawlessness and chicanery of the Anglo-Saxons who ruled the banks and investment houses. It was an irony that reporters were not shy about discussing explicitly. One called the lawyer a "Sicilian immigrant boy." Another remarked on the "primitive faunlike quality in this native of the Italian soil, brought face to face with many scions of the Anglo-Saxon socially [sic] elite." And when politicians as diverse as Montana's progressive senator Burton

Wheeler and President Hoover searched for an analogy to explain their outrage over Mitchell's behavior, they almost invariably invoked the symbol of Southern Italian lawlessness—Al Capone.

However ironic in the context of the Pecora-led hearings, the analogy was natural at the time. Capone was the criminal archetype of the day; for many he was the representative Italian American, and he was a rhetorical favorite of politicians and writers everywhere. One magazine said that Capone was a "bungler by comparison" to Mitchell. When, later that year, Hugh Johnson was promoting the National Recovery Act, he derided the businessmen who opposed it. "Al Capone," he told his audience, "was a poor ignorant Sicilian piker next to these rugged individualists who wanted to prolong the dark ages of human relationships." In reality, Capone was born in Brooklyn, the son of Neapolitan parents, but those facts hardly mattered. Johnson, no doubt, assumed Capone was from Sicily, just one more indication of the durability of the stereotype of Sicilian lawlessness.[15]

The ethnic role reversal brought glee to some, but engendered anger in quite a few others. An outraged citizen wrote to the committee: "In 'his country' that he brags so much about, this Sicilian peasant would be clapped in jail for the part he has played in undermining the price of peoples [sic] stocks. Why such scum is allowed among decent men shows the low hirelings who are paying him." When J. P. Morgan Jr. famously came before the committee in May and June 1933 he was publicly polite, but in private he excoriated Pecora as a "dirty little wop" and "2nd-rate criminal lawyer." Thomas Lamont, Morgan's partner and the real leader of the firm, complained that the hearings were just a "Spanish Inquisition" run by a "young native Sicilian counsel, Ferdinand Pecora." Even the senators weren't immune. Two of Carter Glass's former assistants at Treasury were Morgan partners, and Glass and Pecora had a very public and very heated row over the lawyer's tactics during those hearings. "Glass is a Virginia aristocrat," *Business Week* wrote about the spat, "though he lacks the tolerance and urbanity supposed to go with it. And this young Italian immigrant heckling the loved and revered partners of two of his best friends does not sit at all well with him."[16]

Ultimately, Pecora's masterful performance did little to purge those lingering stereotypes. While much of the press coverage of his work as counsel was complimentary, it remained laced with the stereotypes of the day. A *Barron's* profile of Pecora opened with the line "Ferdinand Pecora is a Sicilian who brought to American citizenship that dramatic instinct characteristic of the Latin race; but added to it in a somewhat larger measure than is frequent—a good brain." Untold articles described him as "swarthy." The *Boston Globe* noted that he had "all the vivacity of his race," and many others wrote about his "sunny" disposition, which, according to the *Christian Science Monitor*, did "not have any of the Anglo-Saxon somberness or severity." One commentator offered that his mixture of Sicilian birth and Protestant religion was "a good combination of potential vindictiveness and austerity."

Maybe it wasn't surprising that newspapers traded in those stereotypes, but Pecora couldn't even change the views of those who saw him up close. Even Pecora's former boss and good friend, Joab Banton, in an effusive article praising Pecora's legal abilities, treated Pecora as something of an anomaly. "Pecora," he wrote, "is a splendid example of the salutary effect of American life upon the artistic temperament of an Italian-born person." Norbeck never really got past his preconceptions of "Latins" as lackadaisical and unintelligent. Pecora had been putting in sixteen- to eighteen-hour days under brutal time pressures, but Norbeck still confided in a colleague that the lawyer was "a man who does not work in an orderly way in his office, but is very good in presenting things when he gets them thoroughly in his mind. . . . I knew he was phlegmatic and took life rather easy—that is apparent from his looks, considering his age." The stereotypes were simply too hard to shake in such a short time.[17]

Still, something transformational was clearly taking place in Room 301. One could almost feel the power and prestige slipping from the Anglo-Saxon financiers who dominated Wall Street.

Many in the Financial District were quite naturally angry, not at Mitchell and Baker, but at their accusers. Quite a few Wall Street denizens thought that the men had been handled too roughly and there was more than a little empathy for the fallen bankers. Many said, at least off the record, that they thought the Washington investigators made Mitchell the scapegoat for the crash and the Great Depression. It was a claim that would get repeated over the years by a host of Pecora's critics. But it wasn't Pecora who drew that causal link; the media had been critical of Mitchell's unalloyed optimism for years. And if anyone in Washington was scapegoating Mitchell, it wasn't Pecora. Senator Carter Glass, the man who took such pains to keep personal accusations out of his own hearings on banking reform, was the first to hurl that charge against Mitchell. "That man more than forty others," Glass charged shortly after the crash, "is responsible for the present situation."[18]

Pecora was certainly not shy about showing all the reckless, inappropriate, and imprudent actions that Mitchell and others at City Bank had taken, but he always treated Mitchell and his ilk as prime examples of what was wrong in commercial and investment banking, not as the single cause for the dire state of the economy. That was certainly the way that most commentators at the time understood the testimony. No one seemed to view the City Bank disclosures as isolated incidents that in and of themselves caused the crash or the Depression. Mitchell was not an aberration; he was representative of bankers as a class.

"This is a sample," the *Philadelphia Record* opined, "of the scruples exercised by the group that whooped up the stock market boom, diverted credit from legitimate business, exercised a controlling hand at Washington, and took the American people for the greatest buggy ride in their history during the last decade." Mitchell was emblematic, according to a St. Louis newspaper, of the "dominant type of American financial overlord. He is one of those upon whom the United States has relied for guidance, for ethical standards. He is one of the handful for whom our laws are written, by whom our institutions are moulded. He is an owner of America. What Mr. Mitchell has done, others have done." Mitchell's testimony condemned "the whole superstructure of American finance."

Pecora had shown that the problems in banking were not limited to smaller banks like the Bank of United States; they went right to the top of the banking structure. That tone at the top, some argued, was actually what caused the problems in the other financial institutions. Out in South Dakota, a paper called *Public Opinion* argued that Mitchell, "as the executive head of one of the greatest banks in the world, was presumed to be of that type of banker and financier in which the public might place absolute confidence. . . . When the greatest of the great was indulging in this sort of manipulation, it is small wonder that exaggerated and aggravated examples of the same scheming were undertaken by thousands of little fellows throughout the nation. The force of example is tremendous."[19]

Everywhere people were shocked at the portrait of Wall Street callousness, of bankers' grasping indifference to ethics. "There is the weakness of America," one paper lamented, "wealth without responsibility, wealth without duty, wealth without a heart-beat." And they were, to be sure, angry at Mitchell in particular. Heywood Broun found Mitchell's conduct particularly galling given the stern warnings the banker gave New York City about cutting its expenses if it wanted to borrow money to ease its financial crisis. "If I were a school teacher," he wrote that Saturday, "and my salary had been cut in order to meet the ideas of civic economy propounded by the big bankers of New York City, I would be a little sore as I read the testimony which is being given before the Senate investigating committee." But he too noted that the testimony had implications beyond Mitchell. "Until a few years ago a fiction went rounds [sic]. High finance, we were told, was an elaborate undertaking carried on by men wholly dedicated to the public weal. That myth has gone." It had been replaced by a more durable conception of Wall Street. The Street wasn't a place that provided capital to help build great companies and fund the American economy; it was a gambling den, and a rigged one at that. "It seems to me," Broun wrote, "that the only thing some of our great financial institutions overlooked during the years of the boom was the installation of a roulette wheel for the convenience of depositors. And, of course, it would have been a wheel with four zeros."[20]

Even the staid and Wall Street–friendly *Commercial & Financial Chronicle* found the City Bank disclosures "depressing." The "ready way in which millions of dollars were passed back and forth between the National City Bank and the National City Company during the period of the speculative craze reveals banking practices which cannot be considered conducive to sound and safe management." The disclosure of Mitchell's wash sale when combined with his enormous bonuses did "not look well taking the most tolerant view of the matter." For a paper that wrote about nothing but the financial community and that had constantly criticized the hearings, it was quite a rebuke, and it reflected a broader outrage that boded well for legislative reform. "Because now also," one young lawyer wrote, "conservative elements are lined up against the bankers: every industrialist whose program for development was retarded by lack of credit facilities; every rentier to whom the National City Co. sold sour bonds; every professional man who lost his shirt in the market; every diehard who took a trimming (& most of them did) will be solidly lined up against the 'money power.'"[21]

Savvier observers saw past the pervading anger. The problem they thought was not so much the scruples of these particular bankers as the ability of anybody to wield so much power with nary a regulatory check. "I don't think I have any animus against Mitchell," the Roosevelt intimate and future Supreme Court justice Felix Frankfurter wrote to Walter Lippmann, probably the most influential columnist of his day. Writing with Roosevelt's approval, Frankfurter, who would go on to a role as a behind-the-scenes architect of New Deal legislation, assured the conservative columnist that he did

> not believe that vice inheres in the rich and virtue in the poor. But for too long we have been largely operating on the assumption that the converse is the truth, and more particularly that the rich are the guardians of wisdom and should control affairs. . . . The crux of the business is not the wickedness of the Mitchells but the power which is wielded by concentration of financial power which they are wholly unworthy—no matter who they are—to wield because of the obfuscations and the arrogances which power almost invariably generates.

A few months later, commenting on the Morgan hearings, Lippmann, who usually toed the Wall Street party line, said much the same thing. "No set of men," he told his readers, "however honorable they may be, and however good their traditions, can be trusted with so much private power."[22]

Roosevelt had to that point only vaguely and indirectly come out in favor of continuing the hearings, but Frankfurter's letter confirms what the public already seemed to think. Pecora was a harbinger for the incoming administration, a signal that power was indeed shifting from the canyons of Lower Manhattan to the corridors of Washington. Although the hearings did not yet bear the new president's imprimatur, Pecora the New Yorker was certainly part of the urban immigrant coalition that had helped bring his party into power. Agnes Meyer saw the same thing when she came to the Morgan hearings a few months later, and something more as well. She was impressed with Pecora, who was "very controlled, patient, sure of his goal." And she chided the Washington elite who tried to discount the significance of the investigation. "The very aspect of this Italo-American immigrant putting J. P. Morgan [Jr.] through his paces has a new American note that

papers seem to overlook. . . . Washington is modern America in essence. The new
stock showing up the hollowness of the old stock." One reporter, Thomas L.
Stokes, thought the "leveling process was never better exemplified."[23]

Norbeck couldn't have been happier. After a year of largely unremitting
criticism, after the personal attacks from Wall Street, and after his lonely
battle to keep the investigation going, he was "immensely gratified" about the
reaction the hearings were finally getting. On Saturday, it became absolutely
certain that the investigation and the leveling process would continue past March
4, 1933. On Friday, just before heading back to New York for the weekend,
Pecora emphasized that because of the severe time constraints under which he
was operating, he would have to limit his questioning to "the main highway of
Wall Street irregularities without going down any of the side streets." The public,
in light of everything that had come out that week, was certainly not going to be
satisfied with that kind of cursory inquiry. Pecora, like Untermyer, knew how to
work the press to his advantage.

Earlier in the week, Senator Edward Costigan, a Colorado Democrat,
introduced a resolution to continue the investigation into the next session
of Congress. Now Senator Duncan Fletcher, the man who, with Roosevelt's
encouragement, would assume control of the committee in the new Congress,
introduced a similar resolution. Resolutions like these are routine under ordinary circumstances. Given the public outcry over the City Bank hearings and
Roosevelt's tacit approval for their continuation, there was no way they would
fail. On Monday morning, before the Senate's formal vote had even taken place,
the committee met in executive session with Pecora to plan its strategy for the
new congressional session.[24]

Mitchell's fall had been nothing short of spectacular. A week earlier he had
been the undisputed leader of City Bank and among the most prominent
figures in the financial community. Now his reputation was in tatters. *Time*
magazine's headline said it all: "The Damnation of Mitchell."

It was a titanic scandal, one that had finally touched the upper echelons of Wall Street, the boardrooms and offices of the men who had largely set financial policy for the nation. A member of the club that ruled the Street was now the subject of a federal criminal investigation. No bank executive, even "the greatest bond salesman who ever lived," could weather that kind of storm. Mitchell did what the banker's code required; he tendered his resignation, as did Hugh Baker. Mitchell's letter to the bank's board was hardly conciliatory. He wrote that his offer to resign was prompted, not by his own inappropriate behavior, but by the "public misunderstanding" of his testimony before "ex-parte hearings." Mitchell's letter downplayed the significance of the disclosures that week and tried to discount the connection that nearly everyone had made between the boom of the 1920s and the Depression. His testimony involved "a period which has passed into history . . . and [which] had little relation to the conditions of the present day." Nonetheless, he did what he thought a gentleman should do: "I personally have been brought under a cloud of criticism from which I conceive that the institution should not be permitted to suffer by my continuance in office." There was no contrition, no recognition that he had done anything wrong, and certainly no apology. It was no wonder that one paper accused Mitchell of "moral obtuseness."[25]

Right after the crash, Percy Rockefeller had ridiculed the notion that Mitchell should resign from the bank, but no one was jumping to Mitchell's defense now. Still the board hesitated, worried that accepting the resignation might further erode already weakening customer confidence in the bank. City Bank's directors reached out to both the current and incoming administrations for advice about what to do with Mitchell, and for once Hoover and Roosevelt found something on which they could agree.

Neither the outgoing nor the incoming president shared Mitchell's surprise or the directors' trepidation. Hoover thought that accepting Mitchell's resignation would almost certainly increase customer confidence in City Bank, not destroy it, as the directors feared. The conduit to the president-elect was William Woodin, the Treasury secretary designate who had sat on the board of the New York Federal Reserve with Mitchell. Roosevelt told Woodin that it was patently obvious that Mitchell should resign immediately and he was surprised that the bankers could even ask the question. Roosevelt had been imbued from an early age with the idea that the well-off had a duty to serve the less fortunate and he was contemptuous of "the grasping speculator." The City Bank scandal had also hit close to home for the incoming president, who had a long personal banking relationship there, and he felt personally aggrieved by the "scandalous" outsize bonuses. "My gosh," he said shortly after he took office, "I feel Charlie took my money." Nor was he sympathetic to the claim that Pecora's investigation was destroying public confidence in the financial sector. "The bankers should have thought of that," he observed, "when they did the things that are now being exposed."

Roosevelt would eventually grow weary of the attacks he received from business leaders as the New Deal progressed. Just a few years into his first term, he lashed out at them, complaining in private that businessmen "were generally very stupid." Their core problem, he concluded, was that they, like the New York newspaper editors, lacked any sense of "moral indignation" about the sins of their colleagues. "Did they denounce Charles Mitchell?" he asked in frustration. "They did not!"

The seeds for Roosevelt's ultimate verdict on the business and banking communities were apparently nurtured that February day in 1933 when he advised Woodin that the bank should accept Mitchell's resignation. After hanging up, the president-elect shook his head in disbelief at the board's hesitation and remarked privately to his aides: "These New York bankers haven't any more notion of public psychology than a chicken."[26]

At midnight on Sunday, Pecora was working in his room at the Hotel Continental trying to prepare for the next day's hearings when the phone rang. It was Guy Cary, the Shearman lawyer and City Bank director. The City Bank board had accepted Mitchell's resignation a half hour earlier, Cary told Pecora. In truth, the board would not meet until the following morning, but after the feedback from Hoover and Roosevelt, acceptance of Mitchell's resignation was a foregone conclusion. Indeed, the next morning's meeting lasted all of ten minutes. James H. Perkins, the president of City Bank's trust affiliate and "an old time banker," would be taking over for Mitchell. It was clear that Perkins had his work cut out for him in trying to restore the bank's now sullied reputation, although he had one important qualification that would help him right the bank and which likely weighed heavily with the City Bank board—he was a personal friend of the president-elect. Even with that link to the new president, "nobody could possibly envy James H. Perkins," the *Nation* wrote. "There has been dumped upon him a mess which was once a great banking institution."

For Perkins, the cleanup started with a significant retrenchment of the bank's mission. Gone was talk of a financial department store and an investment banking powerhouse; his plan was "to conduct things in the most conservative way possible." The bank's primary business, he immediately announced, "is to serve the domestic and foreign commerce and industry of the United States in the field of commercial banking." Perkins was not quite ready to pull the plug on the securities affiliate, but his comments forecast that the National City Company was not long for the world. Pending "legislative determination of the status of securities affiliates, the bank's policy would be to confine the company's activities to government, State, municipal and corporate bonds of the highest character." That conservative note was telling. Pecora had made much of the affiliate's inappropriate trading of the bank's stock. Perkins's statement, however, was more far-reaching. By focusing on the character of the securities the affiliate would underwrite in the future, it seemed to imply that many of its past offerings were unsound. It was a point that neither Mitchell nor Baker had been willing to concede. Both insisted that the staff at the affiliate vigorously reviewed all proposed securities offerings to ensure that they were suitable for investment. With all the ground Pecora had to cover that first week, it was a point that he had not yet probed in detail.[27]

On Sunday Cary did what he could to contain that mess. He ended his phone call with a brief assumption, perhaps hoping to catch Pecora in the shock of the news the investigator had just heard.

"Of course, Mr. Pecora," Cary said, "under the circumstances it won't be necessary for Mr. Mitchell to resume the stand."

"Oh, why do you assume that?" Pecora quickly replied.

Cary argued that there was no more need for Mitchell to testify because he was no longer connected with either the bank or the company. Cary seemed to be suggesting that this was simply about the senators getting a scalp, a sentiment that was echoed in the popular press. "The U.S. Senators got their man," read the caption under one picture of Mitchell that week. Pecora, however, still believed that the hearings were about legislation, not trophies.

"I don't see that that makes any difference at all," Pecora responded. "Let me suggest to you, Mr. Cary, this investigation is not a head hunting expedition; it's a fact-finding expedition. I want to continue to examine Mr. Mitchell to get all the facts I can presented to the committee, consistent with the committee's authority to make an inquiry. Of course, he'll have to resume the stand. . . . I shall look for him tomorrow morning."[28]

Chapter 13

DAY SEVEN: SOUTH OF THE BORDER

The reaction to the news of Mitchell's and Baker's resignations was strangely expectant. At the end of the previous week's testimony, some columnists were already calling for resignations, so when they were officially announced on Monday, they seemed inevitable. "No banking institution," one paper wrote, "not even the next to the largest in the world, could afford even to appear to approve or condone the transactions of which [Mitchell] was the guiding spirit and one of the beneficiaries." The two men were simply paying the requisite and necessary "penalty for mixing the banking business with a stock promotion affiliate." The committee, too, "appeared entirely unmoved" by the news. Pecora refused to be blamed for the "public misunderstanding" Mitchell charged in his resignation letter, explaining, as he did the previous week, that Mitchell had every opportunity to clarify his testimony if he thought anything was misleading.[1]

The high-profile resignations, however, did nothing to slake the public's thirst for change. Oswald Garrison Villard, the publisher of the left-leaning *Nation* and a City Bank shareholder, demanded Rentschler's resignation as well as the resignation "of all directors who knew and countenanced" the bank's and the affiliate's inappropriate activities. But for many even those personnel changes were not enough. Heywood Broun thought that the Banking and Currency Committee had merely won the first "skirmish." An avowed socialist, Broun thought the federal government ought to take over the banking industry entirely. To his way of thinking, with all the Reconstruction Finance Corporation had done to prop up banks, "Washington was already knee-deep in banking." It was a state of affairs Broun sarcastically blamed on "the distress cries of the rugged individualists" who ran the banking system and who pleaded, "Save us or we perish!"

Others, not willing to advocate for governmental control of banking, still thought that Congress should not be satisfied with these high-profile scalps. "More than a change in personnel is needed to restore faith in a bank with such widespread ramifications and power," read a *Philadelphia Record* editorial. "Investigation and prosecutions, new legislation to outlaw securities affiliates and regulate banking more strictly, are called for." Although federal legislation, especially the moribund Glass banking bill, now seemed imminent, some were still warning of the limits of federal legislation to cure the problems Pecora revealed. The editorial sections of the New York papers, in particular, had finally weighed in on the investigation. The *New York Times* sent a mixed message about Mitchell, castigating him for flagrantly violating sound banking methods but praising him for the "loyalty" to the bank that "impelled him to step out." But the editors there still expressed a healthy dose of skepticism about the utility of federal legislation:

Even the best [legislation], however, will require men of the highest ability and utmost probity to manage it successfully. This, after all, is the chief moral to be drawn from the imprudence and irregularities which have been spread before the country by the Senate investigation, and have had so disturbing and unsettling an effect. Capable and conservative bankers can make even a bad system work, but if the established rules of sound banking practice are forgotten or openly violated, if deposits are not regarded as a sacred trust but as material for reckless speculation, if personal motives and a rush to get rich animate the management, there is no safety for anybody, and banks will fall

into merited disrepute and distrust. . . . Frozen assets are not the greatest
handicap of the banks. What is hurting them most is frozen confidence.[2]

D espite Pecora's insistence that Mitchell be present in Washington on Monday morning, the banker was never called to the witness stand that day.
There was no hint of contrition in Mitchell's resignation letter, but Pecora
thought he saw a change in the man who was now sitting in Room 301. Both he
and Baker looked "discomfited" and "chastened." When he first took the job as
president of City Bank, Mitchell wrote that he was "fully mindful of the quasi-
public position which The National City Bank must hold." Whether he believed
it or not when he made this statement, he clearly had not lived up to the standards the sentiment implied. "I think," Pecora recalled, "they were very much
ashamed of the record of their institutions and of their participation in those
happenings. And I think they had good reason to feel that way."[3]

Mitchell may have been planted in the spectators' row, but his policies
were clearly still on trial. Pecora was now ready to challenge the claim to which
Mitchell and Baker had so tenaciously clung in their first week of testimony, the
claim that the affiliate only "manufactured" securities that were "safe and proper"
for investors. And to test that claim, Pecora chose his example carefully. He
picked an offering that was synonymous at the time with worthless securities.
He picked Peruvian bonds, which he regarded as a "spectacular" example of
National City's "disregard of elementary fair play to investors."[4]

Spectacular it may have been, but the testimony on Monday proved to be
anticlimactic, not only because of the high-profile resignations but because
Pecora was treading on familiar ground. A year earlier, the Senate Finance Committee held hearings on foreign bond sales, and the picture that emerged was
not pretty. In fact, Hiram Johnson, chairman of the committee, called it "grotesque and tragic." American investment banks sold billions of foreign bonds
in the 1920s, quickly turning the United States into the world's largest creditor
nation. The vast majority of those bonds plummeted in value with the onset
of the Depression. Some of the worst were the Peruvian bonds, which, after a

revolutionary coup in Peru in August 1930 and a subsequent default, were currently selling for pennies on the dollar.

The Finance Committee investigation was, however, sparked by more than
poor performance. Senator Johnson wanted to explore the government's role in
those bond sales, which every administration since Harding had been urging
investment bankers to make. One of the biggest boosters of foreign investment
was Harding's commerce secretary, Herbert Hoover. Under his direction, the
Commerce Department conducted an extensive program to educate Americans
about the value, as well as the pitfalls, of investing in foreign securities. He urged
bankers to sponsor safe and productive loans that would "bless both the borrower
and the lender."

While Hoover didn't want foreign loans to come directly from the United
States Treasury, he wanted the government to do more than simply provide
educational announcements. Hoover, the man who thought regulating the New
York Stock Exchange was probably unconstitutional, wanted the government
to adopt strict guidelines on what loans could and could not be made. The
business-friendly administration balked at that heavy-handed approach. As a
compromise, the State Department began to informally sign off on foreign loans
before they were made. It wasn't technically approving the bonds, but investment banks made sure to heavily play up the government's involvement as they
tried to sell them. The practice led many customers to believe that the government was vouching for the safety of those bonds, when in fact it wasn't. The
State Department wouldn't object to a loan, one official admitted, even if it "was
absolutely rotten."[5]

Given all the federal encouragement, Mitchell, not surprisingly, told the
Finance Committee that City Bank thought it was the firm's patriotic duty to
participate in these foreign loans. "Many of us," he said, "found a real inspiration
in the fact that in the issuance of this large volume of foreign loans we were
playing a part in the development of American trade and industry. That is our
first motive always." Those high-minded sentiments notwithstanding, underwriting foreign bonds during the halcyon 1920s was one of the biggest drivers of
National City's growth. In fact, participating in foreign loans not only enhanced
a firm's prestige, it earned the bank unusually fat fees and commissions. Both
factors prompted investment banks to fight tooth and nail to win this lucrative

business. Foreign governments were not, in many cases, begging for loans; instead they "were actually besieged by those bankers until they accepted loans." With its far-flung foreign branches, City Bank was in a unique position to capture a good deal of this business, eventually participating in about one-third of all foreign bond offerings. Other investment banks were hardly ready to throw in the towel. One firm paid the son of the president of Peru over $400,000 for his help in winning the right to sell some of the country's bonds. The investment banks politely called the payments "commissions" and said that they were "quite customary" for South American loans.[6]

Thomas Lamont, the J.P. Morgan managing partner, didn't mention City Bank by name, but it was quite clear who he meant when in the late 1920s he rebuked "American banks and firms competing on an almost violent scale" to sell foreign bonds. American investors, he warned, needed to be more circumspect about these bonds. It was an easy thing for Lamont to say; after all Morgan was the most prestigious investment banking firm in the world and could afford to be exceedingly picky in whom it chose to underwrite. City Bank was fighting for what was left, and with the large overhead from its retail sales staff, it was important to keep the pipeline full of new offerings. Lamont's warning, however, was not the only one; others warned average investors away from all foreign offerings, which as a class they considered simply too risky. Despite the warnings, National City went right on selling them and its customers went right on buying them. The company told investors not to worry. As its advertising repeatedly emphasized, the company "buys and offers to investors only such securities as it can recommend after thorough investigation."[7]

If that was the case, how had the bonds failed so spectacularly? Senator Johnson thought it was a massive fraud. The bankers knew or should have known, he claimed, that the securities were worthless and that they were bound to default. The bankers, of course, argued otherwise. No one could possibly expect investment bankers to be prescient. Even the most diligent investigation might prove to be inadequate in hindsight, particularly where there had been a worldwide economic catastrophe like the Great Depression, which might cause even the safest issuers to default. The bankers had a point. To show the kind of fraudulent conspiracy Johnson charged would require more than showing that a bond turned out to be a bad investment. Johnson would have to show that the investment banks were in possession of information before they sponsored the offerings from which they could determine the bonds were bound to fail. That hypothesis seemed far-fetched, massively overestimating both Wall Street's cupidity and its foresight. With Baker, the now former president of National City, back in the witness chair, Pecora seemed bent on demonstrating that the fraud existed.

As he did the week before, Pecora eased into the subject, asking Baker about how the executives of the affiliate evaluated proposed securities offerings. The procedure was the same for foreign bond offerings as for any corporate security. The vice president in charge of a particular field made "an intensive study of economic and political conditions" in which he "tried to determine every important factor connected with that proposed loan." The affiliate would not offer the securities unless the executives unanimously agreed to do so. In the abstract, the process sounded quite rigorous.

Pecora's investigators had carefully pored over these bond offerings, and all morning, he now read into the record a series of the affiliate's internal memoranda. They all seemed to reach precisely the same conclusion—it would be foolhardy to lend the affiliate's good reputation to any Peruvian bond offerings. In the five years before the offering, the affiliate's own South American experts reported that the Peruvian government's finances were "positively distressing." The "government treasury," one report noted, "was flat on its back and gasping for breath." It was unclear "how the government can continue functioning on the basis of its present income." The president of the country was, despite the early reports of bribes, thought to be honest, but he was surrounded by "rascals."

At first, those assessments led National City to decline to participate in any Peruvian bond offerings. The history of Peruvian credit was too shaky; it had "been careless in the fulfillment of contractual obligations" and had defaulted on loans in the past. The political situation was too uncertain. All in all, the "moral risk was not satisfactory." Was there anything, Pecora asked, in these reports that made Peru sound like a good candidate for a bond offering?

"It was not particularly enthusiastic, certainly," Baker granted.[8]

After an improvement in the Peruvian economy, however, National City suddenly decided to offer the country's bonds to its customers, for which the affiliate earned a nice underwriting spread. Was this the fraud Senator Johnson alleged? Pecora wanted it to be and the press thought that "investors seemed destined to take tremendous losses." Didn't the company know these securities were bound to fail? Hadn't they said that Peruvian bonds represented an adverse moral risk?

In truth the fraud didn't seem to be there. People have a remarkable capacity for self-delusion, particularly when those delusions are congruent with their own financial interest. It seemed that the analysts at the company had deluded themselves about the safety and security of Peruvian bonds. With an ever rising market, the lure of fat underwriting commissions, and Mitchell's constant hectoring to keep the pipeline full of new issues, executives at the affiliate were willing to believe that short-term improvements swamped long-term dangers. They were willing, despite Peru's long history of political instability and debt defaults, to believe that this time things were different. "[A]s the great bull market grew greater and greater," Pecora wrote, "as the careless 'New Era' psychology grew more and more pervasive, National City suddenly found nebulous reasons to justify a complete change of attitude."[9]

It was a point that Victor Schoepperle, one of the company's youthful South American experts, would make quite explicitly when he took the stand that afternoon. Just as he had with Baker, Pecora ran Schoepperle through the litany of adverse information in the affiliate's files. Subsequent events, Schoepperle conceded, showed that his earlier assessment that the company should not participate in Peruvian loans was right. He tried, nonetheless, to excuse the optimism that led him to recommend participation as a by-product of those heady days in the late 1920s. "I thought," he said, "like a great many others, that I was in a new era, and I made an honest mistake in judgment." When Pecora pointed out that Schoepperle had seen just as many cons as pros, the banker's only response was that it "was an optimistic era in which optimistic interpretations were put on any situation where the pros were about equal to the cons." And, he might have added, where there was a chance to earn some underwriting fees.[10]

In early 1927, National City participated in its first offering of $15 million of Peruvian bonds, which it very quickly sold. If there was any hesitancy in the buying public, the company's salesmen quickly assuaged it. "Gracious alive," one salesman told a hesitating customer, "we don't lose money for people—we make money for them." Accompanying the offering was a brief prospectus describing the bonds, and Pecora turned from the company's internal documents to what it actually told investors. He was laying the groundwork for the securities legislation that would be offered in the new Congress. His questions fit precisely with Roosevelt's campaign promises to require increased publicity before securities could be marketed to the public.[11]

"Do you find any mention in [the prospectus] whatsoever," he asked Baker, "of the bad credit record of Peru which is embodied in the information I have read into the record from your files?"

"No; I do not see anything."

"No statement or information," Pecora reiterated, "was given to the American investing public . . . concerning the bad debt record of Peru and its being a bad moral and political risk?"

"No, sir," Baker demurely responded.

The company's ads painted a radically different picture. "When you buy a bond recommended by The National City Company," one touted, "you may be sure that all the essential facts which justify the Company's own confidence in that investment are readily available to you." Pecora wanted to know whether Baker knew any reason why this information wasn't conveyed to investors. Baker had no answer. "Do you think it was fair," Pecora then asked, "to the investing public to withhold from it knowledge which the participating bankers had of this issue when they offered it to the public?" Baker seemed to think that, regardless of what the ads said, the affiliate's decision to offer the bonds was all that customers really needed to know.

"You think it was fair to the public to withhold the information which you had or your company had," Pecora asked, "merely because somebody in your company reached the conclusion that the loan would be a sound loan?"

For Baker that was indeed enough: "I think it was fair to present the facts as they existed."

"The facts as they existed included this bad-debt record, did they not?"

Baker quibbled: "I am speaking about the facts that were then currently existing."

"You mean you think it was fair to present a conclusion based upon facts which could not have been more than a year old as against a bad-debt record for many, many years prior thereto?"

Baker finally conceded that "it would have been better if the whole story perhaps were included." Even he now seemed to realize that the affiliate couldn't offer bonds and simply tell investors, "Trust us. If they are good enough for us to offer, they are good enough for you to buy."[12]

The ease of that first sale, Pecora argued, only whetted the company's appetite for more fees (it ultimately netted about $100 million in today's dollars). Here was a ready way to satisfy Mitchell's constant demands that the company manufacture more securities to help cover the costs of its vast retail network. National City kept right on offering Peruvian bonds in 1927 and 1928, even though one of its own South American experts continued to conclude that he had "no great faith in any material betterment of Peru's economic condition in the near future." The political situation, he wrote, was "equally uncertain," with "revolution" a distinct possibility. Would the public have purchased these bonds, Pecora asked, if that information had been included in the bond prospectus? "I doubt if they would," Baker replied.

The company, Pecora showed, didn't even take responsibility for the limited information it did choose to provide investors, and here too Pecora seemed to be laying the basis for the securities legislation that Roosevelt would propose when he took office. Each of the National City Company's prospectuses had for years carried the same disclaimer: "The above statements are based on information received partly by cable from official and other sources. While not guaranteed, we believe them to be reliable, but they are in no event to be construed as representations by us." National City, it seemed, was perfectly happy to collect the fees, but it didn't think it should be on the hook for anything it told or failed to tell investors.[13]

Throughout the day's testimony, Baker was no more cooperative than he had been the previous week. In fact, his public humiliation seemed to make him worse. At one point, Pecora asked the former president about the meaning of a statement issued by an industry group to which he belonged, the Investment Bankers Association, and by his response, it appeared that Baker was denying any ability to comprehend the English language. The professor who wrote the report said he was not at liberty to express his own personal opinions because he was acting as a representative of the IBA. Pecora then asked Baker whether he agreed "with the implications of this statement."

"Well," Baker hesitantly replied, "that depends upon what they are."

Pecora was so surprised at this response that he gave Baker another chance: "Suppose you read them again and see what meaning you attach to them."

"I read it," Baker insisted, "and I told you I don't know what he means."

The two men went back and forth in that manner for some time until an exasperated Pecora finally asked a question that he thought Baker could answer: "And those words are meaningless to you?"

"Well, they are meaningless if you ask me to interpret what was in his mind when he wrote it. I cannot do that."

"Do you think the English used there is so involved that the author did not make himself clear?"

Baker claimed that he didn't know what Pecora was asking him, leading the now thoroughly frustrated lawyer to reply: "I am trying to find out if you attach any meaning at all to that sentence, or if those words are merely a meaningless jumble to you."

"Well," Baker responded, "they do not seem to particularly convey anything to me. I don't know what they mean." Now in his second week facing Pecora, Baker—a man who had once commanded an army of salesmen, a vast, international securities-selling network—was so afraid of this little lawyer from New York he could hardly speak.[14]

The day was filled not only with an inability to grasp the English language, but also with the same kind of casual prejudice that was being directed at Pecora. One of the company's analyses posited that a factor "that will long retard the economic importance of Peru" was its native population of "Indians, two-thirds of whom reside east of the Andes, and a majority [of whom] consume almost no manufactured products." Pecora wanted to know whether, when National City began to offer the country's bonds, the Indian population had changed. To general laughter, Schoepperle remarked, "I imagine it had increased."

"I hope no personal consideration enters into that?" Pecora joked.

"No, I hope you'll admit I had nothing to do with that," Schoepperle replied.

Schoepperle went on to explain: "The state of prosperity of any Indian population is always rather low, because, as you know, they do not hang onto anything very long."

It was some evidence of the ethnic undercurrents in the hearing room— the clash between the olive-skinned Italian American prosecutor and the Anglo-Saxon bankers—that Pecora got a huge laugh when he replied: "Why do you say I know? I am not an Indian."

After the laughter subsided, Schoepperle continued to explain the "notorious" consumption habits of the indigenous Peruvians. Although, he said, there "were some very fine elements" in Peru, he concluded that "a population of that sort is not an especially good moral risk, looking at it from a broad point of view."[15]

The ease with which the two men casually dismissed an entire population is jarring to modern ears, just as jarring in fact as the reporters' comments about Pecora possessing the dramatic instincts of his race or having an unusually good brain for an Italian. Equally shocking are pictures of Pecora from the same time period in black face, performing in minstrel shows. He appeared in his first minstrel performance as a child at St. Peter's and he continued those performances well into the 1930s.

But Pecora was not a racist, at least not by the conventions of the day. *Amos 'n' Andy* (in which two white performers played stereotypical black characters) remained among the most popular radio shows on the air in the 1930s and white performers like Eddie Cantor, Fred Astaire, Judy Garland, and Bing Crosby appeared in blackface into the early 1940s. The truth was that Pecora's own upbringing and his own struggles to overcome Italian American stereotypes had made him unusually sensitive to racial injustices. During World War II, he was chairman of the Legion for American Unity, an organization of naturalized and first-generation Americans who spoke out against racial discrimination and mistrust. "The social snob," he said at that time, "amuses me; the intellectual snob bores me; the racial snob enrages me." His denunciations of racism in the 1940s were hardly novel; he had been publicly denouncing racial prejudice for a decade. Throughout his legal career, he seemed to exhibit little personal prejudice. As a neophyte prosecutor he had gone out of his way to undo the wrongful prosecution of the young Malcolm Wright. The staff he hired for the Senate hearings was a cross-section of many of New York's immigrant communities.[16]

To some, Monday's testimony was anticlimactic, but Pecora professed to be more shocked by these disclosures than anything else in the City Bank testimony. "There was a callous disregard," he recalled some thirty years later, "of the truth when they offered these bonds to the American investor, a complete and callous disregard of it, that even as I reflect on it now continues to shock me."

The senators were mostly quiet on Monday; they seemed to have realized that it was better to simply stay out of the way and let Pecora handle the hearings. The committee members, however, shared his shock and made frequent off-the-record comments that this behavior had to be stopped. In fact, one committee member confided that his own bank had "been misled into buying these Peruvian bonds." If Pecora was trying to create a climate in which reform legislation could pass, he certainly seemed to have succeeded. "I venture to say," Pecora went on, "that without being confronted with this record, you never dreamt that such low ethics, to use a charitable term, would be displayed by important investment banking houses in their dealings with the American investment public."[17]

Former customers of the company echoed those conclusions. Chauncey Overfield of Salt Lake City purchased some of the Peruvian bonds and he praised Pecora's "skilled examination." Overfield bought the bonds because he had "confidence in the integrity of the once high standing National City Bank." He thanked Pecora for all that he had done and was sure that his own expression of gratitude would be "voiced by thousands of others who have been duped in the same manner as I have been duped."[18]

The liberal media shared Pecora's outrage, which of course only increased the pressure for reform legislation. "As a journalist of twenty-six years' experience," Oswald Garrison Villard wrote in the Nation, "I have never recorded any wrongdoing of the representatives of banks, insurance companies and other large corporations that has seemed to me more outrageous than the facts revealed . . .

on the witness stand." Villard, not surprisingly, bought wholeheartedly into the need for federal legislation. "In England corresponding misrepresentations would mean jail for the banking sponsors. But in this country the investor will have to content himself with their expressions of regret and confessions of 'honest error'—after exposure." Even the conservative press was disturbed. They never quite called for legislation, but they concluded that the disclosures required condemnation and punishment "if bankers as a class are to avoid designation by a bitterly cynical word occasionally heard last week, 'banksters.'"[19]

It didn't seem possible, but by the end of the day on Monday, the banking system had grown even more precarious. Pennsylvania and Indiana authorized banks to restrict withdrawals. Banks in nearly twenty Indiana cities and towns immediately did so; now depositors could withdraw only 5 percent of their deposits. With the limitations imposed over the weekend in Ohio, depositors rushed to the banks to get what little money they could. "All day in the Union National Bank bedlam reigned, with hundreds in line clamoring for money," a lawyer watching the scene in Youngstown wrote. "There was no violence but I saw one woman faint." As in any economic calamity, some people sensed a profit-making opportunity and swooped in to take advantage of it. With the onset of the banking crisis, a lively secondary market developed for savings account passbooks. Speculators bought the passbooks from desperate account holders for seventy-five, or fifty, or even twenty-five cents on the dollar—the price contingent on how desperate the depositor was and how unlikely it was that the bank would ever reopen. Ohio newspapers listed passbook quotations right next to the ever falling stock and bond prices.

The week before, Treasury officials were alarmed when tens of millions in aggregate flowed out of the banks each day. On Monday, nearly $200 million came out of circulation, a figure that was matched or exceeded each day over the next three days. Some banks were so beleaguered that they demanded that Washington send money by airplane to prevent their imminent collapse.[20]

In that first week of hearings William Woodin told Roosevelt that the bankers were "hysterical." On Monday, the incoming president saw it for himself. He received a panicky letter from Morgan partner Thomas Lamont, urging him to cooperate with Hoover to quell the banking crisis, which was "far more critical than I had dreamed. I believe in all seriousness that the emergency could not be greater." Lamont begged Roosevelt to consider the human cost of the crisis and he hinted that American civilization and American government might not survive the strain. "It is impossible to contemplate the extent of human suffering, and the social consequences of a denial of currency and credit to our urban populations. Urban populations cannot do without money. It would be like cutting off a city's water supply. Pestilence and famine would follow; with what consequences who can tell?"

It was not enough; even with the leaders of Wall Street predicting the imminent collapse of society, Roosevelt refused to act until he actually held the reins of power. Besides, Roosevelt saw Lamont's missive not as an urgent request to save society, but as a thinly veiled appeal to bail out the bankers, a job Roosevelt had no desire to undertake. Roosevelt didn't see any reason to rescue the bankers; he wanted, he told his aides, "to save the folks."[21]

And the folks, he probably reasoned, could manage for a few more days. Some would panic; the long lines outside banks showed that better than almost anything else. There were tales of hysteria—one family thought it was safer to tape cash to their child's chest than to keep it in the bank. But in the short term most people would do what they had always done in times of crisis—they would adapt. In Minnesota, ministers agreed that they would not pass the collection plate on Sunday. Mary Eloise Green, a young teacher in West Liberty, Ohio, wasn't getting paid because the local school board couldn't access its money. But at least in the short term she neither froze nor starved. The landlord, the coal man, and the grocer all extended her credit. She was grateful, but she knew that "none of those people could have gone on indefinitely."

Bartering, which had taken hold in many places as the Depression worsened, flourished during the banking crisis. A man in Salt Lake City paid for a trolley ride with a pair of pants, fortunately not the pair he was wearing. Ten bushels of wheat were good for a year's subscription to a Montana newspaper. The promoter of the Golden Gloves boxing matches in New York announced that fifty cents, or anything worth fifty cents, would buy a seat in the balcony. Patrons brought neckties and hams, spark plugs and hot dogs, and even a Bible.

In Bronx Traffic Court, twenty-eight people bartered their time—they chose to serve a one-day sentence instead of paying fines, some as low as $2.

Banks that were still open kept a great deal more cash in their vaults to meet the expected crush of withdrawals, and extra police were dispatched throughout the country to prevent robberies. The legendary bank robber John Dillinger managed to steal over $50,000 from an Iowa bank during the crisis, but another would-be robber in Arkansas was thwarted. The bank was so crowded with depositors trying to withdraw their money that the robber could not keep track of everyone. One customer slipped away and warned the sheriff, who promptly arrested the holdup man. "I never got a break in my life," the frustrated robber complained. While some of the stories are amusing, at the time it could not have been pleasant. Those late winter days were fraught with worry, uncertainty, and fear. But it was hardly the doomsday Lamont predicted, at least not yet.[22]

With most Americans muddling through, Roosevelt could wait a few more days to act. On Monday night, however, while three hundred miles to the south Pecora sat in his modest room at the Hotel Continental poring over briefing memos and exhibits, Roosevelt set to work on his Inaugural Address. Raymond Moley had been working on a draft for weeks, and at nine o'clock the two men closeted themselves in the library at Springwood, Roosevelt's Hyde Park home, to revise it. It was a cold night, and the wind rattled the bare branches against the windows, but a roaring fire warmed the room where the two men worked. Moley sprawled on the long couch in front of the fire while Roosevelt sat in a favorite chair at a card table. Spread before him were Moley's draft, a yellow legal pad, and Lamont's letter. The two men sipped whiskey as they revised the draft, shaping and crafting the phrases, sometimes debating each word, trying to pick just the right ones for the new president to offer on that momentous occasion, now less than a week away. As they spoke, Roosevelt wrote out in longhand the now reworked speech, at one point asking Moley, "How do you spell 'foreclose'?" At around eleven, Moley took a moment to scribble a note to himself: "A strong man F.D.R."

Moley's draft had included a biblical reference. "As the money changers were driven from the temple," he wrote, "so it behooves us to restore moral values by driving out—material standards." It was a call to reshape the very fabric of American society, and Roosevelt was unhappy with it. He decided to replace it with the line that had come to him the day before in church. After the shocking practices Pecora uncovered, the weekend's overtures from City Bank about Mitchell's resignation, and Lamont's plea, Roosevelt wanted to sharpen that reference considerably. He didn't want a general reference to long-ago money changers; he wanted a specific reference to current ones, although he was unwilling in the address that would set the tone for his presidency to name names. "The philosophy of the money changers," he wrote, "stands indicted in the court of public opinion, rejected by the hearts and minds of men."

Roosevelt signed his name to the draft speech at one thirty Tuesday morning. Moley, who understood the historical significance that hung over their work that evening, had been trying to choreograph the perfect ending, and his moment had now come. Picking his draft up off the card table, he walked to the fireplace and tossed the sheets into the still hot embers, where they curled and blackened. "This," he told the man who most everyone fervently prayed would lead the country out of depression, "is your speech now."[23]

Chapter 14

DAY EIGHT:
SHORN LAMB

L ouis Howe, Roosevelt's closest political adviser, was so small and homely that he sometimes called himself the Medieval Gnome. He was a frail and sickly man with such severe asthma and bronchitis that his spasmodic and uncontrollable coughing often left him nearly unable to breathe. After years of these violent episodes, he was forced to constantly wear a brace to prevent further damage to his ravaged body. His face was pockmarked and scarred from a childhood bicycle accident that had permanently ground gravel into it. He weighed under a hundred pounds, and his baggy clothes hung loosely from his scrawny body, no doubt dusted with ashes from the Sweet Caporal cigarettes he incessantly smoked, doing nothing to improve his ragged cough. All in all, it would be hard to identify a more unprepossessing or fragile man, or one who had such unswerving loyalty to Franklin Roosevelt. It was Howe who, in 1912 as a reporter covering Albany for the *New York Herald*, first identified a young state senator with a famous last name as a man who could be president, and for the next two decades he unrelentingly worked to make that dream a reality.

Howe's devotion, however, could make him jealous of newcomers to the Roosevelt camp, and compared with him, everyone was a newcomer. After Roosevelt won his party's nomination in Chicago the previous July, Howe, who had been prostrate for days in his sweltering hotel room, spent the night feverishly rewriting the acceptance speech that Moley and his fellow Brain Trusters had been polishing for weeks. Howe could talk to Roosevelt like no one else, and when the candidate arrived in Chicago he insisted that his speech be used instead: "It is much better than the speech you've got right now. You can familiarize yourself with it while you ride to the convention hall."

Roosevelt was uncharacteristically angry: "But dammit Louis, I'm the candidate." Realizing immediately that he had wounded his most loyal aide, Roosevelt rectified the situation in classic fashion—he seamlessly substituted Howe's first page for the first page of the previous draft.

Unlike Moley, Howe wasn't quite ready to turn possession of the Inaugural draft over to Roosevelt. On Tuesday morning, February 28, just hours after Roosevelt and Moley had finished their work, Howe began to edit the speech. But this wasn't just the intermeddling of a needy underling. Howe had spent over forty years as a writer, editor, and political operative, and he could turn a memorable phrase. Howe was an inveterate newspaper reader, and so he was no doubt closely following Pecora's handiwork in Washington. As Howe dictated the entire handwritten draft to a stenographer, he added a slew of new sentences and provided additional bite to existing ones. He apparently, for example, thought the reference to the "philosophy of the money changers" was too soft and he changed it to the "practices of the unscrupulous money changers."

Howe focused most of his energy on the initial paragraphs of the Inaugural Address. Roosevelt, Howe thought, should start with a direct declaration of how he intended to speak to Americans that morning—with candor and without condescension. "This is preeminently the time," Howe dictated, "to speak the truth, the whole truth, frankly and boldly." Lamont was hardly alone in predicting the potential imminent demise of American civilization, so Howe thought Roosevelt needed to make a bold and confident prediction about the future: "This great Nation will endure as it has endured, will revive and will prosper." Howe then gave the speech its most memorable line, one that Americans could believe coming from the man who had faced Zangara's assassination attempt with such aplomb. "So first of all let me assert my firm belief," Howe dictated to the stenographer that morning, "that the only thing we have to fear is fear itself—nameless, unreasoning, unjustified terror which paralyzes the needed effort to bring about prosperity once again."

Roosevelt kept most of Howe's changes, but he balked at the conclusion of Howe's warning to resist the "paralyzing" effects of fear. It was a line that hit close to home for the incoming president, and he changed it, both to make it broader and to project the vision of mobility and progress that was so important to him. Fear, Roosevelt wrote on his typewritten copy of the speech, paralyzed "needed efforts to convert retreat into advance." The call to arms to wage war against the Great Depression, the promise of "action, and action now," and the indictment of Wall Street's elite leaders that would so arouse the Inaugural crowd in Washington on Saturday morning was now largely complete.[1]

As the eighth day of testimony began, Pecora was not quite ready to leave his Latin American excursion. He moved from Peru to Brazil, specifically the state of Minas Gerais (spelled Geraes at the time), a state in the southeast of the country where a good deal of Brazil's major export crop, coffee, was grown. The two Minas Geraes bond offerings, which collectively totaled $16.5 million, had been one of Mitchell's pet projects. They were the Brazilian state's first bond offerings in the United States and they looked as though they were going to be the last. They were currently in default and selling for about twenty cents on the dollar.[2]

In the witness chair to discuss those offerings was Ronald Byrnes, the former head of the foreign bond department at National City. Byrnes was one of the country's many unemployed; he had been out of work for almost two years. Pecora diplomatically asked if he was retired, to which the sardonic Byrnes replied, "You may call it that."[3]

As he did with the Peruvian bonds, Pecora quickly homed in on the language of the prospectus. The document was brief, but one of the things it seemed to be quite clear on was what Minas Geraes was planning to do with the money it raised. "The proceeds of this loan," the summary on the first page of the prospectus read, "will be utilized for purposes designed to increase the economic productivity of the State." It was just what a bond buyer would want to hear. If the state were more productive, it would be that much easier for it to pay back the loan it was getting.

Unfortunately, there was more to it than that. Focusing specifically on the second $8 million bond offering, Pecora asked Byrnes whether he knew that nearly half the offering was instead being "used to pay off existing short-term obligations held by the National City Co." National City was paying itself with the money it raised from investors and, yet again, not telling them anything about it. Byrnes was clearly nervous. He slowly and carefully examined the company's documents, which were piled in front of him on the mahogany table, and then he asked to speak to Pecora "off the record." After a few moments of whispered conversation, in which Byrnes seemed to be worried about his own legal liability, he did his best to distance himself from the offering. It was, he said, "four years ago" and National City got opinions from Shearman & Sterling and from its Brazilian counsel "as to the legality of the issue."

Byrnes also tried to argue that the prospectus had indeed disclosed the relevant information. If an investor turned to the inside pages, he would find a sentence that said that the proceeds were to be used "as provided in law No. 1061," passed in Brazil about a month before the bond offering. The prospectus then listed a few projects that were consistent with the economic development disclosure Pecora had read into the record, investments in the region's railroad, the power company, and the like. But Byrnes pulled a translation of law No. 1061 out of the company's files. That law, it soon became apparent, was not nearly as limited as the prospectus suggested. It said that the government could also use the proceeds to pay back any short-term loans it had outstanding.

When Pecora tried to determine whether the company knew about the contents of that law when it wrote the prospectus, Byrnes made a remarkable pronouncement: "I am informed here that our counsel wrote the law, so to speak, so that I am assuming that would give me greater confidence that it was legally issued."

Pecora was taken aback, unsure of what he had just heard: "You mean that Shearman and Sterling wrote the law for the state of Minas Geraes?"

"No," Byrnes replied, retreating as quickly as he could, "I would hardly say that. I think rather that Momsen and Torres, who were our counsel down there, that they drafted the law, which would be a better way of putting it, than that they wrote the law."

Pecora was unconvinced. "And you might be right in both instances."

"Well," Byrnes conceded, "that would be rather extraordinary to say the least." It was indeed "extraordinary." No matter how delicately Byrnes tried to couch it, the company had dictated the content of a Minas Geraes law in order to ensure the legality of paying itself back with the proceeds of the bonds the company was offering to American investors.[4]

Byrnes continued to insist that this disclosure—an obscure reference to a Brazilian state law with no discussion whatsoever of paying back existing indebtedness—was adequate. It was a losing battle. "Read the information that you say is contained in that circular which informs the public that a substantial part of the proceeds of that loan was to be used to pay back those short-term advances," Pecora demanded. The best the banker could muster was a lame suggestion that the information was "inherent" in the phrase "the proceeds of the loan will be utilized as provided in law 1061."

Eventually, after a good deal of hounding from Pecora, Byrnes reluctantly conceded that the prospectus didn't precisely "contain the direct statement," but he insisted that to include all those details "would have made such prospectus so inordinately long that there would have been no chance that the investor would have read it." Besides, he added, everybody assumed that these loans were used to repay the kind of short-term advances the National City Company had made.

No one seemed to care for that answer. Senator Brookhart pointed out that "it would not have taken much space" to set out the company's interests. Pecora focused on Byrnes's assumption. "Why do you say it is assumed by everybody?" he asked. Byrnes retreated again; perhaps he didn't "know much that is in the mind of the investing public."

Wasn't it true, Pecora continued, that Byrnes only knew about the "trained and sophisticated bond buyer?" Certainly Byrnes wasn't telling the committee "that the mass of the investing public" was aware of these kinds of details? Byrnes again tried to pin some of the blame on the lawyers, but in doing so he, quite conveniently, reiterated one of Pecora's central themes—the reliance the company's customers placed on its advice, expertise, and integrity. "Naturally,"

Byrnes explained, customers "depend upon the bankers to see that the issue is properly made, and the bankers in turn must depend on counsel to see that the necessary legal formalities are set up."

Pecora saw his opening and he did not let it go to waste: "The average investor, the average bond buyer, does not look into these things, does he?"

Byrnes still seemed to think he was pinning the blame on the lawyers, but his answer fit Pecora's needs perfectly. "He depends, first," he repeated, "upon the banker, and they in turn must depend upon their counsel as to the matter of legality."

"And the bond buyer relies considerably upon the prestige of the offering and distributing house, doesn't he?"

"Why, certainly he does," Byrnes replied, not appearing to notice he was hammering one more nail into the coffin of unregulated investment bankers, "not only here but anywhere else that I know of."[5]

How Minas Geraes would use the proceeds of the bond offering was not the only misrepresentation in the prospectus. Pecora put George Train, the man who originally urged National City to underwrite these bonds, on the stand. Train, it seemed, was willing to play fast and loose with other crucial facts in order to get the deal done. In 1927, analyzing Minas Geraes's history of bond offerings in Europe, Train was amazed at the shoddy way that the government had handled its obligations. The "laxness of the State authorities," he wrote in an internal company memorandum, "borders on the fantastic." His review of Minas Geraes's history "shows the complete ignorance, carelessness and negligence of the former State officials in respect to external long-term borrowing." It would, he wrote, "be hard to find anywhere a sadder confession of inefficiency and ineptitude than that displayed by the various State officials." Despite those conclusions, Train wrote in the prospectuses for the bond offerings, "Prudent and careful management of the State's finances has been characteristic of successive administrations in Minas Geraes."[6]

How, Pecora wanted to know, could Train possibly square those statements? Train squirmed and behind him Victor Schoepperle whispered tips, frantically trying to help his colleague. Pecora had no interest in letting Train out of his difficult spot.

"Do you want the help of Mr. Schoepperle in making your answer?" Pecora asked.

Train said that he did not need any help, leading Pecora to announce, "Well, please tell that to Mr. Schoepperle, who seems to think that you do."

Train actually needed quite a bit of help, because the answers he came up with on his own didn't convince anybody. First he tried to explain that his criticisms referred to earlier state administrations, not the ones in power when the bonds were sold. Pecora, who couldn't have had a much easier time with a witness, immediately pointed out that the prospectus referred to "successive administrations." Train quickly switched gears; he only meant to refer to the state's handling of its internal budget matters and not to how the state handled its external finances. But Pecora was again ready for him, turning to the copies he had made from the company's files. Did Train remember, the lawyer asked, a letter from one of his colleagues, which criticized this very language of the draft prospectus? Didn't that colleague point out that this language was problematic "in view of the extremely loose way in which the external debt of the State was managed"? Apparently, even Train's colleagues hadn't bought the argument, although their criticisms were insufficient to get the firm to modify the prospectus's language. Unable to come up with another answer, Train decided to blame it on Rio.

"I was in Brazil and perhaps became, as one often does in that country, a little overenthusiastic with respect to the merits of the particular credit I was investigating," he told Pecora.

Pecora was unwilling to accept that answer either. If it was Train's intention to refer merely to internal finances, why didn't he just say that? Like other witnesses who had painted themselves into corners, Train tried to parse words exceedingly finely. It was straight out of *Alice in Wonderland*.

"Well, of course," Train replied, "it would rest on an interpretation of the word 'finances.'"

Pecora dismissed Train's parsing. "But if you wanted to make a favorable comment on the administration of the internal finances of the State, would it not have been extremely simple to have inserted the word 'internal' before the word 'finances'?"

"I think," Train conceded, "it would have been more accurate."

"And if you wanted to convey to the investing public through the medium of this prospectus what you had learned concerning the 'careless, inefficient, and inept and loose way of the State's management of its external finances,'" Pecora continued, "you would have said so too, would you not, in the prospectus?"

Train continued to squirm, now choosing to blame everything on the citizens of Minas Geraes: "These people in Minas were back-country people, and they had shown, as I stated in my letter, ineptitude in handling—"

Pecora interrupted Train; he was growing impatient with all the evasions and hedging. "Will you answer my question now?" he demanded.

Train insisted that he thought the problems he outlined in his earlier memos involved only "past administrations."

So, Pecora summarized, the company and Train chose to disclose only so much as would make the offering look as good as possible? "You did not go back," he said, "to the point where the administration was loose and inefficient in its handling of its external finances, did you?" Schoepperle was still frantically trying to whisper advice into Train's ear, earning a sharp rebuke from Pecora: "Now, Mr. Schoepperle, he said he did not need your help. . . . Now, what is the answer to that question?"

Train hesitated: "In this prospectus?"

"Of course, in the prospectus."

"No," Train finally admitted, "we did not go back to that point. I did not go back to that point."

Train and Schoepperle were now furiously arguing with each other, leading Pecora to finally interject, "All right. Mr. Train—when you are through quarreling with Mr. Schoepperle, I will ask you a question."[7]

Train's testimony also explained why the company was so eager to advance money to Minas Geraes. It seemed that after the first bond offering two rival investment banks, Kuhn Loeb and Lee Higginson, approached officials there about underwriting a bond offering for the state, a fact that both surprised and perturbed National City. The National City Company, Train explained, "hoped to establish the general relationship, and it was . . . rather disconcerting to find that . . . someone else would come in and have some future financing." The company thought that Lee Higginson was trying to "chisel in."

Pecora was delighted with that phrase. "Chisel in," he exclaimed, "that is not a banker's term, is it?" No, Train conceded to general laughter throughout the room; it was "just an expression." In earlier times, the old-line investment banking firms lived by a strict moral code—it was under most circumstances considered unseemly to poach another firm's clients. Such civilities had long since faded in the hurly-burly of the late 1920s, particularly where foreign bonds were concerned. Thomas Lamont's complaint about the violent competition among investment banks for this business seemed as much a lament for that fading code as a warning for American investors. Code or no code, National City was not happy.[8]

"Naturally," Pecora inquired, "the National City Co. and its co-underwriters in that first loan were unwilling to have these other banking houses 'chisel in,' were they not?"

Train clearly was ruing that he used the phrase, and he demurred: "I would say that they did not like the idea."

Pecora would not be put off, because now it was clear why City Bank had been so insistent on lending to the Brazilian state. "Was it not," Pecora asked, "in order to retain the good will and the favor of the authorities of the State of Minas Geraes that these short-term unsecured advances were made?"

Train would not admit that motivation, but it certainly seemed to be the case. Indeed, the company had all but forced the second bond offering on the state to recoup those advances. State officials insisted that the bond markets were so unsettled at the time the company wanted to make the offering they feared "a new loan would not prove a success." Failure would have been devastating to the state if it ever wanted to go back to the credit markets again. Investors were already wary of Minas Geraes because the bonds from the first offering were trading for less than the offering price. National City insisted on the loan anyway. When one of its executives and the company's lawyers wanted to include language in the prospectus disclosing that the proceeds of the bond offering would be used to repay the company, the company apparently vetoed that suggestion. Byrnes had insisted earlier in the day that "no investor would be in the slightest interested nor his investment in the least affected" by these details. Few of the people in Room 301, certainly not Pecora, seemed to agree.[9]

. . .

The highlight of the day, and perhaps of the entire second week of the City Bank hearings, was the appearance of Edgar D. Brown of Pottsville, Pennsylvania. Brown was brought in to personalize the consequences of the stock market practices Pecora uncovered. He was just forty, but he was not well; although Pecora was ten years his senior, the lawyer was in far better shape. Brown had tuberculosis, was nearly deaf, and although he once had a successful career as a theater owner, he was now destitute, scraping by working as a clerk for the local "poor board" to support his family. Brown described himself as a "shorn lamb," but he was unwilling to take his plight or the plight of any helpless victims meekly. He appears to have been one of Father Cox's Army, the unemployed marchers who descended on Washington from Pennsylvania in January 1932. Just before he arrived for the hearing, a Pottsville grand jury refused to indict him for breaking into the local school in order to shelter a group of students from some nasty weather.[10]

The story Brown was about to tell was heartbreaking. He was a dream witness—earnest, good-humored, and dignified. Pecora knew when to get out of the way, and he asked Brown to tell that story in his own words. In 1927, Brown decided to move to California because of his poor health. He sold his theater chain and with a portfolio of $100,000 in cash and mostly United States government bonds in hand, he came across a City Bank advertisement that seemed perfectly suited to his needs. "Heading out on a long trip?" the bank ad asked. If so, you should contact City Bank, which could help when you were away from "the advice of your local banker." Brown was a successful businessman but, like many Americans at the time, an investment neophyte, and he took the bait.

The close working relationship between City Bank and its securities affiliate was never better demonstrated. Brown was sure that he wrote to City Bank, but he received a reply from a salesman in the National City Company's Philadelphia office named Fred Rummel. Rummel told Brown that his bonds "were all wrong." He should sell the United States government bonds, borrow two or three times the $100,000 he had, and then invest in a wide variety of securities the company recommended.

Brown took the company's advice, insisting only that he wanted bonds instead of stock. Other than that Brown trusted the company implicitly. "I would never buy or sell anything without their sanction and would always act upon any suggestions which they might make." Pecora, especially after all the letters he read from former customers, was not surprised by Brown's faith in the company. "After all," Pecora wrote, "he was not dealing with some fly by night bucket shop or itinerant gold-mining stock peddler, but with the greatest and soundest bank in the world." A bank like this one—at the time the largest in the country—"was supposed to occupy a fiduciary relationship and to protect its clients, not to lead them into dubious ventures; to offer sound, conservative investment advice, not a salesman's puffing patter."[11]

Over the next year a welter of bonds came in and out of Brown's portfolio. There were railroad bonds, utility bonds, and industrial bonds. Brown's foreign bond holdings spanned the globe—Peruvian and Chilean bonds; bonds from the State of Rio Grande do Sul in Brazil; Vienna and Budapest bonds, the bonds of the Belgian National Railroad, Norwegian Hydro, German General Electric, and the Saxon Public Works; Greek, Italian, and Irish bonds. They seemed to have only one thing in common—they all went down in value.

When Brown complained at the end of 1928, Rummel told him, "Well, that is your fault for insisting upon bonds. Why don't you let me sell you some stock?" Brown, like most everyone else, thought the stock market was "continually moving up. So then I took hook, line and sinker and said 'Very well. Buy stock.'" The witness was so deaf that Pecora shouted into Brown's cupped ear, "Did he buy stocks then for your account?" Even Brown laughed, as he tossed a two-inch-thick pile of confirmations onto the mahogany table, replying to the delight of those gathered in Room 301, who roared with laughter, "Might I answer that facetiously—Did he buy stocks?" Brown never knew what he was buying. "I bought," he testified, "thousands of shares of stock on their suggestion which I did not know whether the companies they represented made cake, candy, or automobiles." All he could do was to follow the company's advice; it was, he thought, "the only safe thing to do."[12]

In early 1929, Brown went all the way to 55 Wall Street to complain yet again. Despite the rising stock market, his portfolio had gone down in value. Or, at least he thought it had gone down in value. National City was trading his account so violently, Brown said, he could not tell where he stood. "I told them,"

Brown recounted, "that I was fearful that a reaction in the market might wipe me out and that I had no income on which to depend." The manager in New York recommended even more transactions. Brown should sell everything he had and put all his money in City Bank stock, Anaconda Copper, and a few other stock offerings the company was sponsoring. The audience in the room chuckled again when Brown related the next advice he received, "sit still on that and see what happens."

What happened was the crash. In September 1929, as prices began to dip, Brown went into the company office in Los Angeles and said he wanted to sell everything, not exactly what the salesmen at the company wanted to hear. "I was placed," Brown recalled, "in the category of the man who seeks to put his own mother out of his house. I was surrounded at once by all of the salesmen in the place, and made to know that that was a very, very foolish thing to do."

"That is," Pecora inquired, "to sell your stocks?"

"Especially," Brown said, "the National City Bank stocks." Brown was advised to "sit tight"; the City Bank stock was trading at $525 and was bound to "go to $750 at the very least." When the crash came a month later, the company sold out all of Brown's stock. He had lost nearly everything. "I am now 40 years of age," he wrote the company, "tubercular—almost totally deaf—my wife and family are depending on me solely and alone and because of my abiding faith in the advice of your company I am to-day a pauper." After Brown's testimony, a New York columnist wrote, "When the American banker comes before the public today and says piteously, 'Why don't you trust me?' he should not be surprised if he is greeted with a derisive laugh."[13]

Brown was left with $25,000, and he wanted the company to lend him money so he could buy more Anaconda Copper stock on margin as a way to try to recoup his losses. Brown, it seems by this point in his investing career, had developed some of the same bold gambling instincts as Mitchell. Brown, unlike Mitchell, never got the chance to make the bet, because the company refused to let him borrow. Had he invested, he would have lost virtually everything he had, so perhaps National City was looking out for him in this one instance. Then again, maybe not—the company said his income was no longer sufficient to support the margin loan he requested.[14]

. . .

By the end of Tuesday, seventeen states had legislation already passed or in the works to restrict withdrawals or to close up their banks. In Pennsylvania, the legislature was still drafting the required laws, but troubled banks couldn't wait. Already depositors in Scranton and Erie could only withdraw 5 percent of their money. The First National Bank of Tennessee and People's National Bank of La Follette, Tennessee, mailed notices to all customers immediately restricting withdrawals while a holiday took effect in Memphis. Five banks in Kansas closed their doors for good. A bank in Van Buren, Arkansas, tried to prevent customers from closing out their accounts by paying depositors with silver dollars. It worked with at least one customer who, unable to haul away the fifty-pound bag of coins he was given, handed it back to the teller and stormed out of the bank.[15]

In Maryland, the governor extended the holiday for yet another day, and the situation was beginning to grow more difficult. Relief agencies in the state were already reporting an upswing in requests for food. City workers in Baltimore, who had just received their now useless paychecks, threatened to strike when the mayor announced, "City Hall is not in the check-cashing business." The mayor quickly capitulated to his angry employees.[16]

The panic now spread to Washington, D.C. The capital's fourth largest bank, the Commercial National Bank, closed its doors and placed itself in receivership. Two other banks in the District of Columbia suspended withdrawals. In the scheme of things the Washington closures were small potatoes, but the psychological impact was enormous. "If banks could fail in the shadow of the United States Treasury, at the very door of the R.F.C.," one contemporary commentator wrote, "what then?" Everywhere people gathered they were talking about the fast-collapsing banks. "It seems," one observer wrote that day, "every depositor in the country wants to withdraw his money." And it wasn't just the United States. Bankers in Cuba, where interest in the Senate hearings was enormous, prevailed on military leaders to issue an order prohibiting Cuban newspapers from printing any story about the United States banking crisis, lest the panic spread to the branches of New York banks located there.[17]

That same day, Senator Costigan's resolution to continue the investigation into the next session of Congress came up for a vote. The discussion was brief and focused almost entirely on what Pecora had uncovered in a little over a week rather than what the investigation had done over the preceding year. The disclosures, Costigan argued, "are justly attracting nation-wide attention." Given the outcry, it would have been political suicide to oppose continuing the investigation, a point Costigan made sure to express explicitly on the off chance any of his colleagues failed to see the utterly obvious. "It is assumed," he continued, "that no Member of the Senate will desire to interfere with that highly important investigation at a time when general public agreement is being expressed on the overwhelming necessity for remedial enactments by Congress to guard, so far as humanly possible, against the recurrence of such conditions as have been and are being revealed by the testimony."

Costigan's assumption was spot-on; Congress passed the resolution unanimously.[18]

Chapter 15

DAY NINE: A FREE AND
OPEN MARKET

By the end of Wednesday, Alabama, Kentucky, Louisiana, and Tennessee joined the parade of bank holidays. Kentucky's closures were the most ironic; in order to get the banks closed, state law required Governor Ruby Laffoon to declare official "days of thanksgiving." All told, twelve states—25 percent of the country—had now closed their banks or restricted withdrawals to tiny percentages of deposits. State officials in West Virginia gave individual banks under pressure the option of shutting themselves down.

Other states had not yet acted, but they were ready to do so at a moment's notice. Idaho's governor had the power to shut down banks, while the legislature in Minnesota gave that power to the state's banking commission. Where banks remained open, people searched for any sign the contagion had spread. In Jamestown, New York, just 150 miles northeast of Cleveland's closed banks, the future Supreme Court justice Robert Jackson was nervous. Every morning on his way to his law office he drove out of his way to check if there was a line outside the Bank of Jamestown, where he sat on the board. The bank was in poor shape, and Jackson knew that a run would kill it, ruining both his finances and his reputation. Luckily for Jackson the bank was, so far, quiet.

Reform proposals that were laughed off in Washington as absurd just a few months earlier were now getting a serious hearing in the waning days of the congressional session. As workers hung bunting all around the capital and thousands of inaugural spectators streamed into the city, Michigan senator Arthur Vandenberg renewed calls for a federal guarantee of bank deposits while Texas representative John Patman believed "the Government should consider seriously the proposal of taking over the banks, not as a governmental policy but as a governmental necessity."[1]

The first witness on Wednesday morning was Horace Sylvester, the head of the company's municipal bond department. This was not his first appearance in the limelight. He was a well-known municipal bond expert, but as far as the general public was concerned he was better known as a peripheral player in the molding of an American legend. In October 1926, Sylvester's eleven-year-old son, Johnny, was extremely ill; doctors said he might die. To cheer his ailing son, the banker wired Yankee slugger Babe Ruth, Johnny's idol, asking for a signed baseball. Airmail packages arrived at the Sylvester home carrying balls signed by both World Series combatants, the Yankees and the St. Louis Cardinals. Ruth, however, thought Johnny's plight needed an even bigger gesture. In what quickly became part of Ruth lore, the Babe promised to hit a home run for the boy. Then he went out and hit three. When Johnny recovered, breathless news reports attributed his cure to the Bambino, whose larger-than-life performance raised the boy's spirits. Horace Sylvester's son was suddenly "the most famous little boy in America."[2]

Horace Sylvester could have used something to raise his own spirits on that first day in March 1933. The forty-nine-year-old banker with the round face, thin mustache, and pronounced wattle was in Room 301 to clear up a bit of mysterious testimony that Pecora had elicited the day before. Sylvester's testimony that Wednesday moved the City Bank disclosures from the immoral, unethical, and improper to what seemed like something that, if not outright illegal, showed a complete and utter disregard for City Bank's shareholders, Sylvester's obligations as a corporate officer, and whatever diaphanous tissue separated the bank and the company.

Just after lunch on Tuesday, Pecora briefly suspended his inquiry about the Minas Geraes bonds to put National City's treasurer, Samuel Baldwin, in the witness chair. Baldwin's testimony was brief and cryptic, and what it revealed sounded fishy. In 1931, National City handled a huge $66 million bond offering for the Port Authority of New York. One day shortly after the company completed the offering, Baldwin got a call from Sylvester asking Baldwin to give him $10,200 in cash and to charge the amount as a "syndicate expense" to the Port Authority offering. Baldwin never learned what the cash was for but he testified that it was unusual to pay expenses in cash. "Do you know," Pecora asked, "of any other instance of a similar character where a sum of money amounting to several thousand dollars or more was drawn out in cash and charged to expenses?" Never, Baldwin replied, while he was treasurer. Pecora dropped the subject after establishing that independent auditors never examined the company's accounts, but alerted the committee (and the reporters) that Sylvester would be in Washington the next day.[3]

Now with Sylvester in Room 301, Pecora cleared up the mystery surrounding this odd transaction. Sylvester gave the cash to a City Bank employee named Edward Barrett who in turn "loaned" the money to John Ramsey, the Port Authority's general manager. Ramsey was "in a financial jam" and, although City Bank's policies prohibited it from making an unsecured loan to him, Barrett didn't want to leave his friend in the lurch. Barrett went to Sylvester and the municipal bond manager decided to make this "accommodation" for Ramsey because Ramsey was "a good moral risk." The transaction was never recorded as a loan, Sylvester never knew the terms of the loan, and he never pressed for it to be repaid.[4]

Having exhausted Sylvester's knowledge, Pecora turned to Norbeck. "Mr. Chairman, I ask that a subpoena be issued for Mr. Edward F. Barrett, returnable tomorrow." Before Norbeck could respond, however, Sylvester spoke up, "Mr. Pecora, Mr. Barrett is in the room if you would like to see him." Pecora whirled around, "Oh, is he?"

Barrett took the stand. His story did little to show that City Bank employees were jealously guarding shareholder interests. He claimed to have a note for the loan, but did not know where it was and, in any event, it was a note to Barrett personally, not to the company. The banker did not have a good explanation for why the loan was made in cash rather than by check, other than that Ramsey needed the money right away. Barrett testified that it was supposed to be a temporary loan (just "two or three weeks or a month"), but nearly two years later no interest or principal had ever been repaid and Barrett had not even asked Ramsey to do so. Barrett explained his reluctance: Ramsey's "salary had been cut two or three times, and I knew that he could not make any payment, and I did not want to embarrass John Ramsey."

Ramsey, Pecora asked, received a loan because he was a friend of Barrett's?

"Precisely," Barrett replied. "The one reason that I went to help him was because he was a friend of mine, and a very good friend of mine for ten years' standing, and I have always found him a very high-standing fellow, and I wanted to help him if I possibly could."

Pecora wanted to emphasize just how good a friend Barrett had been: "So you helped him with the funds of the National City Co. with which you were not connected, didn't you?"

Perhaps it truly was a loan; the transaction, after all, occurred about six weeks after National City underwrote the bonds, hardly the ideal time to bribe an official. Sylvester was adamant on that point, pounding the table and denying any wrongdoing. It would have been a silly bribe in any event—Ramsey had no authority to award bond offerings to National City or any other investment bank. Indeed, the Port Authority subsequently refused to accept Ramsey's resignation (he explained that he thought he was receiving a loan personally from Barrett, which was why he made out the note to Barrett). Sylvester was indicted for forgery, but the charges against him were dismissed.

But if it wasn't a bribe it was a blatant misuse of company funds, although one that now hardly seemed surprising. If nothing else, Pecora had shown over the past eight days that City Bank's executives gave little thought to the obligations they owed the bank's shareholders. After the millions in morale loans and the bonuses, $10,200 seemed like nothing, but that $10,200 firmly cemented public perceptions of City Bank. "Of course this was not a bribe, or a bid for future business from the Port Authority," the *Nation* wrote sarcastically. "Heaven forbid! It was just a generous kindly act to take care of a good man who happened to be in a jam. Why not give him $10,200 of the stockholders' money and overlook such matters as collateral and interest? That's the way to make friends for the bank!"[5]

The real star of that second-to-last day of the hearings was not Horace Sylvester; it was the New York Stock Exchange president Richard Whitney, who was making his return engagement in Washington. It had been almost a year since Whitney's previous appearance before the committee. So much had changed in the interim, not only in the success of the investigation and the skill of the lawyer prosecuting it, but in the country at large. A death rattle seemed to be reverberating through the banking sector. The diffuse anger at Wall Street had crystallized into a sharp rage directed at the elite leaders of the financial markets, not just shady short sellers and pool operators. And, with that change in the investigation and that change in the country, there was something of a change in Whitney as well.

A day earlier in Cleveland, Richard Whitney, the man who professed ignorance the previous spring of any illegal activities on the exchange, upbraided the "ephemeral prophets" of the "boom" days. He still could not see that the New York Stock Exchange had ever acted improperly or had failed to protect the people who bought and sold in the securities markets. It was the American people as a group, he asserted, who "were careless of the qualifications of many of those who were entrusted with positions of importance and power." The public was lulled into a false sense of security. It gave its "confidence too readily" and it was too willing to proclaim the heads of profitable companies "business or financial geniuses." Whitney certainly sounded like he was talking about Mitchell, although he never invoked his name. As he told his audience in Ohio, "his remarks were listened to with awe and his lightest statements were accepted as the words of an oracle, without inquiry into his qualifications and training and without much thought of the soundness of his enterprise."

Despite his criticisms of the gullible masses, Whitney sounded downright progressive as he called for more fulsome disclosures, stricter accounting rules, and uniform laws regulating the issuance of securities, all to safeguard the investors who provided capital to industry. It was quite an about-face for a man who, just six month earlier, expressed grave doubts about Congress's ability to adequately frame such laws. "More frank and more complete information," he now conceded, might have avoided the huge run-up before the crash.[6]

But that small concession to the propriety of regulation was about all he could muster. Whitney's "maddeningly unshakable rectitude," his overweening pride in the New York Stock Exchange, in his class, and in himself remained intact. He still ardently defended the exchange and the great service it provided for the United States. "Speculation," he self-righteously declared, "has built this country" and the government had no business regulating it or the market on which it occurred. Indeed, trying to regulate speculation was futile, as Whitney earlier told a House committee. "You are trying to deal with human nature," he explained. "Speculation is always going to exist in this country just as long as we are Americans."

Even the censures in Whitney's Cleveland speech were not nearly so pointed as they at first seemed. Whitney still considered the leaders of Wall Street to be men of honor and conviction—the "ephemeral prophets" he singled out were largely foreigners like Krueger, not American financiers like Mitchell. But after all that had taken place in that hearing room over the previous week and a half and all that had taken place in the country since Michigan had closed its banks, his defense seemed hollow, the remnants of a bygone age.[7]

Not everything had changed in the intervening year, at least not on the other side of the mahogany committee table. Some committee members, in particular Senator Brookhart, learned nothing from Pecora's systematic examination of City Bank. As soon as Whitney took the witness stand Brookhart, who now had only two days remaining in his Senate career, began to hurl seemingly random questions at him, jumping from the Better Business Bureau, to balancing the federal budget, to rehashing testimony Whitney had given the previous spring. Brookhart still had nothing, other than rumor and hunch, to back up his questions, and Whitney continued to easily repel them in the same weary and dismissive tone he exhibited the previous spring. At one point, Brookhart asked Whitney why the Better Business Bureau never complained about the practice of stabilizing bond prices during an offering, to which Whitney disdainfully replied, "I do not claim that that is an unethical practice, Senator Brookhart, as

I have stated." Brookhart's response was suitable for a schoolyard squabble, not a Senate hearing room: "Well, I do."[8]

Pecora had a far more precise plan for his confrontation with Whitney. The only entity capable of policing the exchange was the exchange, and Pecora wanted to know how vigilantly it was walking its beat. Asking Whitney whether the federal government needed to regulate the exchange would elicit a sure negative response. So, instead of asking the question directly Pecora began with a laundry list of precautions and disciplinary actions the exchange never took. The exchange, he asked, never audited the companies that sought to be listed there? No, Whitney replied, but a year earlier it had begun requiring new listings to have an independent audit, although it was unwilling to impose that mandate on existing listings. Did the exchange examine the "character" of a company's officers and directors? Yes, when it was first listed. "And don't you think it would be just as advisable to exercise that same kind of supervision by inquiry even after a corporation had succeeded in having its securities listed?" Pecora asked. Whitney agreed, but explained that at that point the officers and directors were "entirely beyond" the exchange's control. It had no power to remove them; its only power was to remove the company from trading on the exchange, but it almost never did that.

In truth, the New York Stock Exchange's listing standards were the highest in the country. The bigger problems were with other exchanges, where issuers could list their securities without these kinds of disclosures. But even the New York Stock Exchange radically reduced the effectiveness of its required disclosures through its inability or unwillingness to investigate applications for listing. "So lax was the 'self-regulation' of the Exchange authorities," Pecora wrote, "that even the formally condemned abuses were actually detected and punished only on the most infrequent occasions."[9]

Reporters described the confrontation between the two men as "fencing," but it was more like surgery. Pecora's careful cataloging of the limits of exchange enforcement was far more effective than trying to wring either an admission of wrongdoing out of Whitney or a concession that outside regulation was necessary. Whitney, to be sure, tried to argue that no one could stop those bent on outright fraud, not even the federal government. But Pecora, who had little tolerance for Whitney's evasions, was able to show that the exchange failed to take even the most rudimentary steps to police listed companies.

"Mr. Pecora," Whitney explained, "naturally if people wish to be crooked and to make false statements, they may get away with it with any agency or institution."

"But does the New York Stock Exchange take any steps to confirm the statements made by officers of a corporation seeking to list its securities on your exchange?" countered Pecora, who was not buying the impossibility argument.

Whitney said he couldn't answer Pecora's question without referring to some internal exchange documents. An increasingly weary Pecora remained polite but insistent that he wanted Whitney's "own knowledge" as to what really happened, not some canned answer about the exchange's formal procedures.

"My dear sir," Pecora continued, "you have been a member of the exchange for twenty-one years. You have been its president for nearly three years."

"Yes, sir."

"Can't you tell me, from the wealth of knowledge and experience that must have come to you during those years"—Whitney tried to cut in, but Pecora just talked right over him—"whether or not the exchange affirmatively takes any action seeking to check up or to confirm the statements made to it by corporation officers seeking to have their securities listed?"

Whitney admitted that there was no check. "In other words," Pecora continued, "the exchange proceeds upon the assumption that nobody lies to it, does it?"

"The exchange," Whitney insisted, "has got to take people at their face value and that they are honest until they are proved otherwise."

"The presumption is all in favor of the person who makes applications as to honesty and integrity? Is that what you mean?"

"Yes; if you wish it that way."

At no point did Pecora ask Whitney to admit that the exchange was aware of wrongdoing. Pecora surely knew that the self-righteous exchange leader would never do that. But each time Whitney admitted that the exchange could not or did not oversee its listed firms he was making the case that self-regulation was not enough.[10]

Whitney still clung to his belief that the exchange never erred, that it main-tained a perfectly "free and open market" in securities. But, given its lackadaisi-cal methods and the pervasive wrongdoing Pecora had already shown, Whitney's denials were no longer convincing. Pecora, for example, asked him whether he now thought that verifying company information was important. Whitney seemed appalled that Pecora wanted him to question the integrity of the gentle-men who listed their stock on the exchange—verifying information would mean "the presumption of dishonesty rather than honesty."

"In other words, you would rather discover the dishonesty after it has come to light or after its evil effects have been manifested, than prevent the dishonesty beforehand?"

"But that has not happened, Mr. Pecora."

"How do you know it has not happened?"

The answer was self-evident, Whitney replied; because the exchange never found any evidence of problems, they must not exist.[11]

When the exchange did take a look at various types of speculative activity going on in its midst, it appeared to have a rather idiosyncratic definition of what it meant to maintain a "free and open" market. Whitney admitted that stock pools were allowed under exchange rules, but also claimed that the exchange existed for only one purpose—"to allow the ready action of the law of supply and demand."

Pecora could not see how those two statements were compatible. The whole point of a pool was to move prices away from the price the market had set under normal buying and selling conditions. A free and open market, Pecora asked, was not one that was controlled in this way, was it? Whitney said he didn't know what a controlled market was, to which Pecora sarcastically replied, "Well, Mr. Whitney, I am trying to use words that are simple in their meaning, but if I am using words that you do not understand I will try to change them."

Whitney was indignant, no doubt appalled that this immigrant, a former criminal prosecutor far below him on the social scale, would dare speak to him in such an impolite fashion.

"I understand the word 'controlled' completely, Mr. Pecora," he haughtily replied.

Well, if he understood what control meant, Pecora said, then he should be able to say whether it was possible for a pool "to exercise temporarily . . . a control of the market price"?

Whitney said that a pool could exercise that kind of control over price as "long as the stock and their money hold out."

"Now," Pecora asked, "what steps, if any, does the exchange take to prevent that kind of control?"

"I do not know of any, Mr. Pecora."

"When such a pool is operating and effecting such a control, it is restricting a free and open market where honest values can be obtained, is it not?"

"No, sir."

Whitney's denial was simply not credible, and so Pecora asked again, "Is it not?"

"No, sir," the exchange leader repeated.[12]

To be sure, Pecora's naïveté about how stock markets worked was still very much in evidence. The investigator chastised Whitney for not being able to see in 1928 and 1929 that prices were wildly inflated, but it was hardly a fair charge. Bubbles are easy to spot, but usually only after they have burst. "Mr. Pecora," Whitney complained, "you are talking about [the] judgment of hindsight. We did not have it then, nor did but very few, if any, have it then." Pecora remained unconvinced: "Mr. Whitney, don't you think . . . the New York Stock Exchange . . . owes some measure of responsibility to the public to watch those prices and when they get out of line to sound some kind of public warning?"

Whitney was, understandably, incredulous. "If you will tell me, Mr. Pecora, how I, as president of the New York Stock Exchange, might do that I will be glad to have you do so, and will endeavor to act accordingly. But I will say that if the president of the New York Stock Exchange at that time had issued such warnings . . . he would have been laughed at." Whitney was right when he told Pecora that the exchange did not have "either the facility or the ability to be the oracle as to how prices should fluctuate, or to set forth whether a price is too high or too low." It could not be the "dictator of what prices should be" on a daily basis.[13]

Still, Pecora's careful examination of the exchange president was far more successful than the committee's awkward encounter a year earlier. By the end of the day, the picture Pecora painted was not, as Whitney claimed, of a forum in which the forces of supply and demand met freely to determine prices. Pecora saw a darker purpose to the exchange. The exchange "was in reality neither more nor less than a glorified gambling casino where the odds were heavily weighted against the eager outsiders." Pool accounts were rampant. "The public who bought these stocks at dizzily mounting prices," Pecora wrote in his memoirs, "did not do so merely because of impersonal market forces; they were the victims of a determined, organized group of market-wise operators, armed with special information and special facilities and backed generously with bankers' credits."

For his part, Whitney decried such gambling while still trying to defend speculation. Whitney granted that there was a "delicate" line distinguishing the two which turned only on the impossible task of divining the intent of the trader. He insisted that legitimate speculation predominated on the exchange, but in the end even that assertion crumbled in the face of Pecora's skilled questioning.

"So that it is all a matter of intent which controls?" Pecora asked the exchange president.

"It seems to me so, yes."

So, Pecora wanted to know, how did Whitney determine whether a trader intended to speculate or gamble?

Whitney, of course, said that he had no way of divining intent. "Then how are you able to recognize any line that distinguishes an honest or proper kind of speculative trading from an improper kind or gambling kind, if you have no way of ascertaining the intent?" Pecora asked. "[A]s far as you know to the contrary the majority of the speculative buying might be of the gambling variety, might it not?"

In the end, Whitney could resort to nothing but haughty ipse dixit. "I say I do not think so," he replied. "I do not say that it is not. I do not think so."[14]

Federal regulation was needed, Pecora concluded, because Whitney and the other leaders of the New York Stock Exchange were doing nothing about the gambling or the manipulations. Everyone in the country seemed to know that there was a pool in R.C.A. stock organized in March 1929 by Michael Meehan, a specialist and member of the New York Stock Exchange. The pool netted its participants $5 million in one week, but the exchange didn't see the need to investigate it until the summer of 1932, after testimony about it in the Banking and

Currency Committee that spring. Three years on, many of the relevant documents were destroyed. The exchange found no wrongdoing. Since pools didn't violate stock exchange rules, the exchange would have certainly reached the same conclusion if they examined every scrap of paper. It was, to Whitney, just the operation of the free and open market.[15]

With those manipulations and the exchange's hands-off approach, Pecora simply couldn't see that the market performed a legitimate function. But his view was a little too jaundiced. By creating a place where investors could easily sell securities, the market lowered the costs of raising capital for American businesses. Whitney was right—speculation in securities was an essential part of the American economy. All Pecora saw was that this "glorified gambling casino" was unregulated. Pecora had shown that the exchange did not vigorously exercise its regulatory prerogatives and that its prices were not solely the product of supply and demand. To make the case for federal regulation he only needed to underscore the importance of the exchange to the United States economy. Didn't the New York Stock Exchange constitute "the greatest market for securities in this country, if not in the world?" Weren't its quotations accepted "as substantial evidence of the value of securities to which they relate?" Securities were often accepted as collateral for bank loans and, in fact, were more readily accepted because of the active market the exchange created, correct? Whitney, naturally, had no choice but to accept all those propositions.

Well, if all that was true, Pecora continued, then the operation of the stock exchange was "of interest to the entire country," wasn't it? Again, Whitney had no choice but to agree—he had, after all, just proclaimed that speculation on the exchange had built the United States.

Despite the exchange's crucial place in the American economy, Pecora continued, it was "subject to no official regulatory power"? Whitney conceded that there was none. The only logical question after nine days of testimony was, why not?[16]

Chapter 16

DAY TEN: THE END
OF AN ERA

When Pecora recalled the City Bank hearings in his memoirs, his count was off by a full day. "It lasted . . . just nine days," he wrote in 1939, "but in those nine days a whole era of American financial life passed away." Perhaps it was unsurprising that this last day slipped from Pecora's otherwise infallible memory. It was, for the most part, mundane. The investigator's questions were largely perfunctory, and he let his assistants take a good deal of the testimony. In an ideal world, Pecora's flair for the dramatic would no doubt have led him to a more fitting ending. Perhaps the climax could have been Edgar Brown, the personification of the hapless middle-class investor who trusted in City Bank's sterling reputation. Richard Whitney's inveterate self-importance and righteous certitude would also have made a fitting conclusion. Unfortunately, the real world does not come so neatly packaged. Pecora had to tie up some loose ends and was forced to conclude the hearings with a whimper rather than a bang.

Day ten started the same way as day one—with Charles Mitchell. On Sunday evening, when Pecora learned of Mitchell's resignation, he insisted that Mitchell remained under subpoena and that his presence in Washington was crucial. But to anyone watching the hearings, Mitchell now seemed little more than an afterthought. For the last three days the deposed banker had sat in the spectators' row—Pecora didn't call him to the stand once. Instead, Mitchell was forced to sit through hours of testimony about City Bank's South American follies and about the squirrelly loan charged to the Port Authority account. He listened to Edgar Brown's tale of ruin after Brown's encounter with his former financial institution.

After that parade of indiscretions, if not sins, Mitchell continued to look abashed, or at least that was the way it seemed to Pecora. "It was one thing," Pecora wrote in his memoirs, "to manipulate great blocks of stock on the Exchange, to float great bond issues, dealing only with impersonal financial machinery, or professional dealers. It was quite another to be brought face to face with responsibility for the ultimate damage to individual human beings."[1]

On Thursday morning, the last day of the hearings, Pecora was ready to question Mitchell again, but there was no dramatic confrontation between the two men, no Perry Mason moment when Mitchell admitted the error of his ways. Pecora asked Mitchell a few housekeeping questions about when the banker first saw the Lehmann opinion, the opinion by the solicitor general that found securities affiliates violated the National Banking Act. Mitchell could not recall clearly. That was it. Mitchell left the stand in a matter of minutes. So why did Pecora insist that Mitchell remain in Washington? Most likely, he was just being careful. He could not be sure how any of the remaining witnesses would testify. If subsequent testimony implicated Mitchell, Pecora wanted him available. That didn't happen, and now it appeared that Pecora, having insisted that Mitchell remain in Washington, needed to put him briefly on the stand in order to justify his decision.[2]

Over the previous nine days, Pecora had presented nearly all the examples he identified in his investigation "of how a bank should not conduct a stock-selling and stock-speculation business." Now, with that work out of the way, most of the last day was consumed with testimony that Norbeck had wanted the City Bank hearings to address. In the scheme of things, this testimony was not terribly important. There was the consolidation of three farm-equipment manufacturers into a company called Oliver Farm Equipment. National City made a nice profit when it arranged the merger, and there was some unseemly squabbling between it and another Wall Street firm about precisely how those profits should be divided, but there was nothing terribly scandalous in the transaction. The same was largely true of the Lautaro Nitrate Company, a Chilean corporation controlled by the Guggenheim family. When National City offered its securities it never disclosed to prospective investors the profits it would make and it never disclosed substantial risks inherent in the company's business. They were, to be sure, valid points to raise at the hearing, but they were points Pecora had already made several times with the other offerings. Day ten's testimony was simply more of the same.

Pecora wanted to share some of the remaining limelight with his assistants who had worked so hard over the previous six weeks, so Julius Silver handled most of this questioning. Silver was a smart and competent lawyer (he would eventually become the CEO of Polaroid), but only a few minutes after he took the floor, it was clear why the press was so captivated by Pecora. Silver was clinical and dispassionate—he asked the right questions, but there was nothing memorable in his examination.

Pecora's personality came through whenever he asked a question. At one point that afternoon, Pecora interrupted Silver briefly to ask whether National City had sent one of its engineers to Chile to make "a study and survey of that industrial field." The witness was Ronald Byrnes, the man who previously testified about Minas Geraes, and his answer rambled on for some time: "Although we had very great confidence in the acumen and the ability of the Guggenheim organization, so-called, in the engineers whom they had then attached to their organization, we did take the final precaution of sending a man to Chile to study the industry on the ground, in order that we might have somebody in our organization that would understand something about the very technical processes involved."

Pecora waited patiently through Byrnes's long-winded answer, and then he asked, dryly, "And that answer is another way of saying 'Yes' to my question, is it not?"

"I think it is," Byrnes sheepishly replied.

"All right," Pecora responded. "Now we would save time if you would just confine yourself to simple answers." Pecora had style and verve and he could lift the most prosaic questioning into enjoyably political theater.[3]

The only really new information on that last day of testimony involved National City's handling of one of the emerging industries of the 1920s—aviation. In 1928, National City had advised on the merger of the three companies that would eventually become Boeing. The investment banker handling the deal, Joseph Ripley, wanted to make a public offering of Boeing's common and preferred stock, but National City, in an apparent burst of concern for the welfare of the average investor, vetoed that suggestion. The offering, the company decided, "was a little bit too speculative to be spread around to the entire American public." Instead, Mitchell wrote Ripley on October 22, 1928, telling him that National City would buy the stock and "distribution [would] be limited as far as possible to our own officers, key men, directors and special friends." Mitchell, Rentschler, Ripley, and various directors of City Bank were given allocations of Boeing stock. So too were Cary, Winston, and other lawyers from Shearman & Sterling. The biggest chunk went to a partner from J.P. Morgan, who presumably spread the shares around to his fellow partners at the firm.

They were all wealthy and sophisticated and thus could understand and bear the risks associated with investing in such a speculative start-up industry. The company had just floated Minas Geraes and Peruvian bonds, but here at least it seemed National City was indeed only offering securities that were prudent for ordinary investors. Then a funny thing happened. Nine days after the private placement, National City, on behalf of Boeing, requested that the stock be listed for public trading on the New York Curb Exchange (the precursor to the American Stock Exchange), an exchange whose listing standards were far less rigorous than those of the New York Stock Exchange. The next day, National City announced that it had just privately placed a large block of Boeing stock. In the feverish atmosphere of the late 1920s, that announcement could have only one effect. National City insiders, Pecora wrote, "bought plums, not lemons" after all. Boeing's stock price soared, and in no time, National City earned a nearly 50 percent profit, as did Mitchell and the other key men and special friends. In January, the process was repeated with another block of the aviation company's stock with much the same results.

The Boeing disclosures were the final piece of the picture. National City's insiders, Pecora concluded, had "grasped with both hands" the opportunity "for getting in on the ground floor" of the Boeing stock offering. Boeing was "considered too good to be handled in quite the ordinary manner." It became "one of the most familiar tokens of the torrid Wall Street gambles of the period," Pecora wrote. "But before the general public was allowed to enter the game, Mr. Mitchell and his friends had already used their position as officers and directors of the National City to supply themselves with a full set of these tokens . . . at reduced rates." After the bonuses from the management fund and the morale loans, the Boeing testimony was just more evidence that Mitchell and the other officers were running the second largest bank in the country largely "for the profit of themselves and their friends." It was not nearly as dramatic as Edgar Brown or Richard Whitney, but it was, in its own way, a fitting conclusion to Pecora's ten-day economics class.[4]

The lesson Pecora took from those ten days was a simple one. For him, there were two primary culprits that lay at the heart of all the problems he had cataloged—the securities affiliates and the absence of any regulations requiring disclosures to shareholders and investors.

> Without the affiliate to act as an *alter ego* of the Bank, free from the wise restrictions of the National Banking Act, most of the mischief could not even have been initiated. And had there been full disclosure of what was being done in furtherance of these schemes, they could not long have survived the fierce light of publicity and criticism. Legal chicanery and beneficent darkness were the banker's stoutest allies.[5]

Senator Glass's banking bill, which everyone was now predicting would easily be enacted, would address affiliates, and the securities bill that Untermyer was theoretically working on would presumably shine light into the darkness.

On Thursday, the banking system was in its last throes. Before dawn that morning, the telephone rang in Walter Bimson's hotel room in Phoenix. The caller told Bimson, the president of Arizona's Valley Bank and Trust Company, that California had just declared a statewide holiday. California's governor, James Rolph, announced that the holiday was crucial to protect California's banks, and he blamed the panic on "communists who are endeavoring to spread destruction and hysteria."

Arizona's governor, Benjamin Moeur, was staying in the same hotel as Bimson, and the banker rushed to his suite. At first the governor, still in his pajamas and half asleep, did not understand what the problem was. It took Bimson several attempts to explain to Moeur that California banks kept large deposits in Arizona banks. If the California banks all withdrew their money, which was now very likely, the already creaky Arizona banking system would instantly implode. When the governor finally agreed to consult with the state attorney general to determine his authority to declare a holiday, Bimson ran six blocks to the bank's headquarters, where he and the bank's attorney quickly hammered out a draft proclamation. Just before the banks were scheduled to open, Governor Moeur authorized a three-day holiday.[6]

Across the country, there were long lines outside New York's savings banks as fear of the banking crisis reached the city. On Friday those lines grew even longer and soon spread to the large commercial banks. Extra police were called out and did what they could to maintain order, but they were not always successful. An unruly mob at the world's largest savings and loan, the Bowery Savings Bank, forced the bank to close its doors. City Bank was no exception in the panic; its domestic deposits dropped over 10 percent in two days. Enterprising New Yorkers did what they could to make sure they got their money. A woman begged to move to the head of the line at one bank because she had her baby with her. The other customers let her through and then let through the next four women with babies until the bank clerk announced: "This is the fifth time that baby has been here." The mother, it seems, had been renting the baby to anxious depositors for 25 cents a trip.[7]

More states joined the ever growing list of those with full-blown bank holidays or severe restrictions. By the end of the day there were moratoria in Idaho, Nevada, Oregon, Texas, and Washington. Iowa, Mississippi, and Washington, D.C., put restrictions in place. Many of the political dignitaries then flooding into the capital for the inauguration suddenly discovered that their hotels would no longer cash out-of-town checks. On Friday, W. A. Sheaffer, the president of the Sheaffer Pen Company, reported to Raymond Moley that its checks had been refused in twenty-four states. In a few days, he predicted, business would be at "an actual standstill." The "most urgent emergency in the history of our nation," Sheaffer concluded, "is at hand." Over the next two days, the rest of the states would declare their own holidays or restrictions, the two most significant— New York and Illinois—coming in the early hours before dawn on Saturday.

That same morning, Richard Whitney went to the podium overlooking the New York Stock Exchange's immense trading floor and announced that it too would shut down. In Chicago, the commodities exchange, the Board of Trade, closed for the first time in nearly a century, and the streets in the city were eerily quiet. "I do not know how it may have been in other places," one resident recalled, "but in Chicago, as we saw it, the city seemed to have died. There was something awful—absolutely abnormal—in the very stillness of those streets. I recall being startled by the clatter of a horse's hooves on the pavement as a mounted policeman rode past."

On his popular radio broadcast on Thursday evening, Rudy Vallée sang "Let's Put out the Lights (and Go to Sleep)," a song advising that with "no more money in the bank" the best thing to do was simply to crawl into bed. The country's bank leaders once could do no wrong; now everyone was blaming them for the crisis. After the sorry testimony over the last two weeks, Pecora wrote, "the catastrophic collapse of the entire banking structure of the country seemed but the natural climax."[8]

L ate Thursday afternoon, after the last witness testified, Pecora addressed the committee, thanking Norbeck and the other senators for his appointment and the opportunity to serve as counsel. He "accepted the engagement with a high appreciation of the privilege and the honor" it entailed and he thanked his staff "for their devotion, loyalty, industry and integrity." Norbeck returned the compliment. "Speaking for the committee," Norbeck said in gratitude to the little lawyer from New York sitting next to him, "I wish to say that we are well pleased with the progress you have made, Mr. Pecora, in the remarkably short time that you have had a chance to work. The Senate has ordered the committee to continue its work, and there is no doubt in my mind that it will be vigorously prosecuted. I shall not be chairman of the committee very long, but whoever takes charge of the work will go ahead with it I feel certain."[9]

A few minutes later, as the overcast sky grew steadily darker, Pecora and Norbeck were standing in the Senate Office Building engaged in the kind of relaxed small talk that often follows a particularly grueling task. Pecora was no doubt still basking in the warmth of the words with which Norbeck had ended the hearings; it was, after all, just the kind of acclaim that he constantly and desperately craved. The conversation was of "no special importance" and Pecora occasionally glanced out a nearby window. At the base of Capitol Hill he would have seen the Hotel Continental, the bright neon lights on its roof beginning to light up the gloaming sky. He had spent so many sleepless hours there over the past week and a half, studying exhibits, meeting with Silver and Saperstein, getting ready for the next day's examination. It was there—could it have been only a few days ago?—that he picked up his phone and heard Cary tell him that Mitchell had resigned in disgrace from the bank after enduring just four days of his withering questions. Beyond the hotel and across Columbus Plaza was Union Station. It must have seemed remarkable that just a month earlier he had first stepped off the train to meet the senator from South Dakota with whom he was now chatting so casually.

Thirty years later, Pecora reflected on the hearings and the transformation they had wrought in his life. Until this point Pecora likened his experiences to those of "a parish priest," a figure of purely local importance. "I suddenly was thrown into a field of activity which embraced national issues, and matters that had even an international impact." He called it "the most intensive period of my education throughout my entire life." It is easy to believe that although that metamorphosis had only just begun, Pecora had some nascent sense of it as he looked out that window into the fast approaching twilight.

As he stood there, chatting with Norbeck, a figure crossing the windswept plaza caught Pecora's eye, a slump-shouldered man shuffling away from the Senate Office Building toward the train station. Pecora pointed him out to Norbeck, who at first did not recognize him. "That's Mr. Mitchell," Pecora said.

The past ten days had transformed Sunshine Charlie, too, and Pecora couldn't help but think back to when the banker first strutted into the hearing room—a domineering, world-renowned business executive; a leader of Wall Street, surrounded by a bevy of bank executives and lawyers; a man who had nothing but disdain for the people in Washington who were wasting so much of his precious time. The confident, commanding swagger was gone; Mitchell's head was bowed as he made his way across the plaza. The entourage had vanished, too; Mitchell was completely alone, forced to carry his own suitcase as he headed back to New York. Mitchell looked, Pecora thought, like a man completely "wrapped up in his own thoughts."

Norbeck saw the same thing. For all his lack of education, the senator was something of an art aficionado, and he loved to roam the halls of Washington's museums. "There's a famous picture," the senator told Pecora, "that portrays the great Napoleon on his way to St. Helena, on the decks of the steamer conveying him from France." That drawing shows Napoleon standing alone, his gaze fixed on the horizon, totally oblivious to his surroundings, as the ship's officers huddle behind him staring and whispering. Pecora knew the drawing and he agreed with Norbeck—Mitchell looked like a man who was "going into exile." It was the last glimpse the lawyer ever had of the fallen banker.[10]

Just a few hours later, a train rolled in to Union Station, pulling in to the easternmost siding, a gloomy and dimly lit corner of the rail yard. Secret Service men, their hands obviously clutching the pistols in their pockets, quickly surrounded the train, as did a host of policemen in black rubber overcoats, some on foot and others mounted on motorcycles. A steady mixture of sleet and icy rain formed slick, dark pools on the platforms, but it suddenly ceased as soon as President-Elect Roosevelt exited the train and made his way down a gangway to a tightly guarded car waiting nearby. His staff carried a rough draft of a proclamation declaring a nationwide bank holiday. Roosevelt waved to the crowd of about fifteen hundred people and they gave a loud cheer as he departed for the Mayflower Hotel to monitor the final collapse of the banking system and to make the last preparations for the Inaugural Address he would deliver in less than forty-eight hours.

To this point, the incoming president had not breathed a word of the contents of that speech, wanting to heighten the mystery and the drama when he finally delivered it. The typewritten address was in safekeeping with Raymond Moley, who slept with it under his pillow to make sure that it didn't inadvertently fall into the hands of a reporter.[11]

The next day, Union Station was back to its normal bustle as Ferdinand Pecora quietly and unobtrusively boarded a train for New York.

EPILOGUE

Over seventy-five years before Rahm Emanuel, Barack Obama's chief of staff, advised that politicians should never let a good crisis go to waste, the columnist Walter Lippmann wrote that "there are good crises and bad crises." Lippmann had refrained from commenting on Mitchell and City Bank during the hearings, but a week after the inauguration, though he was convinced that Pecora's relentless unmasking of the bank's misdeeds had exacerbated the banking crisis, he nonetheless pronounced that the hearings had been worth it. In a column published in the *New York Herald Tribune*, he wrote:

> The much debated question as to whether the Congressional exposure of Mr. Mitchell's conduct of the National City Bank was in the public interest can now be answered clearly in the affirmative. It is, of course, true that the exposure accelerated the banking crisis by adding to the popular distrust of banks. But the exposure has proved to be a good thing, not merely in the general sense that wrongs should always be exposed whatever the consequences, but in the specific sense that the way has been opened to a more thorough-going reconstruction. The crisis has not only made it possible for the Administration to reform the banking system drastically, but it has pro-

duced, or at least brought into the open, a recognition of evils and a desire
for a reform within the banking community itself.[1]

The new president knew better than anyone the opportunity the banking
crisis created, and he moved quickly to address it. On Sunday, March 5, 1933,
the day after his inauguration, Roosevelt made official what was already a fait
accompli—he declared a national banking holiday. To the *New York Times* it
was the "most drastic" peacetime action that a president had ever taken. Many
others saw it as a necessary breather, a chance for hysterical Americans to simply
calm down. The president had given the country "a sharp slap in the face," the
historian Charles Beard wrote. "By arresting all banking functions, government
removed the sources on which fear might thrive; and it gave the people time to
collect themselves."[2]

Now that the banks were closed, Roosevelt needed to get them back open.
The president rejected calls to nationalize the banking system as completely
impracticable and far too radical. Instead, working off a plan that the Hoover
administration had started, and with Ogden Mills, Arthur Ballantine, and other
Hoover administration officials continuing to pitch in, Roosevelt's staff quickly
drafted the emergency legislation that would permanently close hopeless cases,
prop up shaky ones, and immediately reopen sound banks. Congress passed it
in eight hours with virtually no debate.

A week later, Roosevelt gave his first fireside chat. Trying to restore confidence in the banking sector, he referred only obliquely to the City Bank hearings.
"Some of our bankers," he told the estimated 60 million radio listeners, "had
shown themselves either incompetent or dishonest in their handling of the people's funds. They had used the money entrusted to them in speculations and
unwise loans." Roosevelt was confident that the banking system as a whole was
sound and that the vast majority of bankers were honest. He implored Americans
to have faith. "I can assure you," he told the nation, "that it is safer to keep your
money in a reopened bank than under the mattress." Roosevelt's comforting
words and quick action worked. Money flooded back into the banks and the system quickly righted itself. The New York Stock Exchange reopened and rose 15
percent in the first day's trading. The banking crisis had passed, and the Roosevelt
administration was lauded for its swift and sure-handed response.[3]

With public opinion now even more firmly on his side, Roosevelt was not yet ready to let "the money changers" off the hook. The public was still clamoring for federal legislation. Bankers, as one newspaper put it, needed a "legal straight-jacket" if the country was going to avoid a repeat of the "sickening story of exploitation" Pecora revealed. The president knew that he had to keep that anger alive if he was going to pass real financial reforms, and the way to do that was to keep the pressure on Wall Street. The day after his first fireside chat, Roosevelt met the new chair of the Banking and Currency Committee, the Florida Democrat Duncan Fletcher. Fletcher could have used his seniority to take charge of the powerful Commerce Committee, but over the winter Roosevelt had persuaded him to lead this one instead, a move that prevented Carter Glass, the senator who so hated sensational congressional hearings, from doing so. At his initial meeting with Fletcher, it was Roosevelt who suggested that the next target of the investigation should be the private bankers, especially J.P. Morgan and Company.[4]

Incredibly, Untermyer was still lobbying the president to take over as counsel. He wrote the presidential adviser Raymond Moley that "as soon as the Committee is re-constituted, if it desires to have me go forward with an investigation . . . I shall be prepared to do so." Moley gave Untermyer no encouragement. He thought it was not the administration's role to dictate to a Senate committee who its counsel should be, but he did little to disguise his preference for Untermyer. Moley never really gave Pecora a chance. "He is too blithe on important matters, too ready to dispose by a jest," one contemporary wrote of the Brain Trust coordinator. Moley had worked briefly on the Seabury investigation of Tammany Hall and that experience colored his view of Pecora. It was purely guilt by association. "Untermyer would have been preferable to the man ultimately selected," Moley wrote in his memoirs. "For Ferdinand Pecora's experience had been that of an assistant district attorney in a generally incompetent office."

Not content to lobby just the president, Untermyer wrote again to Norbeck, although he was no longer chair of the committee. Untermyer had "never known the people in such an unsettled, distressed state of mind. I realize as keenly as anyone the necessity for uncovering and uprooting some part of the rottenness of the great financial institutions of New York. I recognize also that this is but a beginning and that the surface has hardly been scratched." The lawyer flattered

Norbeck for his "reckless courage" in uncovering these abuses during "the present terrorized condition of the country" and made his pitch for the job. "It is
hardly necessary for me to repeat that if there is any way in which I can help, the
Committee has only to command, for my heart is and has been for thirteen years
wrapped up in this reform, which should be no longer delayed."

Roosevelt had no intention of switching horses. He was weary of Untermyer's incessant self-promotion and annoyed that the lawyer constantly leaked
news of their meetings in order to bill himself as a crucial adviser. Besides, the
president, who knew a good thing when he saw it, was not about to dump Pecora.
Pecora met with Roosevelt shortly after the inauguration and was reappointed
as counsel on March 13, 1933.[5]

Pecora would guide the hearings for a little more than a year. During that
time all the leading bankers on Wall Street traipsed before the committee,
but the investigation was never more intense than in the spring of 1933, when
J. P. Morgan Jr. came to Washington. The intrepid attorney was now facing off
against Morgan's longtime lawyer, John W. Davis, the man originally considered
to run the short-selling investigation. Davis still abhorred congressional investigations, and he was convinced that Pecora intended this one to be a "witch
hunt." At every turn he opposed Pecora's investigatory efforts. Thomas Lamont,
who just six weeks earlier had pleaded with Roosevelt to intercede in the banking crisis, was now vociferously complaining to the president about Pecora's
handling of the Morgan investigation. None of it was of any use; Roosevelt was
squarely behind the investigation. The president ignored Lamont's protests,
and the committee continually expanded the authorizing resolution, cutting off
Davis's objections.[6]

Public anticipation of the younger J. P. Morgan's appearance before the
committee was tremendous, and when the hearings finally started in late May,
they were a media circus, completely dominating the other news coming out of
Washington. The crowds gathering to see the reclusive Morgan swamped Room
301 and the hearings were moved to the larger and more ornate Senate Caucus
Room down the hall. Overruling Pecora's previous request to ban photographers,
the senators authorized newspapers to attach klieg lights to the room's chande-

liers. Extra telegraph lines were brought into the Senate Office Building so that reporters could get their stories out more easily.

Morgan's last name was filled with mystique, and one newspaper report portrayed him as "the twentieth-century embodiment of Croesus, Lorenzo the Magnificent, [and] Rothschild" all rolled into one, but in reality the shy Morgan was a pale imitation of his legendary father. It was the firm's practices, rather than Morgan himself, that were really on trial.

Despite the hoopla, the hearings were, to some degree, a disappointment. "In truth," Pecora wrote in his memoirs, "the investigation of the Morgan firm elicited no such glaring abuses" as the City Bank hearings. As with Insull, Pecora was again trying hard to prove otherwise, and he ended up skating very close to the line of demagoguery. When he revealed that for two years the Morgan partners paid no income taxes, it was the front-page headline across the country. He neglected to mention that because of their huge capital losses in the Depression, they had no taxes to pay. "It is no criminality," the New York Evening Post observed. "Mr. Pecora only makes it seem so." It may not have been illegal, but if it had been no one at the Internal Revenue Bureau would have noticed. One tax return Pecora put in evidence contained this notation: "Returned without examination for the reason that the return was prepared in the office of J.P. Morgan and Company and it has been our experience that any schedule made by that office is correct."

Other disclosures prompted similar outrage and suggested a market in which the favored few had unerodible advantages over the ordinary investor. Pecora was able to show that the J.P. Morgan firm had preferred lists of clients to whom it doled out financial sure things—stocks that it sold for below market prices. Those recipients of Morgan's generosity were a who's who of the political, social, and financial elite of the day, including the former president Calvin Coolidge, leading bankers (Charles Mitchell among them), former and current cabinet officers (including Roosevelt's Treasury secretary William Woodin), a Supreme Court justice (Owen Roberts) and, for good measure, the aviator Charles Lindbergh and the American World War I hero General John "Black Jack" Pershing. The favors weren't illegal either, but the former Democratic National Committee chairman John J. Raskob's thank-you note seemed to best encapsulate the public's suspicions about what lay behind them. "I appreciate deeply the many courtesies shown me by you and your partners," he wrote, "and sincerely hope the future holds opportunities for me to reciprocate." For Pecora, that sense of obligation ("the silken bonds of gratitude in which it skillfully enmeshed the chosen ranks," as he put it in his memoirs) was one of the key sources of the firm's power.

In the opening statement John Davis penned for him, Morgan defended the private investment banker as "a national asset and not a national danger." Regulation was unnecessary because he conformed his conduct to a far more exacting code than any law could ever articulate. Morgan, Pecora wrote, believed profoundly "in the invincible rectitude of his own regime"; but as the hearings progressed, that view became a minority opinion. "Here was a firm of bankers," the *New York Times* wrote, "perhaps the most famous and powerful in the world, which was certainly under no necessity of practicing the small arts of petty traders. Yet it failed under a test of its pride and prestige." Walter Lippmann, a usually reliable defender of Morgan, now asked Washington to put limits on "the sheer power of so much privately directed money."

Pecora had nothing to do with the incident that, more than anything, evaporated Morgan's air of mystery, although the grilling he was giving the banker precipitated it. Carter Glass had grown annoyed at what he saw as a "Roman holiday" that was diverting attention away from his now reproposed banking bill. Glass began to attack Pecora. The lawyer, he said, was wasting everybody's time asking arcane questions that were of "no significance to a man of ordinary intelligence." Glass's former assistants at Treasury were both partners at the firm, and the senator roared at Pecora that he did "not intend to see any injustice done to the House of Morgan." Senator Couzens came to the investigator's defense. Pounding the table, Couzens barked, "I insist that Mr. Morgan be treated like anyone else here!"

Pecora, who had been working around the clock, no doubt appreciated the support, but he was perfectly capable of taking care of himself. In no mood for Glass's upbraiding of his methods or his motives, he gave as good as he got. "I want to assure Senator Glass," Pecora angrily shot back, "that the compensation of $255 a month which I am receiving for these services is no incentive to me to render these services or continue to render them." The gathered crowd gave a huge round of applause to the feisty counsel, leaving Glass to complain, "Oh yes; that is what it is all about. We are having a circus, and the only things lacking now are peanuts and colored lemonade."

Glass's remark caught the attention of a Ringling Brothers promoter, who brought Lya Graf, the circus's thirty-two-year-old midget, to the hearing room the next day. As the senators on the committee were embroiled in a rancorous executive session, during which Glass wanted to severely curtail Pecora and Pecora threatened to resign, Graf came into the hearing room. After shaking hands with Morgan, at the promoter's suggestion, she promptly plopped down onto the famous banker's lap. The committee implored newspapers not to print the photographs, but only the *New York Times* complied. The iconic pictures of the smiling and grandfatherly Morgan bouncing Graf on his knee humanized Jack and further undermined the view of investment bankers as otherworldly supermen. The fallout for Graf was decidedly worse. She fled to her native Germany in 1935 to escape the constant jokes about the incident. Two years later, the Nazis classified the half-Jewish Graf as a "useless person" and she was eventually killed in the gas chambers at Auschwitz.[7]

Glass failed to squelch the hearings; indeed, Roosevelt himself stood behind the investigator, announcing that he wanted the hearings to "go through without limit." With the Morgan hearings captivating the country and the popular president's benediction, Ferdinand Pecora quickly became a media darling. In the same week in June 1933, the investigator's photograph graced the covers of both *Time* and *Newsweek*. To the editors at *Time*, unaware of Samuel Untermyer's backroom machinations to steal Pecora's job, Pecora was a "Roland for an Untermyer," a reference to Charlemagne's most courageous and loyal knight. Reporters praised Pecora's prosecutorial experience, complimented him on his "penetrating, analytical mind," extolled his relentless cross-examination skills, and fawned over his sparkling dark eyes, "which reveal determination and intelligence." They were gleeful whenever the bantam lawyer transformed "some cocky banker . . . from assurance into a perspiration." They "looked with astonishment at this man who, through the intricate mazes of banking, syndicates, market deals, chicanery of all sorts, in a field new to him, never forgot a name, never made an error in a figure, and never lost his temper." They delighted in reporting that "the sharp rapier of the Senate inquisition," who continued to make a pittance, was facing off against the highest-priced and best-known legal talent in the country.

At times, eager to satisfy the public's voracious appetite for information on the "committee's dynamic little chief investigator," the papers veered into detailing the kind of minutiae normally reserved for puff pieces about movie stars. Pecora stood five feet five inches and weighed 140 pounds. His favorite outdoor sport was golf. He loved to play pinochle. He took "regular sun-lamp treatments." He disliked going to bed and, in fact, did his best work at night. In the middle of eighteen- or twenty-hour days, Pecora liked to refresh himself with a large bowl of ice cream. When he finally made it to bed, he would continue to read while smoking "large expensive cigars."[8]

The *Boston Globe* dubbed him "Fighting Ferdinand"; for others he was the "hellhound of Wall Street" or the "Icy Latin." Although he had been a Democrat for nearly two decades, Will Rogers quipped: "If the Republicans ever decide to enter another Presidential candidate they better hire this little Pecora to run for 'em. He is the best bet I see right now." One enterprising barber in New York who shared the same last name hung this advertisement in his shop window: "D. Pecora, Barber, Let Us Investigate Your Scalp." Few lawyers ever achieve that kind of public acclaim. As for Irving Ben Cooper, the lawyer who quit in a huff after just a week as committee counsel, the rumor around Washington, according to Norbeck, was that he was "quite a little envious of Mr. Pecora's position, and is wondering why he himself is not in the limelight."[9]

With Pecora keeping the pressure on Wall Street, the initial path to federal securities and banking legislation was relatively unobstructed. "The first months of the New Deal," the historian Arthur Schlesinger wrote, "were to an astonishing degree an adventure in unanimity." Roosevelt turned to securities even before the Morgan hearings were held, knowing that the continuing clamor over City Bank and the intense interest in Morgan would ease passage of reform legislation. Before March was out, Roosevelt sent to Congress a draft of a bill regulating how securities were sold to the public. "This proposal," the president wrote, "adds to the ancient rule of *caveat emptor* the further doctrine, 'Let the seller also beware.'" As with the emergency banking legislation, he steered away

from more radical approaches. He rejected proposals from some in his administration to create an agency that would direct the flow of capital in the economy,
deciding which industries and which projects were entitled to funding. Adhering
closely to Brandeis's progressive prescription, Roosevelt wanted to preserve the
markets while regulating their excesses and abuses.

The final bill, drafted by three of Felix Frankfurter's former students (James
Landis, Benjamin Cohen, and Thomas Corcoran, collectively known as the
Happy Hot Dogs), did not require the government to approve new issues or, as
an initial draft had done, give the government the power to revoke securities "not
based upon sound principles." As Roosevelt told Congress, the "Federal Government cannot and should not take any action which might be construed as approving or guaranteeing that newly issued securities are sound in the sense that
their value will be maintained or that the properties which they represent will
earn profit." Instead, the Truth in Securities Act was modeled on the legal requirements already in place in Britain and it put "the burden of telling the whole
truth on the seller." There would be no more skimpy prospectuses like the ones
City Bank distributed to investors. New securities could now only be sold if investors were given all the information they needed to make an informed decision
about whether to buy them. Not only issuers, but their investment bankers as
well, would be liable for any materially false or misleading representations or
omissions in their offering documents. Requiring sunlight, as Brandeis said
twenty years earlier, was the best way to police the markets and the best way to
avoid a repeat of the Minas Geraes and Peruvian bond offerings.

House Speaker Sam Rayburn had the task of moving the securities bill
through Congress, and he was quite conscious of the connection between the
bill and Pecora's confrontation with Mitchell. "Today," he said, "we are forced
to recognize that the hired managers of great corporations are not as wise, not
as conservative, and sometimes not as trustworthy as millions of Americans have
been persuaded to believe. . . . In this bill, we demand not only a new deal, we
also demand a square deal. Less than this no honest man expects nor a dishonest
man should have." Rayburn had comparatively few difficulties. Public opinion
was strongly in favor of the bill, and even such stalwart conservative newspapers
as the *Wall Street Journal* remarked that the bill "is in the main so right in its
basic provisions that the country will insist on its passage."

Investment bankers put up some resistance, but with the political climate so against them, it was comparatively mild. John Foster Dulles, one of the Street's designated spokesmen (and the future secretary of state), was by far the most strident critic, claiming the bill would undermine the entire financial system of the country. No one in Washington seemed to be taking those dire predictions seriously; the groundswell for reform was simply too strong. On May 27, 1933, while Pecora continued to examine J. P. Morgan Jr. in the Senate Caucus Room, the president signed the Securities Act. Advocates for robust federal control of the capital markets continued to deride it as an inadequate "nineteenth-century piece of legislation." But nearly eighty years later, its provisions remain securely in place, and the disclosure philosophy it articulates is still the touchstone for federal regulation of the securities markets.[10]

Three weeks later, near the end of the first hundred days, Roosevelt signed the Banking Act of 1933, more commonly known as Glass–Steagall. The expanded branch-banking features that proved so objectionable the previous winter were still there. Indeed, the bill was even more expansive than the one Huey Long killed in his filibuster. In a direct nod to the City Bank hearings, it gave the Federal Reserve the power to remove officers and directors of national banks if they were operating the bank in an unsafe or unsound manner. There would be no more morale loans either; national banks were barred from loaning money to their own executives. After the trashing Pecora had given securities affiliates, it was not terribly surprising that the ban on them was still firmly in place. Nationally chartered banks were given a year to sever their affiliates, and private investment banks were prohibited from accepting deposits.

When Glass reintroduced his bill on March 9, 1933, some bankers — if only in a vain attempt to restore a semblance of their tattered reputations — were already on board. Winthrop Aldrich, the chairman of Chase National Bank, urged Congress to pass legislation to reform the banking sector and he pledged to divorce Chase from its securities affiliate. "The spirit of speculation," he declared, "should be eradicated from the management of commercial banks." James Perkins, who was doing everything he could to clean up City Bank's sullied image, met with Roosevelt at the White House on the first day of the national banking holiday and promptly announced that his bank would get rid of the National City Company.

Not everyone in the banking community, however, was so amenable to reform. W. C. Potter of the Guaranty Trust called Aldrich's move the "most disastrous" one he had "ever heard from a member of the financial community." J. P. Morgan Jr. predicted that separation of investment and commercial banking would seriously undermine his firm's ability to provide capital for America's future growth. Anger over City Bank's misuse of its affiliate effectively muted these concerns. "To reverse a popular saying of the day," wrote the SEC historian Joel Seligman, "the period of the First Hundred Days of the Roosevelt administration was that rare time when money talked and nobody listened."[11]

Ironically, just as City Bank had created the final impetus for Glass–Steagall, its successor created the final impetus for its repeal more than six decades later. Separation of commercial and investment banking officially remained in place until 1999, when President Clinton signed the law repealing those provisions of Glass–Steagall. Unofficially, strict separation had already slowly begun to erode in the 1980s and 1990s. The financial industry and a chorus of academic critics attacked it as an ill-conceived, anachronistic, and unnecessary restriction standing in the way of financial institutions trying to diversify their businesses and compete on the global stage. In response, federal banking regulators and the courts slowly began to permit commercial banks to engage in securities-related activities and then allowed bank holding companies to acquire investment banking subsidiaries.

Those trends culminated in the 1998 merger of Citibank, as it was then known, and the Travelers Group. Citigroup was immediately the world's largest financial services company, a full-service firm that combined consumer, commercial, and investment banking with insurance and investment management. The scale of this new financial department store—it had nearly $700 billion in assets and $50 billion in revenue at the time the deal was announced—was enormous, far larger than Charles Mitchell could ever have envisioned. Efforts to repeal Glass–Steagall had been kicked around in Congress for a decade, but the announced merger suddenly made them a legislative priority, with Citigroup leading the push for abolition of those Depression-era restrictions. Federal regulators had permitted the merger, but if Glass–Steagall remained the law, they would have required the combined company to shed many of its nonbanking businesses. Repeal foreclosed that contingency, which was all to the good as far as many commentators were concerned. Citigroup, two business writers noted in 2002, "is so well-diversified that there seems little chance of it running into crippling financial problems."[12]

Back in 1933, the most controversial provision of the Glass–Steagall bill was not the elimination of securities affiliates, but the creation of federal deposit insurance. When the Michigan senator Arthur Vandenberg called for a federal deposit guarantee as the City Bank hearings were winding down, it was far from a novel proposal. Over the previous fifty years, 150 bills guaranteeing bank deposits had been introduced in Congress, and every one of them was defeated. Representative Henry Steagall, an Alabama Democrat, introduced one of the last proposals in April 1932, telling then Speaker of the House John Nance Garner that it was a potent political weapon in a climate of cascading bank failures.

"You know," he warned, "this fellow Hoover is going to wake up one day and come in here with a message recommending guarantee of bank deposits, and as sure as he does, he'll be reelected." Hoover, of course, never did, and Steagall's proposal never made it out of the House. Garner, however, was now vice president, and he told Roosevelt the provision was necessary to restore confidence in the banks. "You'll have to have it, Cap'n," Garner told the president. "The people who have taken their money out of the banks are not going to put it back without some guarantee."

Roosevelt disagreed. He held his first press conference before the banks were reopened and he told reporters that he was opposed to deposit insurance. After the Panic of 1907, eight states had tried it and in eight states the system had either collapsed when too many banks failed or the measure had been declared unconstitutional. Like the bankers, Roosevelt saw the proposal as requiring stronger banks to subsidize weaker ones, thereby creating disincentives for prudent management. Throughout the debate, Roosevelt continually threatened to veto any bill that contained an insurance provision, but he eventually succumbed to the overwhelming political pressure. Deposit insurance ultimately proved to be one of the finest innovations of the New Deal. Even the economist and ardent free-market proponent Milton Friedman recognized it as "the most important structural change in the banking system to result from the 1933 panic."[13]

.   .   .

Ever since the inauguration, Richard Whitney, well aware of the strong public distaste for the financial community, had quietly been making the case
that federal regulation of the exchange was unnecessary. Repeating much the
same strategy it had employed with Hoover, the exchange adopted a number of
reforms to head off any proposals. When the Pecora hearings recessed for the
summer, Wall Street stepped up its offensive by launching a direct assault on
the already passed Securities Act. The legislation, it argued, was drying up capital and undermining economic recovery because legitimate investment banks
and issuers were so afraid of liability that they were forgoing offerings. Roosevelt
scoffed at those claims, as did Frankfurter, who argued that Wall Street was looking "not to improve but to chloroform the Act." Indeed, Frankfurter was convinced that the dearth of new securities offerings was not the result of fear of
liability, but the product of a bankers' strike. Roosevelt held firm, even though
more-conservative members of his administration were also urging amendment.
"There will be," the president told reporters, "mighty few changes, if any, in the
Securities Act this winter."

The president could afford to maintain a strong stance against the financial
community because he was still getting plenty of ammunition from Pecora. As
the hearings resumed in the fall of 1933, the lawyer continued to show bankers
behaving badly. Among the most shocking disclosures concerned Albert Wiggin,
the former chairman of Chase National Bank, City Bank's longtime rival. Pecora
carefully showed how Wiggin had used a series of privately owned corporations
to surreptitiously trade Chase's securities. In the midst of the 1929 crash, Wiggin
was part of the group of Wall Street leaders who tried to prop up the market. Or
at least that was what the public thought. In reality, Pecora showed that at the
same time Wiggin was actually shorting Chase's stock (in effect betting that the
price of the stock would continue to drop) on money he borrowed from Chase.
Wiggin had once been one of the most popular bankers on the Street, but the
disclosures thoroughly destroyed his reputation.

Whitney continued trying to thwart Pecora's investigation. The stock exchange president was furious when Pecora hired John Flynn, a reporter and
persistent exchange critic, as an investigator. When Flynn showed up at the

exchange with a questionnaire that Pecora wanted delivered to all exchange members, Whitney was so mad that he actually had to leave the room to compose himself. When he returned he was dismissive. "You gentlemen are making a great mistake," he declared. "The Exchange is a perfect institution."

When the Securities Exchange Act was proposed, in early 1934, Whitney led the fight against it. The atmosphere had changed substantially in a year. The economy's precipitous decline had been arrested, and anger at Wall Street was no longer white-hot, making the exchange leader's efforts all the more effective. Whitney rented a house in Washington (nicknamed the Wall Street Embassy) and railed against the proposed bill, claiming it would "destroy the free and open market for securities" and turn Wall Street into "a deserted village."

Backing Whitney were the leaders of the regional stock exchanges that then dotted the country. Eugene Thompson, head of the Association of Stock Exchanges, testified that the bill was the equivalent of curing a case of hiccups by "severing the head of the patient." Letters and telegrams flooded congressional offices as business leaders, whom Roosevelt had alienated in his first year in office, lined up to oppose the bill. General Electric's chief executive, Gerard Swope, said that passage would be a "national disaster," while the former Federal Reserve chairman Eugene Meyer predicted it would lead to "state control of industry." The Republican congressman Fred Britten was even more hysterical, claiming the object of the bill was to "Russianize everything worthwhile." As the hue and cry intensified, the initially overwhelming editorial support for the bill melted away.

It was, by far, the biggest fight yet against a New Deal measure, and it was at least partially successful. The initial bill was redrafted, some of the provisions that Wall Street found the most objectionable were eliminated or carved back substantially, and Roosevelt even agreed to make the Securities Act less severe. In many controversial areas, the statute mandated nothing, but simply delegated authority to an administrative agency (originally the Federal Trade Commission) to write rules addressing the subject. But Roosevelt refused to back down further, asserting that "the country as a whole will not be satisfied with legislation unless such legislation has teeth in it." Fighting over the bill lingered into the spring, but the president finally signed it on June 6, 1934.

The Securities Exchange Act for the first time required stock exchanges to register with the federal government and submit to the oversight of the new administrative agency the act had just created, the Securities and Exchange Commission. The statute also imposed some federal control over margin trading, restricted stock pools and other forms of manipulation, placed strict limits on corporate insiders trading in their own securities, and created a system under which companies that trade on the exchanges are required to periodically disclose material information to investors. The federal government, Will Rogers noted, had finally managed to put "a cop on Wall Street."[14]

Peter Norbeck was on the sidelines for almost all the action. He lost the chairmanship of the Senate Banking and Currency Committee on March 4, 1933, and moved out of the spacious offices adjoining Room 301. When the committee discussed who the counsel for the investigation should be in the next Congress, Norbeck praised Pecora's work. It was Pecora's efforts, he told the committee, that were responsible for the investigation's excellent results. Still, for all his good words, Norbeck seemed more than a little resentful about the plaudits Pecora was earning. A year earlier Norbeck believed the investigation was his best chance to accomplish something of lasting importance in Washington. Some, like John Flynn, the muckraking financial journalist who worked for Pecora, agreed. "It was Norbeck," Flynn wrote in 1934, "big, honest, calm, filled with common sense, who made this investigation of Wall Street, who kept doggedly at the probe . . . and who, more than any other man, gave to the investigation its tone, its character, and direction."

Even Flynn, however, acknowledged that Norbeck's biggest contribution was his good sense in hiring Pecora. Norbeck was a savvy politician, and he knew who would get credit for Mitchell and for everything else that would thereafter come down the pike. The results, he said, were more important than the credit, but he clearly regretted that despite his hard work he would never be known as the senator who uncovered Wall Street's sins. "It is now being referred to generally as 'Pecora's investigation,'" he wrote Stewart near the end of March 1933, "but that part is natural."[15]

With his move to the minority, Norbeck lost most of his power and influ-

ence. The substantial Democratic majority did not need his vote to pass legislation. He had not supported Roosevelt like some of his progressive colleagues and
so the president had no need to reward him. Old-guard Republicans thoroughly
distrusted him. Peter Norbeck was very much alone in the Seventy-third Congress. Although he came to support much of the New Deal legislation, he was
instrumental in passing none of it, not even Roosevelt's farm relief laws—the
kind of laws he had spent a decade trying to enact. But he was a strong advocate
for Roosevelt's securities legislation, telling his colleagues, "We have got to break
down every crooked organization so that we can throw the fear of God into them
and let them know there is a law in the land."

By 1936, Norbeck had even changed his mind about Roosevelt. He praised
the president for "introducing a little humanity into government . . . where it
has been outlawed from some time." Breaking with his party, the South Dakota
senator endorsed the president's reelection in 1936. It was one of his last political acts. At the time of the endorsement he was battling malignant tumors in
his mouth and jaw, and he died back home in South Dakota on December
20, 1936.[16]

I n March 1938, Richard Whitney was indicted for embezzlement. It was a
 shocking downfall for the face of Wall Street and an enormous scandal for the
financial community given Whitney's veneer of rectitude and his persistent ad-
monitions that federal regulation of the exchange was unnecessary. "Wall Street,"
the Nation wrote, "could hardly have been more embarrassed if J. P. Morgan
had been caught helping himself from the collection plate at the Cathedral
of St. John the Divine." Even Roosevelt was shocked. "Not Dick Whitney!"
the president reportedly exclaimed. "Dick Whitney—Dick Whitney, I can't believe it."

With his New Jersey estate and East Side town house, it was enormously
expensive for Whitney to maintain the lifestyle of a proper country squire. Even
worse, he had an irresistible penchant for speculative stocks. In 1926 Whitney used over $100,000 in securities from his deceased father-in-law's estate
as collateral for a loan to prop up his sagging portfolio. Whitney's money trou-

bles worsened after the crash, even after he borrowed millions from his brother, the Morgan partner George Whitney, and virtually anyone else on the Street he could hit up. In 1930, Whitney, who was treasurer of the New York Yacht Club, took $100,000 of the club's securities as collateral for even more loans. The pattern continued until 1937, when Whitney lifted bonds and cash from the stock exchange's Gratuity Fund, a trust for the widows and orphans of exchange members.

On Monday, April 11, 1938, he was sentenced to five to ten years in New York State prison. On Tuesday, a huge crowd gathered to catch a glimpse of the handcuffed Whitney as he left the Tombs in Lower Manhattan. Five thousand more waited at Grand Central Station, where Whitney was put on a train for the trip up the Hudson River to Sing Sing, along with two extortionists, an armed robber, and a rapist. When he arrived, Whitney passed through yet another crowd surrounding the prison gates. Once inside, he exchanged his blue serge suit, polo coat, and gray felt hat for ill-fitting prison garb and became prisoner 94835. His fellow prisoners were in awe; several raised their caps or stepped aside as he walked past and one sacrificed his sheets so that Whitney, who didn't have any yet, would not have to go without. Even the guards were respectful. "All men who came in Thursday, Friday, Saturday, Monday or Tuesday," one guard growled, "and Mr. Whitney, please step out of the cells."

Whitney was by all accounts a model prisoner—at first assigned to mopping and general cleanup, he eventually taught in the prison school and played first base for the prison baseball team. Indeed, in 1938 Whitney's old Groton headmaster, Endicott Peabody, paid him a visit. Peabody was the same headmaster who led the prep school when the young Franklin Roosevelt was there, and he asked Whitney the same thing that he asked the president when he called—was there anything he could do? "Yes," Whitney replied, "I need a left-handed first baseman's mitt!" Whitney was released from prison in August 1941, the earliest date on which he was eligible for parole. His ever loyal brother, George, paid back everything that Dick Whitney had borrowed or embezzled. Barred from the securities industry, his estate and other properties auctioned off to pay creditors, Dick Whitney briefly managed a Cape Cod dairy. He spent the remainder of his life in Far Hills, New Jersey, and died on December 5, 1974.[17]

. . .

On March 21, 1933, Charles E. Mitchell was arrested at his home for tax evasion. At his arraignment, he proclaimed in a loud, clear voice, "Not guilty." Standing by his side was Max Steuer, the greatest trial lawyer of his day, the man who had twenty years earlier won the acquittal of the owners of the Triangle Shirtwaist Factory on manslaughter charges, the man who had convicted the executives of the Bank of United States, and the man Norbeck's staff wanted to hire to run the investigation. Steuer reportedly made a million dollars a year and, after years of winning one hopeless case after another, he was offered far more cases than he could actually take. He could afford to be choosy. "I take only," he said, "criminal cases when the client is innocent. . . . Having right on my side, I ought to win most of the time." That was not exactly true—sometimes Steuer took cases for the money; the word around Wall Street was that he had demanded a $100,000 retainer from Mitchell and that Mitchell was so strapped for cash that he had to pass the hat among his friends to raise it. Steuer was also known to take cases for the challenge; he took them because no one said they could be won and he won them anyway. And with preachers in New York decrying tax evasion as "unchristian" and "injurious to the spiritual health of the nation," this one certainly looked like a lost cause. Whatever the reason, Steuer the legal magician was now representing Sunshine Charlie.[18]

The lawyer's strategy was to portray Mitchell as a "patriot" and "blameless optimist" who had been wrongly fingered as the scapegoat for the Depression. Mitchell testified that he had acted in good faith; he had relied on Shearman & Sterling, which told him that the tax transactions were perfectly legal. So why was he on trial? Mitchell was a victim. "Mob psychology," argued Steuer, "is now in control. Who is to be made the victim—the little fellow? No, we want big fish. And Charles E. Mitchell is the big fish." Steuer urged the jury not to succumb to that mob mentality. The "law gives you an absolute right to resort to every legal means and device for the purpose of avoiding tax payments," Steuer reasoned, painting Mitchell as no different from the average taxpayer who doesn't want to pay a dime extra to the federal government. Mitchell had engaged in perfectly legitimate "tax avoidance," not illegal "tax evasion."

Steuer, once again, lived up to his reputation. When the jury pronounced

Mitchell not guilty after a six-week trial, Mitchell burst into tears. Steuer was sporting, according to *Newsweek*, a "cat-that-swallowed-the-canary smile" as Mitchell thanked him, and the two men swept out of the Federal Court House and headed over to the Bankers' Club to celebrate, surrounded by a jubilant crowd of Wall Street brokers and runners. The United States attorney general, Homer Cummings, was so shocked by the outcome that he felt compelled to announce he still believed in the jury system. Other commentators saw a classic case of jury nullification—Mitchell seemed like a "good fellow," according to the *New Republic*, and since "every other rich man has sold securities to establish losses" there seemed little reason to throw just this one in jail for it.

The government amended the tax code in 1937 to plug a variety of tax loopholes, and it continued to press civil charges against Mitchell. In 1938, the United States Supreme Court ruled that the banker owed $1.1 million in back taxes and penalties. He could have declared bankruptcy, but claimed it wasn't the "square" thing to do. He eventually settled with the government and paid off everything he owed J.P. Morgan and Company, although he lost the Fifth Avenue mansion and the other houses to foreclosure. At least as far as his debts were concerned, Morgan's assessment seemed to be right—Mitchell was a "good, sound, straight" fellow. In 1934, he formed his own firm and the next year he became chairman of the investment bank Blyth & Co., where he would remain for the next twenty years. On December 14, 1955, he died, again a wealthy and respected Wall Street banker. Those who remembered his dramatic appearance in the Pecora hearings two decades earlier apparently still believed that Sunshine Charlie had unfairly been made the scapegoat of the crash and the Great Depression.[19]

As the hearings came to an end in June 1934, the most important task for Roosevelt was naming the first SEC commissioners. The laws, as Pecora wrote in his memoirs, were neither a "panacea" nor "self-executing." The lawyer told the president much the same thing at the time, commenting when Roosevelt signed the Securities Exchange Act, "It will be a good or bad law depending on the men who administer it." Years later, he denied having any interest in the job, but it is clear that he desperately wanted to be the SEC's first chairman. Perhaps, having been so responsible for its creation, he thought he deserved the job.

In addition to owing him for his work on the investigation, the president owed Pecora a political debt. In the fall of 1933, in an attempt to wrest control of New York politics away from a Tammany Hall weakened by the Seabury investigations, Roosevelt and the Bronx political leader Edward Flynn formed the Recovery Party and put up a slate of candidates to run in that year's citywide elections. Earlier that year, John Curry, the Tammany leader who had thwarted Pecora's ambitions to run for district attorney in 1929, had pleaded with Pecora to run on the Tammany ticket, and Pecora had the satisfaction of turning him down flat. But Pecora could not turn down the president, who personally asked him to accept the Recovery nomination. He campaigned only on weekends so as not to take away from the investigation, and he even managed to win an endorsement from Untermyer, who called him "fearless" and "independent"; but it was to no avail. Tammany lost the mayoral race to the Republican, Fiorello La Guardia. The anti-Tammany vote for district attorney split between Pecora and the Republican candidate and Tammany brazenly stuffed ballot boxes to send its candidate to victory. Pecora said he was glad to have lost the election. Still, seven months later perhaps he now hoped he could use his willingness to run as a lever to get the chairmanship he really wanted.[20]

Raymond Moley, never a fan of the tenacious investigator and increasingly turning in favor of business and away from the New Deal, had other ideas for the SEC chairmanship. Worried that the commission "might fall under the domination of men who had no knowledge of the practical operation of the stock exchange," Moley submitted a list of eight names to the president. Pecora was not on it. A few days later, when he learned of Pecora's interest in the job, Moley "verbally added his name to the list."

At the top of Moley's list was Joseph P. Kennedy, father of the future president. It was a startling choice. Kennedy had made part of his fortune in the stock market, helping to run the kind of manipulative pools that Pecora's investigation exposed. "It is easy to make money in this market," he told a friend at the time. "We'd better get in before they pass a law against it." Ardent New Dealers were stunned at the possibility of having such a man oversee the financial community.

The *Washington Daily News* argued that Roosevelt "cannot with impunity administer such a slap in the face to his most loyal and effective supporters." John Flynn labeled Kennedy a "grotesque . . . economic parasite" and was incredulous that he might lead the commission. "I say it isn't true. It is impossible. It could not happen." Chairman Fletcher urged the president to appoint Pecora, and there was some editorial support for the intrepid investigator, but more for James Landis, the Harvard academic who had helped draft both securities acts.

Roosevelt did not cave. Having angered the financial community so much over the preceding year, Roosevelt decided he needed to mollify it. It was a perfect bit of Roosevelt manipulation from the same man who described his encounter with a Senate delegation this way: "I was good. I saw Barkley and the others, and with my right arm I said, 'Not one inch will I give in, not an inch!' But with my left hand I said, 'Boys, come and get it.'" More pointedly, Roosevelt didn't view Pecora as an administrator; in the president's mind Pecora was always a highly skilled lawyer and investigator, but no more. On June 30, 1934, Roosevelt selected Kennedy with instructions that his fellow commissioners should appoint him as chairman. The Interior secretary, Harold Ickes, who had turned down Pecora's position in January 1933, wrote in his diary that Roosevelt had great confidence in Kennedy. The new chairman was likely to be honest, both because "he has made his pile" and because he "would now like to make a name for himself for the sake of his family." More importantly, Kennedy knew "all the tricks of the trade," or as Roosevelt, smiling, later told those closest to him, "Set a thief to catch a thief."

As for Pecora, the president appointed him to the commission, but gave him the shortest available term, just one year. Pecora had only asked for a one-year appointment—his financial resources were badly depleted and the SEC salary was nearly as puny as the one he made as an investigator—but he was furious about the chairmanship. He thought he had an agreement from the president that he would be chairman. Returning to Washington from New York, the lawyer hoped to prevail on his fellow commissioners to override the president's wishes. Indeed, the rumor swirling around Washington was that if Kennedy were selected as chairman, Pecora would resign at once rather than serve under a man he had exposed in his investigation.

It was over ninety degrees in Washington on the afternoon of July 2 when the newly designated commissioners gathered at the FTC's headquarters, and Pecora was reportedly in a "fighting mood." The commissioners were slated to be sworn in at three, but the session was delayed two hours as Pecora and Kennedy sat intransigently in separate rooms while their fellow commissioner James Landis engaged in shuttle diplomacy between them. Landis finally convinced Pecora not to resign, although in truth it was highly unlikely that the ever loyal Pecora seriously considered embarrassing Roosevelt. The now disappointed investigator dutifully went out to have his picture taken with the new chairman and his fellow commissioners.

Despite the criticism, Kennedy handled the job well, striking a careful balance between enforcing the new statutes and encouraging capital investment. In his first nationally broadcast speech, which was piped in live to the New York Stock Exchange floor, Kennedy reassured the Street that the new agency did not hold "grudges." Nor did the members of the commission, he said, "regard ourselves as coroners sitting on the corpse of financial enterprise. On the contrary, we think of ourselves as the means of bringing new life into the body of the securities business." When Kennedy left the commission late in 1935, even Flynn admitted that he had been its "most useful member." It seems unlikely that Pecora, who at this point inspired nothing but fear and loathing on Wall Street, would have been nearly so effective.[21]

Indeed, Roosevelt was right about Pecora's unsuitability for administrative work and about his unwillingness to reach a cooperative hand out to Wall Street. Although Pecora's relations with Kennedy were amicable, he at times thought the chairman's rapprochement with the financial community went too far, and he constantly found himself taking a harder line when it came to implementing and interpreting the new regulatory structure. After a year and a half of ruthlessly exposing financial wrongdoing, Pecora's "broad faith in human nature" had been forged into a hardened and indelible cynicism. He thought that the corporate form itself had been "twisted out of its original and socially useful character and has become a weapon in the hands of promoters as powerful as machine-guns in the hands of gangsters." Accompanying his deep-seated suspicions was a healthy dose of boredom; he seemed a little lost after the thrill of the investigation in the mundane details of getting the agency up and running. He resigned from the SEC after only six months to take an appointment from New York's governor,

Herbert Lehman, as a judge on New York's Supreme Court, the state's oddly named trial court. Pecora yearned for positions of status as a tangible sign of his accomplishments; it was probably why he wanted the first SEC chairmanship so badly. Appointment to the bench, he said, fulfilled a lifelong ambition.[22]

Less than a year later, Pecora turned down Roosevelt's offer to reprise his Senate inquiry; this time to lead an investigation of American Telephone & Telegraph on behalf of the Federal Communications Commission. Family considerations seemed to play the overwhelming role in his decision to decline the offer. His wife, Florence, wrote a moving and very personal letter to the president, pleading with him to find someone else for the job. "I suffer from extreme nervousness and melancholia and am constantly under medical attention," she told Roosevelt. "More than ever I do need Ferdinand with me. For years I gave him to the public with all good grace. Won't you please let me have him at least at this particular juncture of my life?"

Instead of going back to Washington, Pecora accepted the nominations of both the Democratic and Republican parties for a full fourteen-year term on the court and, for once, he easily coasted to victory that November, a feat he repeated in 1949. In 1938, he became the president of the National Lawyers Guild, an organization of progressive lawyers founded in protest to the American Bar Association's exclusion of African Americans and Jews. As dictatorships proliferated around the world, Pecora responded to critics who said that a sitting judge should not take such a position. "There has been no time," he argued, "when the natural rights of equality before the law, liberty of thought and freedom of speech has been so much in need of preservation by those who believe in democratic principles." Pecora believed reflexively in moderate progressivism and he offered a fiery denunciation of the organization a year later when it became apparent to him that much of the Guild's leadership was linked to the Communist Party.[23]

The year after he won reelection to the bench, the Democratic and Liberal parties nominated Pecora for mayor of New York. It was an ironically bitter three-way race with the Independent candidate Vincent Impellitteri and the Republican Edward Corsi. The famously righteous and independent Pecora was accused of having organized-crime links and was derided as nothing but a Tammany hack. The always energetic and hardworking Pecora was the oldest of the three, and Corsi insisted that "Grandpa Pecora" was too old to be mayor. Pecora defended himself, calling the allegations of mob ties "ridiculous," proclaiming "no political boss has every put a collar on me in thirty years of public service," and demonstrating his vigor with every impassioned speech. True to form, however, he took the high road in the campaign, refusing to sling mud, and ultimately he placed second to Impellitteri. His political career now over, Pecora returned to private practice, but he never gave up the fight to protect the weak and powerless. In 1966, he was one of a group of lawyers and retired judges who fought to prevent the elimination of the New York City Police Department's Civilian Complaint Review Board.[24]

"No memory of having starred," Robert Frost once wrote, "atones for later disregard / Or keeps the end from being hard." Although written thirty-five years earlier, his poem poignantly captured Pecora's life. As he neared his ninetieth birthday, Pecora, the man who lived for acclaim, had little of it. The hearings—his brief moment on the public stage—had long since faded from the public's memory. Even his unsuccessful mayoral campaign lay more than two decades in the past. Pecora died on December 7, 1971, a few months after suffering a heart attack. He spent his last days at the Polyclinic Hospital in New York, where he liked nothing more than to recount for his nurses how he put Wall Street under oath.

In those last days with his nurses, Pecora was trying to reclaim a tiny portion of the admiration and recognition that he had garnered in those hearing rooms in Washington nearly forty years earlier. He would have been gratified to know that his death warranted a long obituary in the *New York Times*, although even the *Times* thought the most memorable incident in the hearings was when Lya Graf sat on J. P. Morgan Jr.'s lap. The forty years since his death did little to bolster his reputation. Indeed, up until the Great Recession that began in late 2007, Pecora's name was virtually unknown, even among those who made their living in and around Wall Street. And to those who had heard of him he was most often not a brilliant and courageous lawyer, but simply a flashy showman.

While the man and his astounding legal performance may be forgotten, his legacy lives on. Every initial public offering, every bond deal, every trade on the New York Stock Exchange or NASDAQ is subject to a regulatory apparatus that did not exist when he took Washington by storm in 1933. Every time companies disclose bad news because securities regulations require them to do so, investors can thank Ferdinand Pecora. And even though financial regulation is in dire need of updating, it remains a vast improvement over the laissez-faire approach that he helped usher offstage. In the turmoil that roiled the financial markets in 2008, bank failures were a small percentage of what they were during the Depression, and there were no bank runs, in large part because Ferdinand Pecora helped blaze the path for federal deposit insurance. The Securities and Exchange Commission has been fairly criticized for its regulatory and enforcement lapses over the last few years, but for most of its history it has been considered one of the ablest of Washington administrative agencies.

Nearly eighty years ago, in the depths of the worst economic crisis in this country's history, Ferdinand Pecora showed what a well-run and well-researched Washington investigation could accomplish, and although congressional hearings too often descend into bluster and posturing, the Pecora hearings remain a model to which future investigations can aspire. All they need is a Hellhound.

ACKNOWLEDGMENTS

I owe a debt of gratitude to the many people who were enormously generous with their time and expertise and who helped make this book a reality. Thanks go to Richard McCulley and William H. Davis, at the National Archives and Records Administration, who fulfilled my many requests for documents from the Senate Banking and Currency Committee hearings. The book would not have been possible without the help of the Oral History Office at Columbia University, which generously allowed me to quote from Ferdinand Pecora's oral history as well as other oral histories in their wonderful collection. Columbia's Rare Book and Manuscript Library was also an important resource, particularly the Edwin Kilroe Collection of materials on the history of Tammany Hall and the papers of Frank Vanderlip and George L. Harrison. Doris Peterson and Sarah Hanson at the University of South Dakota I. D. Weeks Library were especially helpful in my journey through Senator Peter Norbeck's papers. My thanks also go to the staffs at the Franklin D. Roosevelt Presidential Library, the New-York Historical Society, the archives of the New York Stock Exchange, the Museum of the City of New York, the Manuscripts and Archives division of the Yale University Library, and the Library of Congress.

Special thanks go to the librarians at the Rittenberg Law Library at St. John's University School of Law, particularly William Manz, Aru Satkalmi, and Barbara Traub, who cheerfully tracked down for me even the most obscure books and materials. My research assistants, Lisa Dmiszewicki, Lauren Pennisi, Ryan Pratt, and Brandi Sinkovich, were tremendously helpful as well. I thank them all. For a host of small favors and for prompt responses to my various inquiries I'd also like to thank Bruce Baird, Jeff Bridgers, Susan Brinson, Jeff Cane, Brett Carnell, Jordan Costa, Linda Feinberg, Davis Houck, Michael Klausner, Nicholas Natanson, and Lauren Post. Thanks also go to Dean Richard Matasar of New York Law School and his staff and to Samuel Sanchez of the City College Library Archives, both of whom helped locate information about Pecora's time at those schools.

Donald Ritchie, the historian of the United States Senate, was unfailingly generous with both his time and his expertise and graciously agreed to read my manuscript. I want to thank all my colleagues at St. John's, but particularly John Barrett, Christopher Borgen, Vincent DiLorenzo, Luca Melachiona, Keith Sharfman, Michael Simons, and Peggy Turano, who were good sounding boards or who read some or all of the manuscript. Ron and Suzanne Saldarini willingly read very early drafts of several chapters. The comments and suggestions of all these individuals were insightful, and they made the book stronger.

I feel incredibly fortunate that Ann Godoff and Laura Stickney were interested in this project for Penguin Press. It took a leap of faith for them to believe that someone who spent the better part of his career writing inaccessible academic prose about something as arcane as securities regulation could have something to say to a general audience, and I thank them for their willingness to publish the book, for their constant encouragement, and for their many helpful suggestions, all of which improved the book. I could not have asked for a better editorial team. Many thanks also go to my agent, Victoria Sanders, and her staff, and my lawyer, Joseph Gagliano, for guiding me so expertly through the unfamiliar terrain of book publishing. I also got great advice on the publishing world from my friend and publicist Jennifer Richards and her husband, Jamey Ballot.

Last, but most important, thanks go to my wife, Shelley, and my two boys, Joe and John. It is somewhat trite to say that when you write a book it is hardest on your family. That doesn't make it any less true. They all showed infinite humor when I regaled them at dinner with the minutiae of Pecora's life, and infinite patience when I would disappear to my office or on one of my frequent jaunts to some library or archive. Shelley was always there to read drafts and to offer her sage advice. She also knew just how to keep me focused when I tried to make the process way too complex and difficult. I could not have written this book without her and the boys. Thank you.

NOTES

Abbreviations

Colby Papers	Bainbridge Colby Papers, Manuscript Division, Library of Congress
Couzens Papers	James Couzens Papers, Manuscript Division, Library of Congress
CSM	Christian Science Monitor
FDRPL	Franklin Delano Roosevelt Presidential Library, Hyde Park, New York
Hamlin Papers	Charles S. Hamlin Papers, Manuscript Division, Library of Congress
Harrison Papers	George L. Harrison Papers, Rare Books and Manuscripts Library, Columbia University
Hearing Tr.	Stock Exchange Practices, Hearings Before a Subcommittee of the Committee on Banking and Currency, United States Senate, Seventy-second Congress, Second Session, Senate Resolutions 84 and 239
Hearing Tr. (73rd)	Stock Exchange Practices, Hearings Before a Subcommittee of the Committee on Banking and Currency, United States Senate, Seventy-third Congress, First Session, Senate Resolutions 84 and 56
Mills Papers	Ogden Livingstone Mills Papers, Manuscript Division, Library of Congress
Norbeck Papers	Peter Norbeck Papers, Richardson Collection, University of South Dakota, I. D. Weeks Library

NYT   New York Times

NYWT   New York World-Telegram

POH   The Reminiscences of Ferdinand Pecora (1962), in Oral History
                    Collection of Columbia University

PPF   President's Personal File, Franklin D. Roosevelt Presidential
                    Library, Hyde Park, New York

SBCC Minutes   Minutes of the United States Senate Banking and Currency
                    Committee

SEIF   Stock Exchange Investigation Files, National Archives,
                    Washington, D.C.

Vanderlip Papers   Frank A. Vanderlip Papers, Rare Books and Manuscripts Library,
                    Columbia University

Walcott Papers   Frederic Collin Walcott Papers, Manuscripts and Archives, Yale
                    University Library

WSJ   Wall Street Journal

Introduction

1 NYT, March 5, 1933; Conrad Black, *Franklin Delano Roosevelt: Champion of Freedom* (New York: Public Affairs, 2003), 269; Stanley Lebergott, *Americans, An Economic Record* (New York: W.W. Norton, 1984), 447; Amity Shlaes, *The Forgotten Man: A New History of the Great Depression* (New York: HarperCollins, 2007), 144; Edmund Wilson, *Travels in Two Democracies* (New York: Harcourt, Brace and Company, 1936), 43.

2 NYT, March 5, 1933; Drew Pearson and Robert S. Allen, "Washington Merry-Go-Round," United Feature Syndicate, December 16, 1932; Wilson, *Travels in Two Democracies*, 43; Dixon Wecter, *The Age of the Great Depression, 1929–1941* (New York: Macmillan Co., 1948), 25–40; T. H. Watkins, *The Great Depression: America in the 1930s* (Boston: Little, Brown, 1993), 98–107; Donald A. Ritchie, *Electing FDR: The New Deal Campaign of 1932* (Lawrence, KS: University Press of Kansas, 2007), 116–120.

3 NYT, March 5, 1933; Davis W. Houck, *FDR and Fear Itself: The First Inaugural Address* (College Station, TX: Texas A&M University Press, 2002), 64–65, 73.

4 Houck, *FDR and Fear Itself*, 107.

5 Ferdinand Pecora, *Wall Street under Oath: The Story of Our Modern Money Changers* (New York: Simon & Schuster, 1939), 3–4.

6 John Brooks, *Once in Golconda: A True Drama of Wall Street, 1920–1938* (New York: John Wiley & Sons, 1969), 191; Raymond Moley, *After Seven Years* (New York: Harper & Brothers, 1939), 177; Joab H. Banton, "Ferdinand Pecora," *U.S. Law Review* 67 (1933): 302–306.

7 D. B. Hardeman and Donald C. Bacon, *Rayburn: A Biography* (Austin, TX: Texas Monthly Press, 1987), 152; Joel Seligman, *The Transformation of Wall Street: A History of the Securities and Exchange Commission and Modern Corporate Finance* (New York: Aspen Publishers,

3rd edition, 2003), 2; POH, 876; Reminiscences of James McCauley Landis (1964), in Oral History Collection of Columbia University, 199. The hearings are so unknown today that the appellation "Pecora Hearings" led one modern writer to assume that they were the handiwork of "Senator Ferdinand Pecora." Donald Warren, *Radio Priest, Charles Coughlin, the Father of Hate Radio* (New York: Free Press, 1996), 56.

Chapter 1. The Well-Driller and Wall Street

1 Peter Norbeck to D. C. Wallace, November 15, 1932, Norbeck Papers, Box 113, Folder 2; Donald A. Ritchie, *Electing FDR: The New Deal Campaign of 1932* (Lawrence, KS: University Press of Kansas, 2007), 38, 223–224; Gilbert C. Fite, *Peter Norbeck: Prairie Statesman* (Pierre, SD: South Dakota Historical Society Press, 2005), 152–153.

2 *NYT*, November 21, 1932; John T. Flynn, "The Marines Land in Wall Street," *Harper's*, July 1934: 149–155.

3 Peter Norbeck to Theo. J. P. Giedt, July 9, 1932, Norbeck Papers, Box 140, Folder 4; Peter Norbeck to W. R. Ronald, July 11, 1932, Norbeck Papers, Box 105, Folder 13; Fite, *Peter Norbeck: Prairie Statesman*, 167, 186–188; John E. Miller, "Restrained, Respectable Radicals: The South Dakota Farm Holiday," *Agricultural History* 59 (January 1985): 429–447; Herbert H. Schell, *History of South Dakota* (Lincoln, NE: University of Nebraska Press, 2nd edition, 1968), 282–288; Jonathan Alter, *The Defining Moment: FDR's Hundred Days and the Triumph of Hope* (New York: Simon & Schuster, 2006), 149.

4 Ray Tucker, "Those Sons of the Wild Jackasses," *The North American Review* 229 (February 1930): 231–239.

5 Fite, *Peter Norbeck: Prairie Statesman*, 153; Ray Tucker, "Those Sons of the Wild Jackasses," 231–239.

6 Fite, *Peter Norbeck: Prairie Statesman*, 43.

7 Schell, *History of South Dakota*, 278–281.

8 Fite, *Peter Norbeck: Prairie Statesman*, 170–171; Susan Estabrook Kennedy, "Glass, Carter," *American National Biography Online*, http://www.anb.org/articles/06/06-00218.html; *NYT*, May 29, 1946.

9 Joel Seligman, *The Transformation of Wall Street: A History of the Securities and Exchange Commission and Modern Corporate Finance* (New York: Aspen Publishers, 3rd edition, 2003), 8–9; Ritchie, *Electing FDR*, 168; *NYT*, October 16, 1930; Ralph F. de Bedts, *The New Deal's SEC: The Formative Years* (New York: Columbia University Press, 1964), 15.

10 Senator Thomas Connally of Texas, 75th Cong., 1st sess., *Congressional Record* (February 29, 1932), 76, pt. 5:4912.

11 Herbert Hoover, *Memoirs: Great Depression* (New York: Macmillan Co., 1951–52), 16–17; William R. Perkins, "Short Selling: A Reply to the Address of Richard Whitney," October 16, 1931, NYSE Archives; *NYT*, October 15, 1930.

12 Seligman, *The Transformation of Wall Street*, 11–12; de Bedts, *The New Deal's SEC*, 16; Donald A. Ritchie, "The Pecora Wall Street Expose 1934," in *Congress Investigates: A Documented History, 1792–1974*, ed. Arthur M. Schlesinger Jr. and Roger Bruns (New York: Chelsea House Publishers, 1975), 2558; *NYT*, October 16, 1930.

13 *Washington Post*, March 2, 1932; *Time*, March 14, 1932; Drew Pearson and Robert S. Allen, "Washington Merry-Go-Round," United Feature Syndicate, March 13, 1933; Drew Pearson and Robert S. Allen, *More Merry-Go-Round* (New York: Liveright, Inc., 1932), 320–323, 352–357.

14 Peter Norbeck to James Stewart, April 18, 1932, Norbeck Papers, Box 111, Folder 6; *NYT*, March 5, 1932.

15 Peter Norbeck to George W. Pennington, January 26, 1933, Norbeck Papers, Box 2, Folder 2; *NYT*, June 25, 1932.

16 Forrest McDonald, *Insull* (Chicago: University of Chicago Press, 1962), vii; Hiram W. Johnson to Peter Norbeck, September 22, 1932, Norbeck Papers, Box 112, Folder 1; W. Harry King to Peter Norbeck, September 29, 1932, Norbeck Papers, Box 101, Folder 7.

17 McDonald, *Insull*, 309–313; Peter Norbeck to W. Harry King, October 3, 1932, Norbeck Papers, Box 101, Folder 7.

18 Undated memorandum to Peter Norbeck re William Gray, Norbeck Papers, Box 2, Folder 4; *NYT*, November 18, 1932.

19 Ritchie, *Electing Roosevelt*, 124; Eugene Nelson White, *The Regulation and Reform of the American Banking System, 1900–1929* (Princeton, NJ: Princeton University Press, 1983), 14–23.

20 Frederic Walcott to Herbert Hoover, August 5, 1932, Walcott Papers, Box 8; Reminiscences of Eugene Meyer (1953), in Oral History Collection of Columbia University, 684–685.

21 Susan Estabrook Kennedy, *The Banking Crisis of 1933* (Lexington, KY: University Press of Kentucky, 1973), 50–53, 67–74, 212; Richard H. K. Vietor, "Regulation-Defined Financial Markets: Fragmentation and Integration in Financial Services," in *Wall Street and Regulation*, ed. Samuel L. Hayes (Boston: Harvard Business School Press, 1987), 17–18; Rixey Smith and Norman Beasley, *Carter Glass: A Biography* (New York: Longmans, Green and Co., 1939), 182, 301; Ritchie, *Electing FDR*, 124; Francis H. Sisson, "Men, Not Laws, Make Sound Banks," *Nation's Business* 21 (January 1933): 13.

22 Fite, *Peter Norbeck: Prairie Statesman*, 179; Peter Norbeck to E. E. Gelheus, December 31, 1932, Norbeck Papers, Box 140, Folder 4.

Chapter 2. The Best Cross-Examiner in New York

1 POH, 1–2, 6–8, 18, 31; Erik Amfitheatrof, *The Children of Columbus: An Informal History of Italians in the New World* (Boston: Little, Brown, 1973), 137–157; *NYT*, July 29, 1875; George Ripley and Charles A. Dana, *American Cyclopaedia: A Popular Dictionary of General Knowledge*, vol. 11 (New York: D. Appleton and Co., 1875), 644–649; Constantine M. Pannunzio, *The Soul of an Immigrant* (New York: Macmillan Co., 1921), 134.

2 Salvatore J. LaGumina, *New York at Mid-Century* (Westport, CT: Greenwood Press, 1992), 41; Ira A. Glazier and P. William Filby, eds., *Italians to America: Lists of Passengers Arriving at U.S. Ports, 1880–1899*, vol. 2 (Wilmington, DE: Scholarly Resources Inc., 1992), 180, 183.

3 Robert H. Wiebe, *The Search for Order, 1877–1920* (New York: Hill and Wang, 1967); Beverly Gage, *The Day Wall Street Exploded: A Story of America in Its First Age of Terror* (New York: Oxford University Press, 2009); James Green, *Death in the Haymarket: A Story of Chicago, the First Labor Movement and the Bombing That Divided Gilded Age America* (New York: Pantheon Books, 2006).

4 John Higham, *Strangers in the Land: Pattern of American Nativism, 1860–1925* (New Brunswick, NJ: Rutgers University Press, 1983), 55.

5 Higham, *Strangers in the Land*, 55; *NYT*, March 5, 1882.

6 *NYT*, March 5, 1882; Jacob A. Riis, *How the Other Half Lives: Studies Among the Tenements of New York* (New York: Charles Scribner's Sons, 1890), 48–54; Higham, *Strangers in the Land*, 90.

7 Thomas Kessner, *The Golden Door: Italian and Jewish Immigrant Mobility in New York City 1880–1915* (New York: Oxford University Press, 1977), 8; Philip Cannistraro and Gerald Meyer, *The Lost World of Italian American Radicalism: Politics, Labor, and Culture* (Westport, CT: Praeger, 2003), 6; Higham, *Strangers in the Land*, 160.

8 Jerre Mangione and Ben Morreale, *La Storia: Five Centuries of the Italian American Experience* (New York: HarperCollins, 1992), 200–213; Higham, *Strangers in the Land*, 90–91; *NYT*, March 16, 1891.

9 POH, 6–7, 31–32; Cannistraro and Meyer, *The Lost World of Italian American Radicalism*, 12; Donna R. Gabaccia, *From Sicily to Elizabeth Street: Housing and Social Change Among Italian Immigrants* (Albany, NY: State University of New York Press, 1984), 54.

10 POH, 5.

11 Ferdinand Pecora, "Untitled," in *I Am an American*, ed. Robert S. Benjamin (Freeport, NY: Books for Libraries Press, 1970), 101–106.

12 POH, 5–6; Nancy Foner, *From Ellis Island to JFK: New York's Two Great Waves of Immigration* (New Haven: Yale University Press, 2002), 206–207.

13 POH, 5, 20–21, 24–25, 30; Kessner, *The Golden Door*, 14.

14 Charity Organization Society of the City of New York, map showing overcrowding of the buildings on the lots and the consequent lack of light and air space also strongholds of poverty and agencies for betterment in the tenement house district bounded by 22nd Street, 17th Street, 11th Avenue, 6th Avenue (1899), New York Historical Society collection; POH, 12, 29, 53, 94–95.

15 POH, 637.

16 POH, 91–93.

17 POH, 24, 29; Olin Scott Roche, *Forty Years of Parish Life and Work* (New York: Friebele Press, 1930).

18 POH, 3, 10, 39; *NYT*, November 3, 1950.

19 POH, 10–13, 34; Roche, *Forty Years of Parish Life*, 89, 177–178; Reamer Kline, *Education for the Common Good: A History of Bard College the First 100 Years, 1860–1960* (Annandale, NY: Bard College, 1982); *NYT*, June 20, 1896.

20 POH, 13–14,

21 POH, 15–16, 41; Irving Howe and Kenneth Libo, *World of Our Fathers: The Journey of the East European Jews to America and the Life They Found and Made* (New York: Harcourt Brace Jovanovich, 1976), 158; Leon Stein, ed., *Out of the Sweatshop: The Struggle for Industrial Democracy* (New York: Quadrangle, 1977), 20–58.

22 Irving Bernstein, *The Lean Years: A History of the American Worker, 1920–1933* (Boston: Houghton Mifflin Company, 1960), 263.

23 POH, 84–89; Maureen A. Flanagan, *America Reformed: Progressives and Progressivisms, 1890s–1920s* (New York: Oxford University Press, 2007).

24 POH, 105–108; Reminiscences of Thomas E. Dewey (1959), in Oral History Collection of Columbia University, 443.

25 J. Joseph Huthmacher, "Charles Evans Hughes and Charles Francis Murphy: The Metamorphosis of Progressivism," *New York History* 46 (January 1965): 25–40.

26 Nancy Joan Weiss, *Charles Francis Murphy, 1858–1924: Respectability and Responsibility in Tammany Politics* (Northampton, MA: Smith College, 1968), 78–85.

27 Reminiscences of Reuben A. Lazarus (1951), in Oral History Collection of Columbia University, 399–403.

28 POH, 122–123.

29 POH, 123–126; John Jones to Peter Norbeck, January 27, 1933, Norbeck Papers, Box 2, Folder 10.

30 POH, 127–140.

31 POH, 140–43a; 441–457, 478–481; *NYT*, August 23, 1928.

32 POH, 198–254; *NYT*, August 21, 1921.

33 POH, 290, 359–367, 579–581; *NYT*, June 8, 1921; *NYT*, June 11, 1921; *Time*, June 12, 1933.

34 POH, 313–330; *NYT*, June 10, 1922.

35 *NYT*, December 30, 1920; *NYT*, November 7, 1920; *NYT*, July 21, 1923; Peter H. Odegard, *Pressure Politics: The Story of the Anti-Saloon League* (New York: Columbia University Press, 1928), 228–240; K. Austin Kerr, *Organized for Prohibition: A New History of the Anti-Saloon*

League (New Haven: Yale University Press, 1985), 1–11, 121–122; Ron Chernow, *Titan: The Life of John D. Rockefeller, Sr.* (New York: Vintage Books, 1998), 368; POH, 291–303, 308–312, 335–359, 624–628; Joel Seligman, *The Transformation of Wall Street: A History of the Securities and Exchange Commission and Modern Corporate Finance* (New York: Aspen Publishers, 3rd edition, 2003), 21; Reminiscences of William H. Anderson (1950), in Oral History Collection of Columbia University, 61.

36 *NYT*, February 12, 1929; *NYT*, July 7, 1929; *NYT*, August 23, 1929; *NYT*, November 6, 1929; POH, 275–277, 601–610.

37 *NYT*, April 12, 1929; POH, 581–594.

38 POH, 273; Weiss, *Charles Francis Murphy*, 32–33; Warren Moscow, *Politics in the Empire State* (New York: A.A. Knopf, 1948), 44–45.

39 *Time*, April 30, 1934; Weiss, *Charles Francis Murphy*, 125; Alfred Connable and Edward Silberfarb, *Tigers of Tammany: Nine Men Who Ran New York* (New York: Holt, Reinhart and Winston, 1967), 277–278; Herbert Mitgang, *The Man Who Rode the Tammany Tiger: The Life and Times of Judge Samuel Seabury* (Philadelphia: J.B. Lippincott Company, 1963), 164–165; POH, 1026–1027.

40 David Von Drehle, *Triangle: The Fire That Changed America* (New York: Atlantic Monthly Press, 2003), 306; POH, 582, 643.

41 POH, 590–594; *NYT*, August 9, 1929.

42 *NYT*, January 1, 1930.

43 POH, 633–635.

44 POH, 619–620, 633–638.

Chapter 3. Sitting on the Lid

1 Peter Norbeck to W. E. Briggs, April 26, 1932, Norbeck Papers, Box 139, Folder 2.

2 Hugo L. Black, "Inside a Senate Investigation," *Harper's Monthly Magazine* 172 (February 1936): 275–86.

3 William H. Harbaugh, *Lawyer's Lawyer: The Life of John W. Davis* (New York: Oxford University Press, 1973), 321.

4 *NYT*, March 7, 1932; *NYT*, March 9, 1932; *NYT*, March 10, 1932; *NYT*, March 12, 1932; Drew Pearson and Robert S. Allen, *More Merry-Go-Round* (New York: Liveright, Inc., 1932), 355.

5 Donald A. Ritchie, *Electing FDR: The New Deal Campaign of 1932* (Lawrence, KS: University Press of Kansas, 2007), 168; Donald A. Ritchie, "The Pecora Wall Street Expose 1934," in *Congress Investigates: A Documented History, 1792–1974*, ed. Arthur M. Schlesinger Jr. and Roger Bruns (New York: Chelsea House Publishers, 1975), 2559; SBCC Minutes, April 8, 1932; *NYT*, April 9, 1932; *NYT*, April 10, 1932; Peter Norbeck to J. D. Coon, April 11, 1932, Norbeck Papers, Box 139, Folder 5; *Public Papers of Herbert Hoover* (Washington, D.C.: U.S. Government Printing Office, 1977), 1175; Pearson and Allen, *More Merry-Go-Round*, 355–356.

6 John Brooks, *Once in Golconda: A True Drama of Wall Street 1920–1938* (New York: John Wiley & Sons, 1969), 61–62, 142; Steve Fraser, *Every Man a Speculator* (New York: HarperCollins, 2005), 417; Ormonde de Kay, "Debt Before Dishonor: How Richard Whitney Went down the Drain and up the River," *Quest* (February 1988): 40–47.

7 *Washington Post*, April 9, 1932; Joel Seligman, *The Transformation of Wall Street: A History of the Securities and Exchange Commission and Modern Corporate Finance* (New York: Aspen Publishers, 3rd edition, 2003), 15; Brooks, *Once in Golconda*, 142.

8 POH, 662; Ritchie, "The Pecora Wall Street Expose 1934," 2560; Seligman, *The Transformation of Wall Street*, 15.

9 Brooks, *Once in Golconda*, 144.

10 WSJ, April 23, 1932; *Tatler and American Sketch*, May 1, 1932; P. M. Cushing to Editors, *New*

York Evening Post, May 10, 1932; Gilbert C. Fite, *Peter Norbeck: Prairie Statesman* (Pierre, SD: South Dakota Historical Society Press, 2005), 176–177.

11 *NYT*, April 27, 1932.

12 Peter Norbeck to Lydia Norbeck, June 2, 1932, Norbeck Papers, Box 61, Folder 2; "*Short Selling*" *on Stock Exchanges—Limit of Expenditures*, 72nd Cong., 1st Sess., S.R. 239, *Congressional Record*, 75, pt. 12:13235-13236; Undated memorandum to Peter Norbeck re William Gray, Norbeck Papers, Box 2, Folder 4.

13 Richard Whitney to Ogden Mills, September 2, 1932, Mills Papers, Box 11; Statement of Richard Whitney in Regard to the Investigation of Stock Exchange Practices, August 24, 1932, NYSE Archives; Vincent P. Carosso, *Investment Banking in America: A History* (Cambridge, MA: Harvard University Press, 1970), 324; *Commercial & Financial Chronicle*, April 30, 1932.

14 Herbert Mitgang, *The Man Who Rode the Tammany Tiger: The Life and Times of Judge Samuel Seabury* (Philadelphia: J.B. Lippincott Company, 1963), 207–214; Henry F. Pringle, *Big Frogs* (New York: Macy-Masius, 1928), 139–160; *Washington Post*, April 2, 1932; Reminiscences of Benjamin J. Buttenwieser (1981), in Oral History Collection of Columbia University, 341.

15 Raymond Moley, *After Seven Years* (New York: Harper & Brothers, 1939), 176–177; Raymond Moley with Elliot A. Rosen, *The First New Deal* (New York: Harcourt, Brace & World, 1966), 309.

16 *NYT*, January 9, 1933.

17 Harold L. Ickes, *The Autobiography of a Curmudgeon* (New York: Reynal & Hitchcock, 1943), 258–271; T. H. Watkins, *Righteous Pilgrim: The Life and Times of Harold L. Ickes 1874–1952* (New York: Henry Holt & Co., 1990), 280; Linda J. Lear, *Harold L. Ickes: The Aggressive Progressive 1874–1933* (New York: Garland Publishing, 1981), i–ii, 120, 180, 316–319, 328, 360–362, 397–398.

18 Reminiscences of Morris Lincoln Strauss (1951), in Oral History Collection of Columbia University, 320.

19 Mitgang, *The Man Who Rode the Tammany Tiger*, 174, 186–187; Peter Norbeck to Irving Ben Cooper, January 6, 1933, Norbeck Papers, Box 2, Folder 2; SBCC Minutes, January 10, 1933; *NYT*, January 11, 1933; *NYT*, March 20, 1962; *Washington Post*, January 11, 1933.

20 *NYWT*, January 12, 1933.

21 Peter Norbeck to Nils Okland, January 16, 1933, Norbeck Papers, Box 115, Folder 4; William E. Leuchtenburg, *Franklin D. Roosevelt and the New Deal* (New York: Harper & Row, 1963), 25; Benjamin Roth, *The Great Depression: A Diary*, ed. James Ledbetter and Daniel B. Roth (New York: Public Affairs, 2009), 81–83.

22 Frank Partnoy, *The Match King: Ivar Kreuger, the Financial Genius Behind a Century of Wall Street Scandals* (New York: Public Affairs, 2009); *NYT*, January 13, 1933.

23 *NYWT*, January 12, 1933; *NYT*, January 14, 1933; *NYT*, January 19, 1933; Mitgang, *The Man Who Rode the Tammany Tiger*, 180; Seligman, *The Transformation of Wall Street*, 20; Peter Norbeck to Irving Ben Cooper, January 13, 1933, Norbeck Papers, Box 2, Folder 2.

24 *NYT*, March 20, 1962; *NYT*, March 21, 1962; *NYT*, June 14, 1962.

25 *NYT*, January 18, 1933; *NYT*, January 19, 1933.

26 *NYWT*, January 18, 1933; *NYT*, January 19, 1933; Mitgang, *The Man Who Rode the Tammany Tiger*, 275.

27 Sidney W. May to Peter Norbeck, January 19, 1933, SEIF, Box 81, Cooper, Irving Ben Folder; R. H. Nelson to Peter Norbeck, January 20, 1933, SEIF, Box 81, Cooper, Irving Ben Folder.

28 POH, 655.

29 Seligman, *The Transformation of Wall Street*, 21; David S. Levin, "Regulating the Securities Industry: The Evolution of a Government Policy" (Ph.D. diss., Columbia University, 1969), 196; Peter Norbeck to O. L. Brownlee, August 23, 1934, Norbeck Papers, Box 116, Folder 1; Bainbridge Colby to Duncan Fletcher, January 25, 1933, Colby Papers, Box 5; POH, 655.

Chapter 4. A Short-Term Job

1 Gilbert C. Fite, *Peter Norbeck: Prairie Statesman* (Pierre, SD: South Dakota Historical Society Press, 2005), 167, 186–188.

2 POH, 656–657; Merlo J. Pusey, *Charles Evans Hughes* (New York: Macmillan Co. 1951), 132–168; Charles Evans Hughes, *The Autobiographical Notes of Charles Evans Hughes*, ed. David J. Danelski and Joseph S. Tulchin (Cambridge, MA: Harvard University Press, 1973), 119–127; J. Joseph Huthmacher, "Charles Evans Hughes and Charles Francis Murphy: The Metamorphosis of Progressivism," *New York History* 46 no. 1 (January 1965): 25–40.

3 POH, 657–661.

4 Ferdinand Pecora, *Wall Street under Oath: The Story of Our Modern Money Changers* (New York: Simon & Schuster, 1939), 5.

5 NYT, January 25, 1933; NYT, January 29, 1933; POH, 664; Ferdinand Pecora to Peter Norbeck, January 28, 1933, Norbeck Papers, Box 2, Folder 10.

6 POH, 664–666, 704–606; NYT, January 26, 1933; NYT, January 29, 1933; NYT, September 6, 1953.

7 Peter Norbeck to W. L. Baker, March 21, 1933, Norbeck Papers, Box 1, Folder 3.

8 Rixey Smith and Norman Beasley, *Carter Glass: A Biography* (New York: Longmans, Green and Co., 1939), 85; NYT, January 6, 1933; NYT, January 25, 1933; WSJ, January 5, 1933; Drew Pearson and Robert S. Allen, "The Washington Merry-Go-Round," United Feature Syndicate, December 8, 1932; Pearson and Allen, "The Washington Merry-Go-Round," December 16, 1932.

9 Richard D. White Jr., *Kingfish: The Reign of Huey P. Long* (New York: Random House, 2006), 65, 143–146, 171–172; Alan Brinkley, *Voices of Protest: Huey Long, Father Coughlin and the Great Depression* (New York: Vintage Books, 1983), 22–23, 42–45, 77; NYT, May 29, 1946; Lawrence Sullivan, *Prelude to Panic: The Story of the Bank Holiday* (Washington, D.C.: Statesman Press, 1936), 3; Pearson and Allen, "The Washington Merry-Go-Round," January 14, 1933; Pearson and Allen, "The Washington Merry-Go-Round," February 16, 1933.

10 Brinkley, *Voices of Protest*, 55–56; White, *Kingfish*, 172–173; NYT, January 11, 1933; NYT, January 17, 1933; NYT, January 19, 1933; NYT, January 22, 1933; *Washington Post*, January 13, 1933; *Washington Post*, January 14, 1933; Theodore G. Joslin, *Hoover Off the Record* (Freeport, NY: Books for Libraries Press, 1971), 339–340; Pearson and Allen, "The Washington Merry-Go-Round," December 8, 1932; Pearson and Allen, "The Washington Merry-Go-Round," January 14, 1933.

11 NYT, January 17, 1933; *Literary Digest*, January 21, 1933, 10; William E. Leuchtenburg, *Franklin D. Roosevelt and the New Deal* (New York: Harper & Row, 1963), 28.

12 Katharine Graham, ed., *Katharine Graham's Washington* (New York: Alfred A. Knopf, 2002), 393.

13 NYT, January 26, 1933; NYT, January 31, 1933; John Marrinan to Florence N. Wright, January 25, 1933, SEIF, Box 81, Gray, William A., Correspondence File; Memorandum from Florence Wright to John Marrinan, January 25, 1933, SEIF, Box 83, Wright, Florence M., Correspondence File; Peter Norbeck to Ferdinand Pecora, January 25, 1933, SEIF, Box 82, Norbeck Correspondence File.

14 NYT, February 1, 1933; *Milwaukee Leader*, February 7, 1933. Privately, Pecora also said that his goal for the hearings was to provide the basis for the first federal legislation of the stock markets. William O. Douglas to George E. Bates, April 7, 1933, in *The Douglas Letters: Selections from the Private Papers of Justice William O. Douglas*, ed. Melvin I. Urofsky (Bethesda: Adler & Adler, 1987), 18.

Chapter 5. Sunshine Charlie

1 POH, 669; Donald A. Ritchie, "The Pecora Wall Street Expose 1934," in *Congress Investigates: A Documented History, 1792–1974*, ed. Arthur M. Schlesinger Jr. and Roger Bruns (New York: Chelsea House Publishers, 1975), 2652; NYT, June 5, 1932.

2 Harold van B. Cleveland and Thomas F. Huertas, *Citibank, 1812–1970* (Cambridge, MA: Harvard University Press, 1985), 9–15, 32–49.

3 Ibid., 88; Ana Robeson Burr, "The Portrait of a Great Banker," *World's Work* 54 (September 1927): 482–495.

4 Cleveland and Huertas, *Citibank*, 85–87; Vincent P. Carosso, *Investment Banking in America: A History* (Cambridge, MA: Harvard University Press, 1970), 96, 105.

5 Frederick Lewis Allen, *The Lords of Creation* (New York: Harper & Brothers, 1935), 311; Julian Sherrod, *Scapegoats* (New York: Brewer, Warren & Putnam, 1931), 14; Edmund Wilson, *Travels in Two Democracies* (New York: Harcourt, Brace and Company, 1936), 56; *Barron's*, March 5, 1923; ibid., May 14, 1923; ibid., November 19, 1923; *Newsweek*, August 17, 1935; *Time*, March 3, 1933; *NYT*, May 4, 1921; *NYT*, December 15, 1955; *WSJ*, May 18, 1923.

6 Allen, *The Lords of Creation*, 311; Charles R. Geisst, *Wall Street: A History* (New York: Oxford University Press, 1997), 117–121; *Barron's*, March 5, 1923; *WSJ*, March 5, 1923; Maury Klein, *Rainbow's End: The Crash, 1929* (New York: Oxford University Press, 2001), 51; Bruce Barton, "Is There Anything Here That Other Men Couldn't Do?" *American Magazine*, February 1923, 16–17, 128–135.

7 Cleveland and Huertas, *Citibank*, 138–139.

8 Ibid., 137–138; Stephen Fox, *The Mirror Makers: A History of American Advertising and Its Creators* (New York: William Morrow, 1984), 78–117; William E. Leuchtenburg, *Franklin D. Roosevelt and the New Deal* (New York: Harper & Row, 1963), 20.

9 Cleveland and Huertas, *Citibank*, 137–152; Carosso, *Investment Banking in America*, 244.

10 Cleveland and Huertas, *Citibank*, 136; Carosso, *Investment Banking in America*, 243.

11 Cleveland and Huertas, *Citibank*, 99–107; Anonymous, *The Mirrors of Wall Street* (New York: G.P. Putnam's Sons, 1933), 156.

12 Charles Mitchell to Frank Vanderlip, May 7, 1921, Vanderlip Papers, Box A68.

13 *NYT*, January 17, 1922; *WSJ*, May 18, 1923; Cleveland and Huertas, *Citibank*, 107–112.

14 Cleveland and Huertas, *Citibank*, 114, 153; *Literary Digest*, May 19, 1928, 76.

15 National City Bank Annual Reports, 1927–1928; Cleveland and Huertas, *Citibank*, 113–158; *Literary Digest*, December 15, 1926, 50; Hearing Tr., 1885–86.

16 Cleveland and Huertas, *Citibank*, 133; *NYT*, September 20, 1929; *NYT*, September 22, 1929.

17 Anonymous, *The Mirrors of Wall Street*, 151–152.

18 William K. Klingaman, *1929: The Year of the Great Crash* (New York: Harper & Row, 1989), 134–135; Klein, *Rainbow's End*, 58; Ron Chernow, *The House of Morgan: An American Banking Dynasty and the Rise of Modern Finance* (New York: Grove Press, 1990), 255; Christian R. Sonne & Chiu yin Hempel, eds., *Tuxedo Park: The Historic Houses* (Tuxedo Park, NY: Tuxedo Park Historical Society, 2007), 66–67, 250–253; Cleveland Amory, "Tuxedo Park—Black Tie," *Harper's Magazine*, September 1952, 82–90.

19 Joel Seligman, *The Transformation of Wall Street: A History of the Securities and Exchange Commission and Modern Corporate Finance* (New York: Aspen Publishers, 3rd edition, 2003), 4; John Kenneth Galbraith, *The Great Crash, 1929* (Boston: Houghton Mifflin Company, 1955), 24–42; Klein, *Rainbow's End*, 181; *NYT*, March 29, 1929; *NYT*, April 3, 1929.

20 Cleveland and Huertas, *Citibank*, 132–133, 382–383.

21 *NYT*, March 30, 1929.

22 Klein, *Rainbow's End*, 201, 205, 215; Galbraith, *The Great Crash, 1929*, 88–127; William K. Klingaman, *1929*, xiii, 56–57, 238.

23 *NYT*, November 29, 1929; *New Yorker*, December 14, 1929, 42; Sherrod, *Scapegoats*, 92–93.

24 Anonymous, *The Mirrors of Wall Street*, 157; William K. Klingaman, *1929*, 223; Bernard Baruch, *The Public Years* (New York: Holt, Rinehart and Winston, 1960), 224–225.

25 *NYT*, November 13, 1929; *Nation*, January 1, 1930, 11; Clifford Reeves, "A Brief for Bankers," *American Mercury*, September 1932, 20–29.

26 *NYT*, August 21, 1930; Edward Robb Ellis, *A Nation in Torment: The Great American Depression 1929–1939* (New York: Coward–McCann, 1970), 140–141.

27 Edward Robb Ellis, *The Epic of New York City* (New York: Old Town Books, 1990), 532; *Nation's Business*, December 1932, 59; *American Experience: The Crash of 1929*, DVD, produced by Ellen Hovde and Muffie Meyer (PBS, 1990), http://www.pbs.org/wgbh/americanexperience/crash/.

28 *Time*, March 6, 1933; *NYT*, September 26, 1923; *NYT*, September 29, 1929; Gerald D. Nash, "Herbert Hoover and the Origins of the Reconstruction Finance Corporation," *Mississippi Valley Historical Review* 46 (1959): 455–468; *NYWT*, January 10, 1933; *NYT*, January 6, 1933; *NYT*, January 11, 1933; *Washington Post*, January 11, 1933.

29 Drew Pearson and Robert S. Allen, *More Merry-Go-Round* (New York: Liveright, Inc., 1932), 14–15; Alan Brinkley, *Voices of Protest: Huey Long, Father Coughlin and the Great Depression* (New York: Vintage Books, 1983), 110; David H. Bennett, *Demagogues in the Depression: American Radicals and the Union Party, 1932–1936* (New Brunswick, NJ: Rutgers University Press, 1969), 36–37, 43; Donald Warren, *Radio Priest, Charles Coughlin, the Father of Hate Radio* (New York: Free Press, 1996); Clifford Reeves, "A Brief for Bankers," *American Mercury*, September 1932, 20–29.

30 *NYT*, February 28, 1932; *Time*, January 2, 1933; *Literary Digest*, January 28, 1933, 11; *Father Coughlin's Radio Discourses* (Royal Oak, MI: Radio League of the Little Flower, 1932), 218.

31 Ferdinand Pecora to Peter Norbeck, February 4, 1933, SEIF, Box 82, Norbeck Correspondence File; Charles Mitchell to Ferdinand Pecora, February 3, 1933, SEIF, Box 146, General Correspondence/National City Co. File; New York Landmarks Preservation Commission, *National City Bank Building* (New York: Landmarks Preservation Commission, 1999), 5–6.

32 M. R. Werner and John Starr, *Teapot Dome* (Clifton, NJ: Augustus M. Kelley Publishers, 1973), 187, 227–228, 292–293.

33 Hugo L. Black, "Inside a Senate Investigation," *Harper's Monthly Magazine*, 172 (February 1936), 275–286; Ferdinand Pecora to Peter Norbeck, February 4, 1933, SEIF, Box 82, Norbeck Correspondence File.

34 Ferdinand Pecora to Peter Norbeck, February 4, 1933, SEIF, Box 82, Norbeck Correspondence File; Ivan Lashins Handwritten Notes, February 1, 1933–February 4, 1933, SEIF, Box 150, National City Company Conference Memoranda; Memorandum from J. F. O'Hanlon to George K. Watson, May 23, 1932, SEIF, Box 144, Anaconda Copper Mining Company File.

35 *NYT*, February 2, 1933.

36 Walter K. Earle and Charles C. Parlin, *Shearman and Sterling: 1873–1973* (New York: Private Imprint, 2nd edition, 1973), 208–211; *NYT*, July 7, 1922.

37 POH, 704–709.

38 Ferdinand Pecora to Peter Norbeck, February 4, 1933, SEIF, Box 82, Norbeck Correspondence File; Ferdinand Pecora to Charles Mitchell, February 2, 1933, SEIF, Box 149, Mitchell, Charles E., File; *NYT*, February 3, 1933.

39 John Marrinan to Ferdinand Pecora, February 4, 1933, SEIF, Box 150, National City Company Conference Memoranda.

40 John E. Miller, "Restrained, Respectable Radicals: The South Dakota Farm Holiday," *Agricultural History* 59 (July 1985): 429–447.

41 SBCC Minutes, February 7, 1933; *NYT*, February 8, 1933; *NYT*, February 9, 1933.

Chapter 6. A Mine of Information

1 William E. Leuchtenburg, *Franklin D. Roosevelt and the New Deal* (New York: Harper & Row, 1963), 2–3, 19–21; Michael Vincent Namorato, ed., *The Diary of Rexford G. Tugwell: The New Deal, 1932–1935* (New York: Greenwood Press, 1992), 30; Robert A. Caro, *The Power Broker: Robert Moses and the Fall of New York* (New York: Vintage Books, 1974), 323, 336; Edward Robb Ellis, *The Epic of New York City* (New York: Old Town Books, 1990), 531–39; Studs Terkel, *Hard Times: An Oral History of the Great Depression* (New York: Pantheon

Books, 1970), 5, 20, 303, 381–382; T. H. Watkins, *The Great Depression: America in the 1930s* (Boston: Little, Brown, 1993), 13, 54; Irving Bernstein, *The Lean Years: A History of the American Worker, 1920–1933* (Boston: Houghton Mifflin, 1960), 326, 360–363; *NYT*, January 13, 1933.

2 *NYT*, December 11, 1932; *NYT*, December 17, 1932; *NYT*, February 12, 1933.

3 POH, 13–15, 41–42, 853.

4 POH, 853–855; Ron Chernow, *The House of Morgan: An American Banking Dynasty and the Rise of Modern Finance* (New York: Grove Press, 1990), 86–87.

5 POH, 44–46, 59.

6 Jerold Auerbach, *Unequal Justice: Lawyers and Social Change in Modern America* (New York: Oxford University Press, 1976), 14–129.

7 Robert B. Stevens, *Law School: Legal Education in America from the 1850s to the 1980s* (Chapel Hill, NC: University of North Carolina Press, 1983), 27, 101; Auerbach, *Unequal Justice*, 117; Joseph M. Proskauer, *A Segment of My Times* (New York: Farrar, Straus and Co., 1950), 179–180.

8 POH, 46–50, 63–67; Alfred Z. Reed, *Training for the Public Profession of the Law* (New York: Carnegie Foundation, 1921), 320, 452; Auerbach, *Unequal Justice*, 94–101; Deborah L. Rhode, "Moral Character as a Professional Credential," *Yale Law Journal* 94 (1985): 491.

9 POH, 90–91, 95–97; *Newsweek*, June 10, 1933; *NYT*, June 17, 1906; *NYT*, July 1, 1906; *NYT*, July 8, 1906; *NYT*, July 29, 1906; *NYT*, December 2, 1910.

10 Reminiscences of Morris Lincoln Strauss (1951), in Oral History Collection of Columbia University, 317; Reminiscences of Harold R. Medina (1977), in Oral History Collection of Columbia University, 553–556; Susan L. Brinson, *Personal and Public Interests: Frieda B. Hennock and the Federal Communications Commission* (Westport, CT: Praeger, 2002), 150, 159; Tyler Abell, ed., *Drew Pearson Diaries, 1949–1959* (New York: Holt, Rinehart and Winston, 1974), 425.

11 *CSM*, February 21, 1934; *Time*, June 12, 1933.

12 Donald A. Ritchie, *Electing FDR: The New Deal Campaign of 1932* (Lawrence, KS: University Press of Kansas, 2007), 46; *Time*, March 6, 1933; United States Immigration Commission, *Dictionary of Races or Peoples* (Washington, D.C.: U.S. Government Printing Office, 1911), 81–85; Edward Alsworth Ross, "Italians in America," *Century Magazine* 87 (July 1914): 443–445; Salvatore J. LaGumina, *Wop! A Documentary History of Anti-Italian Discrimination* (Toronto: Guernica Editions, 1999), 183.

13 Federal Writers' Project, *The Italians of New York* (New York: Random House, 1938), 138.

14 POH, 668–669; Harold van B. Cleveland and Thomas F. Huertas, *Citibank, 1812–1970* (Cambridge, MA: Harvard University Press, 1985), 54; *55 Wall Street: A Working Landmark* (New York: Citibank, 1979), 15–18. In his oral history, Pecora recalls this trip occurring the next week, after he had finished the Insull hearings. Contemporary records, both newspaper accounts and Pecora's travel records during the period, suggest that it was on February 9, a week earlier. *NYT*, February 10, 1933; Donald A. Ritchie, "The Pecora Wall Street Expose 1934," in *Congress Investigates: A Documented History, 1792–1974*, ed. Arthur M. Schlesinger Jr. and Roger Bruns (New York: Chelsea House Publishers, 1975), 2562.

15 James B. Stewart, *The Partners* (New York: Simon & Schuster, 1982), 24–25; Walter K. Earle and Charles C. Parlin, *Shearman and Sterling: 1873–1973* (New York: Private Imprint, 1973).

16 POH, 669–670.

17 *NYT*, February 10, 1933; POH, 671.

18 POH, 671–672.

19 POH, 670–672, 676; Ferdinand Pecora to Julian Sherrod, February 11, 1933, SEIF, Box 83, Telegrams Folder; Julian Sherrod to Ferdinand Pecora, February 14, 1933, SEIF, Box 83, Telegrams Folder; David S. Jordan to Ferdinand Pecora, January 27, 1933, SEIF, Box 81, Jordan, David S. File.

20 SBCC Minutes, July 28, 1932; James E. Stewart to Peter Norbeck, October 3, 1932, Norbeck Papers, Box 2, Folder 1.

21 Unsigned memorandum, December 5, 1932, Norbeck Papers, Box 2, Folder 2; Drew Pearson and Robert S. Allen, *The Washington Merry-Go-Round*, United Feature Syndicate, December 30, 1932; "Editor's Note," *The Washington Merry-Go-Round*, United Feature Syndicate, December 30, 1932; *Hartford Courant*, March 28, 1933; *Washington Post*, March 28, 1933; *NYT*, June 16, 1933.

22 Gilbert C. Fite, *Peter Norbeck: Prairie Statesman* (Pierre, SD: South Dakota Historical Society Press, 2005), 181; *NYT*, February 10, 1933; *Hartford Courant*, February 10, 1933.

23 Although Olson's specific charges did not pan out, he was not the only one to raise suspicions about Mellon's taxes. In the coming years, the Roosevelt administration pursued a series of tax cases against the former Treasury secretary. David Cannadine, *Mellon: An American Life* (New York: Vintage Books, 2008), 505–515, 523–35, 583–585; *Washington Post*, July 18, 1933.

24 *NYT*, February 10, 1933; *Washington Post*, February 10, 1933; *Hartford Courant*, February 10, 1933; *CSM*, February 11, 1933.

25 Ralph Blumenthal, *The Stork Club: America's Most Famous Nightspot and the Lost World of Café Society* (Boston: Little, Brown, 2000), 65–79, 127–129.

26 Raymond Moley, *First New Deal* at 310; Henry F. Pringle, *Big Frogs* (New York: Macy-Masius, 1928), 141; Samuel Untermyer to Peter Norbeck, February 23, 1933, Norbeck Papers, Box 2, Folder 2.

27 *NYT*, February 10, 1933; Fite, *Peter Norbeck: Prairie Statesman*, 180.

28 F. A. Loitch to Peter Norbeck, February 9, 1933, Norbeck Papers, Box 2, Folder 10; James B. Nue to Peter Norbeck, February 9, 1933, Norbeck Papers, Box 2, Folder 10.

29 *NYWT*, February 2, 1933; Fite, *Peter Norbeck: Prairie Statesman*, 181; *Boston Post*, January 21, 1933.

30 *CSM*, February 11, 1933; Frederic Walcott to Herbert Hoover, August 5, 1932, Walcott Papers.

31 *CSM*, February 11, 1933; Paul Mallon, *The National Whirligig*, McClure News Syndicate, February 23, 1933; *Hartford Courant*, February 11, 1933; *Norfolk Way*, February 11, 1933.

32 Peter Norbeck to H. C. Barton, February 13, 1933, Norbeck Papers, Box 2, Folder 10; George Norbeck to Peter Norbeck, February 15, 1933, Norbeck Papers, Box 65, Folder 3; Peter Norbeck to F. A. Loitch, February 13, 1933, Norbeck Papers, Box 2, Folder 10; Peter Norbeck to C. W. Robertson, February 11, 1933, Norbeck Papers, Box 129, Folder 9; Peter Norbeck to J. J. Linehan, February 14, 1933, Norbeck Papers, Box 65, Folder 2.

33 *NYT*, February 12, 1933; John Marrinan to Peter Norbeck, February 11, 1933, SEIF, Box 82, Norbeck Correspondence File.

34 *Aurora Monitor*, February 25, 1933.

Chapter 7. Junior

1 *NYT*, February 15, 1933; *Washington Post*, February 15, 1933; Peter Norbeck to Col. J. W. McIntosh, February 4, 1933, Norbeck Papers, Box 115, Folder 3; Drew Pearson and Robert S. Allen, *The Washington Merry-Go-Round*, United Feature Syndicate, February 23, 1933.

2 POH, 688–690; Frederic Lewis Allen, *The Lords of Creation* (New York: Harper & Brothers, 1935), 272–278.

3 Darwyn H. Lumley, *Breaking the Banks in Motor City: The Auto Industry, the 1933 Detroit Banking Crisis and the Start of the New Deal* (Jefferson, NC: McFarland & Co., 2009), 11.

4 Charles R. Geisst, *Wall Street: A History* (New York: Oxford University Press, 1997), 202–203.

5 Susan Estabrook Kennedy, *The Banking Crisis of 1933* (Lexington, KY: University Press of Kentucky, 1973), 1–5.

6 *Federal Reserve Bulletin*, September 1937, 907–908; Dixon Wecter, *The Age of the Great Depression, 1929–1941* (New York: Macmillan Co., 1948), 62; Gerald D. Nash, "Herbert

Hoover and the Origins of the Reconstruction Finance Corporation," *Mississippi Valley Historical Review* 46 (1959): 455–468; *Literary Digest*, January 21, 1933, 7; Kennedy, *The Banking Crisis of 1933*, 74; Charles Calomiris and Joseph Mason, "Contagion and Bank Failures During the Depression: The June 1932 Chicago Banking Panic," *American Economic Review* 87 (1997): 863–883; Lawrence Sullivan, *Prelude to Panic: The Story of the Bank Holiday* (Washington, D.C.: Statesman Press, 1936), 71; Calvin W. Coquillette, *Hoover, the Banks, the Depression: The Iowa Experience, 1930–1933* (Ph.D. diss., University of Iowa, 1997), 306–307; *NYT*, October 5, 1932.

7 Marcus Nadler and Jules I. Bogen, *The Banking Crisis: The End of an Epoch* (New York: Dodd, Mead & Company, 1933), 134; William E. Leuchtenburg, *Franklin D. Roosevelt and the New Deal* (New York: Harper & Row, 1963), 23.

8 Kennedy, *The Banking Crisis of 1933*, 75–76; James L. Butkiewicz, "The Reconstruction Finance Corporation, the Gold Standard and the Banking Panic of 1933," *Southern Economic Journal* 66 (1999): 271–293; Federal Reserve Bank of Boston, *Closed for the Holiday: The Bank Holiday of 1933* (Boston: Federal Reserve Bank of Boston, 1996), 13.

9 Elmus Wicker, *The Banking Panics of the Great Depression* (New York: Cambridge University Press, 1996), 121; Arthur A. Ballantine, "When All the Banks Closed," *Harvard Business Review* 26 (1948): 129–143; Barrie A. Wigmore, *The Crash and Its Aftermath: A History of Securities Markets in the United States, 1929–1933* (Westport, CT: Greenwood Press, 1985), 429–431; Nadler and Bogen, *The Banking Crisis: The End of an Epoch*, 1.

10 Timothy Walch and Dwight M. Miller, *Herbert Hoover and Franklin D. Roosevelt: A Documentary History* (Westport, CT: Greenwood Press, 1998), 130, 135.

11 Jonathan Alter, *The Defining Moment: FDR's Hundred Days and the Triumph of Hope* (New York: Simon & Schuster, 2006), 168–177; Raymond Moley with Elliot A. Rosen, *The First New Deal* (New York: Harcourt, Brace & World, 1966), 65–69.

12 *Time*, February 27, 1933.

13 POH, 695; Hearing Tr., 1397–1398; *Time*, February 27, 1933; Forrest McDonald, *Insull* (Chicago: University of Chicago Press, 1962), 276.

14 Hearing Tr., 1515–1516, 1519; Josephine Young Case and Everett Needham Case, *Owen D. Young and American Enterprise* (Boston: David R. Godine, 1982), 595–616.

15 Hearing Tr., 1430–1431; *NYT*, February 16, 1933.

16 Hearing Tr., 1521, 1523.

17 Edward A. Goedeken, "Dawes, Charles Gates," *American National Biography Online*, http://www.anb.org/articles/06/06-00144.html.

18 Conrad Black, *Franklin Delano Roosevelt: Champion of Freedom* (New York: Public Affairs, 2003), 232.

19 McDonald, *Insull*, 278.

20 Peter Norbeck to W. L. Dyce, February 3, 1932, Norbeck Papers, Box 140, Folder 1; Clyde B. Stovall to John Marrinan, February 16, 1933, SEIF, Box 149, Mitchell, Charles E. (Elizabeth R.), Income Tax Folder; Hearing Tr., 1529–1544; *NYT*, February 17, 1933; *Time*, February 27, 1933.

21 Forrest McDonald, *Insull*, 204–205, 315; Vincent P. Carosso, *Investment Banking in America: A History* (Cambridge, MA: Harvard University Press, 1970), 95–96, 102, 259.

22 Hearing Tr., 1626–1627, 1644; *Washington Post*, February 18, 1933.

23 Julian M. Pleasants, "Reynolds, Robert Rice," *American National Biography Online*, http://www.anb.org/articles/06/06-00552.html; Pearson and Allen, *The Washington Merry-Go-Round*, United Feature Syndicate, February 23, 1933.

24 Carosso, *Investment Banking in America*, 51–78, 255–270; *United States v. Morgan*, 118 F. Supp. 621 (S.D.N.Y. 1953); Hearing Tr., 1662–1673.

25 *NYT*, February 19, 1933.

26 James McMullin, *The National Whirligig*, McClure News Syndicate, February 23, 1933.

Chapter 8. Day One: Unimpeachable Integrity

1 Russell Senate Office Building, 1909–2009, http://www.senate.gov/RSOB/.

2 Ferdinand Pecora, *Wall Street under Oath: The Story of Our Modern Money Changers* (New York: Simon & Schuster, 1939), 71; POH, 686–687, 852–853; *Baltimore Sun*, February 26, 1933; Julian Sherrod, *Scapegoats* (New York: Brewer, Warren & Putnam, 1931), 14; *Newsweek*, June 3, 1933.

3 *Time*, March 6, 1933.

4 POH, 714–716.

5 Vincent Carosso, "Washington and Wall Street: The New Deal and Investment Bankers, 1933–1940, *The Business History Review* 44 (Winter 1970): 425–445; Lawrence Sullivan, *Prelude to Panic: The Story of the Bank Holiday* (Washington, D.C.: Statesman Press, 1936), 94–96; NYT, February 22, 1933.

6 James Grant, *Money of the Mind: Borrowing and Lending in America from the Civil War to Michael Milken* (New York: Farrar, Straus and Giroux, 1992), 222; Pecora, *Wall Street under Oath*, 71; Sherrod, *Scapegoats*, 12–13.

7 POH, 858–859; Drew Pearson and Robert S. Allen, *More Merry-Go-Round* (New York: Liveright Inc., 1932), 357.

8 E. W. Morriss to Ferdinand Pecora, February 8, 1933, SEIF, Box 152, Remedies NCB and NCC File; Thomas Stovall to Ferdinand Pecora, February 11, 1933, SEIF, Box 152, Remedies NCB and NCC File.

9 Helen Kirst to Peter Norbeck, SEIF, Box 152, Remedies NCB and NCC File.

10 A. H. Nicander to Senate Banking Committee, February 20, 1933, SEIF, Box 152, Remedies NCB and NCC File.

11 Christopher Lane to Ferdinand Pecora, February 18, 1933, SEIF, Box 152, National City Bank Remedies Folder.

12 William E. Leuchtenburg, *Franklin D. Roosevelt and the New Deal*, (New York: Harper & Row, 1963), 19; Frances Murphy to Ferdinand Pecora, February 2, 1933, SEIF, Box 152, National City Bank Remedies Folder.

13 Hearing Tr., 1762–1767.

14 *WSJ*, February 22, 1933.

15 Hearing Tr., 1762–1767, 1774; Memorandum prepared by David Saperstein, February 16, 1933, SEIF, Box 149, National City, Check List Preliminary to Final Examination File; POH, 682.

16 Thomas L. Stokes, *Chip off My Shoulder* (Princeton, NJ: Princeton University Press, 1940), 348.

17 Harry Barnard, *Independent Man: The Life of Senator James Couzens* (New York: Scribner, 1958); Drew Pearson and Robert S. Allen, *The Washington Merry-Go-Round*, United Feature Syndicate, May 29, 1933; ibid., May 19, 1936.

18 Barnard, *Independent Man*, 88–93, 168, 192.

19 David Cannadine, *Mellon: An American Life* (New York: Vintage Books, 2008), 343–347; Barnard, *Independent Man*, 158–167; *WSJ*, February 2, 1927, *WSJ*, February 22, 1933; *NYT*, March 29, 1925.

20 Susan Estabrook Kennedy, *The Banking Crisis of 1933* (Lexington, KY: University Press of Kentucky, 1973), 86–88; James L. Butkiewicz, "The Reconstruction Finance Corporation, the Gold Standard and the Banking Panic of 1933," *Southern Economic Journal* 66 (1999): 271–293; NYT, February 15, 1933; Reminiscences of James Paul Warburg (1952), in Oral History Collection of Columbia University, 855.

21 Sherrod, *Scapegoats*, 13.

22 This figure, as well as the other comparisons between dollar figures from the hearings and today's equivalents, are based on the relative share that those figures represent of the total gross domestic product (GDP) of the United States economy. Samuel H. Williamson, "Six Ways to Compute the Relative Value of a U.S. Dollar Amount, 1774 to Present," MeasuringWorth, 2009, http://www.measuringworth.com/uscompare/.

23 Pecora, *Wall Street under Oath*, 72; Sherrod, *Scapegoats*, 19.

24 Barnard, *Independent Man*, 50–51; Joel Seligman, *The Transformation of Wall Street: A History of the Securities and Exchange Commission and Modern Corporate Finance* (New York: Aspen Publishers, 3rd edition, 2003), 26; Pecora, *Wall Street under Oath*, 114.

25 Hearing Tr., 1774–1775.

26 Hearing Tr., 1775–1776; Pecora, *Wall Street under Oath*, 73.

27 Sherrod, *Scapegoats*, 13.

28 Hearing Tr., 1787–1788; Sherrod, *Scapegoats*, 92.

29 Pecora, *Wall Street under Oath*, 116.

30 Robert A. Caro, *The Power Broker: Robert Moses and the Fall of New York* (New York: Vintage Books, 1974), 323; T. H. Watkins, *The Great Depression: America in the 1930s* (Boston: Little, Brown, 1993), 70; Donald A. Ritchie, *Reporting from Washington: The History of the Washington Press Corps* (New York: Oxford University Press, 2005), 3; Edmund Wilson, *The American Earthquake: A Documentary of the Twenties and Thirties* (New York: Farrar, Straus and Giroux, 1958), 226; *NYT*, February 22, 1933.

31 Hearing Tr., 1778.

32 Hearing Tr., 1779.

33 POH, 672; Harold van B. Cleveland and Thomas F. Huertas, *Citibank, 1812–1970* (Cambridge, MA: Harvard University Press, 1985), 184.

34 Hearing Tr., 1785–1786; Pecora, *Wall Street under Oath*, 119.

35 Louis D. Brandeis, *Other People's Money: And How the Bankers Use It* (New York: Frederick A. Stokes, 1914), 92; Leonard Baker, *Brandeis and Frankfurter: A Dual Biography* (New York: Harper & Row, 1984), 283.

36 Hearing Tr., 1801–1802, 1806; Thomas K. McCraw, *Prophets of Regulation: Charles Francis Adams, Louis D. Brandeis, James M. Landis, Alfred E. Kahn* (Cambridge, MA: Belknap Press of Harvard University Press, 1984); 166.

37 Hearing Tr., 1808.

38 Pearson and Allen, *The Washington Merry-Go-Round*, January 9, 1934; ibid., April 15, 1934; Gilbert C. Fite, *Peter Norbeck: Prairie Statesman* (Pierre, SD: South Dakota Historical Society Press, 2005), 173; Ray Tucker and Frederick R. Barkley, *Sons of the Wild Jackass* (Boston: L.C. Page & Co., 1932), 346; *NYT*, November 16, 1944; Reminiscences of Eugene Meyer (1953), in Oral History Collection of Columbia University, 455; Seligman, *The Transformation of Wall Street*, 9.

39 Hearing Tr., 1807; 1811–1813; *NYT*, February 22, 1933; Pearson and Allen, *The Daily Washington Merry-Go-Round*, January 23, 1933.

40 Hearing Tr., 1811–1814.

41 Pecora, *Wall Street under Oath*, 113.

42 *NYT*, February 22, 1933; *Washington Post*, February 22, 1933; *WSJ*, February 22, 1933; *Philadelphia Record*, February 24, 1933.

43 Memorandum on "Michigan Banking Events," undated, Couzens Papers, Box 141; John Kenneth Galbraith, *The Great Crash, 1929* (Boston: Houghton Mifflin Company, 1955), 157; *NYT*, February 23, 1933; Pearson and Allen, *The Washington Merry-Go-Round*, March 10, 1933.

44 Reminiscences of Eugene Meyer (1953), in Oral History Collection of Columbia University, A39, A79.

Chapter 9. Day Two: Morale

1 *NYT*, February 23, 1933.

2 Letter to Committee from S. J. Smelts, February 22, 1933, SEIF, Box 81, Criticisms, General File.

3 Harry Barnard, *Independent Man: The Life of Senator James Couzens* (New York: Charles Scribner's Sons, 1958), 242; Theodore G. Joslin, *Hoover Off the Record* (Freeport, NY: Books

for Libraries Press, 1971), 360; Liaquat Ahamed, *Lords of Finance: The Bankers Who Broke the World* (New York: Penguin Press, 2009), 422–448; Memorandum: Meeting of Federal Reserve of New York Board of Directors, February 23, 1933, Harrison Papers, Box 23

4 Harold van B. Cleveland and Thomas F. Huertas, *Citibank, 1812–1970* (Cambridge, MA: Harvard University Press, 1985), 106–109; National City Bank 1923 Condensed Statement of Condition.

5 Hearing Tr., 1838.

6 Hearing Tr., 1788–1790, 1793–1794; Ferdinand Pecora, *Wall Street under Oath: The Story of Our Modern Money Changers* (New York: Simon & Schuster, 1939), 121.

7 Hearing Tr., 1795–1796.

8 *Washington Daily News*, March 1, 1933.

9 Hearing Tr., 1796–1799; Pecora, *Wall Street under Oath*, 123.

10 Hearing Tr., 1831–1833.

11 Hearing Tr., 1830.

12 Hearing Tr., 1833–1835, 1837.

13 Hearing Tr., 1840–1846.

14 Hearing Tr., 1862–1863; NYT, February 23, 1933.

15 Cleveland and Huertas, *Citibank*, 108–109; *Newsweek*, March 4, 1933; NYT, March 5, 1948.

16 *Newsweek*, March 31, 1934; Hearing Tr., 1868–1871.

17 Hearing Tr., 1871; *Hartford Courant*, February 23, 1933.

18 Hearing Tr., 1872–1875; E. H. Adams to Peter Norbeck, February 19, 1933, SEIF, Box 152, Remedies National City Bank and National City Company File; Pecora, *Wall Street under Oath*, 129.

19 Hearing Tr., 1877; Pecora, *Wall Street under Oath*, 129.

20 Hearing Tr. (73rd), 111–112; Senate Committee on Banking and Currency, *Stock Exchange Practices*, 73rd Cong., 2nd Sess., 1934, S. Rept. 1455, 60; Ron Chernow, *The House of Morgan: An American Banking Dynasty and the Rise of Modern Finance* (New York: Grove Press, 1990), 356.

21 John Kenneth Galbraith, *The Great Crash, 1929* (Boston: Houghton Mifflin, 1955), 151–152; Julian Sherrod, *Scapegoats* (New York: Brewer, Warren & Putnam, 1931), 78–79, 82; NYT, November 8, 1929; Anonymous to Peter Norbeck, February 22, 1933, SEIF, Box 146, Cuban Sugar Bonds General Correspondence File; Hearing Tr., 1875.

22 Drew Pearson and Robert S. Allen, *More Merry-Go-Round* (New York: Liveright, 1932), 114–154; Peter Norbeck to Ogden Mills, February 2, 1933, Norbeck Papers, Box 2, Folder 10; SBCC Minutes, February 21, 1933, March 13, 1933.

23 POH, 832–833; Reminiscences of James Paul Warburg (1952), in Oral History Collection of Columbia University, 187; Reminiscences of Eugene Meyer (1953), in Oral History Collection of Columbia University, 691; Pearson and Allen, *More Merry-Go-Round*, 138.

24 Reminiscences of Morris Strauss (1951), in Oral History Collection of Columbia University, 317–318; Reminiscences of Reuben A. Lazarus (1951), in Oral History Collection of Columbia University, 399–402.

25 NYT, November 20, 1950.

26 Ferdinand Pecora to Franklin Roosevelt, June 24, 1935, PPF 2818, Pecora, Ferdinand, Folder, FDRPL.; Ferdinand Pecora to Franklin Roosevelt, November 22, 1937, PPF 2818, Pecora, Ferdinand, Folder, FDRPL.

27 POH, 846–847.

28 POH, 723–725.

Chapter 10. Day Three: Manipulation

1 NYT, September 25, 1929; NYT, December 20, 1939; NYT, December 16, 1964; WSJ, April 4, 1929.

2 *Washington Post*, February 24, 1933; *Washington Herald*, February 24, 1933; Hearing Tr., 1893.

3 POH, 682; Hearing Tr., 1917.

4 Hearing Tr., 1881–1882, 1940.

5 Hearing Tr., 1879, 1884–1886; Julian Sherrod, *Scapegoats* (New York: Brewer, Warren & Putnam, 1931), 50.

6 Hearing Tr., 1881–1882.

7 NYWT, February 23, 1933; NYT, February 24, 1933.

8 Hearing Tr., 1920.

9 A. E. Budell to Peter Norbeck, February 25, 1933, SEIF, Box 149, National City Bank Press Clippings File.

10 Hearing Tr., 1925–1926.

11 Hearing Tr., 1939, 1942–1943.

12 Hearing Tr., 1953–1954.

13 Hearing Tr. (73rd), 114; NYT, February 24, 1933; *Time*, April 3, 1933.

14 *Nation*, March 8, 1933.

15 Joseph P. Kennedy, *I'm for Roosevelt* (New York: Reynal & Hitchcock, 1936), 93.

16 NY *Inquiry*, March 5, 1933; *Nation*, March 8, 1933.

17 Raymond Moley, *After Seven Years* (New York: Harper & Brothers, 1939), 377; *Philadelphia Record*, February 23, 1933; *Hartford Courant*, February 24, 1933; WSJ, February 24, 1933.

18 Paul W. Doyle to Peter Norbeck, February 28, 1933, SEIF, Box 152, National City Bank Remedies Folder; John S. Campen to Peter Norbeck, February 24, 1933, SEIF, Box 149, National City Bank Press Clippings Folder; H. W. Frund to Ferdinand Pecora, February 26, 1933, SEIF, Box 152, National City Bank Remedies Folder; Dr. J. W. Gould to Ferdinand Pecora, March 1, 1933, SEIF, Box 152, National City Bank Remedies Folder; Ferdinand Pecora to Dr. J. W. Gould, March 10, 1933, SEIF, Box 152, National City Bank Remedies Folder.

19 Silas Green to Peter Norbeck, February 2, 1933, SEIF, Box 152, National City Bank Remedies Folder.

20 Edmund Wilson, *The Thirties: From Notebooks and Diaries of the Period* (New York: Farrar, Straus and Giroux, 1980), 324; NYT, June 20, 1930.

21 NYT, February 24, 1933; NYWT, February 24, 1933; *Congressional Record*, 72nd Cong., 2nd Sess., 1933, 76, pt. 5:4769-4780.

22 *Public Papers of President Herbert H. Hoover, Volume 4: 1932–33* (Washington, D.C.: U.S. Government Printing Office, 1977), 1048–1049.

23 Reminiscences of Eugene Meyer (1953), in Oral History Collection of Columbia University, A119.

Chapter 11. Day Four: Legal Legerdemain

1 NYT, February 25, 1933.

2 John Marrinan to Ferdinand Pecora, February 4, 1933, SEIF, Box 149, Mitchell, Charles E. (Elizabeth R.) Income Tax File; Ambrose W. Hussey to Peter Norbeck, February 23, 1933, SEIF, Box 149, Mitchell, Charles E. (Elizabeth R.) Income Tax File.

3 NYT, February 25, 1933; John H. Highfill to Senator Joseph T. Robinson, March 20, 1933, quoted in Pamela Webb, "The Bank Holiday in Arkansas," *Arkansas Historical Quarterly* 39 (1980): 247–261; Digest of Diary of Charles S. Hamlin, February 24, 1933, Hamlin Papers, Reel 21.

4 Hearing Tr., 1965–1966.

5 Hearing Tr., 1970–1971.

6 Edwin J. Perkins, "The Divorce of Commercial and Investment Banking: A History," *Banking Law Journal* 88 (1971): 483–528; Eugene Nelson White, *The Regulation and Reform of the American Banking System, 1900–1929* (Princeton, NJ: Princeton University Press, 1983).

7 Richard H. K. Vietor, "Regulation-Defined Financial Markets: Fragmentation and Integration in Financial Services," in *Wall Street and Regulation*, ed. Samuel L. Hayes III (Boston: Harvard

Business School Press, 1987), 12; Harold van B. Cleveland and Thomas F. Huertas, *Citibank, 1812–1970* (Cambridge, MA: Harvard University Press, 1985), 358; Ferdinand Pecora, *Wall Street under Oath: The Story of Our Modern Money Changers* (New York: Simon & Schuster, 1939), 76.

8 Pecora, *Wall Street under Oath*, 80; Hearing Tr., 1995.

9 Hearing Tr., 2007–2008; Perkins, "The Divorce of Commercial and Investment Banking," 488.

10 Hearing Tr., 2010.

11 Julian Sherrod, *Scapegoats* (New York: Brewer, Warren & Putnam, 1931), 16.

12 Pecora, *Wall Street under Oath*, 89.

13 Hearing Tr., 2019–2020.

13 Hearing Tr., 2020.

14 Hearing Tr., 2025.

15 Sherrod, *Scapegoats*, 22–23, 39; NYT, January 18, 1920; Edmund Wilson, *Travels in Two Democracies* (New York: Harcourt, Brace and Company, 1936), 55–56; Maury Klein, *Rainbow's End: The Crash, 1929* (New York: Oxford University Press, 2001), 56.

16 James C. German Jr., *Taft's Attorney General: George W. Wickersham* (New York: New York University, 1969), 47.

17 Hearing Tr., 2027–2044; Pecora, *Wall Street under Oath*, 77, 80–81.

18 NYT, February 6, 1942; Hearing Tr., 2043.

19 German, *Taft's Attorney General*, 26.

20 Henry F. Pringle, *The Life and Times of William Howard Taft: A Biography* (New York: Farrar & Rinehart, 1939), 676.

21 Cleveland and Huertas, *Citibank*, 66–67; Pringle, *The Life and Times of William Howard Taft*, 677.

22 Perkins, "The Divorce of Commercial and Investment Banking," 488, 491–495; Vietor, "Regulation-Defined Financial Markets," 12; Vincent P. Carosso, *Investment Banking in America: A History* (Cambridge, MA: Harvard University Press, 1970), 272–273.

23 NYT, February 24, 1933; NYWT, February 24, 1933; Drew Pearson and Robert S. Allen, *The Washington Merry-Go-Round*, United Feature Syndicate, March 11, 1933.

24 Marcus Nadler and Jules I. Bogen, *The Banking Crisis: The End of an Epoch* (New York: Dodd, Mead & Company, 1933), 44.

25 NYT, May 10, 1932; NYWT, February 24, 1933; NY American, February 25, 1933; John Marrinan to Ferdinand Pecora, February 27, 1933, SEIF, Box 82, Marrinan, John Correspondence File.

26 POH, 852; *Nation*, July 1, 1939; George J. Benston, *The Separation of Commercial and Investment Banking: The Glass-Steagall Act Revisited and Reconsidered* (New York: Oxford University Press, 1990).

Chapter 12. Days Five and Six: Intermission

1 Darwyn H. Lumley, *Breaking the Banks in Motor City: The Auto Industry, the 1933 Detroit Banking Crisis and the Start of the New Deal* (Jefferson, NC: McFarland & Co, 2009), 84–85; Roy Chapin to James Couzens, February 25, 1933, Couzens Papers, Box 139.

2 Elmus Wicker, *The Banking Panics of the Great Depression* (New York: Cambridge University Press, 1996), 126–127; Ellen N. Lawson, "Banking," *The Encyclopedia of Cleveland History*, http://ech.cwru.edu/index.html; Lawrence Sullivan, *Prelude to Panic: The Story of the Bank Holiday* (Washington, D.C.: Statesman Press, 1936), 98, 101–104; NYT, February 25, 1933; WSJ, February 25, 1933; Jo Ann E. Argersinger, *Toward a New Deal in Baltimore: People and Government in the Great Depression* (Chapel Hill, NC: University of North Carolina Press, 1988), 17–19.

3 Reminiscences of Eugene Meyer (1953), in Oral History Collection of Columbia University, A92; Digest of Diary of Charles S. Hamlin, February 25, 1933, Hamlin Papers, Reel 21;

Harold van B. Cleveland and Thomas F. Huertas, *Citibank, 1812–1970* (Cambridge, MA: Harvard University Press, 1985), 407.

4 Reminiscences of Eugene Meyer, A92–A93.

5 *NY Evening Post*, February 25, 1933.

6 Fred W. Sargent to Peter Norbeck, February 27, 1933, Norbeck Papers, Box 115, Folder 4; William Purnell to Peter Norbeck, February 27, 1933, SEIF, Box 81, Criticisms General File.

7 *Washington Herald*, February 25, 1933; CSM, February 27, 1933; Frank E. Karelsen Jr. to Peter Norbeck, February 28, 1933, Norbeck Papers, Box 2, Folder 2.

8 Reminiscences of James Paul Warburg (1952), in Oral History Collection of Columbia University, 135.

9 *Literary Digest*, April 8, 1933.

10 *Business Week*, March 8, 1933; *Baltimore Sun*, February 26, 1933.

11 NYT, February 26, 1933.

12 *Washington Herald*, February 25, 1933; *Newsweek*, March 4, 1933.

13 Eli Wald, "The Rise and Fall of the WASP and Jewish Law Firms," *Stanford Law Review* 60 (2008): 1803; Samuel Untermyer to Peter Norbeck, February 25, 1933, Norbeck Papers, Box 2, Folder 2; Raymond Moley with Elliot A. Rosen, *The First New Deal* (New York: Harcourt, Brace & World, 1966), 310; Allan H. MacLean to Peter Norbeck, February 27, 1933, Norbeck Papers, Box 2, Folder 10.

14 Richard O. Boyer, *Max Steuer: Magician of the Law* (New York: Greenberg, 1932), 11; James McMullin, *The National Whirligig*, McClure News Syndicate, February 23, 1933.

15 *Commonweal*, March 15, 1933; CSM, February 21, 1934; Arthur M. Schlesinger Jr., *The Age of Roosevelt: The Coming of the New Deal* (Boston: Houghton Mifflin Company, 1958), 120.

16 CSM, February 21, 1934; *Boston Globe*, May 21, 1933; *Literary Digest*, June 10, 1933; *Time*, March 6, 1933; Charles N. Camp, undated, SEIF, Box 82, Miscellaneous Correspondence File; Ron Chernow, *The House of Morgan: An American Banking Dynasty and the Rise of Modern Finance* (New York: Grove Press, 1990), 361–362; *Business Week*, June 7, 1933.

17 Joab H. Banton, "Ferdinand Pecora," *U.S. Law Review* 67 (1933): 302–306; *Barron's*, September 17, 1934; *Boston Globe*, May 21, 1933; *Literary Digest*, June 10, 1933; *Time*, March 6, 1933; *Newsweek*, June 10, 1933; Ralph F. de Bedts, *The New Deal's SEC: The Formative Years* (New York: Columbia University Press, 1964), 94; Peter Norbeck to James E. Stewart, March 24, 1933, Norbeck Papers, Box 134, Folder 5.

18 Thomas F. Huertas and Joan L. Silverman, "Charles E. Mitchell: Scapegoat of the Crash?" *Business History Review* 60 (1986): 81–103; NYT, October 25, 1929.

19 *Philadelphia Record*, February 24, 1933; *Public Opinion*, February 25, 1933; *St. Louis Star and Times*, February 24, 1933.

20 *St. Louis Star and Times*, February 24, 1933; NYWT, February 25, 1933.

21 *Commercial & Financial Chronicle*, February 25, 1933; Max Freedman, ed., *Roosevelt and Frankfurter: Their Correspondence, 1928–45* (Boston: Little, Brown, 1967), 123.

22 Freedman, *Roosevelt and Frankfurter*, 114–117; Ronald Steel, *Walter Lippmann and the American Century* (Boston: Little, Brown, 1980), 289–290.

23 Reminiscences of Eugene Meyer (1953), in Oral History Collection of Columbia University, A119–A120; Thomas L. Stokes, *Chip off My Shoulder* (Princeton, NJ: Princeton University Press, 1940), 347.

24 John Marrinan to Ferdinand Pecora, February 25, 1933, SEIF, Box 82, Marrinan, John Correspondence File; NYT, February 26, 1933; NYWT, February 27, 1933.

25 *Literary Digest*, March 11, 1933 (quoting *Troy Record*).

26 *Public Papers of President Herbert H. Hoover, Volume 4: 1932–33* (Washington, D.C.: U.S. Government Printing Office, 1977), 1054–1055; William E. Leuchtenburg, *Franklin D. Roosevelt and the New Deal, 1932–1940* (New York: Harper & Row, 1963), 36; Raymond Moley, *After Seven Years* (New York: Harper & Brothers, 1939), 143, 377; Edward M.

Lamont, *The Ambassador from Wall Street: The Story of Thomas W. Lamont, J.P. Morgan's Chief Executive* (Lanham, MD: Madison Books, 1994), 338; Ernest K. Lindley, *The Roosevelt Revolution: First Phase* (New York: Viking Press, 1933), 75–76.

27 CSM, February 27, 1933; NYT, February 27, 1933; Cleveland and Huertas, *Citibank*, 186–188.

28 POH, 678–679.

Chapter 13. Day Seven: South of the Border

1 NYT, February 28, 1933; *Washington Daily News*, March 1, 1933.

2 *Philadelphia Record*, March 2, 1933; NYWT, February 28, 1933.

3 POH, 682.

4 Ferdinand Pecora, *Wall Street under Oath: The Story of Our Modern Money Changers* (New York: Simon & Schuster, 1939), 100.

5 Vincent P. Carosso, *Investment Banking in America: A History* (Cambridge, MA: Harvard University Press, 1970), 248–249; Joel Seligman, *The Transformation of Wall Street: A History of the Securities and Exchange Commission and Modern Corporate Finance* (New York: Aspen Publishers, 3rd edition, 2003), 10–11.

6 Harold van B. Cleveland and Thomas F. Huertas, *Citibank, 1812–1970* (Cambridge, MA: Harvard University Press, 1985), 145–153; Seligman, *The Transformation of Wall Street*, 10–11; Carosso, *Investment Banking in America*, 262.

7 James Grant, *Money of the Mind: Borrowing and Lending in America from the Civil War to Michael Milken* (New York: Farrar, Straus and Giroux, 1992), 174; Cleveland and Huertas, *Citibank*, 145; John Brooks, *Once in Golconda: A True Drama of Wall Street, 1920–1938* (New York: John Wiley & Sons, 1969), 103; Carosso, *Investment Banking in America*, 251.

8 Hearing Tr., 2053–2063.

9 NYWT, February 27, 1933; Pecora, *Wall Street under Oath*, 101.

10 Hearing Tr., 2115.

11 David Bristow to Peter Norbeck, February 21, 1933, SEIF, Box 149, National City Remedies File.

12 Hearing Tr., 2067–2068.

13 Hearing Tr., 2069, 2071, 2076.

14 Hearing Tr., 2085–2086.

15 Hearing Tr., 2106.

16 NYT, May 20, 1934, NYT February 12, 1942; *Washington Post*, November 11, 1943.

17 POH, 817–818, 827–828; Peter Norbeck to George A. Perley, April 17, 1933, Norbeck Papers, Box 115, Folder 4.

18 Chauncey Overfield to Ferdinand Pecora, February 28, 1933, SEIF, Box 152, Remedies NCB and NCC File.

19 *New York Herald Tribune*, February 27, 1933; *Nation*, February 27, 1933; *Nation*, March 15, 1933.

20 Benjamin Roth, *The Great Depression: A Diary*, ed. James Ledbetter and Daniel B. Roth (New York: Public Affairs, 2009), 93; Theodore G. Joslin, *Hoover off the Record* (Freeport, NY: Books for Libraries Press, 1971), 360; Lawrence Sullivan, *Prelude to Panic: The Story of the Bank Holiday* (Washington, D.C.: Statesman Press, 1936), 104.

21 Thomas W. Lamont to Franklin D. Roosevelt, February 27, 1933, PPF 70, Lamont, Thomas File, FDRPL; Michael Vincent Namorato, ed., *The Diary of Rexford G. Tugwell: The New Deal, 1932–1935* (New York: Greenwood Press, 1992), 82.

22 Susan Estabrook Kennedy, *The Banking Crisis of 1933* (Lexington, KY: University Press of Kentucky, 1973), 133, 161; Interview of Mary Eloise Green, The Ohio State University Oral History Project, http://hdl.handle.net/1811/478; *Literary Digest*, March 25, 1933; Pamela Webb, "The Bank Holiday in Arkansas," *Arkansas Historical Quarterly* 39 (1980): 247–261; Federal Reserve Bank of Boston, *Closed for the Holiday: The Bank Holiday of 1933* (Boston: Federal Reserve Bank of Boston, 1996), 10; Calvin W. Coquillette, *Hoover, the Banks, the*

Depression: The Iowa Experience, 1930–1933 (Ph.D. diss., University of Iowa, 1997), 310–311; William H. Jervey Jr., "When the Banks Closed: Arizona's Bank Holiday of 1933," in *Hitting Home: The Great Depression in Town and Country,* ed. Bernard Sternsher (Chicago: Ivan R. Dee, 1989), 219–246.

23 Davis W. Houck, *FDR and Fear Itself: The First Inaugural Address* (College Station, TX: Texas A&M University Press, 2002), 96–116; Raymond Moley with Elliot A. Rosen, *The First New Deal* (New York: Harcourt, Brace & World, 1966), 113–120.

Chapter 14. Day Eight: Shorn Lamb

1 Davis W. Houck, *FDR and Fear Itself: The First Inaugural Address* (College Station, TX: Texas A&M University Press, 2002), 98–99, 117–124; Raymond Moley with Elliot A. Rosen, *The First New Deal* (New York: Harcourt, Brace & World, 1966), 113–120; Alfred B. Rollins Jr., *Roosevelt and Howe* (New Brunswick, NJ: Transaction Publishers, 2002), 338–348; Geoffrey C. Ward. "Howe, Louis McHenry," *American National Biography Online,* http://www.anb.org/articles/06/06-00295.html.

2 Charles R. Geisst, *Wall Street: A History* (New York: Oxford University Press, 1997), 214–215; Hearing Tr., 2123.

3 Hearing Tr., 2119–2120.

4 Hearing Tr., 2134–2135.

5 Hearing Tr., 2136–2138.

6 Hearing Tr., 2155.

7 Hearing Tr., 2157–2160.

8 Vincent P. Carosso, *Investment Banking in America: A History* (Cambridge, MA: Harvard University Press, 1970), 101.

9 Hearing Tr., 2163–2166; *NYT,* March 1, 1933.

10 *Newsweek,* March 11, 1933; *Pottsville Republican,* February 27, 1933; Irving Bernstein, *The Lean Years: A History of the American Worker, 1920–1933* (Boston: Houghton Mifflin Company, 1960), 432.

11 Ferdinand Pecora, *Wall Street under Oath: The Story of Our Modern Money Changers* (New York: Simon & Schuster, 1939), 85, 89.

12 *Newsweek,* March 11, 1933.

13 *NYWT,* February 28, 1933.

14 Hearing Tr., 2170–2182.

15 Susan Estabrook Kennedy, *The Banking Crisis of 1933* (Lexington, KY: University Press of Kentucky, 1973), 144; Pamela Webb, "The Bank Holiday in Arkansas," *Arkansas Historical Quarterly* 39 (1980): 247–261.

16 Jo Ann E. Argersinger, *Toward a New Deal in Baltimore: People and Government in the Great Depression* (Chapel Hill, NC: University of North Carolina Press, 1988), 17–19.

17 Lawrence Sullivan, *Prelude to Panic: The Story of the Bank Holiday* (Washington, D.C.: Statesman Press, 1936), 108; Benjamin Roth, *The Great Depression: A Diary,* ed. James Ledbetter and Daniel B. Roth (New York: Public Affairs, 2009), 93, 96; *NYT,* March 1, 1933; *CSM,* March 1, 1933.

18 S.R. 371, 72nd Cong., 2nd Sess., *Congressional Record,* 76, pt. 5:5212–5214.

Chapter 15. Day Nine: A Free and Open Market

1 Susan Estabrook Kennedy, *The Banking Crisis of 1933* (Lexington, KY: University Press of Kentucky, 1973), 144; Elmus Wicker, *The Banking Panics of the Great Depression* (New York: Cambridge University Press, 1996), 108; Reminiscences of Robert H. Jackson (1952), in Oral History Collection of Columbia University, 237; *NYT,* March 1, 1933; *Washington Post,* March 1, 1933.

2 *NYT*, October 8, 1926, Jan 11, 1990.

3 Hearing Tr., 2141–2151; *NYT*, March 22, 1933.

4 Hearing Tr., 2183–2196.

5 Hearing Tr., 2196–2202; *NYT*, March 1, 1933; *NYT*, March 22, 1933; *NYT*, April 12, 1933; *NYT*, October 8, 1933; *Nation*, March 15, 1933.

6 *Baltimore Sun*, February 28, 1933; *NYT*, March 1, 1933; *WSJ*, March 1, 1933.

7 Arthur M. Schlesinger Jr., *The Age of Roosevelt: The Crisis of the Old Order, 1919–1933* (Boston: Houghton Mifflin Company, 1957), 461–462; Report of Richard Whitney to NYSE Governing Committee, August 24, 1932, NYSE Archives; Hearing Tr., 2262.

8 Hearing Tr., 2203–2213.

9 Joel Seligman, *The Transformation of Wall Street: A History of the Securities and Exchange Commission and Modern Corporate Finance* (New York: Aspen Publishers, 3rd edition, 2003), 46–47; Ferdinand Pecora, *Wall Street under Oath: The Story of Our Modern Money Changers* (New York: Simon & Schuster, 1939), 264.

10 Hearing Tr., 2206–2210; 2247–2248.

11 Hearing Tr., 2249.

12 Hearing Tr., 2219–2224.

13 Hearing Tr., 2234, 2257.

14 Hearing Tr., 2263–2264.

15 Charles R. Geisst, *Wall Street: A History* (New York: Oxford University Press, 1997), 183; Pecora, *Wall Street under Oath*, 263.

16 Hearing Tr., 2227–2228.

Chapter 16. Day Ten: The End of an Era

1 POH, 682; Ferdinand Pecora, *Wall Street under Oath: The Story of Our Modern Money Changers* (New York: Simon & Schuster, 1939), 88.

2 Hearing Tr., 2265–2269.

3 Hearing Tr., 2269–2323.

4 Hearing Tr., 2323–2343; POH, 763; David S. Levin, "Regulating the Securities Industry: The Evolution of a Government Policy" (Ph.D. diss., Columbia University, 1969), 207; Pecora, *Wall Street under Oath*, 123–126.

5 Pecora, *Wall Street under Oath*, 130.

6 William H. Jervey Jr., "When the Banks Closed: Arizona's Bank Holiday of 1933," in *Hitting Home: The Great Depression in Town and Country*, ed. Bernard Sternsher (Chicago: Ivan R. Dee, 1989), 219–246; *San Mateo Times*, March 2, 1933.

7 Edward Robb Ellis, *A Nation in Torment: The Great American Depression 1929–1939* (New York: Coward–McCann, 1970), 265; *Literary Digest*, March 25, 1933.

8 Reminiscences of James Paul Warburg (1952), in Oral History Collection of Columbia University, 102; Pecora, *Wall Street under Oath*, 71; Harold van B. Cleveland and Thomas F. Huertas, *Citibank, 1812–1970* (Cambridge, MA: Harvard University Press, 1985), 189; William A. Leuchtenburg, *Franklin D. Roosevelt and the New Deal*, (New York: Harper & Row, 1963), 39–40; Edward Robb Ellis, *A Nation in Torment*, 265–266; Michael E. Parrish, *Anxious Decades: America in Prosperity and Depression 1920–1941* (New York: W.W. Norton, 1992), 290.

9 Hearing Tr., 2344–2345.

10 POH, 685–686, 851.

11 *NYT*, March 3, 1933; Arthur M. Schlesinger Jr., *The Age of Roosevelt: The Crisis of the Old Order, 1919–1933* (Boston: Houghton Mifflin Company, 1957), 479; Susan Estabrook Kennedy, *The Banking Crisis of 1933* (Lexington, KY: University Press of Kentucky, 1973), 144; Davis W. Houck, *FDR and Fear Itself: The First Inaugural Address* (College Station, TX: Texas A&M University Press, 2002), 117–134.

Epilogue

1 Adam Cohen, *Nothing to Fear: FDR's Inner Circle and the Hundred Days that Created Modern America* (New York: Penguin Press, 2009), 276; *New York Herald Tribune*, March 10, 1933; Ronald Steel, *Walter Lippmann and the American Century* (Boston: Little, Brown, 1980), 280.

2 Cohen, *Nothing to Fear*, 73; Charles A. Beard and George H. A. Smith, *The Old Deal and the New* (New York: Macmillan Co., 1940), 78.

3 Conrad Black, *Franklin Delano Roosevelt: Champion of Freedom* (New York: Public Affairs, 2003), 274–279; Susan Estabrook Kennedy, *The Banking Crisis of 1933* (Lexington, KY: University Press of Kentucky, 1973), 152–202.

4 *Literary Digest*, March 11, 1933.

5 Raymond Moley with Elliot A. Rosen, *The First New Deal* (New York: Harcourt, Brace & World, 1966), 309–310; POH, 698; Samuel Untermyer to Peter Norbeck, March 6, 1933, Norbeck Papers, Box 2, Folder 10; Joel Seligman, *The Transformation of Wall Street: A History of the Securities and Exchange Commission and Modern Corporate Finance* (New York: Aspen Publishers, 3rd edition, 2003), 52; Arthur M. Schlesinger Jr., *The Age of Roosevelt: The Coming of the New Deal* (Boston: Houghton Mifflin Company, 1958), 440.

6 Thomas Lamont to Franklin D. Roosevelt, April 11, 1933, PPF 70, Lamont, Thomas File, FDRPL.

7 Seligman, *The Transformation of Wall Street*, 30–38; Donald A. Ritchie, "The Pecora Wall Street Expose 1934," in *Congress Investigates: A Documented History, 1792–1974*, ed. Arthur M. Schlesinger Jr. and Roger Bruns (New York: Chelsea House Publishers, 1975), 2564–2569; Ron Chernow, *The House of Morgan: An American Banking Dynasty and the Rise of Modern Finance* (New York: Grove Press, 1990), 346–377; POH, 732–748; NYT, May 30, 1933.

8 *Time*, June 12, 1933; Flynn, "The Marines Land in Wall Street," 149; *Newsweek*, May 27, 1933; *Newsweek*, June 10, 1933; *Time*, June 12, 1933; Drew Pearson and Robert S. Allen, *The Washington Merry-Go-Round*, United Feature Syndicate, May 31, 1933; ibid., June 4, 1933.

9 *Barron's*, September 17, 1934; *Boston Globe*, May 21, 1933; NYT, May 21, 1933; NYT, May 28, 1933; NYT, June 2, 1933; WSJ, June 23, 1933; Peter Norbeck to James E. Stewart, May 6, 1933, Norbeck Papers, Box 115, Folder 4.

10 Schlesinger, *The Coming of the New Deal*, 423, 439–442; D. B. Hardeman & Donald C. Bacon, *Rayburn: A Biography* (Austin, TX: Texas Monthly Press, 1987), 154; Seligman, *The Transformation of Wall Street*, 39–72; Donald A. Ritchie, *James M. Landis: Dean of Regulators* (Cambridge, MA: Harvard University Press, 1980), 43–61; WSJ, March 31, 1933; Peter Norbeck to James E. Stewart, May 6, 1933, Norbeck Papers, Box 115, Folder 4.

11 Franklin D. Roosevelt to James H. Perkins, March 9, 1933, PPF 54, Perkins, James H. File, FDRPL; Schlesinger, *The Coming of the New Deal*, 442–443; Kennedy, *The Banking Crisis of 1933*, 203–223; Seligman, *The Transformation of Wall Street*, 66; Harold van B. Cleveland and Thomas F. Huertas, *Citibank, 1812–1970* (Cambridge, MA: Harvard University Press, 1985), 197.

12 Melanie L. Fein, *Securities Activities of Banks* (New York: Wolters Kluwer, 3rd edition, 2009); Ingo Walter, ed., *Deregulating Wall Street: Commercial Bank Penetration of the Corporate Securities Market* (New York: John Wiley & Sons, 1985); Amey Stone and Mike Brewster, *King of Capital: Sandy Weill and the Making of Citigroup* (New York: John Wiley & Sons, 2002), 217–244, 254–257.

13 Kennedy, *The Banking Crisis of 1933*, 203–223; Milton Friedman and Anna Jacobson Schwartz, *A Monetary History of the United States, 1867–1960* (Princeton, NJ: Princeton University Press, 1963), 434–442.

14 Seligman, *The Transformation of Wall Street*, 73–100; Schlesinger, *The Coming of the New Deal*, 461–467; Michael R. Beschloss, *Kennedy and Roosevelt: The Uneasy Alliance* (New York: W.W. Norton, 1980), 83–91.

15 Peter Norbeck to Ferdinand Pecora, March 10, 1933, Norbeck Papers, Box 2, Folder 2; John T. Flynn, "The Marines Land in Wall Street," *Harper's* 169 (July 1934): 148–153; Peter Norbeck to James E. Stewart, March 24, 1933, Norbeck Papers, Box 134, Folder 5; Gilbert C. Fite, *Peter Norbeck: Prairie Statesman* (Pierre, SD: South Dakota Historical Society Press, 2005), 182–183.

16 Fite, *Peter Norbeck: Prairie Statesman*, 182, 192–208.

17 Ormonde de Kay, "Debt Before Dishonor: How Richard Whitney Went down the Drain and up the River," *Quest* (February 1988), 40–47; Seligman, *The Transformation of Wall Street*, 169; John Brooks, *Once in Golconda: A True Drama of Wall Street, 1920–1938* (New York: John Wiley & Sons, 1969), passim; *NYT*, April 12, 1938; *NYT*, April 13, 1938; *NYT*, April 15, 1938; *NYT*, December 6, 1974.

18 Richard O. Boyer, *Max Steuer: Magician of the Law* (New York: Greenberg, 1932), 43; Frank Vanderlip to Julian Street, May 31, 1933, Vanderlip Papers, Box B-1-10; Assaf Likhovski, "The Duke and the Lady: *Helvering v. Gregory* and the History of Tax Avoidance Litigation," *Cardozo Law Review* 25 (2003–2004): 954–1018.

19 *Newsweek*, June 24, 1933; ibid., July 1, 1933; *NYT*, March 23, 1933; *NYT*, June 22, 1933; *NYT*, December 15, 1955; *New Republic*, July 5, 1933.

20 POH, 790–795; Edward J. Flynn, *You're the Boss* (New York: Viking Press, 1947), 133–138; Warren Moscow, *What Have You Done for Me Lately? The Ins and Outs of New York City Politics* (Englewood Cliffs, NJ: Prentice-Hall, Inc., 1967), 171; *NYT*, October 9, 1933; *NYT*, November 8, 1933.

21 Raymond Moley, *After Seven Years* (New York: Harper & Brothers, 1939), 285–290; Schlesinger, *The Coming of the New Deal*, 557; Beschloss, *Kennedy and Roosevelt*, 60, 83–91; David E. Koskoff, *Joseph P. Kennedy: A Life and Times* (Englewood Cliffs, NJ: Prentice-Hall, 1974), 55–63; Reminiscences of James McCauley Landis (1964), in Oral History Collection of Columbia University, 192–193; Ralph F. de Bedts, *The New Deal's SEC: The Formative Years* (New York: Columbia University Press, 1964), 96–111; *New Republic*, July 18, 1934; *New York Evening Post*, July 2, 1934; ibid., July 3, 1934; ibid., July 5, 1934.

22 de Bedts, *The New Deal's SEC*, 104–105; Koskoff, *Joseph P. Kennedy*, 62–63; POH, 852.

23 *NYT*, March 27, 1938; *NYT*, February 23, 1939; *NYT*, September 17, 1939; Florence Louise Pecora to FDR, August 20, 1935, PPF 2818, Pecora, Ferdinand Folder, FDRPL.

24 *NYT*, December 8, 1949; October 6, 1950.

INDEX